Let's
Meet up!

ANGLAIS 1re B1-B2

DIRECTION D'OUVRAGE ET AUTEUR :

Erwan GOURAUD
FORMATEUR
ENSEIGNANT AU LYCÉE JEAN-JACQUES ROUSSEAU, SARCELLES (95)

AUTEUR·E·S :

Bryce ANGOT
ENSEIGNANT DANS L'ACADÉMIE D'AMIENS (80)

Hugues AZAÏS
ENSEIGNANT AU LYCÉE DÉODAT DE SÉVERAC, TOULOUSE (31)

Joël CASCADE
ENSEIGNANT AU LYCÉE BELLEPIERRE, SAINT-DENIS-DE-LA-RÉUNION (974)

Mélanie CUBERTAFOND
ENSEIGNANTE AU LYCÉE SUD MÉDOC, LE TAILLAN-MÉDOC (33)

Élodie DAVO-VERDAVOIR
ENSEIGNANTE AU LYCÉE SAINTE-MARIE GRAND LEBRUN, BORDEAUX (33)

Véronique DORGET
ENSEIGNANTE AU LYCÉE LOUIS LAPICQUE, ÉPINAL (88)

Sylvie DOUGLADE-VAL
FORMATRICE
ENSEIGNANTE AU LYCÉE CLAUDE GELLÉE, ÉPINAL (88)

Françoise DU
FORMATRICE
ENSEIGNANTE AU LYCÉE BREQUIGNY, RENNES (35)

Pierre GUENDOUZ
FORMATEUR
ENSEIGNANT AU LYCÉE JACQUES DUHAMEL, DOLE (39)

Axel JACOBIN
FORMATEUR
ENSEIGNANT AU LYCÉE MONTALEMBERT, COURBEVOIE (92)

Amal NAVAILH
ENSEIGNANTE AU LYCÉE JACQUES PRÉVERT, BOULOGNE-BILLANCOURT (92)

Isabelle VALENTIN
FORMATRICE
ENSEIGNANTE AU LYCÉE DES MÉTIERS PIERRE DORIOLE, LA ROCHELLE (17)

Fatima ZAÂZOUI
ENSEIGNANTE AU LYCÉE LÉO LAGRANGE, BONDY (93)

Avec la participation de Cathy LIRIA
ENSEIGNANTE AU LYCÉE JEAN STURM, STRASBOURG (67)

Hatier

Merci à tou·te·s les enseignant·e·s qui nous ont aidé·e·s à élaborer cette nouvelle collection lors des rencontres à Paris et avec nos délégué·e·s pédagogiques, en particulier Véronique JAUBERT et Sandy LOCKHART pour leurs relectures et leurs conseils avisés.

Conception graphique : Primo&Primo, Gudrun Challe
Mise en page : Gudrun Challe
Édition : Annika Sanchez, Pauline Gaberel, Catherine de Bernis, Kyllian Ménard
Illustrations : Philippe Gady, Nicolas Haverland, Louise Plantin
Infographies : Olivier Damiens
Iconographie : Véronique Foz, Hatier illustration
Cartographie : L'atelier cartographik
Droits : Andréa Freire

Les auteur·e·s tiennent également à remercier tou·te·s les élèves qui ont testé les unités du manuel en classe.

ISBN : 978-240-1-05298-7

Discover the English-speaking world and improve your skills!

Bienvenue dans votre manuel !

Nous avons pensé ce manuel autour de vous, de votre expérience d'élève de première qui rentrez de plein pied dans le cycle terminal - celui de vos épreuves communes pour le baccalauréat.

Ce manuel est conçu pour s'adapter à votre niveau de compétence dans chaque activité langagière. Vous travaillerez toutes ces activités langagières à travers l'étude des documents de chaque unité ! Nous incluons également des propositions de médiation, à l'articulation de ces activités langagières.

Dès la page d'ouverture, vous pourrez comprendre quel est l'angle d'attaque de l'unité, c'est-à-dire sa problématique. Des mots-clés sous forme de **hashtags** vous indiqueront l'orientation que prendra votre unité.

Les rubriques **Improve your writing skills**, qui reviennent sur des points-clés d'écriture, et les activités proposées en grammaire (**Practise your grammar**) et en phonologie (**Improve your pronunciation**) ainsi que pour travailler le lexique (**Build up your vocabulary**) vous permettront de consolider vos compétences à l'écrit et à l'oral. À la fin de chaque axe, vous pourrez faire le bilan sur ce que vous avez compris grâce à la page **Let's RECAP**, aller plus loin avec la page **GO4IT** et vous entraîner aux nouvelles épreuves du baccalauréat grâce aux pages **BAC in sight**.

Votre manuel est imaginé pour vous permettre de progresser tout au long de l'année. Ainsi, les logos *Pédagogie différenciée* vous indiquent que vous, ou votre professeur·e, pouvez choisir votre parcours, celui qui est le plus adapté à vos compétences à un moment précis de l'année. Cela vous permettra de gagner en confiance et en compétences, et cela facilitera, *in fine*, votre progression au cours de l'année.

Vous verrez que le manuel vous propose de multiples aides pour la langue, la culture et la méthodologie. Il ne reste plus qu'à vous servir !

Enfin, ce manuel, c'est aussi et surtout une invitation au voyage, à la découverte. Grâce à des documents, tous authentiques, nous explorons les axes du programme qui constituent le socle de la culture anglo-saxonne aujourd'hui.

En somme, avec **Let's Meet Up!**, nous vous proposons tous les ingrédients pour que votre année de première soit une réussite.

Les auteur·e·s

Quelques pistes pour bien utiliser

Pour vous repérer

Réception

Compréhension écrite

Compréhension orale

Production

Expression écrite

Expression orale

Interaction écrite

Interaction orale

Médiation

Expliquer un discours lu et entendu

Pédagogie différenciée

Pédagogie différenciée

› Deux **approches différentes** d'un même document pour arriver à la même conclusion.
› Plusieurs documents de niveaux différents pour **travailler en groupes**.

Mémorisation active

Memory Challenge

Une manière originale de retenir les contenus essentiels de chaque double-page.

Pour vous entraîner

Dans votre manuel :

grammaire, phonologie, écriture et vocabulaire pour chaque séquence.

Practise your grammar
› L'essentiel de la règle
› Un ou deux exercices

Improve your prononciation
› L'essentiel de la règle
› Des exemples fournis en MP3
› Un ou deux exercices

Work on your writing skills
› Une démarche simple accompagnée d'exemples en contexte
› Un ou deux exercices

Build up your vocabulary
› Une carte mentale
› Des exercices en contexte
› Quizlet

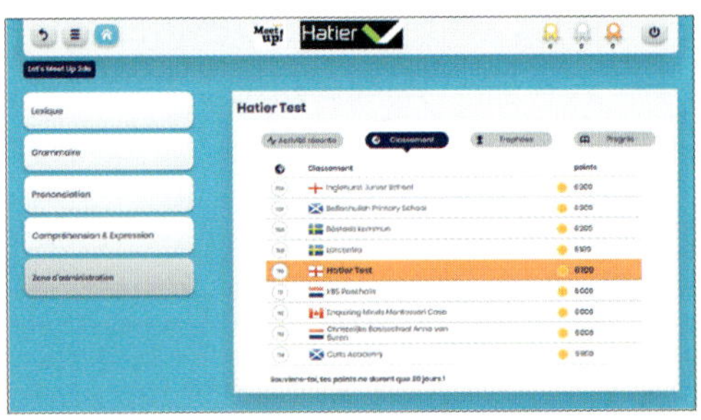

Sur la plateforme : lexique, grammaire, prononciation, compréhension et expression orales ou écrites.

www.reussirenlangues.fr/Letsmeetup1re

› Une **interface** très fonctionnelle et facile à utiliser
› Des **activités** ludiques en lien avec les contenus de chaque séquence
› Un **enregistreur** pour la production orale
› La possibilité d'envoyer **vos productions** directement à votre enseignant·e
› Un **suivi de vos résultats**

Pour vous évaluer

Auto-évaluation

› Un quiz interactif pour mesurer vos acquis et préparer l'évaluation.

Préparation des épreuves

› Compréhension orale, compréhension écrite et expression écrite : des sujets pour préparer les épreuves communes du BAC !

LET'S MEET UP!

Pour lire, écouter de l'anglais en dehors du cours

La classe inversée Classe inversée

› Un **document** accompagné d'une **fiche du E-workbook** (à télécharger) pour préparer la mise en commun en classe et/ou travailler à votre rythme.

› Ces éléments sont disponibles en ligne en tapant la mini-URL indiquée dans la boîte !

E-workbook
Classe inversée
hatier-clic.fr/lmu1040

Go4it

› **Des conseils pour prolonger la séquence** : lectures, séries, films, romans graphiques, chansons…
Il y en a pour tous les goûts – la priorité est votre immersion dans la langue anglaise !

Le site de téléchargement :

Retrouvez tous les MP3 et les fiches du *E-workbook* en un seul clic !

https://langues-eleves.editions-hatier.fr

Sommaire des MP3

Sommaire des annexes

AXE 1 Identities and exchanges Identités et

SÉQUENCE 1 How did tea become a part of British identity?

Le thé : héritage de l'Empire et marqueur social.

Project #1: Prepare a tour of the Twinings Museum.

Project #2: Create a leaflet to introduce a new brand of tea called "Heritage".

Texts

The birth of a global economy, NPR; *The great tea robbery: how the British stole China's secrets and seeds*, South China Morning Post; *One beverage for all*, BBC

Videos

Tea War: The Adventures of Robert Fortune; Tea time

SÉQUENCE 2 How can jazz bring people together?

De *New Orleans* aux clubs de jazz pendant le *Blitz* : une musique qui unit les gens face à l'adversité.

Project #1: During your summer trip to New Orleans, you went to an exhibition on jazz. Make a presentation to the class.

Project #2: Prepare a quiz show about jazz! In pairs, write 10 questions. In class, mix all the flash cards and start playing.

Texts

How jazz was born, acloserwalknola.com; *South London Memories*, South London Press; *A revival through jazz*, ThinkProgress

Video

City of Jazz; Swinging into the Blitz, BBC2

Axe 2 Private space and public space Espace

SÉQUENCE 1 How are women detectives represented in

L'évolution du rôle des femmes détectives dans les romans, les films et les séries.

Project #1: Film your pitch for a new Sherlock Holmes TV series with a female actor playing Sherlock.

Project #2: You are the screen-writer of *Shirley Holmes, female detective*. Prepare a presentation of the first episode of the series!

Texts

The No. 1 Ladies' Detective Agency, Alexander McCall Smith; *Depraved Heart*, Patricia Cornwell; *Why do we enjoy reading about female detectives?*, The Independent

Videos

Prime Suspect 1973; Trailer for FBI TV series

SÉQUENCE 2 How do Hollywood love stories reflect social

Hollywood : miroir des évolutions du couple et de la famille.

Project #1: Review a Hollywood love story reflecting the evolution of the couple in the USA for your YouTube channel.

Project #2: Prepare a plot summary for an adaptation of a classic Hollywood love story.

Texts

Remembering Hollywood's Hays Code, NPR; *LGBTQ representation in Hollywood is still 'bleak,'* Entertainment Weekly

Videos

Mrs. Doubtfire; The Back-up Plan

échanges

privé et espace public

Axe 3 Art and power Art et pouvoir

SÉQUENCE 1 How does art boost British cities' economy?

L'art et l'architecture comme moteurs de croissance des villes britanniques.

Project #1: You have designed an artwork or a building to boost your city's economy. Give a speech explaining its positive impact.

Project #2: Make a flyer presenting an artwork or a building in the UK and explaining how it helps to boost the city's economy.

Texts

Street art: Crime, grime or sublime?, BBC; *Hastings Pier*, ARCHDAILY.COM

Videos

Stik in Shoreditch, THE GUARDIAN; *Birmingham*

SÉQUENCE 2 How did US artists relate the Great Depression?

Comment les artistes des années 30 se sont emparés de la Grande Dépression dans leur art.

Project #1: Prepare a presentation of an artwork for an exhibition on the Great Depression.

Project #2: Write an email to the curator of an exhibition on the Great Depression. Convince him or her to include your favourite artwork.

Text

The Grapes of Wrath, JOHN STEINBECK

Videos

America after the Fall, ART INSTITUTE OF CHICAGO; *The art of Edward Hopper*

Axe 4 Citizenship and virtual worlds Citoyenneté

SÉQUENCE 1 What is the Americans' relationship to the

De l'hyper-concentration des médias aux *fake news* : le rapport des Américains à leurs médias.

Project #1: Act out a discussion between a journalist and an expert about the evolution of the media and the dangers of fake news.

Project #2: Write a post about the changing face of the news on an online forum about journalism in the USA.

Texts

Real news vs fake news; How to spot fake news, INTERNATIONAL FEDERATION OF LIBRARY ASSOCIATIONS AND INSTITUTIONS; *Teens' views on the news*, THE ATLANTIC

SÉQUENCE 2 Is online activism effective in the USA?

L'activisme en ligne aux USA : un nouvel outil de lutte ?

Project #1: Live stream on Instagram to speak about your experience as an activist.

Project #2: Launch an online petition for a cause that is important to you.

Texts

This Is What Social Media Had to Say About the March for Our Lives, VOGUE US; *Philanthropy That Comes From a Click*, THE NEW YORK TIMES

Video

How online social movements become offline results, PBS

P. 64			Options pédagogiques
Pictures *Upfest street art festival; The ArcelorMittal Orbit; Hastings Pier*	**Grammaire** l'infinitif en *to*, les indénombrables **Phonologie** l'accentuation des adjectifs composés **Écriture** la ponctuation de la phrase **Vocabulaire** le street art, l'architecture	BAC in sight P. 82 Let's RECAP P. 80 AUTO évaluation P. 70 GO4IT P. 81	Pédagogie différenciée P. 65 Classe inversée P. 66 Médiation P. 66

P. 72			Options pédagogiques
Pictures *Family walking on highway,* Dorothea Lange; *Hooverville,* James Patrick Lee; *Classic Landscape,* Charles Sheeler; *The Park Bench,* Reginald Marsh	**Grammaire** le prétérit en *be* + V-*ing*, la phrase complexe **Phonologie** les liaisons **Écriture** le journal intime **Vocabulaire** l'art, la crise économique	BAC in sight P. 84 Let's RECAP P. 80 AUTO évaluation P. 78 GO4IT P. 81	Pédagogie différenciée P. 73 Classe inversée P. 75 Médiation P. 72

et mondes virtuels

media? P. 88			Options pédagogiques
Videos *This is an Apple,* CNN; *The Fifth Estate* **Graph** *American Government: Power and Purpose*	**Grammaire** les quantifieurs (1), l'aspect *be* + V-*ing* **Phonologie** l'accentuation d'un mot et de ses dérivés **Écriture** l'apostrophe **Vocabulaire** les médias, l'information	BAC in sight P. 106 Let's RECAP P. 104 AUTO évaluation P. 94 GO4IT P. 105	Pédagogie différenciée P. 90 Classe inversée P. 88 Médiation P. 89, P. 91

P. 96			Options pédagogiques
Audio *The effects of #MeToo,* NPR **Picture** *Caption from* Change.org **Cartoon** *Cartoon by* La Montagne	**Grammaire** les quantifieurs (2), les adjectifs en -*ed* et -*ing* **Phonologie** l'accent de phrase **Écriture** les faux amis **Vocabulaire** le militantisme, les actions	BAC in sight P. 108 Let's RECAP P. 104 AUTO évaluation P. 102 GO4IT P. 105	Pédagogie différenciée P. 98 Classe inversée P. 99 Médiation P. 96

Axe 5 Fictions and realities Fictions et réalités

SÉQUENCE 1 How close to reality can dystopia be?

La frontière fine entre la réalité et l'imaginaire dystopique.

Project #1: Audition for a role in a dystopian series. Deliver a speech explaining the problems in this society.

Project #2: Take part in a creative writing competition. Write the beginning of a dystopia.

Bookcovers

Brave New World, Aldous Huxley; ***It Can't Happen Here,*** Sinclair Lewis; ***1984,*** George Orwell; ***Fahrenheit 451,*** Ray Bradbury

Texts

1984, George Orwell; ***The Handmaid's Tale,*** Margaret Atwood

SÉQUENCE 2 How did British pirates inspire fiction?

Entre mythes et réalité, le personnage du pirate, un élément clé de la culture anglosaxonne.

Project #1: Show visitors around the Pirates of Nassau Museum and tell them about the lifestyles of pirates.

Project #2: Create a leaflet depicting a fictional pirate, to win the Cayman Islands Pirates Week Festival contest.

Texts

Privateers, nmrn.org.uk; ***Pirates in the Age of Sail,*** Robert J. Antony; ***Printing the legend,*** BBC; ***Treasure Island,*** Robert Louis Stevenson

Videos

True Caribbean Pirates, The History Channel; ***Black Sails***

Axe 6 Scientific innovations and responsibility

SÉQUENCE 1 How far are Americans willing to let AI into

Objets connectés, androïdes : que cache l'intelligence artificielle ?

Project #1: Participate in a debate about the place artificial intelligence has and will have in our lives.

Project #2: Write an article for *Tech Insider* about what life will be like in 2050 thanks to AI and how to prepare for it.

Texts

Regulate before it's too late, The Guardian; ***AI for security,*** The Telegraph

Videos

Meet Sophia the robot, Tech Insider; ***ElliQ The Active Aging Companion,*** Intuition Robotics

SÉQUENCE 2 How important is the Space Race for the USA?

Hier la Lune, aujourd'hui Mars : la conquête de l'espace est-elle le nouvel eldorado ?

Project #1: Interview an American astronaut. Discuss the possibility and the consequences of sending humans to Mars.

Project #2: Write a speech about the Space Race for a conference at a famous US university.

Videos

Fascination for Mars, National Geographic; ***We're going to Mars***

Texts

Collier's; Apollo 11: the first men on the moon, space.com; ***Mars City,*** The Telegraph

Innovations scientifiques et responsabilité

Axe 7 Diversity and inclusion Diversité et inclusion

SÉQUENCE 1 How far is the USA from Martin Luther King

Le mouvement *Black Lives Matter* est-il l'héritier de la *Freedom March* ?

Project #1: Deliver a speech on the situation of black Americans since the Civil Rights Movement to celebrate Black History Month.

Project #2: Create a poster on an inspiring black American figure to celebrate Black History Month.

Texts

Black Americans mostly left behind by progress since Dr. King's death?, The Conversation; ***A place to come together***, National Geographic Magazine

Videos

I am not your Negro, Raoul Peck; ***Oprah Winfrey's speech***

SÉQUENCE 2 How do social realist films question British

Depuis les années 60 et les *Angry Young Men* à Ken Loach aujourd'hui, portrait d'un cinéma de lutte purement Britannique.

Project #1: Act out an interview between a film student and the director of a social realist film. They discuss the director's vision of British society.

Project #2: Write the review of a British social realist film for a special edition of a film magazine.

Texts

Where to begin with kitchen-sink drama, bfi.org; ***This is England review***, watershed.co.uk; ***Filmmaker Amma Asante on race, Brexit and meeting Prince***, The Financial Times

Axe 8 Territory and memory Territoire et mémoire

SÉQUENCE 1 How strong is the UK's link to its territories?

Les *British Overseas Territories* : joyaux ou enfants oubliés de la couronne britannique ?

Project #1: Make a video promoting one of the BOTs to win a competition set up by the tourism agency VisitBritain.

Project #2: Following an article on BBC News, exchange a few tweets about the independence of British Overseas Territories.

Texts

The rise and fall of the British Empire, The Washington Post; ***Blaming mainland Britain***, The Independent

Videos

Britain's Treasure Islands, Warehouse 51 Productions; ***The Iron Lady***, Phyllida Lloyd

SÉQUENCE 2 How is slavery commemorated in the English-

Un regard sur le passé de l'esclavage toujours important dans les sociétés anglo-saxonnes aujourd'hui.

Project #1: Give a speech to convince the citizens of Liverpool to place a monument commemorating slavery in the main square.

Project #2: Songwriting contest: write the lyrics of a new song commemorating slavery.

Texts

What's Juneteenth?, Vox; ***Redemption song***, Bob Marley

Videos

Today's TMJ4; The Ark of Return, United Nations; ***Amazing Grace***, Michael Apted

AXE 1

Identities and exchanges

Identités et échanges

SÉQUENCE 1

How did tea become a part of British identity?

Projects

Project #1: Prepare a tour of the Twinings Museum.

Project #2: Create a leaflet to introduce a new brand of tea called "Heritage".

Tools

Grammaire	les structures causatives, le *past perfect*
Phonologie	les sons /ɪ/ et /aɪ/
Écriture	le tiret et le trait d'union
Vocabulaire	le thé, le commerce

SÉQUENCE 2

How can jazz bring people together?

Projects

Project #1: During your summer trip to New Orleans, you went to an exhibition on jazz. Make a presentation to the class.

Project #2: Prepare a quiz show about jazz! In pairs, write 10 questions. In class, mix all the flash cards and start playing.

Tools

Grammaire	le gérondif, le pluriel des noms
Phonologie	les sons /dʒ/ et /tʃ/
Écriture	l'orthographe américaine
Vocabulaire	la musique, les sentiments

#identity #mobility #hospitality

#worldeconomy #socialgroups

Keep calm and drink tea

#culturalexchanges #sharing

#crossingborders #solidarity

New Orleans Jazz & Heritage Festival, Louisiana

SÉQUENCE 1 How did tea become a part of British identity?

A Tea trade

The birth of a global economy

Professor Woodruff Smith, a historian, says [...] there's evidence[1] that much of the same health claims[2] about tea – that it cleared the head and improved spirits[3], without the debauchery of alcohol – were also being made about coffee around the turn of the 18th century. But coffee came from countries like Yemen and Eritrea — "places beyond European control and with little capacity to expand production," Smith writes. So when demand for coffee rose, prices did, too.

Tea, on the other hand, came from China — which had in place a sophisticated commerce system that could respond quickly to rising demand, Smith says. That demand was coming from the British and Dutch East India companies, which were already in China buying spices, silks[4] and other goods for trade. As interest in tea grew back home, Smith says, the companies were in good position to ship[5] large, reliable[6] quantities at affordable[7] prices "and therefore make tea a popular fad[8] — and beyond a fad."

"What you're seeing is the global economy being constructed," Smith says. [...]

As Lord Beckett, the villainous, tea-and-sugar-sipping agent of the British East India Company in the *Pirates of Caribbean* movies might have put it, "it's just good business."

✦ Maria Godoy, www.npr.org, April 7, 2015

1. proof 2. affirmations 3. moods 4. precious textile fabric 5. send by boat 6. here: enough 7. reasonable 8. popular trend

Pédagogie différenciée

TRAIL A

1 Read the first paragraph. Find the drinks the professor talks about.

2 Pick out the names of countries that produced coffee. Use the expression "little capacity" (l. 8) to explain why it was expensive.

3 Read from l. 10 to l. 15. List all the goods traded from China. Explain why China was a great trading partner.

4 Read from l. 15 to l. 22. Pick out adjectives showing that Chinese commerce made tea popular in Britain. Explain this popularity.

TRAIL B

1 Read the first paragraph. List the effects of drinking tea or coffee.

2 Explain the quote: "So, when demand for coffee rose, prices did, too." (l. 8-9).

3 Read the second paragraph. Explain the advantage of the Chinese commerce system and list the products traded.

4 Explain the causes and the consequences of the success of the tea trade.

Meet up! Using all the information you have gathered from the text, explain the last paragraph.

Grammar Spot

The past perfect TOOLS → p. 20

"They **had** tried to show the Chinese emperor many objects in order to persuade him."

Word Spot

- delegation: group of people
- supply and demand: economic rule, the more you demand a product, the more the product costs
- monopoly
- industrial secret
- industrial theft: industrial espionage
- lucrative: profitable
- trade: do business
- expand: get bigger
- influence
- transport: dispatch

B Trading with China

Audio
CD1 piste 02

✦ *The Reception of the Diplomatique and his Suite at the Court of Pekin* by James Gillray, 1792

1 Describe the engraving. Imagine what is written in the letter in the middle of the picture.

2 Listen to the first sentence and explain what was special about China in the 19th century.

3 Listen to the whole recording and note down the problems encountered by the British and the solution they found.

4 Write a short paragraph to sum up the tea trading problems between Great Britain and China.

C A dangerous mission

Vidéo
DVD

1 Watch the beginning of the video without the sound. Observe the environment and the people. Guess where Robert Fortune is and what he is doing.

2 Watch the full video with the sound.

a. Check your guesses.

b. Focus on his appearance and explain the reasons for his transformation.

E-workbook
Fiche à imprimer
hatier-clic.fr/lmu1001

3 Describe the role of Robert Fortune for the British Empire and show why he is a legend.

4 ***PAIR WORK*** One of you is Robert Fortune; the other works for the East India Company. Write your telegraphic exchanges during Fortune's secret mission.

✦ *Tea War: The Adventures of Robert Fortune*, 2016

Prepare your project

You are on a boat set to China to buy tea. Write an entry in your diary explaining what you intend to do to come back to Britain with tons of tea.

Grammar Tip Précis → p. 244

Use the **present perfect** to describe new experiences.

Memory Challenge

Choose five words that sum up what Great Britain did to bring tea home.

D The tea spy

Classe inversée

E-workbook
Classe inversée
hatier-clic.fr/lmu1002

The great tea robbery: how the British stole China's secrets and seeds[1]

China dominated the tea trade until the East India Company sent Scottish botanist Robert Fortune on a secret mission to steal its plants and tea-processing technique.

The East India Company believed that with the best Chinese seeds, together with the secrets of production, it could grow precious tea in the British colony of India. "The task required a plant hunter, a gardener, a thief, a spy," writes Sarah Rose in her book *For All the Tea in China*.

The East India Company gave Fortune his mission impossible in May 1848. By September 1848, Fortune was travelling from Shanghai to China's green-tea regions. It was a laborious three-month trek south-west by river junk[2], sedan chair and foot, accompanied by two trusty servants. On their recommendation, Fortune had his hair shaved off, had a faux queue attached to the back of his head and wore the clothes of a local nobleman or wealthy merchant. "I am Chinese from a distant province beyond the Great Wall," he would say to local people in hesitant Chinese.

Fortune had collected 13,000 plants and 10,000 seeds but it was now winter and the fragile and vulnerable tea seeds had to be transported to the Indian Himalayas via Hong Kong and Calcutta. Fortune organised the recruitment of experienced tea growers and producers who would manage production in India. Fortune left Shanghai for Hong Kong with his mission accomplished.

✦ Stuart Heaver, *South China Morning Post*, May 27, 2017 (adapted)

1. grain 2. Chinese sailing boat

1 Focus on the introduction and the first paragraph. Find as many elements as possible on Fortune, then write a short description.

2 In the second paragraph, pick out elements linked to travelling and disguise and write a short paragraph about the conditions of Fortune's journey.

3 In the last paragraph, pick out numbers, nationalities and places and describe what Fortune did with his plants.

4 Explain why Fortune was an early James Bond (mission, disguise...).

E Tea time

Vidéo
hatier-clic.fr/lmu1003

1

2

1 Study the photographs and match "low tea" and "high tea" to the correct photograph. Justify your choice.

2 Watch part one of the video and pick out three situations where tea is drunk in everyday life.

3 Watch part two of the video and explain the difference between low tea and high tea.

4 Prepare a short speech to convince your teacher to organise an afternoon tea party.

Grammar Spot

Causative verbs TOOLS → p. 20

"Tea **makes** people **feel** better."

Word Spot

- finger sandwich: small sandwich
- the British way of life
- a tea-drinking nation
- unnoticed: undetected
- convivial
- cultural
- soothing: making sb feel calm
- uplifting: making sb feel better
- complete a mission
- wear a disguise: wear a costume

F One beverage for all

Anthropologist Kate Fox writes in her book *Watching the English* that there are several clear messages sent whenever[1] a Brit makes a cuppa[2]. She observes that the strongest brews[3] of black tea — with the largest doses of molecules — are typically drunk by the working class. The brew gets progressively weaker[4] as one goes up the social ladder.

Milk and sweetener[5] have their own codes. "Taking sugar in your tea is regarded by many as an infallible lower-class indicator: even one spoonful is a bit suspect (unless you were born before about 1955); more than one and you are lower-middle at best; more than two and you are definitely working class," she writes. Other rules involve when and how milk is added, if any. […] Fox writes, "Tea-making is the perfect displacement activity: whenever the English feel awkward[6] or uncomfortable in a social situation (that is, almost all the time), they make tea."

✦ Veronique Greenwood, www.bbc.com, June 3, 2016

1. each time 2. + 3. cup(s) of tea 4. less strong 5. sugar or aspartame 6. embarrassed

1 Draw the ladder in your notebook and complete it with the different social classes.

lower middle class - upper class - working class - upper middle class

2 Pick out words connected to tea and match them to a social class. Explain Kate Fox's observation about the use of sugar and complete the ladder with the correct amount of sugar.

more than one spoonful - no sugar - more than two spoonfuls

3 You are a British person explaining the importance of tea to a foreign visitor. Be as specific as possible (ingredients, social role of tea, moments when it is drunk...).

Prepare your project

PAIR WORK Prepare and act out an interview with an expert about the role of tea in British life.

Student A Ask questions about the origins and the history of tea.

Student B You are an expert on British tea. Answer the questions. You can use the following words: afternoon tea, high tea, social ladder, British habits.

Grammar Tip Précis → p. 256

Don't forget to use **relative clauses** to add information.

Memory Challenge

You have 30 seconds to write as many elements as possible on high tea and low tea or on the origins of tea on a piece of paper. Then compare it with your partner.

Tools in the Spotlight

Entraînez-vous sur la plateforme ***Let's Meet Up!***
reussirenlangues.fr

Practise your grammar

Précis grammatical, p. 216

Les structures causatives

• *Make* et *have* peuvent avoir un sens causatif. Ils se traduisent par « **faire faire quelque chose à quelqu'un** ». Même si le sujet est à l'origine de l'action, il ne l'accomplit pas lui-même. Le verbe causatif *make* exprime plus une idée de **contrainte**.

The servants ***made*** *Fortune* ***eat with chopsticks.***

The servants : responsable de l'action — ***made*** : verbe causatif — *Fortune* : celui qui fait l'action — ***eat with chopsticks*** : l'action réalisée

Les serviteurs ont fait manger Fortune avec des baguettes.

The servants ***had*** *Robert Fortune* ***meet tea farmers.***

The servants : responsable de l'action — ***had*** : verbe causatif — *Robert Fortune* : celui qui fait l'action — ***meet tea farmers*** : l'action réalisée

Les serviteurs ont fait rencontrer des producteurs de thé à Robert Fortune.

• *Make* peut aussi être employé avec un adjectif seul, au sens de « rendre ».

This story made me happy.

1 Remettez les éléments dans l'ordre.

a. didn't understand / Robert Fortune / their sentences / so he had / Chinese very well / them repeat

b. made / the East India Company / the secret of tea from Imperial China / Robert Fortune / steal

c. us / my mother / had / for the guests / high tea / prepare

d. the British / another solution / the refusal by the Emperor / made / to get the secret of tea / look for

2 Complétez les phrases en utilisant les structures causatives (*make* ou *have*) au temps qui convient.

a. Some studies ... Kate Fox think that tea has its own codes.

b. Five trips to China ... Robert Fortune familiar with Chinese culture.

c. They ... Fortune look like a Chinese man.

d. Opium ... people addicted quite rapidly.

e. The East India Company ... Fortune go to China to steal tea.

Le *past perfect*

Le *past perfect* a divers emplois. Il se traduit souvent par un plus-que-parfait français.

• Il sert généralement à faire un **bilan** ou à créer un **retour en arrière** sur le passé.

Fortune went to India in 1850. He ***had stayed*** *in China in 1848.*

• Il peut créer un **lien** entre **deux moments du passé**.

When I met Robert Fortune, he ***had spent*** *three months in China.*

Passé → Présent

he ***had spent*** *three months in China* — *I met Robert Fortune*

• Il peut exprimer l'**irréel**.

If the Chinese emperor ***had agreed*** *to sell tea, China would have been rich.*

Le *past perfect* se forme à l'aide de l'auxiliaire *had* et du participe passé.

3 Complétez les phrases avec un verbe conjugué au *past perfect* ou au prétérit.

a. In the 1880s drinking tea (become) fashionable in high society and it continued after that.

b. The British (not – try) to talk to the Emperor because they (try) before.

c. Robert (already – shave) his head when he (start) working as a spy.

d. Juliet (visit) the best tearooms in London in 2013, then she (discover) a new one in 2017.

e. Yesterday I (not – want) another cup of tea because I (already – have) two.

4 Complétez les phrases en utilisant un verbe conjugué au *past perfect*.

a. When he arrived in India, Robert Fortune ... .

b. The Chinese emperor wished he ... .

c. By the time I got to the tea room, everyone ... .

Improve your pronunciation

Précis de phonologie, p. 262

Les sons /ɪ/ et /aɪ/

Audio
CD1 piste 03
MP3 n° 02

- Le son /ɪ/ peut correspondre à la graphie :
  - age (*village*, *cottage*, *sausage*)
  - i (*milk*, *mix*, *fix*)
  - ui (*biscuit*, *building*)
  - o (*women*)
  - y (*myth*, *symbol*)

- De manière générale, la lettre i, suivie d'une consonne et de la voyelle e, se prononce /aɪ/ : *like*, *mine*, *dive*, *five*, *site.* Mais le son /aɪ/ peut aussi correspondre à la graphie :
  - ai (*aisle*)
  - ei (*height*)
  - ey (*eye*)
  - igh (*high*)
  - uy (*buy*)
  - y (*cry*, *shy*, *dry*)

5 **Écoutez les mots et classez-les selon la prononciation de la lettre *i* soulignée.**

Audio
CD1 piste 04
MP3 n° 03

mind, scientific, instrument, tired, Twinings
China, finger, sign, ship, milk, drink, disguised

/ɪ/	/aɪ/
big ...	eye ...

6 **Prononcez les mots suivants, puis écoutez l'enregistrement pour vérifier.**

Audio
CD1 piste 05
MP3 n° 04

a. file • fill
b. bite • bit
c. kit • kite
d. fit • fight
e. lick • like
f. knit • knight

Work on your writing skills

Le tiret et le trait d'union

Un tiret (*dash*) **sépare** des mots du reste de la phrase, tandis qu'un trait d'union (*hyphen*) **relie** deux ou plusieurs mots. Le trait d'union n'a pas d'espaces autour, alors qu'un tiret a un espace de chaque côté. Le tiret est plus long que le trait d'union.
This – is a dash. This - is a hyphen.

- **Le tiret** permet de réaliser une pause à l'intérieur même d'une phrase. C'est une forme de parenthèse. Ex : *[...] and therefore make tea a popular fad – and beyond a fad.*

Il sert aussi à distinguer les personnages dans un dialogue, à séparer les parties d'une énumération, à indiquer une interruption du discours dans un dialogue ou à insister sur un fait.

- **Le trait d'union** sert à :
  - former des noms et des adjectifs composés : *lower-class*, *a tea-drinking nation* ;
  - écrire les nombres de 21 à 99 : *twenty-one*, *eighty-nine* ;
  - relier deux mots ou une particule et un mot : *set-up* ;
  - écrire les fractions : *two-fifths*, *one-third*.

7 **Si nécessaire, insérez un tiret ou un trait d'union.**

a. Britain is really a tea ... drinking nation.
b. Robert Fortune was a great ... nineteenth ... century botanist.
c. Robert ... where has he gone? ... I would like to meet him.
d. She might come to the Twinings Museum ... you never know.
e. The landscapes, the lifestyle, the traditions ... this is what brought them to China.
f. It was a laborious three ... month trek southwest.
g. One thing's for sure ... the British Empire was very powerful.
h. Bob and Jane like ... tea very much.
i. A group of 10 ... year ... old schoolboys visited the museum yesterday.
j. Diana submitted a 6 ... page document.

Build up your vocabulary

Audio
CD1 piste 06

Tea

Habits and tradition MP3 n°05

institution
traditional
most common
most ordinary
date back to + date
symbolise

Spying MP3 n°06

costume
industrial secret
industrial theft: industrial espionage
unnoticed: undetected
complete a mission
wear a disguise: wear a costume

Tea time MP3 n°07

the British way of life
a tea-drinking nation
tea: word for the evening meal in some parts of the UK
cultural
convivial
soothing: making sb feel calm
uplifting: making sb feel better
depend on (social class)
go up the social ladder: go from a lower class to an upper class

Food MP3 n°08

meal: lunch, dinner
dish: starter, main course
dessert
meat pies
vegetables
bread
finger sandwiches
scones
pastries: cakes
homemade cakes
cream tea
clotted cream
exotic

Trade MP3 n°09

trade: commercial exchange
trading company
delegation: group of people
monopoly
supply and demand: economic rule, the more you demand a product, the more the product costs
manufactured products
lucrative: profitable
expensive ≠ cheap, inexpensive
exchange: trade (buying and selling)
do business
increase
expand: get bigger
influence
transport: dispatch
trade: buy and sell goods and services

Apprenez et révisez le vocabulaire !

Utilisez Quizlet pour vous entraîner en vous amusant.

Quizlet
hatier-clic.fr/lmu1004

Utilisez le vocabulaire en contexte.

1 Complétez les phrases suivantes avec des mots de la carte mentale.

a. In the 18th century ... ... between Britain and China developed and became essential as exotic products were in great demand.
b. The trading companies were in a situation of ... and sent delegations to China to sign treaties and agreements.
c. In China the British East India Company traded spices, silk, china, and tea. These products were bought by the people of the ... .
d. As the ... increased tea became affordable.

2 Complétez ces phrases en utilisant des mots de la carte mentale.

a. Robert Fortune ...
b. Low tea ...
c. The people at the top of the social ladder ...
d. Many people think that tea ...

AUTO évaluation

Faites le quiz interactif en ligne et suivez les conseils pour vous préparer à l'évaluation.

Quiz
hatier-clic.fr/lmu1005

Project #1

Prepare a tour of the Twinings Museum.

1 Explain the origins of tea.

- ✓ Use dates to give a historical perspective.
- ✓ Add the country where tea was produced.

2 Add fun facts.

- ✓ Go on the internet if needed to find some fun facts about tea.
- ✓ Talk about Robert Fortune's secret mission.
- ✓ Use the **preterite** to talk about the past.

3 Show the difference between high tea and low tea.

- ✓ Use linking words like **contrary to** or **whereas** to underline the differences between the two.
- ✓ Give details about the food associated with both.

4 Talk about the importance of tea in the UK.

- ✓ Say when and how people drink tea in the UK.
- ✓ State why tea is an important element in any social situation in the UK.

➤ Fiches de méthodologie N°5 p. 276 N°18 p. 296

Project #2

Create a leaflet to introduce a new brand of tea called "Heritage".

1 Focus on the product.

- ✓ Explain why tea is essential in the UK (amount of tea drunk in a year, types of tea, moments when it's drunk).
- ✓ Use the **simple present** to talk about habits.
- ✓ Use hashtags with keywords to highlight important information.

2 Tell the public about the origin of the brand.

- ✓ Explain what the name of the brand means.
- ✓ Add a few historical facts to link your brand to the history of tea in Great Britain.

3 Advertise the product.

- ✓ Say where customers can find your brand of tea.
- ✓ Find a catchy slogan to make people remember the product.
- ✓ Use **superlatives** to make the product sound unique.

4 Focus on the layout of the leaflet.

- ✓ Make it attractive by adding colours and nice pictures.
- ✓ You can use online tools.

➤ Fiche de méthodologie N°20 p. 300

SÉQUENCE 2

How can jazz bring people together?

A How jazz was born

Congo Square is an open square located in Louis Armstrong Park in New Orleans, Louisiana.
Congo Square is one of the most hallowed[1] sites in American music history. This area, once a grassy commons behind the original city rampart (now Rampart Street), was one of several gathering places for enslaved people from Africa and their descendants. In the 1700s, under French and Spanish colonial rule, slaves were permitted to buy and sell goods on Sundays. They also played African-style musical instruments and performed dances that originated from their native homes. After New Orleans became part of the United States in the early 1800s, a city ordinance[2] limited gatherings of slaves to this spot, and only until sunset. Still, the weekly ritual sustained a continuum of African culture in the New World, with profound implications for the future of music.
The African and Caribbean cultural expressions that thrived[3] there sowed the seeds[4] of New Orleans' jazz, second-line[5], and Mardi Gras Indian[6] traditions. Participants came from different African nations, and played a variety of styles of music. The spectacle of hundreds of people drumming and dancing the Bamboula and the Calinda attracted all kinds of visitors, from domestic workers and free people of color to curious outsiders likely including composer Louis Moreau Gottschalk. Music and dance here served vital functions: they were a spiritual practice and a form of resistance, which made them a threat to the American racial order. As a result, the gatherings were shut down for good in 1851.

✦ acloserwalknola.com

✦ Statue of Buddy Bolden, Louis Armstrong Park, New Orleans, Louisiana

1. venerated 2. rule 3. prospered 4. started 5. brass instrument parade 6. African Americans participating in the Mardi Gras carnival parade

1 Look at the photo. Imagine why the statue was placed in this park.

2 Read the text and spot the different groups of people who used to come to Congo Square.

3 Explain the role of music and dance in the 1800s in Congo Square.

4 The New Orleans tourist office is going to put a memorial plaque at the entrance of Congo Square. Write a short text about the history of the place.

Culture Tip

Charles Joseph "Buddy" Bolden was the biggest cornetist in New Orleans around 1900. He developed a New Orleans style of music called "jass", which later became "jazz".

Grammar Spot

The gerund Tools → p. 28

"The spectacle of hundreds of people **drumming** and **dancing** the Bamboula and the Calinda attracted all kinds of visitors"

Word Spot

band: orchestra
brass instruments: trumpet, trombone, cornet
drums: percussion
beat: rhythm /rɪðəm/
track: tune, song
gig: concert
jam session: improvised concert
venue /venjuː/: concert hall
trend: fashion
entertaining: enjoyable
perform: sing / play on stage
praise: compliment
clap (hands): applaud
have a good time: enjoy oneself
on stage: in front of an audience

B City of jazz

Vidéo
hatier-clic.fr/lmu1006

1 Introduce Tim Curran and his two passions.

2 Use the following words from the video to show Ben Jaffe's love for jazz.

DNA - share - connect - music

3 Define the historical importance of Congo Square for Ben Jaffe.

4 Tim Curran writes about his trip to New Orleans on his band's blog. Imagine his short text.

C Painting jazz

Audio
CD1 piste 07

E-workbook
Fiche à imprimer
hatier-clic.fr/lmu1007

✦ Archibald Motley, *Nightlife*, 1943

1 Find information about Motley, the importance of music in Chicago and the origin of its new inhabitants.

2 List the activities African Americans did in Chicago.

3 Pick out the words used by the professor to describe Motley's work at the end of the recording. Use them to describe *Nightlife*.

4 Explain how Motley managed to capture the Jazz Age in his paintings.

D I love jazz

Audio
CD1 piste 08

E-workbook
Fiche à imprimer
hatier-clic.fr/lmu1008

1 Spot words explaining why Louis Armstrong and other people loved jazz.

2 Pick out words related to the origins and evolution of jazz.

3 Define how jazz makes people feel, according to Louis Armstrong.

4 Explain what this song is about to a classmate, in French or in English.

Culture Tip

At the beginning of the 20th century, African Americans left the south because of segregation and poverty.
They moved to cities like **New York** and **Chicago**, making **jazz** fashionable in northern states.
Louis Armstrong was born in New Orleans but he joined a band in Chicago in 1922 and later moved to New York.

Prepare your project

Write the first paragraph of an ad for a one-week trip to New Orleans and Chicago, the cities of jazz!

Grammar Tip

Précis → p. 231

Use **superlatives** to show how amazing this trip is.

Memory Challenge

Look at Motley's painting for ten seconds, then close your book. List as many words as you can in 30 seconds.

E Dancing the Blitz away

Vidéo
hatier-clic.fr/lmu1009

Pédagogie différenciée

TRAIL A

1 Explain how successful jazz was in London during the Second World War.

2 Name two types of places where people could listen to jazz.

3 Read the Culture Tip. Explain why the word "escape" is used twice in the video.

TRAIL B

1 Explain the historical context and pick out words showing people enjoyed jazz at the time.

2 Create a mind map to draw links between jazz, Café de Paris and the BBC.

3 Say how jazz helped people cope and survive during the war.

Meet up! In a secondhand shop, you find an old postcard. The sender wrote about life in London during the Second World War but also about new music trends. Imagine his or her text.

Culture Tip

The Blitz refers to the nighttime bombing raids against London and other major British cities led by Nazi Germany during World War II. The raids destroyed houses, factories as well as infra-structures and caused heavy civilian casualties.

F Keep swinging despite the bombing!

In 1940, Adelaide embarked on a concert tour that brought her to South London. On the evening of Monday, August 26, just days before the official start of the Blitz, she topped the bill[1] at Lewisham Hippodrome with her piano accompanist Gerry Moore.

In the middle of her act, the air raid siren sounded, but most of the audience remained seated. When the raid started everyone in the theatre could hear the screaming bombs falling and exploding, and the bursts of anti-aircraft machine gun fire.

Though the building was strongly constructed, the sound of exploding bombs close by was clearly felt in the auditorium.

Adelaide encouraged the nervous audience to join her in some community song numbers and she later recalled: "We — the performers and the audience — were told that no one could leave the theatre because it was too dangerous. Outside everything was burning. So, we just carried on and I managed to get the audience to join in many of the songs."

On the night of August 26-27, for four hours, with bombs exploding outside the Lewisham Hippodrome, Adelaide helped to entertain[2] the nervous audience until the all-clear[3] sounded at 3.45am.

Later that day, Gerry Moore commented that his fingers ached[4] so much from playing that he could hardly move his hands.

Though Adelaide could barely speak, in defiant mood she returned to the stage of the Hippodrome the following evening to perform her act as scheduled.

✦ *South London Memories – Jazz singer Adelaide Hall sang as bombs fell, South London Press*, July 3, 2018

1. was the star 2. sing for and distract 3. end of warning 4. hurt

1 Pick out words describing the atmosphere inside the Hippodrome and the events that happened outside that night.

2 Explain what the performers did to comfort the audience.

3 Explain what the last sentence of the text shows about Adelaide and the pianist.

4 The following morning, a journalist on the radio relates what happened at the concert at the Hippodrome. Act out the report.

Grammar Spot

Plural nouns TOOLS → p. 28
"the absence of musicians"
"their families"

Word Spot

bombing: air raid
casualties: victims
(physical) pain: suffering
grief: sorrow: (emotional) pain
hardship: difficulty
relief: aid
funding: financing
donations: gifts
injured, wounded: hurt
carefree ≠ anxious
cope: deal with problems
recover: get better, improve
feel relieved: reassured
comfort: reassure
cheer sb up: make sb happy
look forward to V-ing

G A revival through jazz

Classe inversée

'Tremé Was Empty': How Musicians Are Helping New Orleans Heal From Katrina

No matter where you've heard about it, New Orleanians consider Tremé a multicultural epicenter of a city known for its rich musical heritage. Its famed Congo Square, now a large park, is where slaves once gathered to socialize, sell goods, and dance. It's the site of funeral marches, parades, and infamous second lines. It's home to the Mardi Gras Indians, who dance in the streets in beautiful, flamboyant costumes every year.

But on August 29, 2005, the beloved neighborhood was flooded[1] like the rest of the city, and the vibrant neighborhood was left in shambles. The physical destruction caused by the storm was devastating, and the absence of musicians meant the pulse and soul of the city was gone. Ten years after the mass exodus, the music scene in Tremé and the rest of New Orleans is trying to find its footing.

Benny Jones, the creator and bandleader of the Treme Brass Band, was born in the vivacious community 72 years ago. Over the years, he's carried on a longstanding brass band tradition, and the people of Tremé consider him and the band a cherished symbol of the community's musical legacy. […]

After the Category 5 hurricane hit the city back in 2005 — displacing 1 million people in the Gulf, killing 1,833, and decimating 80 percent of New Orleans, alone — musicians were among those forced to flee[2] the city. […]

It took about a year for the Treme Brass Band to get up and running again, Jones says, and it no longer had standing gigs[3] like it used to. "When we [came] back to the city, a bunch of the clubs were closed down." […]

As we talked in Club Soul, Jones explained the role that music played in healing[4] the city in the aftermath of the storm.

"Music did [help rebuild the city] in a way, it really did," he said. "Music relieved the pain, it kinda eased their mind a little bit. They'd come out to the club, listen to music, and talk about what happened — the hurricane, what they went through." To this day, the music is inspired by the storm. "[Each] musician has a different story to tell about Katrina. They relive what happened to their families. My story was about how I left, how my house was damaged and I had to take my family way out."

The recovery process has been a long one, and the city still has a long way to go before it's back to what it once was — for musicians and non-musicians alike.

✦ Carimah Townes, ThinkProgress.org, August 26, 2015

1. submerged 2. escape 3. concerts 4. helping get better

✦ Residents of the 9th Ward neighbourhood and Treme Brass Band honouring the victims of Hurricane Katrina, New Orleans, Louisiana, May 29, 2006

E-workbook
Classe inversée
hatier-clic.fr/lmu1010

1 Pick out words describing the city, groups of people and music. Link your findings to the consequences of Hurricane Katrina.

2 Explain what part musicians played after Hurricane Katrina. Use the photo to prove your point.

3 ***PAIR WORK*** After a charity event, Benny Jones is interviewed about the role of musicians after the hurricane. Act out the interview.

Prepare your project

Imagine the short speech given by a jazz musician before the concert for a charity event. He or she explains how it can help people.

Grammar Tip Précis → p. 257

You can use **in order to** ou **so as to + V** to explain your goal.

Memory Challenge

In pairs, list three positive things music and musicians can do to bring people together.

Tools in the Spotlight

Entraînez-vous sur la plateforme *Let's Meet Up!*
reussirenlangues.fr

Practise your grammar

Précis grammatical, p. 216

Le gérondif

• Le gérondif est représenté par la forme du verbe en *-ing*. C'est une **nominalisation**, c'est-à-dire la transformation du verbe en nom. On peut donc utiliser le gérondif là où un nom est possible.

• Le gérondif peut être employé comme **sujet** d'une phrase.

__Listening__ to jazz was fashionable in New Orleans at the beginning of the 20th century.

• On peut aussi employer le gérondif **après une préposition**.

Gerry Moore commented that his fingers ached so much from __playing__ that he could hardly move his hands.

• On trouve aussi le gérondif **après des verbes de sentiments** tels que *like, love, prefer* pour des événements déjà vécus.

This singer likes __playing__ Louis Armstrong's jazz solo improvisations.

1 Choisissez le gérondif ou l'infinitif en *to*.

a. I look forward to **(going / to go)** to this jazz concert.
b. I would like **(learning / to learn)** how to play the trumpet.
c. **(Going / To go)** to the Cotton Club in Harlem was popular with jazz lovers in the late 1920s.
d. After **(opening / to open)** the Cotton Club in New York in 1927, jazz musicians also promoted jazz in the Grand Terrace Cafe in Chicago the following year.

2 Transformez les phrases suivantes en utilisant le gérondif du verbe proposé entre parenthèses.

a. He enjoyed *The Great Gatsby*. **(read)**
b. The description of the Roaring 20s usually includes jazz. **(describe)**
c. During the Prohibition in the 1920s Americans were keen on jazz in speakeasies. **(listen to)**
d. I prefer a record by Bessie Smith! She was the most famous blues singer in the 1920s. **(buy)**

Le pluriel des noms

• Le pluriel des **noms réguliers** comptables s'obtient, de manière générale, par l'ajout de ***s*** au nom singulier.

musician → musicians

• Cependant, il existe des **graphies différentes** selon la terminaison des mots au singulier :

– singulier en ***x*** → pluriel en ***es***
box → boxes
– singulier en ***s*** → pluriel en ***es***
pass → passes
– singulier en ***f*** ou ***fe*** → pluriel en ***ves***
leaf → leaves *life → lives*
– singulier en ***y*** → pluriel en ***ies***
family → families

• Certains mots ont des pluriels irréguliers.

man → men *tooth → teeth*
woman → women *foot → feet*
child → children *criterion → criteria*
crisis → crises *phenomenon → phenomena*

3 Indiquez le pluriel irrégulier dans les phrases suivantes.

a. The criteria which explained this jazz musician's choices are numerous.
b. Some of the main phenomena in the 1920s in the USA were jazz and art.
c. Both women and men went to speakeasies to listen to their favourite jazz singers.
d. Jazz can survive and thrive in times of crises.
e. Put your feet up after this long trip across Louisiana!

4 Mettez les mots soulignés au pluriel et faites les modifications nécessaires dans les phrases suivantes.

a. A man and a woman were sitting on a bench in Louis Armstrong Park in New Orleans.
b. A child was playing near the statue of Buddy Bolden.
c. There was a leaf next to the bench.
d. You can often listen to a jazz singer in New Orleans.
e. Just leave your bus pass in this box before you leave New Orleans.

Improve your pronunciation

Précis de phonologie, p. 262

Les sons /dʒ/ et /tʃ/

Audio
CD1 piste 09
MP3 n° 10

- Les sons /dʒ/ et /tʃ/ sont tous les deux composés de **deux phonèmes** prononcés en même temps, donc en un seul son :
  - /d/ + /ʒ/ pour le son /dʒ/
  - /t/ + /ʃ/ pour le son /tʃ/
- Le **son** /dʒ/ correspond en général à la graphie :
  - ***dge*** comme dans *badge*
  - ***j*** comme dans *jazz*, *enjoy*
  - ***g*** suivi de ***e*** ou ***i*** comme dans *dangerous* ou *ginger*
- Le **son** /tʃ/ correspond à la graphie :
  - ***tch*** comme dans *match*
  - ***ch*** comme dans *charity*, *cheer*, *rich*
  - ***t*** suivi de ***ion*** ou ***ure*** comme dans *question* ou *picture*

5 Indiquez s'il s'agit du son /dʒ/ ou du son /tʃ/ dans les mots suivants, puis vérifiez avec l'enregistrement.

Audio
CD1 piste 10
MP3 n° 11

joke • choice • badge • cherry • research • gesture • Jane • chin • jail

6 Indiquez le son /dʒ/ et /tʃ/ dans les phrases suivantes, puis répétez les phrases après l'enregistrement.

Audio
CD1 piste 11
MP3 n° 12

a. The question is why they have chosen the major statue of Buddy Bolden.
b. Naturally, the weekly ritual sustained a mix of African culture.
c. Let's take a picture of this jazz musician in Chicago!
d. Archibald Motley managed to capture the Jazz Age in his paintings.

Work on your writing skills

L'orthographe américaine

L'anglais américain connait quelques **variantes orthographiques** par rapport à l'anglais britannique. En voici quelques exemples.

🇬🇧		🇺🇸	
-re	cent**re** theat**re**	**-er**	cent**er** theat**er**
-our	col**our** neighb**our**	**-or**	col**or** neighb**or**
-se	advertis**e** critici**se**	**-ze**	adverti**ze** critici**ze**
-ence	def**ence** lic**ence**	**-ense**	def**ense** lic**ense**
-ll-	trave**ll**ed trave**ll**ing	**-l-**	trave**l**ed trave**l**ing
-ogue	dial**ogue** catal**ogue**	**-og**	dial**og** catal**og**
-amme	progr**amme**	**-am**	progr**am**
-que	che**que**	**-ck**	che**ck**

7 Trouvez l'intrus dans chacune des phrases suivantes, et indiquez si elle est écrite en anglais britannique ou américain.

a. The neighbour apologised for his behaviour and his bad sense of humor.
b. This dialog in defense of humour is often played in theaters.
c. They travelled to the centre of this country for its colours and flavors.
d. The experts analysed the behavior and the labour of workers.

8 Réécrivez les phrases suivantes en anglais américain.

a. Travelling to the centre of this country requires a licence.
b. They recognised that it was an honour to appear in this catalogue.
c. The modernised harbour emphasised the splendour of the neighbourhood.
d. She cancelled her programme when she realised it was an offence there.

Build up your vocabulary

Audio
CD1 piste 12

Charity actions
MP3 n°13

donations: gifts
relief: aid
funding: financing
raise money: collect funds
comfort: reassure
recover: get better, improve
each cloud has a silver lining: bad times lead to better days

The Blitz
MP3 n°14

bombing: air raid
World War II (WWII): the Second World War
siren /saɪərən/
shelter: refuge
casualties /kæʒjuəltiz/: victims
(physical) pain: suffering
hardship: difficulty
injured, wounded /wu:ndɪd/: hurt
alive

Music
MP3 n°17

band: orchestra
brass instruments: trumpet, trombone, cornet, tuba, saxophone
piano /piænəʊ/
drums: percussion
beat: rhythm /rɪðəm/
track: tune, song
trend: fashion
trendy: fashionable
entertaining: distracting
enjoyable: pleasant

Jazz

Feelings
MP3 n°15

grief: sorrow: (emotional) pain
≠ joy: delight
carefree ≠ anxious
cope: deal with problems
cheer sb up: make sb happy / happier
feel relieved: reassured
have a good time: have a blast: enjoy oneself
look forward to V-ing: feel happy in anticipation

Concerts
MP3 n°16

gig: concert
jam session: improvised concert
venue /venju:/: concert hall
audience: spectators
perform: sing / play / act on stage
clap (hands): applaud
praise: compliment
on stage: in front of an audience

Apprenez et révisez le vocabulaire !

Utilisez Quizlet pour vous entraîner en vous amusant.

Quizlet
hatier-clic.fr/lmu1011

Utilisez le vocabulaire en contexte.

1 Complétez le texte suivant avec des mots de la carte mentale à la forme qui convient.

On 8 March, 1941, during an … …, dozens of people were … and about 35 were killed.
The Café de Paris was a popular jazz … in London where the famous … leader 'Snakehips' Johnson used to … .
The night of the …, the audience felt … and was … … . They were having a good time.

2 Le ou la manager d'un groupe de jazz écrit un message à ses musiciens et musiciennes pour leur annoncer leur participation à un concert pour une association caritative.
Écrivez son texte en utilisant cinq mots de la catégorie *Music* ou *Concert* et cinq mots de la catégorie *Charity actions* de la carte mentale.

AUTO évaluation

Faites le quiz interactif en ligne et suivez les conseils pour vous préparer à l'évaluation.

Quiz
hatier-clic.fr/lmu1012

Project #1

During your summer trip to New Orleans, you went to an exhibition on jazz. Make a presentation to the class.

1 Prepare an introduction for your presentation.

- ✓ Find information about jazz in New Orleans in the unit or on the internet, using acloserwalknola.com for example.
- ✓ Get ready to describe the city, the jazz venues, the atmosphere…

2 Pick two objects you saw in the exhibition.

- ✓ You can choose instruments, clothes, awards, signed pictures, posters or records.
- ✓ Go to the website of New Orleans Jazz Museum for inspiration: nolajazzmuseum.org/collections.
- ✓ Think about the reasons why these objects struck your attention.

3 Choose a jazz artist you discovered.

- ✓ Pick a famous jazz artist: Louis Armstrong, Adelaide Hall, Ella Fitzgerald, Miles Davis…
- ✓ Search online for information about him or her (bands, concerts, awards…).
- ✓ List the reasons why he or she is a great jazz artist.

4 Get ready for your presentation!

- ✓ Select some photos of the objects and the jazz artist to show the class and a song to play.
- ✓ Think about linking words to present your arguments: **what's more**, **in addition**; and examples: **for instance**, **namely**.
- ✓ Use superlatives to show your enthusiasm!

➤ Fiche de méthodologie N°18 p. 296

Project #2

Prepare a quiz show about jazz! In pairs, write 10 questions. In class, mix all the flash cards and start playing.

1 Search for information about jazz places and people in the unit and on the internet.

- ✓ Find biographies of jazz stars: Louis Armstrong, Duke Ellington, Miles Davis, Ella Fitzgerald…
- ✓ Look for facts about New Orleans, Chicago, New York City, London and famous jazz venues.

2 Choose data that is relevant.

- ✓ Select facts from the unit (about famous musicians and events) that other students know or can have heard of.
- ✓ For each event, specify the date and the place where it happened.

3 Check the grammar.

- ✓ Make sure your questions are clear and simple. Check their syntax: **Wh- / How + auxiliary + subject + verb (+ object)?** or **Auxiliary + subject + verb (+ object)?**
- ✓ Questions do not need to be long: the shorter the better! Remember the other students need to understand them at once.

4 Create the flash cards.

- ✓ Write one question and its answer on each card.
- ✓ Depending on how hard each question is, decide how many points it is worth.

➤ Fiche de méthodologie N°5 p. 276

Let's RECAP

Lisez les questions-clés et complétez la fiche bilan avec des exemples et des documents que vous avez étudiés ou découverts.

AXE 1 | Identities and exchanges

SÉQUENCE 1 How did tea become a part of British identity?

E-workbook
Bilan à compléter
hatier-clic.fr/lmu1013

How is tea linked to British history?
How has it become a synonym of Britishness?

#mobility
How did the British steal tea from the Chinese?

#worldeconomy
What part has tea played in the economy of Great Britain? How did the British consumption of tea favour the world economy?

#identity
What importance does tea have in Great Britain?

#socialgroups
What role does tea have in British social life? How can it be a marker of social class?

#hospitality
How is tea part of British hospitality?
What does offering a cup of tea mean?

SÉQUENCE 2 How can jazz bring people together?

E-workbook
Bilan à compléter
hatier-clic.fr/lmu1014

How has this music style travelled around the world and throughout the ages?
How does it shape a sense of belonging among communities where it has spread?

#sharing
What do jazzmen share when they play?
What do audiences find so appealing about jazz?

#solidarity
How has jazz helped people cope with war or disasters?

#culturalexchanges
How has the jazz culture shaped communities in the USA?
How was jazz influenced by southern African-American culture?

#crossingborders
How have jazz musicians managed to popularise jazz across the USA?
How did it become popular in the UK?

GO4IT!

Lisez et écoutez de l'anglais en dehors de la salle de classe ! Voici quelques conseils en lien avec votre séquence.

SÉQUENCE 1

Books and article

For All the Tea in China, SARAH ROSE, 2009

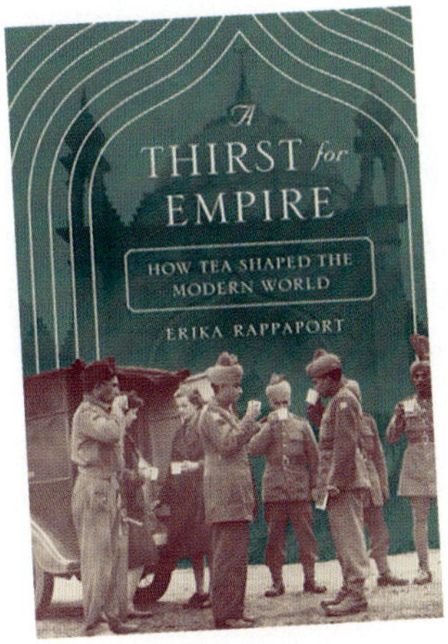

A Thirst for Empire, How Tea Shaped the Modern World, ERIKA RAPPAPORT, 2017

The history of tea in Britain: Google celebrates the cuppa with a Doodle, THETELEGRAPH.CO.UK, 2016
http://bit.ly/2Ih7slD

Film

Song

English Tea, PAUL MCCARTNEY, 2005

Videos

Journey with a Tea Master, PURE LEAF ICED TEA, BBC
http://bit.ly/2FBuhyX

Blessed are the Tea Makers, YORKSHIRE TEA
http://bit.ly/2eUoJzq

How to make tea the British way, BBC
http://bit.ly/1Ss62nd

SÉQUENCE 2

Books

Tales of the Jazz Age, F. SCOTT FITZGERALD, 1922

Jazz, TONI MORRISON, 1992

Jazz: An Introduction to the History and Legends Behind America's Music, BOB BLUMENTHAL, 2008

The Jazz Palace, MARY MORRIS, 2016

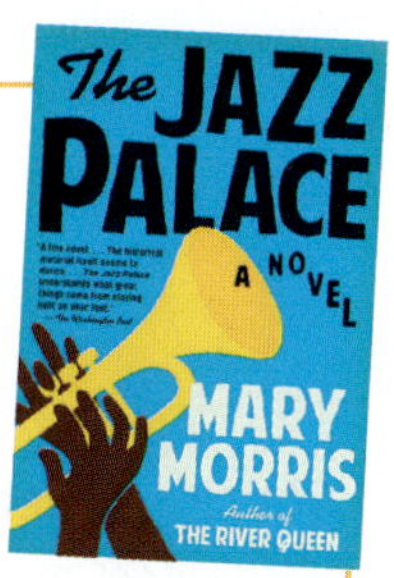

Songs

Sing Sing Sing, BENNY GOODMAN, 1937

Strange Fruit, BILLIE HOLIDAY, 1939

So What, MILES DAVIS, 1959

Take Five, DAVE BRUBECK QUARTET, 1959

What a Wonderful World, LOUIS ARMSTRONG, 1967

Websites

Preservation Hall, New Orleans http://preservationhall.com/hall/music

Jazz FM http://www.jazzfm.com

Films

TV series

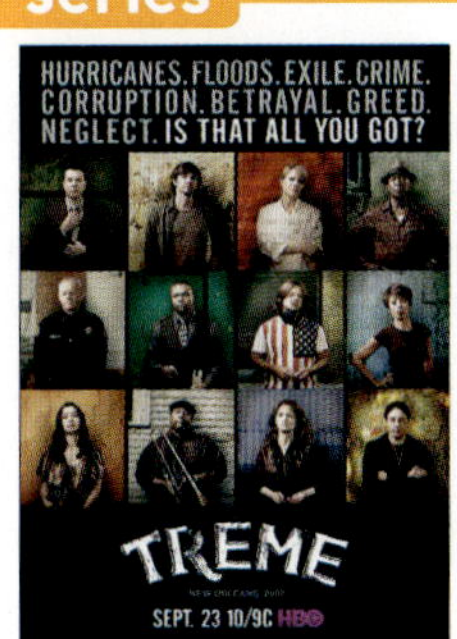

BAC in sight

ÉPREUVE 1

COMPRÉHENSION ORALE

Audio
CD1 piste 13

How the business of tea between Britain and China evolved in the 19th century.

Tips
- Try to identify the number of speakers, the type of document.
- Focus on people, places, time and the main subject by picking out key words.

Fiche de méthodologie N°15 p. 290 Compréhension orale

EXPRESSION ÉCRITE

SUJET 1 Imagine the letter from Britain to the Emperor of China as their business relationships get complicated.

OU

SUJET 2 Should there be restrictions on what companies are allowed to sell for profit?

Tip
- Use the preterite to write about the past.

Fiche de méthodologie N°20 p. 300 Expression écrite

✦ Weighing a tea chest in Canton, 1750

Pour l'épreuve

Questions
Fiche modifiable
hatier-clic.fr/lmu1015

Évaluation
Grille à imprimer
hatier-clic.fr/lmu1016

ÉPREUVE 2

EXPRESSION ÉCRITE

SUJET 1 Write the note James Cuninghame could have left with the box.

OU

SUJET 2 How important is it for a nation to share the same values?
Use examples from the unit and give your personal opinion.

Tip
- Use linking words to add information.

Fiche de méthodologie N°20 p. 300 Expression écrite

✦ The four members of the Beatles posing with cups of tea, October 1965

COMPRÉHENSION ÉCRITE

The oldest tea in Britain

The oldest tea in Britain, a box of leaves and flowers neatly labelled "a sort of tea from China" more than 300 years ago, has turned up in the stores of the Natural History Museum in London.

When it was brought back by James Cuninghame, a Scottish surgeon and amateur naturalist in the late 17th century, tea was still a fabulous rarity, sold at between six and 60 shillings a pound, 10 times the price of even the best coffee. Cuninghame was a passionate plant hunter and may have collected his samples at Amoy in Fujian province, or on the island of Chusan where he described tea growing wild and the local farmers preparing the leaves for the drink.

Academics from Queen Mary University London uncovered his samples while researching the history of the exotic import which rapidly became the British national drink, for a book to be published this summer. They yearned[1] to taste it but were not even allowed to touch the tea. Instead, the glass lid of the small cardboard box was lifted, and they were permitted to sniff the contents.

"It had a very faint scent of hay[2]," one of the academics, Matthew Mauger, said. "In the 18th century, writers struggling to describe this exotic new drink do refer to the smell of hay," his co-author Richard Coulton said. However, he added: "Fresh tea really doesn't last very long – I doubt very much that it would be drinkable."

Cuninghame corresponded with an even more passionate and far wealthier[3] medicine man and plant collector, Hans Sloane. Sloane had introduced England to another exotic brew. By adding milk to ground cocoa beans from Jamaica he reduced the bitterness and gave birth to drinking chocolate. Like chocolate, tea was first promoted for its medicinal value. […]

✦ Culture and preparation of tea, China, 1847

From the start despite, or because of, the enormous cost, tea drinking spread rapidly among the wealthy. By 1660 Samuel Pepys recorded: "I did send for a cup of tee (a China drink) of which I never had drank before." The porcelain cups and tea pots came in with the leaves, used as ballast to counteract the problem for shippers of a very bulky but very light cargo.

The drink became cheaper in the 19th century when the East India Company began to import in bulk tea grown on land it controlled in India, instead of entering into fractious[4] negotiations with Chinese merchants. […]

Tea became an emblem of domestic virtue and temperance[5] – though the temperance movement was initially suspicious of its dangerously stimulant qualities – and the tea break the joyful mandatory pause in an exhausting day's industrial labour.

✦ Maev Kennedy, *The Guardian*, May 26, 2015

1. desire (want) 2. dried grass 3. richer 4. hard
5. sobriety (teetotaller)

Tip

➤ Before you start, identify the main elements of your text: the title, the introduction, the source of the text and when it was published.

➤ Fiche de méthodologie N°16 p. 292 Compréhension écrite

Pour l'épreuve

Questions
Fiche modifiable
hatier-clic.fr/lmu1017

Évaluation
Grille à imprimer
hatier-clic.fr/lmu1018

BAC in sight

ÉPREUVE 1

COMPRÉHENSION ORALE

Audio
CD1 piste 14

Jazz has dramatically evolved in recent years. The following interview explains the complexity of this genre.

✦ Nate Chinen, *Playing Changes: Jazz for the New Century*, 2018

Tips
- Pay attention to the number of voices. Try to identify who the journalist is.
- Guess how people are connected and whether what they say is similar or contradictory.

➤ Fiche de méthodologie N°15 p. 290 Compréhension orale

EXPRESSION ÉCRITE

SUJET 1 In your opinion, will jazz be popular with teenagers in years to come?

OU

SUJET 2 Write an article explaining how jazz could enjoy a type of renaissance.

Tips
- Double-check verbs: are you writing about the past, the future or the present?
- Use adjectives that sound specific, not only adjectives like "important" or "big"!

➤ Fiche de méthodologie N°20 p. 300 Expression écrite

Pour l'épreuve

Questions
Fiche modifiable
hatier-clic.fr/lmu1019

Évaluation
Grille à imprimer
hatier-clic.fr/lmu1020

ÉPREUVE 2

EXPRESSION ÉCRITE

SUJET 1 How can new musical genres emerge today? You can discuss jazz as well as other new trends and artists.

OU

SUJET 2 A young artist meets a jazz veteran who has played on the stages of many festivals. They discuss the evolution of music over the years.

✦ Students playing jazz in the streets of New Orleans

Tips
- Find appropriate ice-breakers to start your dialogue: "How are you?"; "Where did you last...?"; etc.
- Think about interesting tips the jazz veteran can give the young musician: "I think you should..."

➤ Fiche de méthodologie N°20 p. 300 Expression écrite

COMPRÉHENSION ÉCRITE

The British jazz explosion: meet the musicians rewriting the rulebook

For many of us, jazz has seemed like something other people listened to. But in the past few years, the genre has had a serious overhaul[1]. When Kendrick Lamar released his landmark album *To Pimp a Butterfly* in 2015, one of its most extraordinary aspects was its liberal use of jazz, which dovetailed[2] with hip-hop and opened it up for a new generation. Not only did it immediately feel more accessible but, played by the likes of strikingly cosmic characters such as Thundercat and Kamasi Washington, it looked commandingly cool.

In the UK, a new and thrilling jazz movement has evolved. As with Lamar, Thundercat and Washington, it is born out of fresh experimentalism, is reaching far younger, more diverse audiences and doesn't care for snootiness[3]. Unlike in previous waves, these musicians are in their 20s and early 30s, come from diverse backgrounds and, as with grime, have created their own community outside of major labels and concert halls. Their music, meanwhile, pulls liberally from other genres, whether hip-hop, neo-soul, UK club sounds such as broken beat, or from the African and Caribbean diaspora. And it's not just at gigs that you can hear it but, much like in the acid jazz days, nightclubs too. British DJs such as Bradley Zero and Floating Points have liberated jazz for the dancefloor to the extent that it's now not unheard of for a 10-minute Pharaoh Sanders odyssey to be spun on the decks to an appreciative, twenty-something crowd.

Notable, too, is how prolific this wave is, with jazz musicians infiltrating summer music festival listings, signing to indie[4] labels or taking their sound abroad. The sheer volume of talent is being recognised across the world. "Wherever I'm travelling, whether it's in the States, Argentina, Japan, or all over Europe, everyone is talking to me about the British invasion," says DJ and broadcaster Gilles Peterson [...].

The movement hasn't just sprung out of nowhere. In London especially there is the sense that today's jazz musicians have come up together over the past few years. They are collaborative, constantly threading through one another's projects, and jamming together at a number of DIY stomping grounds [...]. Broadcaster Teju Adeleye says: "The artists don't feel like inaccessible superstars, they come to all the gigs and jam nights."

Adeleye is one of the new crop of radio hosts who are supporting jazz's rising stars on internet stations such as NTS and Worldwide FM. "Having affordable spaces where people can go and experiment in front of audiences is important," she says. "It fosters something genuine in a city where so much is driven by corporate ventures." [...]

Perhaps what's most exciting, though, is the sense that this generation is wresting jazz from its gatekeepers and making it their own. With this scene, says Adeleye, "not everyone is classically or formally trained", and as a result "there's an accessible, anti-hero energy that feels like sweet vindication[5] for a music that should be for everyone, but has felt locked away and preserved only for a few. They've liberated the sound."

✦ Kate Hutchinson, *The Guardian*, April 8, 2018

1. massive evolution 2. mixed 3. arrogance 4. independent 5. justification

✦ Kamasi Washington performing at Monterey Jazz Festival in California

Tips

➤ Focus on places, list the names of musicians or bands and the words used to qualify their music.

➤ Categorise musical genres and find what differentiates them from one another.

➤ Fiche de méthodologie N°16 p. 292 Compréhension écrite

Pour l'épreuve

Questions — Fiche modifiable — hatier-clic.fr/lmu1021

Évaluation — Grille à imprimer — hatier-clic.fr/lmu1022

AXE 2

Private space and public space

Espace privé et espace public

SÉQUENCE 1 How are women detectives represented in fiction?

Projects

Project #1: Film your pitch for a new Sherlock Holmes TV series with a female actor playing Sherlock.

Project #2: You are the screen-writer of *Shirley Holmes, female detective*. Prepare a presentation of the first episode of the series.

Tools

Grammaire	le génitif, les pronoms relatifs
Phonologie	les sons /æ/ et /ɑː/
Écriture	le paragraphe argumentatif
Vocabulaire	la fiction policière, les stéréotypes

SÉQUENCE 2 How do Hollywood love stories reflect social progress?

Projects

Project #1: Review a Hollywood love story reflecting the evolution of the couple in the USA for your YouTube channel.

Project #2: Prepare a plot summary for an adaptation of a classic Hollywood love story.

Tools

Grammaire	les verbes prépositionnels, l'ordre des adjectifs
Phonologie	les mots commençant par *h*
Écriture	la ponctuation du dialogue
Vocabulaire	les films, la société

#genderequality #socialchange
#womensemancipation #workingwomen

Priyanka Chopra as Alexandra Parrish, *Quantico*, ABC Studios, 2015

#traditions #education
#emancipation
#familylaw #representinglove

The film set of *Gone with the Wind*, 1939

SÉQUENCE 1

How are women detectives represented in fiction?

A Evolving figures

GROUP WORK

GROUP A

GROUP B

GROUP C

GROUP D

1 Describe how the woman detective is depicted in your document (clothes, facial expression, setting).

2 Match one of these publication dates with your document. Explain your choice.

1930 - 1967 - 1990 - 2012

3 Imagine the story of the book, film or TV series corresponding to your document in 30 words maximum.

4 Present the book, film or TV series corresponding to your document to the class. Indicate why it looks modern or not.

B A stereotypical detective

Audio
CD1 piste 15

1 List some of the qualities of detectives and some stereotypes about spinsters.

2 Explain how Amelia Butterworth helps Detective Inspector Bryce.

3 For your new detective novel, create a stereotypical character: a spinster detective. Write a short paragraph describing her appearance and her interview techniques.

Culture Tip

"A **spinster** is a woman who is not married, especially a woman who is no longer young and seems unlikely ever to marry." (Cambridge dictionary)
Some spinsters, like Agatha Christie's **Miss Marple**, became famous both in print and on TV.

Grammar Spot

Genitive TOOLS → p. 44

The No.1 Ladies' Detective Agency

Word Spot

investigation: enquiry
evidence: proof
professional ≠ amateur
active ≠ passive
traditional ≠ modern
unconventional: unusual
unfair: unjust
equal ≠ unequal
determined
nosy: gossipy
cunning: clever
be shown in action
solve a crime
look for clues
in the foreground ≠ in the background

C A masculine atmosphere

Vidéo
hatier-clic.fr/lmu1023

E-workbook
Fiche à imprimer
hatier-clic.fr/lmu1024

1 Present the main character.

2 Rearrange the jumbled words and explain why the producer chose them. Use them to describe how Jane is considered in her job.

WORLD – 'S – WOMAN – A – MEN – IN – A

3 Jane calls her sister to tell her about her first day at work. Imagine what she says about her feelings, her relationship with her co-workers and the atmosphere.

Culture Tip

Prime Suspect 1973 is a British television detective drama series set in London.
It tells the story of 22-year-old Jane Tennison's first days in the police force.

D The No.1 Ladies' Detective Agency

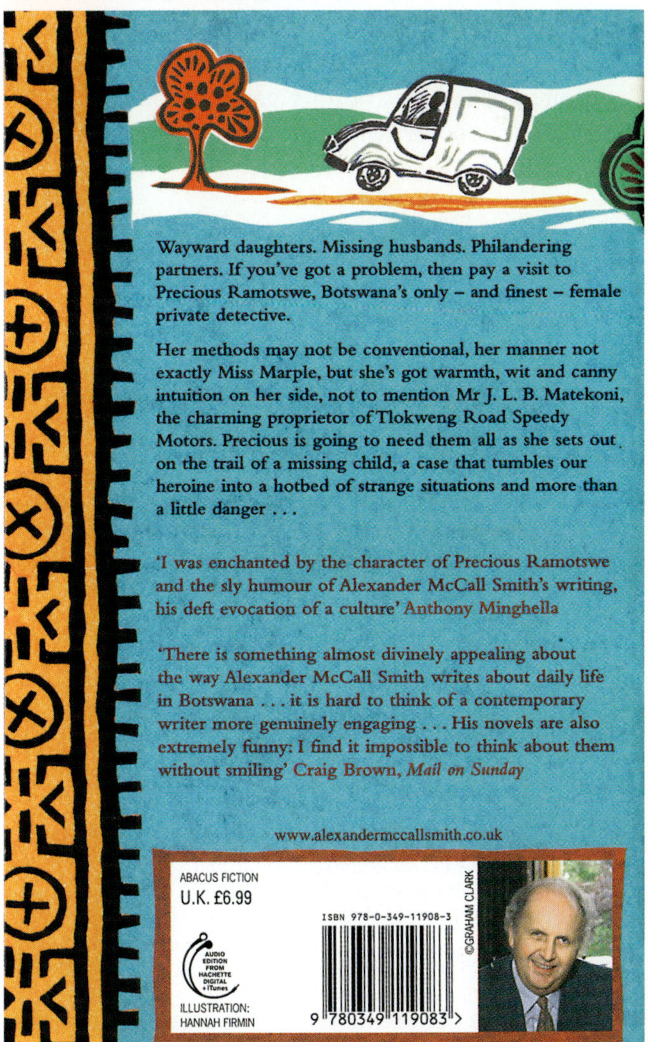

Wayward daughters. Missing husbands. Philandering partners. If you've got a problem, then pay a visit to Precious Ramotswe, Botswana's only – and finest – female private detective.

Her methods may not be conventional, her manner not exactly Miss Marple, but she's got warmth, wit and canny intuition on her side, not to mention Mr J. L. B. Matekoni, the charming proprietor of Tlokweng Road Speedy Motors. Precious is going to need them all as she sets out on the trail of a missing child, a case that tumbles our heroine into a hotbed of strange situations and more than a little danger . . .

'I was enchanted by the character of Precious Ramotswe and the sly humour of Alexander McCall Smith's writing, his deft evocation of a culture' Anthony Minghella

'There is something almost divinely appealing about the way Alexander McCall Smith writes about daily life in Botswana . . . it is hard to think of a contemporary writer more genuinely engaging . . . His novels are also extremely funny: I find it impossible to think about them without smiling' Craig Brown, *Mail on Sunday*

www.alexandermccallsmith.co.uk

ABACUS FICTION
U.K. £6.99
ISBN 978-0-349-11908-3
ILLUSTRATION: HANNAH FIRMIN
©GRAHAM CLARK

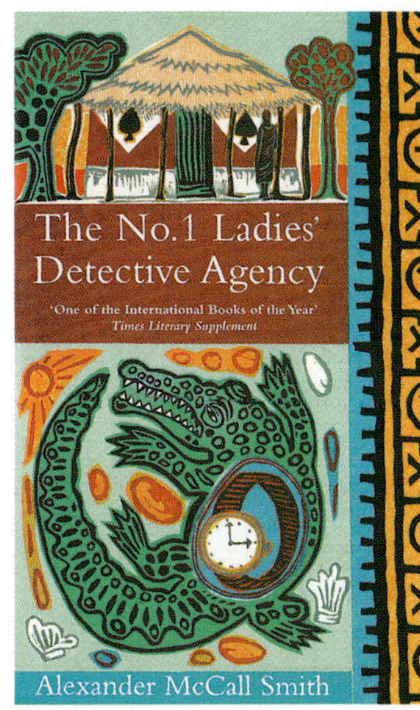

✦ Alexander McCall Smith, *The No.1 Ladies' Detective Agency*, 1998

1 Comment on the graphic elements on the cover. Choose one that strikes you as unusual for a detective novel.

2 Read the back cover and pick out elements which make *The No.1 Ladies' Detective Agency* unique.

3 You are a member of a book club. Present this book using five adjectives that best define it.

Prepare your project

Imagine a modern detective novel where the main character is a woman. Write a short paragraph for the back cover.

Grammar Tip Précis → p. 239

Use the **simple present** to write about the detective and the story.

Memory Challenge

Look at p. 40-41 for two minutes then close your book. In groups, you have five minutes to go through the alphabet with as many words about female detectives as you can.
Ex: A for agency, B for book...

How are women detectives represented in fiction?

E A newcomer

I was the chief medical examiner of Virginia, the first woman to hold that position. I'd become Lucy's caretaker after my selfish sister Dorothy decided to unload her on me. What was presented as a short impromptu visit turned into forever and the timing for when it all began couldn't have been worse.
My first summer in Richmond and it was under siege as a serial killer strangled women in their own homes, in their own beds. The murders were escalating and becoming increasingly sadistic. We couldn't catch him. We didn't have a clue. I was new. The press and politicians thundered down on me like an avalanche. I was a misfit. I was chilly and aloof[1]. I was peculiar. What kind of woman would dissect dead bodies in a morgue? […]
The exhilaration of being one of the first female chiefs in the United States quickly lost its thrill […]. The former chief medical examiner was a misogynistic bigoted alcoholic who died suddenly and left a disastrous legacy. No seasoned[2] board-certified forensic pathologist with a decent reputation wanted to take his place. So a bright idea occurred to the men in charge. What about a woman?
Women are good at cleaning up messes. Why not find a female forensic expert? It doesn't matter if she's young and missing the requisite experience to head a statewide system. As long as she's a qualified expert in court and minds her manners she can grow into the position. How about an overeducated detail-addicted work-obsessed perfectionistic Italian woman who grew up dirt poor, has everything to prove, is turbo-driven and divorced with no kids?

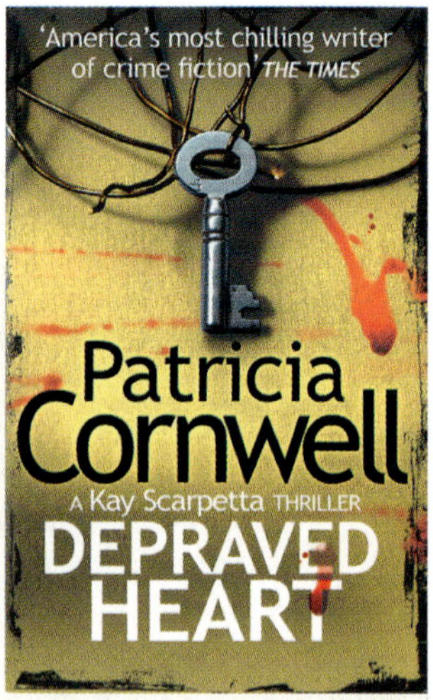

✦ Patricia Cornwell, *Depraved Heart*, 2015

1. distant 2. experienced

1 Find details about the life and job of Kay Scarpetta, the narrator.

2 Pick out the words linked to the former Chief Medical Examiner and guess what Kay Scarpetta thinks of him.

3 You are the editor of *Forensics Magazine*. Write a short article announcing the arrival of Kay Scarpetta at Virginian CME: why she came, who she replaces, her qualities, her career…

Culture Tip

Patricia Cornwell wrote her first novel, *Post-mortem* (1990), while working as a computer analyst at the Office of the Chief Medical Examiner in Richmond, Virginia. It was the first authentic forensic thriller.

F Inside the FBI

Classe inversée

✦ Trailer for *FBI* TV series, CBS, 2018

Vidéo
hatier-clic.fr/lmu1025

E-workbook
Classe inversée
hatier-clic.fr/lmu1026

1 Study how female characters appear in the scenes.

2 Use the following words to describe what the FBI director says in the office.

authoritarian - self-confident - manager

3 Choose one of the two female characters. Comment on her tone, her choice of words and her expectations.

Grammar Spot

Relative pronouns TOOLS → p. 44
"the female detective who is part of a police team"

Word Spot

sleuth: investigator
subordinate
forensic science
scientist
offence: crime
issue: problem
feeling: emotion
cliché: stereotype
pioneer /paɪənɪəʳ/
strength: force
skill: ability: talent
deduction
superiority ≠ inferiority
skilled: qualified
feminist
manage: lead
be in charge

G Reading about female detectives

Why do we so enjoy reading about female detectives?

Part of the enjoyment, I suspect, lies[1] in the satisfaction that we derive from seeing women, who have suffered so much from male arrogance and condescension, either outwitting[2] men or demonstrating that they are just as capable as men of doing something that may have been seen as a male preserve. We live today in a society in which gender equality has been, to a very large extent, realised. At the time at which *The Female Detective* was written, in 1864, of course, things were very different. The relegation of women to a subservient[3] position within society — a position in which they were outsiders to the male-dominated worlds of work and affairs — meant that for women to be involved in the investigation of crime was a novel thing. Today one might expect that novelty to have faded[4], as women do all the jobs previously monopolised by men. Yet the idea of the female detective as being special or unusual still persists in literary and cinematic treatments of criminal investigation. […]

There are other factors, though, that I suspect lie behind[5] the popularity of the female detective. One is that the woman sleuth is often portrayed as the outsider in the male world of policing and criminal investigation. This operates in two ways: one where the woman is a member of a police force, and one where she is the freelance who operates either at the request of the official investigators or as a well-meaning bystander. In the case of the female detective who is part of a police team, the outsider status results from the fact that women police detectives frequently operate in a male-dominated force. They are frequently portrayed as having to deal with sceptical and sexist superiors who are only too eager to detect weakness […].

✦ Alexander McCall Smith, *The Independent*, 2012

1. is found 2. being more clever than 3. inferior 4. diminished 5. are the hidden causes of

Culture Tip

With ***The Female Detective***, published in 1864, British writer James Redding Ware created the first professional female detective character, opening the way for other famous female sleuths such as Miss Marple and Nancy Drew.

Pédagogie différenciée

TRAIL A

1 Pick out words and phrases referring to women in the first part of the text (l. 1-19). Classify them in two columns: past and present. Explain the situation of women in the past.

2 Focus on lines 14 to 19 and say whether women sleuths are still seen as special today.

3 Focus on lines 20 to 33 and explain why women detectives are always seen as outsiders.

TRAIL B

1 Compare the life of female detectives in the past and in the present. Focus on lines 1 to 19.

2 Explain whether the "novelty" has "faded" (l. 15).

3 Explain which factor behind the popularity of female detectives is mentioned at the end of the text (l. 20-33).

Meet up! "We live today in a society in which gender equality has been, to a very large extent, realised." (l. 6) Write a short paragraph to explain how this is true in detective fiction.

Prepare your project

Record a one-minute audio for your blog where you talk about a female detective you know. Explain why she is a typical female detective.

Grammar Tip Précis → p. 236

Use the modal **can** to demonstrate the detective's skills.

Memory Challenge

In pairs, write down all the words you can link to female detectives in fiction, then compare your list with your classmate's. May the best win!

Tools in the Spotlight

Entraînez-vous sur la plateforme *Let's Meet Up!*
reussirenlangues.fr

Practise your grammar

Précis grammatical, p. 216

Le génitif

- Le génitif permet d'établir un rapport de **possession**.
  - nom singulier + ***'s*** + nom

It is the detective's bag.

  - nom pluriel se terminant par un ***s*** + ***'*** + nom

The No.1 Ladies' Detective Agency

  - nom pluriel irrégulier + ***'s*** + nom

Children's books include a lot of detective stories.

- Le génitif peut aussi être employé pour les **expressions de temps** (jour, mois, année).
  - expression de temps au singulier + ***'s*** + nom

The film Blue Steel *was advertised in yesterday's newspaper.*

1 Remplacez l'adjectif possessif souligné par un génitif en utilisant les mots entre parenthèses.

a. This study room is <u>their</u> room. (the inspectors)
b. <u>His</u> detective is called Philip Marlowe in *The Big Sleep*. (Raymond Chandler)
c. <u>Their</u> detectives are similar to heroes. (British authors)
d. <u>Their</u> reading choices include a lot of detective fiction. (Children)
e. <u>His</u> essay deals with fictional detectives. (James)
f. <u>Their</u> house is located in Brumley in *An Inspector Calls*. (The Birlings)

Les pronoms relatifs

Who, which, that, whose sont des pronoms relatifs.

On distingue les **propositions relatives descriptives** (ou appositives : encadrées par des virgules) qui apportent un complément d'information et peuvent donc être omises, et les **propositions relatives déterminatives** qui définissent l'antécédent et sont donc essentielles pour l'identifier.

- ***who*** → pour une personne

*The detective, **who** has found out the truth, will be rewarded.* (personne + relative descriptive)

*In the case of the female detective **who** is part of a police team, the outsider status results from the fact...* (personne + relative déterminative)

- ***which*** → pour une chose

*The bag, **which** had been forgotten, was brought to the police station.* (chose + relative descriptive)

- ***that*** → pour une chose (ou une personne dans le cas d'une relative déterminative)

*The car **that** was parked opposite the station was the murderer's.* (chose + relative déterminative)

*The man **that** was found in the park may be the murderer.* (personne + relative déterminative)

- ***whose*** → pour établir un rapport de possession

*The inspector, **whose** car is blue, has just arrived.*

2 Complétez les énoncés suivants par le pronom relatif qui convient et Ø si l'omission du pronom relatif est possible.

Ex: The books ... I like best are detective stories.
→ The books **that / Ø** I like best are detective stories.

a. Inspectors, ... role is crucial in revealing what has actually happened, are always admired by readers ... are looking forward to discovering the name of the murderer.
b. The plot, ... is often a complex strategy, can be highly unexpected.
c. This man, ... wife is an inspector, has been living in Baker Street for quite a few years.
d. The problem ... the detective has been trying to solve secretly for a while has finally been revealed to the readers.

3 Utilisez un pronom relatif pour réunir les deux phrases en une seule.

a. In Patricia Cornwell's story, Kay Scarpetta has been promoted. She is a young American woman.
b. The murderer has been arrested. His flat was searched by the police yesterday.
c. Sir Arthur Conan Doyle wrote *A Study in Scarlet* in 1887. The book introduces us to Sherlock Holmes.
d. CSI investigated a recent murder. The murder had been committed by a young woman.

Improve your pronunciation

Précis de phonologie, p. 262

Les sons /æ/ et /ɑː/

Audio
CD1 piste 16
MP3 n° 18

• La voyelle /æ/ est une voyelle **courte**.
Le son /æ/ correspond, en général, à la graphie ***a*** dans les cas suivants :
- graphie ***a*** suivie de ***c*** + ***k*** (*back*, *pack*)
- graphie ***a*** suivie d'une seule consonne (*bat*, *can*)

⚠ Si ***a*** est suivie d'une seule consonne puis de la seule lettre ***e***, on ne prononce pas /æ/, mais /eɪ/ comme dans *female*. Mais dans le cas d'un mot dont la dernière syllabe de termine par *-age*, la syllabe se prononce /ɪdʒ/ (*manage*, *encourage*).

• La voyelle /ɑː/ est une voyelle **longue**. En phonétique, les /ː/ qui suivent une voyelle indiquent qu'elle est longue. Le son /ɑː/ peut correspondre aux graphies suivantes :
- graphie ***a*** suivie de ***s***, ***f***, ***nce***, ***th*** (*class*, *staff*, *lance*, *path*)
- graphie ***a*** suivie de ***r*** (*Marple*)
- graphie ***a*** suivie de ***lm*** ou ***lf*** (*palm*, *half*)
- graphie ***au*** (*laugh*)
- graphie ***ea*** suivie de ***r*** (*heart*)

4 Écrivez les phrases et indiquez si la graphie soulignée se prononce /æ/ ou /ɑː/, puis écoutez l'enregistrement pour confirmer vos réponses.

Audio
CD1 piste 17
MP3 n° 19

a. This article from January on female detectives in charge of murders is heartbreaking.
b. Their active participation turns these amateur sleuths into real dramatic characters.
c. Indeed, Agatha Christie's Miss Marple is so talented in her quest for truth!
d. This man argues that he is not an amateur. And he is very classy!

5 Écrivez les mots et indiquez si la graphie soulignée se prononce /æ/ ou /ɑː/, puis écoutez l'enregistrement pour confirmer vos réponses.

Audio
CD1 piste 18
MP3 n° 20

Agatha • Marple • drama • character • amateur • heart • talented • fast

Work on your writing skills

Le paragraphe argumentatif

• Le paragraphe argumentatif sert à défendre une **thèse** (une idée ou un point de vue) à l'aide d'**arguments** illustrés par des **exemples**.

TIP Avant de rédiger, écrivez au **brouillon** votre thèse et vos arguments, puis barrez les moins convaincants et ceux qui se recoupent. Trouvez des exemples pour justifier chaque argument.

• On utilise des **mots de liaison** pour articuler un paragraphe argumentatif.
- Commencer : *To begin with... First of all...*
- Ajouter une idée : *In addition... What's more... Furthermore... Also...*
- Exprimer un contraste : *On the contrary... On the other hand... However... Whereas... While...*
- Donner un exemple : *For example... For instance...*
- Exprimer la conséquence : *As a consequence... Consequently... As a result... That's why...*
- Donner son opinion : *To me... As for me... In my opinion... I think... I believe...*
- Conclure : *So... In conclusion... To conclude...*

6 Remettez les phrases dans l'ordre.

a. In my opinion, there is no doubt that female detectives have improved the quality and the plots of past and modern works of fiction.
b. That's why we can consider women detectives should be more present in fiction.
c. First of all, do women characters in detective novels, films or TV series make them more interesting?
d. For instance, in its latest series adaptation, the female version of Watson helps the main character express his feelings more freely.

7 Écrivez un court paragraphe argumentatif pour répondre à la question : *Should Sherlock Holmes become a woman in the next film adaptation?* **Vous devrez utiliser au moins cinq mots de liaison.**

Build up your vocabulary

Audio
CD1 piste 19

Women detectives

Characteristics MP3 n°21

skill: talent: ability
clever: smart
ingenious
subtle
determined
self-confident
strong: tough /tʌf/
authoritarian
skilled: qualified
talented
professional ≠ amateur /æmətəʳ/

Tasks MP3 n°22

forensic science: study of crime scenes
investigation: enquiry
offence: crime, murder
issue: problem
evidence: proof
look for clues
solve a crime
manage: lead
be in charge

Stereotypes MP3 n°26

spinster
cliché: stereotype
strength: force
deduction
feeling: emotion
sensitive
nosy: gossipy
cunning /kʌnɪŋ/: sly
traditional ≠ modern
unconventional: unusual
stereotypical

Jobs MP3 n°23

sleuth /sluːθ/: detective
subordinate: person who has a lower position
police officer: cop (*informal*)
policeman / policewoman
sergeant, captain
Crime Scene Investigator
chief medical examiner
scientist

Gender equality MP3 n°25

evolution
emancipation
social change
superiority ≠ inferiority
pioneer /paɪənɪəʳ/
feminist
unfair: unjust
equal ≠ unequal
active ≠ passive
be on an equal footing

Fiction MP3 n°24

novel
trailer
screenwriter
scenario
character
plot
cliffhanger
twist

Apprenez et révisez le vocabulaire !

Utilisez Quizlet pour vous entraîner en vous amusant.

Quizlet
hatier-clic.fr/lmu1027

Utilisez le vocabulaire en contexte.

1 Complétez les phrases suivantes avec des mots de la carte mentale à la forme qui convient.

Women detectives are ... and show ... . They are as ... as men. Their image in literature has evolved throughout the years. They were ... at the beginning, but they progressively became ... . In novels and series nowadays, they are not ... but ... . One can say it is the end of a stereotyped approach to ... stories, in other words it is the end of ... about female detectives.

2 Écrivez une courte annonce pour une nouvelle série télévisée policière avec les traductions anglaises de ces mots, que vous trouverez dans la carte mentale.

résoudre un crime — pionnière — déterminée — émotion — policière

AUTO évaluation

Faites le quiz interactif en ligne et suivez les conseils pour vous préparer à l'évaluation.

Quiz
hatier-clic.fr/lmu1028

Project #1

Film your pitch for a new Sherlock Holmes TV series with a female actor playing Sherlock.

1 Introduce the topic.

- ✓ Show why the "cop show" genre needs to evolve.
- ✓ Use linking words: **because**, **since**, **that's why**...

2 Find at least three arguments.

- ✓ Using the documents you read or watched in this unit, imagine the audience targeted and compare successful TV series.
- ✓ Justify your opinion using: **in my opinion**, **to my mind**, **to me**, **I believe**, **I think**...

3 Provide relevant examples.

- ✓ Show how female cops have been portrayed in books, films and TV series.
- ✓ Use **more / less** + long adjective **+ than** or adjective **+ -er + than** to compare the way actresses act, their personality, their life...

4 Organise your ideas.

- ✓ Select five linking words that you will be using while improvising your pitch: **in addition**, **what's more**, **besides**...

5 Try to make an impression.

- ✓ Don't stick to traditional models! Be creative!

➤ Fiche de méthodologie N°11 p. 284

Project #2

You are the screenwriter of *Shirley Holmes, female detective*. Prepare a presentation of the first episode of the series.

1 Create a striking character.

- ✓ Find character traits that make her stand out!
- ✓ Use adjectives to describe her investigation style: **professional ≠ amateur**, **determined**, **unconventional**, **modern ≠ traditional**...

2 Do some research.

- ✓ Find inspiration from the content of the unit or from other fictional characters. How is your character's life (relationships, lifestyle)?

3 Prepare the plot.

- ✓ Imagine what the investigation is about and how your character will lead it.
- ✓ Use linking words to show the progress of the investigation: **firstly**, **secondly**, **then**, **all of a sudden**, **finally**.

4 Make up secondary characters.

- ✓ Think about your heroine's team if she has one. Do her male colleagues help her?

5 Create cliffhangers.

- ✓ Add some twists to surprise the viewers. You want them to watch episode 2!

➤ Fiche de méthodologie N°20 p. 300

SÉQUENCE 2

How do Hollywood love stories reflect social progress?

A Are love stories evolving?

GROUP WORK

GROUP A ✦ dir. by Victor Fleming, 1939

GROUP B ✦ dir. by Nora Ephron, 1993

GROUP C ✦ dir. by James Cameron, 1997

GROUP D ✦ dir. by Sanaa Hamri, 2006

GROUP E ✦ dir. by Peyton Reed, 2006

GROUP F ✦ dir. by Damien Chazelle, 2016

1 Describe your group's poster (place, colours, characters, title, attitudes...).

2 List typical and atypical elements of Hollywood love stories in your poster.

3 Prepare questions about your classmates' posters (title, director, situation...).

E-workbook
Fiche à imprimer
hatier-clic.fr/lmu1029

4 Answer your classmates' questions on your group's poster.

Word Spot

- rom-com: romantic comedy
- director /daɪrektəʳ/
- decorum: appropriate behaviour
- epic
- classic
- progressive
- fall in love with sb
- get together: become a couple
- be in a relationship ≠ be single
- break up: split up
- argue /ɑːgjuː/: have an argument
- censor
- break the standards
- be released
- find Mr or Ms Right

Grammar Spot

Prepositional verbs TOOLS → p. 52

"his organization finally **shifted from** restricting filmmakers to alerting audiences"

Project #1

Film your pitch for a new Sherlock Holmes TV series with a female actor playing Sherlock.

1 Introduce the topic.
- ✓ Show why the "cop show" genre needs to evolve.
- ✓ Use linking words: **because**, **since**, **that's why**...

2 Find at least three arguments.
- ✓ Using the documents you read or watched in this unit, imagine the audience targeted and compare successful TV series.
- ✓ Justify your opinion using: **in my opinion**, **to my mind**, **to me**, **I believe**, **I think**...

3 Provide relevant examples.
- ✓ Show how female cops have been portrayed in books, films and TV series.
- ✓ Use **more / less** + long adjective **+ than** or adjective **+ -er + than** to compare the way actresses act, their personality, their life...

4 Organise your ideas.
- ✓ Select five linking words that you will be using while improvising your pitch: **in addition**, **what's more**, **besides**...

5 Try to make an impression.
- ✓ Don't stick to traditional models! Be creative!

Fiche de méthodologie N°11 p. 284

Project #2

You are the screenwriter of *Shirley Holmes, female detective*. Prepare a presentation of the first episode of the series.

1 Create a striking character.
- ✓ Find character traits that make her stand out!
- ✓ Use adjectives to describe her investigation style: **professional ≠ amateur**, **determined**, **unconventional**, **modern ≠ traditional**...

2 Do some research.
- ✓ Find inspiration from the content of the unit or from other fictional characters. How is your character's life (relationships, lifestyle)?

3 Prepare the plot.
- ✓ Imagine what the investigation is about and how your character will lead it.
- ✓ Use linking words to show the progress of the investigation: **firstly**, **secondly**, **then**, **all of a sudden**, **finally**.

4 Make up secondary characters.
- ✓ Think about your heroine's team if she has one. Do her male colleagues help her?

5 Create cliffhangers.
- ✓ Add some twists to surprise the viewers. You want them to watch episode 2!

Fiche de méthodologie N°20 p. 300

SÉQUENCE 2

How do Hollywood love stories reflect social progress?

A Are love stories evolving?

GROUP WORK

GROUP A ✦ dir. by Victor Fleming, 1939

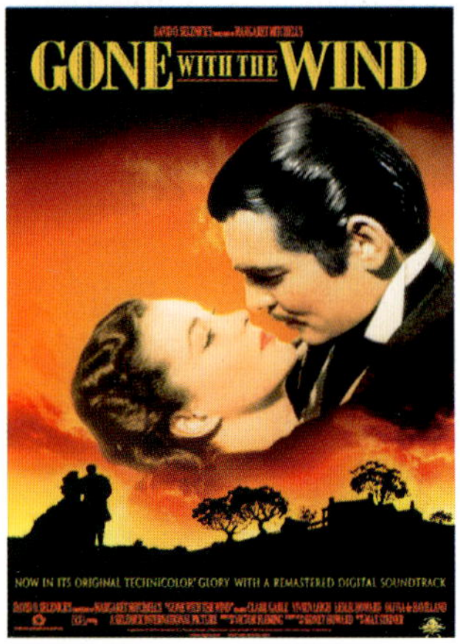

GROUP B ✦ dir. by Nora Ephron, 1993

GROUP C ✦ dir. by James Cameron, 1997

GROUP D ✦ dir. by Sanaa Hamri, 2006

GROUP E ✦ dir. by Peyton Reed, 2006

GROUP F ✦ dir. by Damien Chazelle, 2016

1 Describe your group's poster (place, colours, characters, title, attitudes...).

2 List typical and atypical elements of Hollywood love stories in your poster.

3 Prepare questions about your classmates' posters (title, director, situation...).

E-workbook
Fiche à imprimer
hatier-clic.fr/lmu1029

4 Answer your classmates' questions on your group's poster.

Grammar Spot

Prepositional verbs TOOLS → p. 52

"his organization finally **shifted from** restricting filmmakers **to** alerting audiences"

Word Spot

- rom-com: romantic comedy
- director /daɪrektəʳ/
- decorum: appropriate behaviour
- epic
- classic
- progressive
- fall in love with sb
- get together: become a couple
- be in a relationship ≠ be single
- break up: split up
- argue /ɑːgjuː/: have an argument
- censor
- break the standards
- be released
- find Mr or Ms Right

B Influencing the moral codes

From 1930 to 1968, major Hollywood studios had to use a set of moral guidelines which was called the Motion Picture Production Code. It was also known under the name of the Hays Code after Will H. Hays.

For decades, it's true, the major film studios were governed by a production code requiring that their pictures be "wholesome[1]" and "moral" and encourage what the studios called "correct thinking."

But that code, which was officially abandoned 40 years ago this year, was the result of a nationwide backlash — an outraged reaction to a Hollywood that by 1922 had come to seem like a moral quagmire[2] [...]

"The code sets up high standards of performance for motion-picture producers," Hays proclaimed when the new code was unveiled. "It states the considerations which good taste and community value make necessary in this universal form of entertainment."

Among those considerations: that no picture should ever "lower the moral standards of those who see it" and that "the sympathy of the audience shall never be thrown to the side of crime, wrongdoing, evil or sin."

There was an updated, much-expanded list of "don'ts" and "be carefuls," with bans on nudity, suggestive dancing and lustful[3] kissing.

The mocking of religion and the depiction of illegal drug use were prohibited, as were interracial romance, revenge plots and the showing of a crime method clearly enough that it might be imitated. [...]

✦ *Wife, Husband And Friend*, 1939

Now, the Production Code was voluntary for film companies, who figured it was a nifty[4] way to avoid government censorship. But it was mandatory for filmmakers, if they wanted their films to play in American theaters. [...]

By 1959, the man charged with enforcing the rules conceded that if a "moral conflict" provided "the proper frame of reference," a Code-approved film could deal with pretty much any topic but homosexuality. [...]

A year after *Some Like It Hot* was released, the head of the MPA[5] began suggesting that some sort of classification system might work better than a censorship system that no one was paying attention to. In 1968, his organization finally shifted from restricting filmmakers to alerting audiences, using the film-ratings system we know today. [...] And it took just two years after that for *Midnight Cowboy* to be re-rated from X to R, without a single frame being altered. Community standards had changed — as they invariably do.

✦ Bob Mondello, *Remembering Hollywood's Hays Code, 40 Years On*, NPR, August 8, 2008

1. with nothing immoral 2. immoral place 3. passionate 4. excellent 5. Motion Picture Alliance was an American organisation for the preservation of American Ideals

Pédagogie différenciée

TRAIL A

1 Pick out words that explain the aims of the Hays Code.

2 Name at least three things that you see on screen today which were prohibited with the Hays Code.

3 From line 21 to 31, find the sentence that proves that Hollywood filmmakers were forced to accept this production code.

4 Explain the difference between the Hays Code and the 1968 system. Use the following key words.

rate - censorship - end - warn - the public

TRAIL B

1 Find the reasons why the Hays Code was created.

2 List the elements which were prohibited on screen at the time of the Hays Code.

3 Identify the reason why this production code cannot really be called "voluntary".

4 Show the difference between the Hays Code and the 1968 system.

Meet up! Post a recap of the article for the readers of your blog. Make sure you mention the main points.

Prepare your project

Prepare a review on one of the films of p. 48 for your school's film club. Explain if it is a typical or atypical Hollywood love story.

Grammar Tip Précis → p. 224

When preparing your review, make sure you put the adjectives in the **correct order**. Remember OFTACOAM!

Memory Challenge

Choose one of the film posters and describe it to your classmates without mentioning the title nor any of the following words: couple, kiss, classic and love story.

C Divorcing in Hollywood

Vidéo
hatier-clic.fr/lmu1030

✦ *Mrs. Doubtfire*, dir. by Chris Columbus, 1993

1 Find information about the characters, their relationships and the situation.

2 List the elements which make us think that Mrs. Doubtfire is an unusual character.

3 Explain how the couple and the family are represented.

4 Using the trailer, write the synopsis of this film.

D New ways to start a family

Classe inversée

✦ *The Back-up Plan*, dir. by Alan Poul, 2010

Vidéo
hatier-clic.fr/lmu1031

E-workbook
Classe inversée
hatier-clic.fr/lmu1032

1 Guess what you can expect in the film based on what is written on this poster.

2 Watch the trailer. Identify the elements making the film both a traditional and an unconventional Hollywood love story.

3 In your own words, explain how the film diverts from the "traditional" life plan.

4 ***PAIR WORK*** Act out a short interview of the film director talking about his intentions for this film (breaking stereotypes, independent women, etc.).

Grammar Spot

Adjective order Tools → p. 52

"*Love, Simon* is your **typical teenage romantic** comedy"

Word Spot

representation: visibility
bond: emotional tie
IVF: in vitro fertilisation
single parent
lover: boyfriend/girlfriend
household chores /tʃɔːrz/
cross-dessing: wearing clothes of the opposite sex
complicated ≠ easy
inclusive
smitten: in love
stark: severe
date: spend time with sb
you have a romantic relationship with
get pregnant
keep a relationship private / a secret
get divorced
have custody /kʌstədi/
release: come out in cinema
coming of age: becoming an adult
love at first sight

E LGBT representation

E-workbook
Fiche à imprimer
hatier-clic.fr/lmu1033

2017 was a particularly dismal[1] year for LGBTQ representation in major studio films, according to GLAAD[2]'s annual Studio Responsibility Index. The advocacy organization released its sixth annual report Tuesday, examining LGBTQ representation in every major Hollywood release of 2017. This year, GLAAD found a "significant drop" in the number of studio films with a lesbian, gay, bisexual, transgender, or queer character: Only 14 of the 109 films released by the major studios in 2017 included a LGBTQ character, or 12.8 percent. Not only is that down 5.6 percentage points from 2016, but it's the worst percentage recorded since GLAAD launched its yearly investigation in 2012. […] The GLAAD report analyzed each of the seven major studios' 2017 film releases and assigned each one a grade: failing, poor, insufficient, good, or excellent. Twentieth Century Fox and Universal performed best, with "insufficient" ratings, while Paramount, Sony, and Disney earned "poor" ratings. Lionsgate and Warner Bros. both fared the worst, receiving "failing" grades.

GLAAD also noted that not a single studio film in 2017 included a transgender character.

The report did, however, praise[3] several indie[4] releases for their accurate and inclusive LGBTQ representation, like the Chilean transgender drama *A Fantastic Woman* and Luca Guadagnino's *Call Me By Your Name*. Also, GLAAD said that 2018 has already seen a number of positive depictions of LGBTQ characters in films like *Love, Simon; Annihilation*; and *Blockers*.

Still, the report concludes, the film industry has a long way to go, and GLAAD is asking studios to commit to making sure 20 percent of their releases include LGBTQ characters by 2021, and 50 percent by 2024. "If Hollywood wants to remain relevant with these audiences and keep them buying tickets, they must create stories that are reflective of the world LGBTQ people and our friends and family know," Ellis said.

✦ Devan Coggan, *LGBTQ representation in Hollywood is still 'bleak,' GLAAD report finds*, *Entertainment Weekly*, May 22, 2018

1. bad 2. Gay and Lesbian Alliance Against Defamation
3. speak highly of something/someone 4. independent movies

1 Explain what GLAAD does every year.

2 Use the figures to explain GLAAD's dissatisfaction and demands.

3 Write GLAAD's tweet demanding that major film studios reflect today's couples in their love stories. (280 characters)

F Rom-coms for everyone

Audio
CD1 piste 20

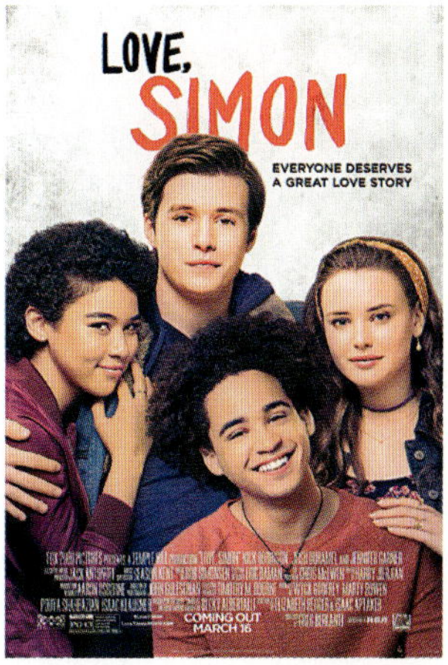

1 ***PAIR WORK*** Listen to Greg Berlanti, the director of *Love, Simon*, interviewed on NPR (National Public Radio).

Student A
a. List the elements which make this film a typical teenage rom-com.
b. Prepare questions about the differences with a typical rom-com and ask them to your partner.

Student B
a. Find the elements making this film different from a typical rom-com.
b. Prepare questions about the similarities with a typical rom-com and ask them to your partner.

2 Identify the reasons why the director released this film.

3 After the interview, NPR takes calls from the audience. Call to explain why you think it is important to watch this film.

Prepare your project

PAIR WORK You and your friend have just watched one of the films on p. 50 or 51. Discuss how it shows that Hollywood love stories have evolved.

Grammar Tip Précis ➔ p. 231

To compare two things use: short adj.**-er** + **than** or **more** + long adj. (+ 2 syll.) + **than**

Memory Challenge

Choose two words below and write them down. Close your textbook and use them to explain how Hollywood rom-coms have evolved.

divorce - LGBT representation - character - movie - love story - Hollywood film

Tools in the Spotlight

Entraînez-vous sur la plateforme ***Let's Meet Up!***
reussirenlangues.fr

Practise your grammar

Précis grammatical, p. 216

Les verbes prépositionnels

• Un verbe prépositionnel est un verbe qui est suivi d'une préposition, elle-même **obligatoirement** suivie d'un **nom** ou d'un **pronom**.

The audience ***is listening to*** *the actress's speech.*

verbe — préposition — nom

Emma Stone ***walked across*** *the catwalk.*

• Le sens d'un verbe peut être modifié selon la préposition employée.

look : sembler **mais** ***look for*** : chercher
look at : regarder ***look after*** : s'occuper de

Voici d'autres exemples de verbes prépositionnels : *depend on, apologise for, listen to, congratulate on*.

⚠ Si la préposition est suivie d'un verbe, celui-ci est au gérondif (V+-*ing*).

His organization finally ***shifted from*** *restricting filmmakers* ***to*** *alerting audiences.*

L'ordre des adjectifs

• L'ordre des adjectifs en anglais correspond à une logique allant du plus **subjectif** vers le plus **objectif**.

• Les adjectifs d'opinion se placent en premier, viennent ensuite les adjectifs exprimant une caractéristique.

It's a ***fantastic American*** *film.*

opinion subjective — caractéristique — nom

Love, Simon *is your* ***typical teenage romantic*** *comedy.*

• De manière générale, l'ordre des adjectifs est le suivant :

OTAFCOAM : **O**pinion – **T**aille – **A**ge – **F**orme – **C**ouleur – **O**rigine – **A**utre qualité – **M**atière

A ***wonderful modern American*** *film.*

O A O

• Les noms peuvent parfois être utilisés comme adjectifs, surtout pour définir une caractéristique ou un sous-groupe.

Hollwood films include famous ***disaster*** *films and some interesting* ***adventure*** *films as well.*

Disaster et *adventure* se placent au plus près du nom *film*, car ils définissent une caractéristique objective en créant une sous-catégorie de films.

1 Complétez ces verbes prépositionnels par la préposition qui convient.

on • at • about • for • to • up • after • to • with • to

a. We looked ... almost all the stars on Hollywood boulevard.
b. She apologised ... not playing cards with us because but she preferred watching *Mrs. Doubtfire* on TV. It's a classic film which refers ... divorce.
c. I've listened ... this interview, Kate Winslet was talking ... her job and the film *Titanic*.
d. The babysitter looks ... the children when their parents go to the cinema.
e. I went ... Griffith Park and walked ... to the top of Mount Lee where the Hollywood sign is located.
f. The film *Brooklyn* deals ... an Irish girl who wants to fulfill the American dream.
g. The film industry largely depended ... the Hays Code to know what they were allowed to show in their films.

2 Réécrivez la phrase avec la bonne réponse.

a. *Gone With the Wind* is an ... film.
1. old American **2.** American old
b. *Titanic* is a ... film.
1. disaster famous **2.** famous disaster
c. *Sleepless in Seattle* is a ... comedy.
1. romantic American **2.** American romantic
d. In *La La Land* Emma Stone plays a ... actress who falls in love in L.A.
1. wonderful young **2.** young wonderful

3 Écrivez la phrase en mettant les mots dans l'ordre.

a. The (**American / major / film**) studios were governed by the Hays Code.
b. The (**film / best / Hollywood**) companies have made a fortune.
c. This is a poster of my (**progressive / favourite**) film.
d. *The Back-up Plan* is a (**love / 2010 / American**) story.

Improve your pronunciation

Précis de phonologie, p. 262

Les mots commençant par *h*

Audio
CD1 piste 21
MP3 n° 27

• De manière générale, les mots commençant par la lettre *h* sont aspirés, c'est-à-dire que le son /h/ doit être prononcé.

how /haʊ/	*husband* /hʌzbənd/
Hollywood /hɒliwʊd/	*his* /hɪz/
Hays /heɪz/	*humorist* /hjuːmərɪst/

• Il existe des exceptions, pour lesquelles le son /h/ ne sera pas prononcé.

hour /aʊər/	*honesty* /ɒnəsti/
honour /ɒnəʳ/	*heir* /eəʳ/
honest /ɒnɪst/	

4 **Indiquez si le *h* est prononcé dans les mots suivants, puis écoutez l'enregistrement pour confirmer votre réponse.**

Audio
CD1 piste 22
MP3 n° 28

hotel • hospital • hour • holiday • horrible • honest • hilarious • humour

5 **Indiquez dans les phrases suivantes si le *h* est aspiré ou non, puis écoutez l'enregistrement pour confirmer votre réponse.**

Audio
CD1 piste 23
MP3 n° 29

a. There are plenty of hotels in Hollywood.
b. Most humorists have an excellent sense of humour.
c. Honestly, it was a horrible experience, not an honourable one!
d. It will take you less than two hours to drive to the Hollywood studios.

Work on your writing skills

La ponctuation du dialogue

• En anglais, les dialogues ne sont jamais précédés d'un tiret. On ouvre et on ferme généralement chaque réplique avec ces guillemets : " ".

• À l'intérieur d'un dialogue on utilise les guillemets simples ' '.

• Il faut ajouter une virgule avant de fermer les guillemets quand la phrase est affirmative.

"Well, you should go to the cinema and see it for yourself," Nina replied.

• Pour écrire un dialogue, il faut utiliser les verbes introducteurs (*say, exclaim...*) au prétérit simple.

• Contrairement au français qui inverse souvent le verbe et le sujet, en anglais, le sujet est suivi du verbe.

• Il est possible d'utiliser un adverbe ou un verbe en *-ing* pour préciser de quelle façon la personne parle.

*"Do you really think Hollywood filmmakers have changed over the years?" Jamie asked **hesitantly**.*

TIP Utilisez les verbes de cette liste pour varier vos verbes introducteurs : *admit, add, answer, exclaim, agree, announce, stutter, insist, declare*.

6 **Recopiez ces deux dialogues en ajoutant la ponctuation et en vous assurant de respecter les règles de présentation du dialogue anglais.**

a. You know I have just watched *Love, Simon* and I'm really happy that the LGBT community is more visible today she said enthusiastically.
You're right it took time but now we've made it to Hollywood he said jokingly.

b. Hi she said joyfully.
Get away from me! the woman screamed. I don't know you.

7 **Écrivez une conversation entre deux personnages d'un des films que vous avez étudiés en classe.**

Build up your vocabulary

Audio CD1 piste 24

Movies and society

Social evolution — MP3 n°30

household chores /tʃɔːrz/
representation: visibility
single parent
LGBT: Lesbian, Gay, Bisexual, Transgender
IVF: in vitro fertilisation
uncommon
progressive: forward thinking
inclusive: comprehensive
stark: severe
get divorced
have custody of children /kʌstədi/: have the legal right to care for the children

Modern rom-coms — MP3 n°31

bond: emotional tie
teenage rom-coms
complicated ≠ easy
typical ≠ atypical
usual ≠ unusual /ʌnjuʒuəl/
argue /ɑːgjuː/: have an argument
break up: split up
keep a relationship /rɪleɪʃənʃɪp/ private
keep a secret
coming of age: becoming an adult

Production codes — MP3 n°32

censorship
decorum: appropriate behaviour
moral code /kəʊd/
moral guidelines
classic
break the standards
prohibit: forbid
censor
rate: grade /greɪd/

Classic love stories — MP3 n°33

date: rendezvous
couple
lover: boyfriend ≠ girlfriend
kiss
traditional
wholesome: moral
smitten: in love
be in a relationship ≠ be single
fall in love with sb
date: spend time with sb you have a romantic relationship with
get together: become a couple
get married
get pregnant
be pregnant: expect a child
find Mr or Ms Right

The film industry — MP3 n°34

audience
character
plot: story
director /daɪrektəʳ/
filmmaker
producer
genre /ʒɒnrə/
popular
epic
release: allow a film to be shown in cinemas
be released: come out in cinemas

Apprenez et révisez le vocabulaire !

Utilisez Quizlet pour vous entraîner en vous amusant.

Quizlet hatier-clic.fr/lmu1034

Utilisez le vocabulaire en contexte.

1 Complétez les phrases suivantes avec des mots de la carte mentale à la forme qui convient.

a. Mia … … … with Sebastian the first time they met.
b. The Hays Code was used to … Hollywood films for more than 30 years.
c. The main character in *The Back-up Plan* is … and she wants to … … all by herself.
d. In this … … … film, the teenager learns about the difficulties of adulthood.
e. We need more representation of the … community in today's films.

2 Utilisez les traductions des mots français suivants pour expliquer quelle est votre comédie romantique préférée et pourquoi.

lien — atypique — protocole — briser les conventions — se mettre ensemble — épris·e

AUTO évaluation

Faites le quiz interactif en ligne et suivez les conseils pour vous préparer à l'évaluation.

Quiz hatier-clic.fr/lmu1035

Project #1

Review a Hollywood love story reflecting the evolution of the couple in the USA for your YouTube channel.

1 Choose the Hollywood love story you want to review.

- Watch the film or the trailer, or read a summary on imdb.com.
- Write a few key words to prepare your notes.
- Choose a particular scene or character you want to focus on.

2 Introduce yourself and present your YouTube channel.

- Invent your identity.
- Prepare an introduction for your video: **Hello everyone! You're watching... and today, we're talking about... Welcome back everyone! Today's film is...!**

3 Take notes and practise.

- Give general information about the film. **It deals with... It takes place in... It is directed by... It's set in...**
- Say what you liked or did not like. Use: **like**, **dislike**, **be keen on**...
- Show how it mirrors today's society. Use words from p. 54.

4 Time for filming!

- Check your pronunciation first. Use an online dictionary like wordreference.com for example.
- Do not read your notes.
- Make sure you do not spoil the movie!

Fiche de méthodologie N°11 p. 284

Project #2

Prepare a plot summary for an adaptation of a classic Hollywood love story.

1 Choose a classic love story.

- Choose a classic love story. Make sure it is a typical Hollywood romantic comedy.
- You can look for references on imdb.com or rottentomatoes.com.

2 Choose what you want to change.

- Find one or two aspects you can modify in the film to modernise it (same-sex couples, divorce, stepfamily, interracial love stories...).
- Compare it with previous rom-coms.
  – **more** + long adjective (more than 2 syllables) + **than**
  – short adjective + **-er** + **than**
- Be creative and be respectful of the plot!

3 Write a draft version.

- Look for examples of plot summaries on the internet (imdb.com).
- Use adjectives to describe both the action and the characters.

4 Prepare your plot summary!

- Proofread your production for grammar and spelling mistakes.
- Use an online dictionary for the words you are unsure of.

Fiche de méthodologie N°20 p. 300

Let's RECAP

Lisez les questions-clés et complétez la fiche bilan avec des exemples et des documents que vous avez étudiés ou découverts.

AXE 2 | Private space and public space

SÉQUENCE 1 How are women detectives represented in fiction?

E-workbook
Bilan à compléter
hatier-clic.fr/lmu1036

How have female detectives been portrayed through time in literature, films and TV series in the English-speaking world?
How does that reflect a social evolution?

#socialchange
Has any social progress been achieved for women?

#genderequality
Do women and men enjoy the same rights and opportunities in English-speaking detective fiction?

#womensemancipation
How have the role and image of women evolved in English-speaking detective fiction?

#workingwomen
Are women detectives treated the same as men at work?
Do they have to fight harder to earn their place?

SÉQUENCE 2 How do Hollywood love stories reflect social progress?

E-workbook
Bilan à compléter
hatier-clic.fr/lmu1037

How has the representation of couples and families in Hollywood evolved throughout the last century?
How do they mirror changes taking place in the American society?

#traditions
How has the traditional image of the couple and the family progressively changed in Hollywood films?

#familylaw
How are social evolutions in couples and families shown in Hollywood films?

#emancipation
How do Hollywood films show the emancipation of women and minorities in the American society?

#education
Can films educate people to accept the evolution of social norms?

#representinglove
How have love stories been represented in Hollywood films through time?

GO4IT!

Lisez et écoutez de l'anglais en dehors de la salle de classe ! Voici quelques conseils en lien avec votre séquence.

SÉQUENCE 1

Books

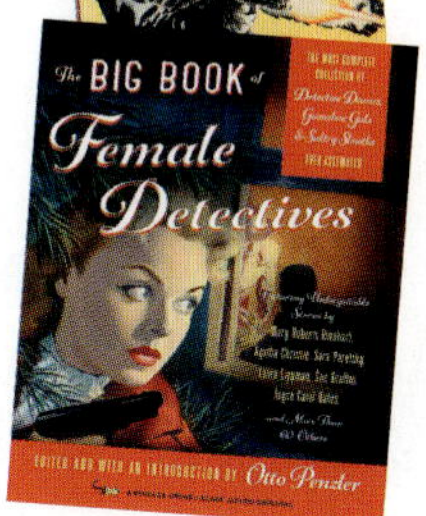

Miss Marple - The Complete Short Stories, AGATHA CHRISTIE, 1930

Trixie Belden and the Secret of the Mansion, JULIE CAMPBELL, 1948

Ms. Tree, MAX ALLAN COLLINS AND TERRY BEATTY, 1981

Post-Mortem, PATRICIA CORNWELL, 1990

The Big Book of Female Detectives, OTTO PENZLER, 2018

Articles

America's 'Mrs Holmes'
http://bit.ly/2KXyRtG

CIS: The First Female Detectives
https://bit.ly/2tWCjyC

Films

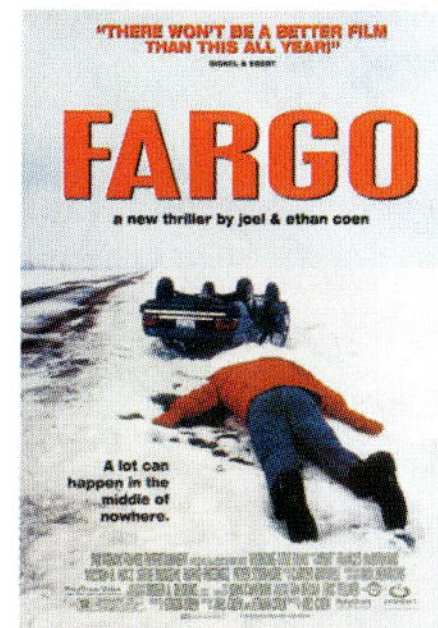

TV series

SÉQUENCE 2

Books

Jane Eyre, CHARLOTTE BRONTË, 1847

The Great Gatsby, F. SCOTT FITZGERALD, 1925

Me Before You, JOJO MOYES, 2012

Songs

I Will Always Love You, WHITNEY HOUSTON, 1992

Love Song, SARA BAREILLES, 2007

Diane, CAM, 2017

Films

(500) Days of Summer, DIR. BY MARC WEBB, 2009

Her, DIR. BY SPIKE JONZE, 2013

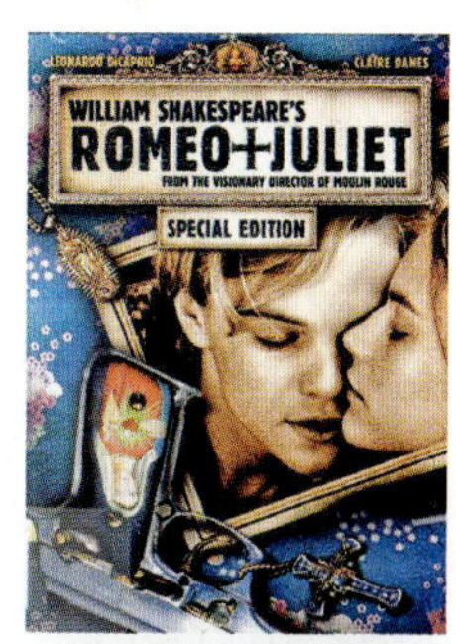

BAC in sight

ÉPREUVE 1

COMPRÉHENSION ORALE

Vidéo
hatier-clic.fr/lmu1038

Patricia Cornwell talks about the character she created, Dr. Kay Scarpetta.

Tips
➤ Be active and take notes right from the start of the first viewing.
➤ Write down the words that are stressed.

➤ Fiche de méthodologie N°15 p. 290 Compréhension orale

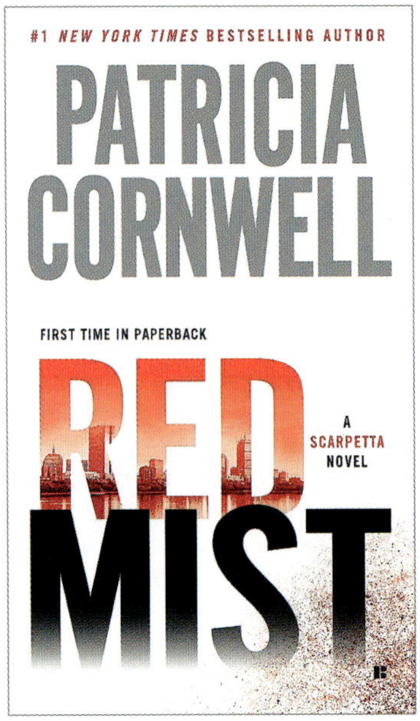

✦ Patricia Cornwell, *Red Mist*, 2011

EXPRESSION ÉCRITE

SUJET 1 Imagine the end of the interview when the journalist and Patricia Cornwell discuss the need for more women detectives in fiction.

OU

SUJET 2 Do you think there should be more women in detective films, TV series and books?

Tip
➤ Review how to write a dialogue in English.

➤ Fiche de méthodologie N°20 p. 300 Expression écrite

Pour l'épreuve

Questions
Fiche modifiable
hatier-clic.fr/lmu1039

Évaluation
Grille à imprimer
hatier-clic.fr/lmu1040

ÉPREUVE 2

EXPRESSION ÉCRITE

SUJET 1 Gillian Anderson, the leading female character in *The Fall*, is interviewed about her role and how women make good detectives. Write the interview.

OU

SUJET 2 Why is it important to have unstereotyped women detectives in TV series and films?

✦ Gillian Anderson as Stella Gibson, *The Fall*, BBC Two, 2013-2016

Tips
➤ Use linking words to structure your text.
➤ Find examples in the unit to support your arguments.

➤ Fiche de méthodologie N°20 p. 300 Expression écrite

COMPRÉHENSION ÉCRITE

The Fall: The Most Feminist Show on Television

The BBC drama stars Gillian Anderson as a detective investigating a serial killer, but the series' treatment of women defies the genre's conventions.

A crime drama about a psychosexual serial killer who stalks, tortures, and murders young women doesn't sound like an obvious choice for the most feminist show on television. Especially given that the writers, directors, and producers of that show are all men. But that's just one of the ways *The Fall* — the BBC hit set in Northern Ireland whose second season began streaming for American audiences on Netflix last week — upends[1] TV conventions and deserves to be the first binge-watched[2] show of 2015. [...]

But the debate over *The Fall*'s first season obscured the show's revolutionary treatment of women and the topic of sexual power. In fact, I haven't seen another program that so directly challenges and rewrites the traditional conventions of crime dramas, starting with Anderson as DSI[3] Stella Gibson, a highly-regarded London cop who gets called to Belfast because investigators there need her expertise on a murder case.

Refreshingly, none of the tropes[4] we've been trained to expect in a story about a powerful woman play out. Nobody resents[5] Gibson's appearance on the scene or questions her authority. Her gender is a non-issue; subordinates hop to when she enters a room and they follow her commands without question. Gibson doesn't try to submerge her femininity and stomp around barking out orders. In Anderson's restrained yet compelling performance, Gibson is cool, calm, and always chic, with the most fabulous coat in detectivedom.

When a shooting happens at the station, it's Gibson who smoothly takes charge while also tending to a male colleague in shock. As she begins to suspect that the murder they've been investigating is linked to subsequent killings, Gibson presses for the creation of a task force and firmly makes the case that she should lead it.

But this isn't to say that it doesn't make a difference that Gibson is a woman. Early on, she tells a colleague to leave the word "innocent" out of a statement about the victims. "What if he kills a prostitute next? Or a woman walking home drunk?" She asks. "The media loves to divide women into virgins and vamps, angels or whores[6]. Let's not encourage them." It's she who notices the victims' painted nails, and who appears at a press conference with her own nails painted bright red as a signal to the serial killer that she's on to him.

More importantly, while Gibson is very good at her job, she isn't portrayed as having sacrificed her personal life in exchange. That's long been a frustrating trope about powerful women on television, including Sarah Linden, the detective on *The Killing* whose obsessive commitment to cases came at the cost of relationships with her fiancé and son. But neither does Gibson try to escape the stress and trauma of her job with damaging addictions. She has a glass of wine to unwind in the evening, and she swims every morning as discipline and release. [...]

The Fall is an intelligent show with tremendous acting, shot as beautifully as anything else you'll watch on television this year. [...] But *The Fall*'s most remarkable achievement will be if it turns out to be the first show of many to present a new normal for women on television.

✦ Amy Sullivan, *The Atlantic*, January 23, 2015

1. reverses 2. watched for hours, one episode after the other 3. Detective Superintendent (a top officer) 4. recurring themes 5. is angry about 6. prostitutes

Tips

➤ Read the introduction carefully: it will help you understand the text.

➤ Focus on the main character: look for her job, relationships, attitudes...

➤ Fiche de méthodologie N°16 p. 292 Compréhension écrite

Pour l'épreuve

Questions — Fiche modifiable — hatier-clic.fr/lmu1041

Évaluation — Grille à imprimer — hatier-clic.fr/lmu1042

BAC in sight

ÉPREUVE 1

COMPRÉHENSION ORALE

Audio
CD1 piste 25

In 2018, the guests of this National Public Radio programme discuss rom-coms and try to decide if the genre is really dead today.

✦ *To All the Boys I've Loved Before*, dir. By Susan Johnson, 2018

Tips
- ➤ Be active and take notes right from the start.
- ➤ Pay attention to the words that are stressed.
- ➤ Use abbreviations to be quick when you take notes.

➤ Fiche de méthodologie N°15 p. 290 Compréhension orale

EXPRESSION ÉCRITE

SUJET 1 Write a letter to defend rom-coms explaining why they are great and how much they have changed over time.

OU

SUJET 2 Do you think rom-coms can do better at mirroring American society?

Tip
- ➤ What type of written expression is it? A dialogue, an essay... Apply the COOL methodology.

➤ Fiche de méthodologie N°20 p. 300 Expression écrite

Pour l'épreuve

Questions
Fiche modifiable
hatier-clic.fr/lmu1043

Évaluation
Grille à imprimer
hatier-clic.fr/lmu1044

ÉPREUVE 2

EXPRESSION ÉCRITE

SUJET 1 Write an interview between Rebel Wilson and a journalist, where she explains why she chose this role and how important it is for Hollywood to reflect today's society.

OU

SUJET 2 Do American rom-coms reflect how society has evolved? Give examples of Hollywood films to support your answer.

✦ Rebel Wilson plays Natalie in *Isn't It Romantic*, dir. by Todd Strauss-Schulson, 2019

Tips
- ➤ Read the instructions two or three times.
- ➤ Highlight the key words and write down synonyms or words related to them.

➤ Fiche de méthodologie N°20 p. 300 Expression écrite

COMPRÉHENSION ÉCRITE

'Isn't It Romantic?' is only pretending to be a different kind of rom-com

Isn't It Romantic? will have you know that it is not like other rom-coms.

Its heroine, Natalie (Rebel Wilson) doesn't look like most other rom-com heroines. She does not have a lavish[1] apartment, or an adorable wardrobe, or even an Instagram-ready pet. She isn't especially interested in finding love. And she definitely doesn't like rom-coms themselves. "All these movies are lies," she huffs. "So unrealistic!"

In truth, though, *Isn't It Romantic?* is, in almost all respects, exactly like other rom-coms, down to the sugar-coated[2] morals it wants to feed you. It's just one that loudly calls attention to the tropes[3] it's using before using them, and then pats itself on the back for turning them on their heads — never mind that most of those "subversions" have themselves been rom-com staples[4] for years.

The film opens in the "real" version of New York, so gloriously gross and sticky that it made this former New Yorker feel positively homesick. After Natalie hits her head, however, she enters a candy-colored version of the city littered with cupcake shops and bridal stores, and populated by pretty people in flattering clothes.

Even as the film winks and nudges to let you know it's in on the joke, it borrows enough of the genre's tricks to deliver a passable imitation. Liam Hemsworth is a hoot as the guy who's too "CW[5] hot" to be true — and almost as dim as he is sexy. And some of its observations about rom-com silliness are, if not exactly original, at least pretty amusing. Slow-motion sprints to grand romantic gestures *are* inherently silly!

Plus, there's a gratuitous karaoke moment that really works, even if it's just because it's hard to go wrong with "I Wanna Dance With Somebody." It is one of the few moments of *Isn't It Romantic?* that achieves the fluffy transcendence of the films it's trying to parody. Not coincidentally, it's also one of the few that's played relatively straight.

Where *Isn't It Romantic?* runs into trouble is when it tries to go beyond winking at stereotypical rom-com details and trying to comment on deeper issues — like gay male best friends, jealous female frenemies, a lack of diversity, and the general concept of finding happily ever after in a man — while acting completely oblivious to the fact that dozens of earlier rom-coms have tackled them already.

Films take years to develop, produce, and market, and it's possible that had *Isn't It Romantic?* come out even two years ago, when the traditional rom-com movie seemed all but dead, it'd have felt fresher. Its premise might have felt more novel, its insights more trenchant, its smugness[6] easier to stomach.

Unfortunately for *Isn't It Romantic?*, it's coming right as the genre is on the rise again, and looking more heterogeneous than ever. In the past year, movies like *Love, Simon*, *Set It Up*, *Crazy Rich Asians*, and *To All the Boys I've Loved Before* have put their own spins[7] on well-worn conventions, and addressed a lot of *Isn't It Romantic?*'s critiques in the process — to say nothing of shows like *Crazy Ex-Girlfriend*, *Jane the Virgin*, and *You're the Worst*, which have been doing so for seasons already.

In that company, *Isn't It Romantic?* feels like a missed opportunity. It *is* revolutionary to have plus-sized woman like Wilson in a romantic lead role. It *is* worth acknowledging that these movies are selling a fantasy, some of them toxic. It *is* equally worth trying to convince the timid and the skeptical to consider opening themselves up to the world. We *could* use a romantic comedy that acknowledges those things, and expands our ideas of what this genre can be.

But *Isn't It Romantic?* does not, in the end, manage to forge something new from those elements. It's so busy working to remind you of everything it's trying not to be, that it never quite gets around to figuring out what it actually is.

✦ Angie Han, mashable.com, February 12, 2019

1. extravagant 2. embellished 3. recurrent themes 4. regular 5. US TV Channel 6. self-satisfaction 7. given their own interpretation

Tips

➤ Highlight in different colours the elements for typical and atypical rom-coms. Classify them in a grid.

➤ Pay attention to the journalist's opinion in the conclusion.

➤ Fiche de méthodologie N°16 p. 292 Compréhension écrite

Pour l'épreuve

Questions — Fiche modifiable — hatier-clic.fr/lmu1045

Évaluation — Grille à imprimer — hatier-clic.fr/lmu1046

AXE 3

Art and power

Art et pouvoir

SÉQUENCE 1 How does art boost British cities' economy?

Projects

Project #1: You have designed an artwork or a building to boost your city's economy. Give a speech explaining its positive impact.

Project #2: Make a flyer presenting an artwork or a building in the UK and explaining how it helps to boost the city's economy.

Tools

Grammaire	l'infinitif en *to*, les indénombrables
Phonologie	l'accentuation des adjectifs composés
Écriture	la ponctuation de la phrase
Vocabulaire	le street art, l'architecture

SÉQUENCE 2 How did US artists relate the Great Depression?

Projects

Project #1: Prepare a presentation of an artwork for an exhibition on the Great Depression.

Project #2: Write an email to the curator of an exhibition on the Great Depression. Convince him or her to include your favourite artwork.

Tools

Grammaire	le prétérit en *be* + V-*ing*, la phrase complexe
Phonologie	les liaisons
Écriture	le journal intime
Vocabulaire	l'art, la crise économique

#streetart #freedomofcreation #publicart #architecture #economicpower

Queen Elizabeth Olympic Park and Canary Wharf, London

#painting #economicpower #photography #literature #politicalexpression

Unemployed men queueing outside a soup kitchen in Chicago, Illinois, 1931

SÉQUENCE 1

How does art boost British cities' economy?

A The impact of street art

GROUP WORK

GROUP A Upfest, a street art festival in Bristol

✦ Front cover of the book *Upfest 2: The Urban Paint Festival*, designed by Jody Thomas, 2016

Upfest is Europe's largest free street art and graffiti festival. It is held every summer in Bristol (UK), and attracts over 400 British and international artists. Visitors can also take part in art sales, concerts and art workshops.
The festival was created in 2008, as street art was rehabilitated in the early 2000s. It started with just nine artists. Bristol, the birthplace of Banksy, has an international reputation for its street art.

Grammar Spot

The *to*-infinitive TOOLS → p. 68

"Arty areas — such as Brixton — attract more cafes and restaurants that in turn **attract** the art-loving crowd **to move in**."

Word Spot

- district: neighbourhood
- passer-by
- tourist: sightseer
- house value: price of a house
- growth: development
- economic boom
- open-air
- attractive
- arty: artistic
- derelict: in bad condition
- wander: walk around
- tag a wall
- increase: go up
- improve: make better
- rehabilitate
- beautify: make more beautiful

GROUP B Stik, a London street artist

✦ *Stik in Shoreditch: the artist's hidden tribute to a sold-off London*, *The Guardian*, 2016

Vidéo
DVD

"Last year, the street artist Stik got permission for a major new mural in his neighbourhood, an area of the East End of London that now embodies gentrification at its most extreme." (*The Guardian*)

GROUP C Views on street art

It's an age when you can awake in the morning to find your house value increased overnight with the emergence of a Banksy on your wall — or even something a bit like a Banksy on your wall.
Public perception appears to have changed.
People used to scrub the art away[1], but nowadays the first reaction seems to be "is it worth money?"
Street artist Neil Morris agrees this is the case with some, but "these are the people who never have and never will appreciate the work. These people are middle-aged, middle-manager types that think the art is offensive to others without actually asking anyone. And it's money that has changed perception. Money changes everything."
Fellow artist Jadryk Brown argues that the high prices street art can fetch[2] means "rich people don't find it scary any more. Nothing's scary if money could be involved". [...]
A study from the University of Warwick indicates that street art in London is generally now associated with improving economic conditions of urban neighbourhoods.
It's partly down to a "loop effect"[3]. Arty areas — such as Brixton — attract more cafes and restaurants that in turn attract the art-loving crowd to move in.
Areas outside London can also see graffiti affecting property prices — in both directions.
Prof Clay says it can polarise opinion: "To most people street art is either an indicator of an area that is vibrant or of one that is run-down[4] and in need of better policing. It very much depends on individuals' broader opinions about acceptable behaviours in public space, but it seems clear to me that more and more people regard street art as a positive phenomenon. Hence, it appears to be being more widely tolerated by public authorities". [...]
The creative urge to leave one's mark in public space crosses the boundaries of class, gender, sexuality, ethnicity and religion. It always has and it always will.

✦ Bethan Bell, *Street art: crime, grime or sublime?*, *BBC News*, December 16, 2016

1. rub in order to clean 2. be sold for 3. virtuous circle 4. in a bad state

Pédagogie différenciée GROUP WORK

1. Study your group's document. Give examples of places where you can find street art.
2. Show how street art has evolved.
3. Choose one spokesperson in your group who will tell the rest of the class about your findings.
4. Write an ad to promote a street art tour in London or Bristol.

Prepare your project

PAIR WORK A street artist is interviewed at a press conference about the place and the impact of urban art in British cities. Imagine the interview.

Grammar Tip Précis → p. 251

Review how to form questions:
(Wh- or How) + auxiliary + subject + verb (+ object)?

Memory Challenge

In groups, write your top two arguments in favour of street art in cities. Use graffiti style!

B Reshaping London's cityscape

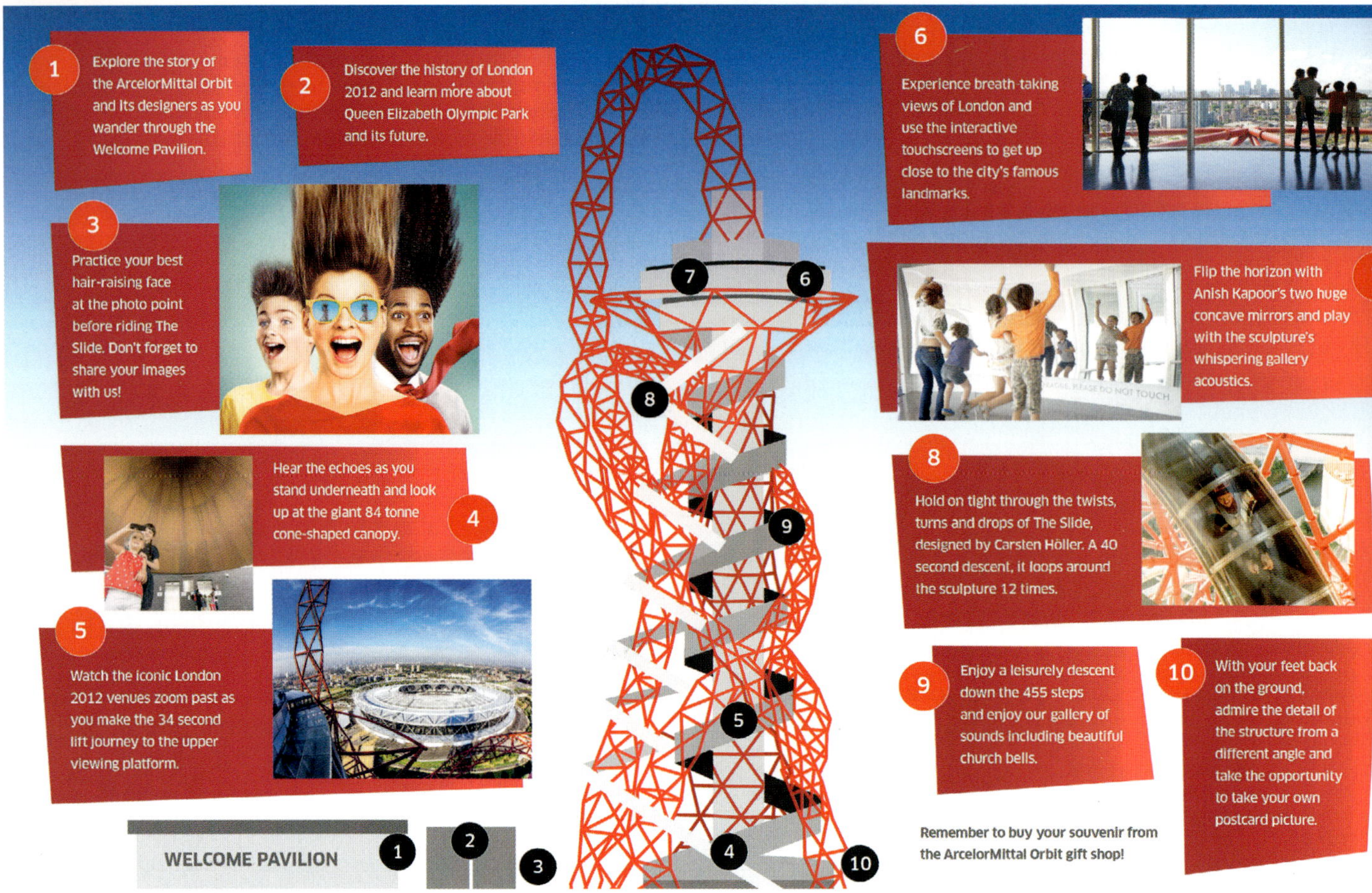

✦ The ArcelorMittal Orbit, designed by Anish Kapoor and Cecil Balmond, London, 2018

1 Find out where the ArcelorMittal Orbit is located and who designed it.

2 Explain what makes people go and visit it.

3 You want to visit this attraction. Explain what it is to your host family in England.

C Modern Birmingham

Classe inversée

Vidéo
hatier-clic.fr/lmu1048

E-workbook
Classe inversée
hatier-clic.fr/lmu1049

1 Say why the following places are mentioned.

Birmingham - Birmingham Library - Birmingham Grand Central - The UK - The Midlands - Liverpool

2 Explain how Birmingham has changed lately.

3 Using elements from the video, make a list of slogans promoting Birmingham as the capital of modern British architecture.

Grammar Spot

Uncountable nouns TOOLS → p. 68
"the evolution of architecture"

Word Spot

inhabitant
artwork: piece of art: art piece
masterpiece
achievement: breakthrough
revival: rebirth
amazing: striking
remarkable: outstanding
innovative: creative
shortlisted
stand out: attract attention
be in sharp contrast: be opposed
award: give a prize
change: evolve
regenerate: rejuvenate: renew

D Regenerative architecture: Hastings Pier

✦ Hastings Pier, 2009

✦ Hastings Pier, 2018

London-based architects dRMM have been announced as the winners of the 2017 RIBA Stirling Prize for their renovation of Hastings Pier. [...]

"Hastings Pier is a masterpiece in regeneration and inspiration. The architects and local community have transformed a neglected wreck[1] into a stunning, flexible new pier to delight and inspire visitors and local people alike," said RIBA President and Stirling Prize jury chair Ben Derbyshire.

Designed as "a strong, well-serviced platform that could support endless uses," the new Hastings Pier has completely transformed the town's waterfront from a neglected "shantytown"[2] into a life-filled space for gathering and entertainment. The project was spurred[3] into action after the pier was destroyed by fire in 2010. "There was no sense in trying to reconstruct it as a 19th century pier — that typology[4] had gone with the fire. There was an opportunity to reuse and reinvent the pier and give it a new future," commented Alex de Rijke, dRMM Founding Director.

✦ Patrick Lynch, *dRMM's Hastings Pier Wins 2017 RIBA Stirling Prize*, archdaily.com, October 31, 2017

1. building that has been badly damaged 2. very poor district 3. encouraged 4. type

1 Look at the two photos and say what has changed.

2 Pick out from the text five words starting with the prefix "re-". Use them to explain how Hastings Pier has changed.

3 List all the positive words used to qualify the new pier. Use them to explain the advantages of this new building.

4 You are a tour guide. Explain to visitors why the pier has been awarded the Stirling Prize.

Culture Tip

The **Royal Institute of British Architects (RIBA) Stirling Prize** is an annual prize that has been awarded to the best building in the UK since 1996. It is the most prestigious architecture prize in the United Kingdom.

Prepare your project

Imagine that the ArcelorMittal Orbit, Hastings Pier or one of Birmingham's new buildings has won a prize. Write a short article about it in the column "News in brief" of the local newspaper.

Grammar Tip

Précis → p. 252

Use **direct speech** to report the artist's or architect's words (as in the article above).

Memory Challenge

In groups or in pairs, list 10 adjectives to describe one of the buildings from p. 66-67. The first student who completes his or her list is the winner!

Tools in the Spotlight

Entraînez-vous sur la plateforme *Let's Meet Up!*
reussirenlangues.fr

Practise your grammar

Précis grammatical, p. 216

L'infinitif en *to*

- On utilise l'infinitif en *to* :
  – après des verbes de **volonté** et d'**ordre** comme ***want, would like, wish, prefer, advise, tell, order***.

*I **would like** you **to take** a picture of Banksy's street art.*

  – après les verbes exprimant une visée comme ***intend, plan, expect, attract***.

*Arty areas **attract** the art-loving crowd **to move** in.*

- L'infinitif en ***to*** sert également à introduire une proposition de but, ainsi que ***in order to*** ou ***so as to***, pour des sujets identiques.

*I am going to Birmingham **to / in order to / so as to** see its modern architecture.*

→ Le sujet de ***go*** et de ***see*** est le même : ***I***.

⚠ On emploie ***so that*** s'il y a deux sujets différents.

*I've invited you to Bristol **so that** you can attend the famous street art lectures on Banksy.*

→ ***I*** est le sujet de ***invite*** et ***you*** celui de ***attend***.

1 Utilisez l'infinitif en *to* ou le gérondif.

a. Paul Smith, the English fashion designer, had every intention of (**to become / becoming**) well known with his multi-coloured striped clothes.
b. I would like (**to go / going**) to this exhibition on British street artists because I want (**to see / seeing**) Nick Walker's art.
c. She wants (**to rent / renting**) a house in Liverpool, because she likes its modern architecture.

2 Complétez par *in order to* ou *so that*.

a. Robert needs to leave the museum by 4 pm ... arrive on time at the station.
b. Museums are open throughout the year, ... visitors can discover paintings by the most famous artists.
c. ... make sure that photographs were allowed, she asked the guide as soon as she walked in.
d. Jane parked her car near the exhibition, ... her children didn't need to walk too far.

Les indénombrables

Les indénombrables singuliers

- Ce sont des noms au **singulier**, dont le verbe s'accorde au singulier, mais qui ont un sens **pluriel** : ***advice*** (des conseils), ***information*** (des renseignements), ***fruit*** (des fruits), ***furniture*** (des meubles).
Ils ne peuvent pas figurer avec l'article **a / an**.

- Pour extraire un seul élément, l'anglais a recours à un **dénombreur** : ***a piece of***. On a donc :
a piece of advice (un conseil), ***a piece of information*** (un renseignement), ***a piece of fruit*** (un fruit), ***a piece of furniture*** (un meuble).

- Il existe aussi des indénombrables qui acceptent difficilement le pluriel et sont au **singulier** en général.

*the evolution of **architecture***

Les indénombrables pluriels

- Ces noms sont toujours au **pluriel** : ***clothes, jeans, glasses, scissors.*** On peut utiliser un **dénombreur** pour désigner un seul élément : ***an article of clothing, a pair of jeans, a pair of glasses, a pair of scissors.***

3 Mettez les mots soulignés au singulier.

a. I would like some information about Upfest, the street art festival in Bristol.
b. That Brixton artist wears jeans all the time!
c. If I have some advice to give you, don't miss Banksy's street art when you are in Bristol.
d. They left their luggage at the reception desk of their hotel in Birmingham.

4 Complétez par le dénombreur qui convient.

a. Could you get me ... fruit, please? There's a grocer's shop next to the gallery.
b. This ... furniture is very modern. Do you know which artist made it?
c. I would like to get ... evidence to show what really qualifies as modern architecture.
d. You don't wear ... shorts to go to an art gallery, do you? Please put on ... trousers instead!

Improve your pronunciation

Précis de phonologie, p. 262

L'accentuation des adjectifs composés

Audio CD1 piste 26 MP3 n° 35

- Un adjectif composé est formé d'au moins deux mots qui gardent leur accentuation initiale. Mais l'adjectif composé comporte un **accent tonique** noté ˈ devant la syllabe portant l'accentuation la plus forte et un **accent secondaire** noté ˌ devant l'autre syllabe accentuée.
- Pour les adjectifs composés dont le deuxième élément est un nom (+ éventuellement *-ed*), l'accent tonique porte, en général, sur le **deuxième élément**.

a 15-minute /fɪfˌtiːnˈmɪn.ɪt/ *break*

old-fashioned /ˌəʊldˈfæʃənd/ *architecture*

- Pour les adjectifs composés dont le deuxième élément est un verbe en *-ing* ou un participe passé, l'accent tonique porte, en général, sur le **premier élément**.

art-loving /ˈɑːtˌlʌvɪŋ/ *cone-shaped* /ˈkəʊnˌʃeɪpt/

5 **Écrivez les adjectifs composés suivants et soulignez les syllabes qui portent l'accent tonique, puis écoutez l'enregistrement pour confirmer vos réponses.** Audio CD1 piste 27 MP3 n° 36

green-eyed • bad-mannered • meat-eating • low-necked • Bristol-based • five-minute • one-armed • oil-producing • one-year

6 **Prononcez les groupes nominaux suivants en veillant à les accentuer correctement, puis écoutez l'enregistrement pour vérifier l'accentuation.** Audio CD1 piste 28 MP3 n° 37

a. a wheat-producing region
b. a bad-tempered neighbour
c. a word-processing programme
d. a three-week holiday
e. a London-based exhibition

Work on your writing skills

La ponctuation de la phrase

- Les phrases se terminent par un **point final** (*full stop*), un **point d'interrogation** (*question mark*) ou un **point d'exclamation** (*exclamation mark*).
- La **virgule** (*comma*) s'utilise :
  - pour séparer les différentes parties d'une phrase.
  In 2017, the Stirling Prize was awarded to Hastings Pier.
  - pour séparer les éléments d'une liste.
  Hastings Pier is a strong, flexible and well-serviced platform.
  - pour ajouter une information supplémentaire.
  Arty areas, such as Brixton, attract more and more cafés.
- Le **point-virgule** (*semicolon*) s'emploie pour transformer deux phrases (reliées par leur sens) en une seule.
People used to disregard street art; nowadays, perception has completely changed.
- Les **deux-points** (*colon*) servent à introduire une liste ou une explication.
Visitors can take part in different activities: art sales, concerts and art workshops.
Street art helps to boost urban areas: it gives value to derelict neighbourhoods.

7 **Remplacez les virgules ou les points par deux-points quand c'est possible.**

a. Hastings Pier has all kinds of advantages. It is strong, flexible and multi-functional.
b. Enjoy seeing the whole of London, riding the slide, listening to our gallery of sound, and so much more. Visit the ArcelorMittal Orbit.
c. Upfest is Europe's largest free street art and graffiti festival. It attracts over 400 British as well as international artists, painting 50 venues in the city.

8 **Complétez les phrases par des virgules ou des points-virgules.**

a. Thanks to art ... we can make our cities diverse ... inspirational places.
b. Rogue One is a street artist with a realistic style ... his artworks often look like photos.
c. Street art acts as an antidote to online images ... it is an authentic ... thought-provoking art form.
d. Riders will experience the twists ... turns and drops of the world's longest tunnel slide in the ArcelorMittal Orbit.

Build up your vocabulary

Audio
CD1 piste 29

Art and power

Neighbourhoods
MP3 n°38

district: neighbourhood
local community
inhabitant
tourist: sightseer
passer-by
art-loving crowd
shantytown: cheaply built houses
neglected: shabby
run-down: decrepit
vibrant: lively

Architecture
MP3 n°39

achievement: breakthrough /breɪkθruː/
wreck: ruin /ruːɪn/
revival: rebirth
derelict /derəlɪkt/: in bad condition
shortlisted
innovative: creative
change: evolve
regenerate: rejuvenate: renew /rɪnjuː/
rehabilitate
reinvent
award: give a prize

Street art
MP3 n°42

evolution
positive phenomenon
masterpiece
public space
urban /ɜːbən/ art
artwork: piece of art: art piece
spray-painted
open-air
arty: artistic
amazing: striking
remarkable: outstanding
illegal
tag a wall
beautify: make more beautiful

Economic development
MP3 n°40

economic boom
economic conditions
property prices
real estate: land and buildings
gentrification
tourist industry
growth: development /dɪveləpmənt/
house value: price of a house
increase: go up

Cityscapes
MP3 n°41

building
horizon: skyline
pier /pɪəʳ/
structure
waterfront
breathtaking views
attractive
improve: make better
reshape
stand out: attract attention
walk around: wander
be in sharp contrast to / with: be opposed to

Quizlet
hatier-clic.fr/lmu1050

Apprenez et révisez le vocabulaire !

Utilisez Quizlet pour vous entraîner en vous amusant.

Utilisez le vocabulaire en contexte.

1 Complétez les phrases suivantes avec des mots de la carte mentale à la forme qui convient.

a. In many neighbourhoods, street art is seen as a … … as it causes the … of the tourist industry.
b. Urban art can … city walls in run-down districts.
c. One of Anish Kapoor's great … is the ArcelorMittal Orbit which offers … … of London.
d. The London City … has changed thanks to the inclusion of new high buildings in Canary Wharf.
e. Most of Birmingham's … are in favour of the new architecture in their city.
f. The emergence of street art has caused … as housing value tends to … and so lower-class and middle-class people can't afford to stay.

2 Écrivez l'interview d'un·e architecte ou d'un·e artiste de rue qui parle de l'impact de son œuvre dans une ville britannique. Utilisez au moins 10 mots de la carte mentale.

AUTO évaluation

Faites le quiz interactif en ligne et suivez les conseils pour vous préparer à l'évaluation.

Quiz
hatier-clic.fr/lmu1051

Project #1

You have designed an artwork or a building to boost your city's economy. Give a speech explaining its positive impact.

1 **Search the internet or the unit to find an artwork or building you like.**

- ✓ Decide on the type of art that interests you most: street art, architecture...
- ✓ Look for an original artwork or building, focusing on its aesthetic value and its benefits for the city.

2 **Make a list of arguments showing why it is inspiring and is likely to revive the city.**

- ✓ Find arguments about the artwork or building itself and its impact on the city.
- ✓ Look at the arguments used in this unit and add your own touch.

3 **Reorder your arguments to have a structured plan showing your reasoning.**

- ✓ Use linking words: **first**, **to start with**, **then**, **finally**, **to conclude**, **as a matter of fact**, **actually**, **besides**, **what's more**...
- ✓ Use greetings such as: **Ladies and gentlemen**, **(Dear) Mr / Ms Mayor**, **Members of the City Council** and end politely: **I would like to thank you for...**

4 **Practise your speech and deliver it!**

- ✓ Practise giving your speech at home or to a friend.
- ✓ Look at the audience and do not depend on your notes when delivering your speech.
- ✓ Be enthusiastic and convincing!

Fiche de méthodologie N°18 p. 296

Project #2

Make a flyer presenting an artwork or a building in the UK and explaining how it helps to boost the city's economy.

1 **Search the internet or this unit to find a work of public art, street art or architecture that inspires you.**

- ✓ Select some photos of the artwork or building and its location.
- ✓ Find out information about the artwork or building and its positive impact on the city.

2 **Observe the flyer about the ArcelorMittal Orbit (p. 66).**

- ✓ Pay attention to its different parts and its layout, as you will use it as a model.

3 **Write a short caption for each photo.**

- ✓ Start your captions with verbs such as: **explore**, **discover**, **enjoy**...
- ✓ Mention the name of the work and its creator in large letters.

4 **Decide on a layout to make an attractive, efficient flyer.**

- ✓ Select the title, colours, fonts, size of the photos... Be creative!
- ✓ If you want to make a digital flyer, you can find some help on the following sites: **desygner.com**, **about.easil.com**.

Fiche de méthodologie N°20 p. 300

SÉQUENCE 2 How did US artists relate the Great Depression?

A Paintings of the 1930s

Vidéo
DVD

✦ Grant Wood, *Young Corn*, 1931

1 Note down keywords about the changes that took place in society.

2 Identify what the paintings you see have in common.

3 Describe what the regionalists painted and their goal. Explain whether they succeeded or not.

4 In art class, explain in French or in English what inspired American painters in the 1930s. Use elements from the video and the Culture Tip.

Culture Tip

The Great Depression was a period of economic crisis in the 1930s which began with the stock market crash of October 1929. It was one of the most difficult times in American history. Thousands of people lost their jobs.

B Forced to leave

✦ Dorothea Lange, *Family walking on highway, five children*, 1938

1 Describe the photograph (landscape, people's expressions and clothes).

2 Read the Culture Tip. Imagine why these people are on the road.

3 Explain Dorothea Lange's message to the visitors of a museum.

Culture Tip

The **Dust Bowl** was a region of the USA where there were dust storms due to successive years of drought (lack of rain). In the 1930s, thousands of farmers had to leave their homes to find better land.

Word Spot

the stock market: Wall Street
rural exodus
journey
migrant /maɪgrənt/
crowd /kraʊd/
belongings: possessions
optimism ≠ pessimism
exhausted: very tired
anxious: worried
desperate
bankrupt: unable to pay debts
unemployed ≠ employed
homeless
flee: escape
rise ≠ fall

Grammar Spot

Preterite *be* + V-*ing* TOOLS → p. 76
"Democracy wasn't working"

C The migrants' road

Highway 66 is the main migrant road. 66 — the long concrete[1] path across the country, waving gently up and down on the map, from Mississippi to Bakersfield — over the red lands and the gray lands, twisting up into the mountains, crossing the Divide and down into the bright and terrible desert, and across the desert to the mountains again, and into the rich California valleys. 66 is the path of a people in flight[2], refugees from dust and shrinking[3] land, from the thunder of tractors and shrinking ownership, from the desert's slow northward invasion, from the twisting winds that howl up[4] out of Texas, from the floods[5] that bring no richness to the land and steal what little richness is there. From all of these the people are in flight, and they come into 66 from the tributary side roads, from the wagon tracks and the rutted[6] country roads. 66 is the mother road, the road of flight. [...]

Danny wants a cup of water.

People in flight along 66. And the concrete road shone like a mirror under the sun, and in the distance the heat made it seem that there were pools of water in the road.

Danny wants a cup of water.

He'll have to wait, poor little fella.[7] He's hot. Nex' service station. Service station, like the fella says.

Two hundred and fifty thousand people over the road. Fifty thousand old cars — wounded,[8] steaming. Wrecks[9] along the road, abandoned. Well, what happened to them? What happened to the folks in that car? Did they walk? Where are they? Where does the courage come from? Where does the terrible faith come from?

✦ John Steinbeck, *The Grapes of Wrath*, 1939

1. macadam 2. escape 3. getting smaller 4. make a very long sound 5. inundations 6. damaged 7. (*informal*) man 8. damaged (but usually for people) 9. badly damaged cars

Pédagogie différenciée

TRAIL A

Part 1 (l. 1-14)

1 Identify at least four expressions used to describe highway 66.

2 Find examples of the word "from" and explain what the people on the road are escaping from.

Part 2 (l. 15-24)

3 Find words that suggest that the travel conditions are difficult.

TRAIL B

Part 1 (l. 1-14)

1 Find words from the text to describe highway 66.

2 Explain the different reasons why the characters are fleeing.

Part 2 (l. 15-24)

3 Show how the author describes the difficulty of travelling on highway 66.

Meet up! "Well, what happened to them?" (l. 23) "Where are they?" (l. 24)
Try to answer these questions. Share your answers with the class.

Prepare your project

You are a photo journalist and you have taken pictures of migrants on the road. Write an entry in your diary describing what you saw and what you wanted to show with your pictures.

Grammar Tip Précis → p. 241
Use the **preterite** to describe what you saw.

Memory Challenge

Write down as many words to do with the Great Depression as you can in one minute.

D Welcome to Hooverville

✦ James Patrick Lee, *Homeless shantytown known as Hooverville*, Seattle, Washington, 1937

James Patrick Lee took several photographs of homeless people in this Hooverville near Seattle. Hoovervilles were shantytowns (towns of poor quality houses) built on the periphery of cities by homeless people during the stock market crash of 1929. They were named after Herbert Hoover who was president from 1929 to 1933.

1 Describe the photograph: compare the foreground and the background.

2 Read the text. Explain who lived there and why.

3 Write the presentation plate of this photograph for an exhibition. State the artist's message.

E The new classic American landscape

PAIR WORK

✦ Charles Sheeler, *Classic Landscape*, 1931

E-workbook
Fiche à imprimer
hatier-clic.fr/lmu1052

1 **Student A** Describe the foreground and background to your partner.
Student B Describe the colours and shapes to your partner.

2 Look at the title. Imagine what a classic American landscape looked like before this one.

3 Read the Culture Tip. Act out a short interview of Charles Sheeler about his intentions with this painting.

Culture Tip

Charles Sheeler (1883-1965) celebrated modern industry in his artworks. His paintings are dominated by rational organisation, efficiency and the veneration of industrial architecture. He was hired to document Ford's great new automobile plant in 1927.

Word Spot

plant: factory
feeling: sensation
anxiety /æŋzaɪəti/: panic
alienation: separation from others
shanty: poor quality house
vivid light ≠ dim light
straight lines
vertical ≠ horizontal ≠ diagonal /daɪægᵊnᵊl/
representative: illustrative
entitled: named
still: motionless
lonely
wretched: miserable
depict: portray
intend: want to
convey: express
shed light upon: clarify
surround: encircle
make do: live with what you have

Grammar Spot

Complex sentences Tools → p. 76

They were named after Herbert Hoover who was president from 1929 to 1933.

F Until the crisis is over

✦ Reginald Marsh, *The Park Bench*, 1933

Culture Tip

Reginald Marsh (1898-1954) was very much affected by the human side of the Great Depression. He chose to capture the resignation and immobilism of American citizens in the 1930s.

1 ***PAIR WORK***

Student A Describe the painting to your partner: focus on the location and background.

Student B Describe the painting to your partner: focus on the people and their attitudes.

2 Read the Culture Tip. In a few words, use the title to imagine why Reginald Marsh chose to represent different members of society.

3 Explain the artist's message using these words.

all categories of society - despair - stillness - resignation

G Loneliness in the city

Classe inversée

✦ Edward Hopper, *New York Movie*, 1939

Vidéo hatier-clic.fr/lmu1053

E-workbook Classe inversée hatier-clic.fr/lmu1054

1 Observe the painting, its title and date. Guess the themes explored by Edward Hopper in his paintings.

2 Watch the video and take notes to develop your answers to question 1.

3 Explain Edward Hopper's technique to make the viewer contemplate America in the 1930s.

4 ***PAIR WORK*** You and a friend have both just seen an exhibition on Edward Hopper. Discuss your impressions and the artist's intention on a messaging app.

Prepare your project

The museum you work for is organising an exhibition on the Great Depression. Choose one of the artworks you have studied and indicate why it is a good representation of the Great Depression.

Grammar Tip

Précis → p. 239

Use the **present simple** to explain the artist's message. Don't forget to add an **-s** with the 3rd person (he, she).

Memory Challenge

In pairs, speak about a painting or photograph from p. 74-75 without saying its title or author. Your partner has to guess which artwork you are talking about.

Tools in the Spotlight

Entraînez-vous sur la plateforme ***Let's Meet Up!***
reussirenlangues.fr

Practise your grammar

Précis grammatical, p. 216

Le prétérit en *be* + V-*ing*

- Le prétérit en *be* + V-*ing* indique qu'un événement était en cours dans le passé. On l'utilise pour insister sur le **déroulement de l'action** par rapport à un événement bref, ponctuel dans le passé (au prétérit simple).

*This artist **was finishing** his painting when he received an offer from a museum.*

→ Le tableau n'était pas encore terminé au moment où il a reçu une proposition d'un musée.

- Lorsque le prétérit en *be* + V-*ing* apparaît seul, sans autre événement au prétérit simple, il renvoie à une **période bien précise** au cours de laquelle l'événement a eu lieu.

*Democracy **wasn't working**.*

→ Pendant la période en question (sous-entendu : *during that time*), il n'y avait guère de fonctionnement démocratique.

La phrase complexe

- La phrase complexe est une phrase comprenant au moins deux parties : une **proposition principale** et une **proposition subordonnée**. Seule la principale est obligatoire pour que l'énoncé soit grammaticalement bien formé. La subordonnée apporte un complément d'informations.

They were named after Herbert Hoover,
proposition principale

who was president from 1929 to 1933.
proposition subordonnée

- La **proposition principale** est *They were named after Herbert Hoover*. Cette phrase est correctement formée sur le plan grammatical.

- Ce qui suit apporte un complément d'informations. Il s'agit d'une **proposition subordonnée relative** : *who was president from 1929 to 1933.*

1 Choisissez le prétérit simple ou en *be* + V-*ing*.

a. During the Great Depression, American rural areas (**lost / were losing**) a lot of their inhabitants.
b. Californian cities (**were regarded / were being regarded**) as magnets.
c. She (**read / was reading**) *The Grapes of Wrath* by John Steinbeck when I called her.
d. American artists (**depicted / were depicting**) the Great Depression in their masterpieces.

2 Utilisez le prétérit simple ou en *be* + V-*ing*.

a. He (**not - study**) American art when he was young. He (**study**) history at Berkeley.
b. She (**visit**) a Norman Rockwell exhibition when she (**come across**) *The Runaway*.
c. She (**count**) the numbers of cans in Andy Warhol's *Campbell's Soup Cans*. That's why she (**spend**) a lot of time in the US Pop Art section.
d. (**think**) she of *The Circus* when she (**mention**) American sculptor Alexander Calder?

3 Décomposez les phrases complexes suivantes en deux parties : proposition principale et proposition subordonnée.

a. Although the Great Depression was a difficult period, all the paintings are just beautiful.
b. Farmers left their plots of land in order to move to California.
c. Roosevelt's New Deal programme between 1933 and 1938 targeted the poorest people, so that the US economy could be boosted.
d. I prefer Isaac Soyer's painting, whereas my sister likes Edward Hopper's best.

4 Repérez la proposition principale dans les phrases suivantes.

a. Contrary to Edward Hopper's paintings, whose windows vanish, Norman Rockwell's paintings are quite powerful, because they give glass a texture and make it look more authentic.
b. Although highway 66 used to be the main migrant road, it has now become a tourist attraction, as opposed to the farmers' lands in Oklahoma.

Improve your pronunciation

Précis de phonologie, p. 262

Les liaisons

Audio
CD1 piste 30
MP3 n° 43

• Faire des liaisons entre deux mots permet de **fluidifier le débit**, de rendre la phrase plus naturelle, sans interruption artificielle.

• De manière générale, on fait une liaison lorsqu'un **son consonne est suivi d'un son voyelle**. Tout se passe comme s'il n'y avait pas de séparation graphique entre les deux mots, qui se trouvent accolés sur le plan phonétique. La consonne finale du mot est donc prononcée avec la voyelle qui la suit. Cependant, cette liaison doit être discrète.

His canvasses are clean.

In this way, there's just enough room.

Her brother is an artist.

They are only finishing their paintings.

5 **Faites la liaison entre les deux mots, puis écoutez l'enregistrement pour confirmer votre réponse.**

Audio
CD1 piste 31
MP3 n° 44

a. Paint it!
b. After all...
c. Read it!
d. Watch out!

6 **Indiquez les liaisons dans les phrases suivantes, puis vérifiez avec l'enregistrement.**

Audio
CD1 piste 32
MP3 n° 45

a. Perhaps it's Hopper who painted it, after all!
b. You are always right, but watch out all the same!
c. It isn't attractive, but I like it.
d. These boxes are ideal for erasers.

Work on your writing skills

Le journal intime

• Un **journal intime** (*diary*) ou **de voyage** (*travel diary*) présente le récit de la vie et les opinions et sentiments de son auteur·e.

• Il est écrit à la **1re personne du singulier**. L'auteur·e commence par la **date** et écrit parfois ***Dear Diary***, comme s'il ou elle écrivait une lettre à son journal.

• Dans ce type de texte, on emploie souvent plusieurs temps :
– le **prétérit simple** pour les actions passées.
*Yesterday I **went** to... I **enjoyed** visiting...*
– le ***present perfect*** pour faire un bilan.
I have finished...
– le **présent simple** pour les sentiments actuels.
*I **feel** happy about...*
– le **futur** en *will* + V ou en *be going to* + V pour les intentions, les résolutions.
I will visit... I am going to visit...

TIP Si vous devez écrire un journal à la place d'un personnage, mettez-vous à sa place et imaginez ce qu'il pense et ce qu'il ressent. **Qui** est-il ? **Où** et **quand** écrit-il ? **Quels événements** va-t-il raconter ? **Quel registre de langue** va-t-il utiliser ?

7 **Repérez et faites une liste des éléments typiques d'un journal intime (présentation, thèmes, temps verbaux).**

September 3rd, 1931

Dear Diary,
Yesterday Dad came home from the farm and told us his boss had to let him go because there wouldn't be any work for him tomorrow. Mommy felt horrible and cried all evening. Our family is so sad at the moment, I feel I can't do anything to help and it hurts.
I hope this crisis will come to an end and that we'll be able to have a normal family life again, with a house, a garden and a car. And maybe even a dog or a horse!
I'm glad I can write this down because I can't say this to anyone at the moment.
Maybe I'll talk about happy things tomorrow!

8 **Écrivez une note de journal intime de 80 mots environ après avoir visité une exposition sur la Grande Dépression.**

Build up your vocabulary

Audio
CD1 piste 33

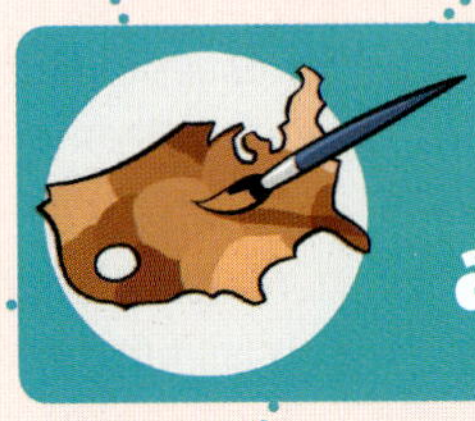 1930s artists

The rural exodus — MP3 n°51

crowd /kraʊd/
migrant /maɪgrənt/
belongings: possessions
Dust Bowl
drought /draʊt/ : lack of rain
highway
journey
exhausted: very tired
wretched: miserable
anxious: worried
desperate
flee: escape
travel

Hoovervilles — MP3 n°46

shanty: poor quallity house
shantytowns
periphery: suburbs
homeless
make do: live with what you have

The Great Depression — MP3 n°47

democracy
difficult times
anxiety /æŋzaɪəti/: panic
optimism ≠ pessimism
poverty
economic crisis
crash
stock market: Wall Street
bankruptcy
bankrupt: unable to pay debts
unemployed: jobless ≠ employed
rise ≠ fall

Modernisation — MP3 n°50

plant: factory
modern industry
industrial architecture /ɑ:kɪtektʃəʳ/
efficiency
rational organisation
alienation: separation from others
still: motionless
surround: encircle

American artists — MP3 n°49

regionalists
message
intention
political expression
feeling: sensation
entitled: named
representative: illustrative
celebrate
capture /kæptʃəʳ/
convey: express
relate: describe
depict: portray
intend to: want to
shed light on / upon: clarify

Artworks — MP3 n°48

painting
sculpture
photograph (image)
≠ photography (art)
literature
diary
form: shape
texture /tekstʃəʳ/
colour: shade
brightness ≠ darkness
vivid light ≠ dim light
straight lines
vertical ≠ horizontal
≠ diagonal /daɪægᵊnᵊl/
in the background
≠ in the foreground

Apprenez et révisez le vocabulaire !

Utilisez Quizlet pour vous entraîner en vous amusant.

Quizlet
hatier-clic.fr/lmu1055

Utilisez le vocabulaire en contexte.

1 Complétez les phrases suivantes avec des mots de la carte mentale à la forme qui convient.

a. Route 66 is a famous ... that goes from Chicago to Santa Monica.
b. In the 1930s, people had a deep feeling of ... and ... about the economic situation in the USA.
c. Hoovervilles were towns of ... that were built with cheap or reused materials.
d. Edward Hopper's paintings ... the loneliness of city life.
e. The region which farmers fled from because of drought is called the ... .

2 Utilisez cinq mots de la catégorie *American Artists* de la carte mentale pour écrire une ou deux phrases sur les intentions des artistes des années 1930.

AUTO évaluation

Faites le quiz interactif en ligne et suivez les conseils pour vous préparer à l'évaluation.

Quiz
hatier-clic.fr/lmu1056

Project #1

Prepare a presentation of an artwork for an exhibition on the Great Depression.

1 Choose an artwork.

- Do some research on artic.edu, moma.org or metmuseum.org. Look for American artists of the 1930s.
- Select artworks that are representative of the period and choose one you like.

2 Introduce the painting or photograph.

- Briefly present the artist and give some information about his or her life and work.
- Describe the artwork using the present be + V-ing.
- Say what type of art it is: movement, style.

3 Explain the artist's message.

- Give the social, cultural and historical context of the time.
- Use the preterite to talk about the past.
- Explain what it tells us about the 1930s.

4 Justify your choice.

- Say what made you choose this particular artwork.
- Explain why it is special and what you appreciate about it.
- Vary the adjectives to avoid repetitions and to give a complete description.

Fiche de méthodologie N°8 p. 280

Project #2

Write an email to the curator of an exhibition on the Great Depression. Convince him or her to include your favourite artwork.

1 Choose the best American artwork to represent the Great Depression.

- Use your copybook to find ideas of artworks. You can find more on the internet: www.artic.edu/exhibitions/1952.
- Choose a picture, a painting or a sculpture and find an image online.

2 Prepare your arguments.

- Introduce and describe the artwork (artist, date, theme, message).
- Use the superlative and the comparative to compare the artwork you chose with others from the unit: **This is the most thought-provoking painting because... It is more interesting than...**

3 Prepare your draft.

- Do not forget to greet the curator of the museum: **Dear Sir or Madam**.
- Use linking words to organise your ideas: **whereas**, **moreover**, **however**...
- Remember to use final greetings to conclude your email: **Best regards**, **Yours sincerely**.
- Add your name at the end.

4 Send your email to the chief curator.

- Check your email and look for spelling and grammar mistakes. You can use online tools: wordreference.com, oxfordlearnersdictionaries.com.
- Attach the image of the artwork and write: **Please find attached...**

Fiche de méthodologie N°20 p. 300

Let's RECAP

Lisez les questions-clés et complétez la fiche bilan avec des exemples et des documents que vous avez étudiés ou découverts.

AXE 3 | Art and power

SÉQUENCE 1 How does art boost British cities' economy?

E-workbook
Bilan à compléter
hatier-clic.fr/lmu1057

How do public art, street art and architecture help to promote urban space in the UK?
What is their economic impact?

#streetart
How do street artists or festivals hype British cities?

#architecture
How can architects regenerate cities with their creations?
How are new architectural forms changing the face of British cities?

#publicart
What is the use of public art in urban space?

#freedomofcreation
Are economic objectives an obstacle to freedom of creation?

#economicpower
What is the economic impact of urban art and architecture?

SÉQUENCE 2 How did US artists relate the Great Depression?

E-workbook
Bilan à compléter
hatier-clic.fr/lmu1058

How have American artists provided lasting memories of life in the 1930s?
How did US artists denounce the American people's living conditions during the Great Depression?

#politicalexpression
How can art be used to express an artist's political views?
To what extent can we say that art is not only for aesthetic purposes?

#economicpower
Can art be considered a counter power?

#painting
How can paintings express mood and feelings?
To what extent are paintings a testimony of a period in a nation's history?

#photography
How does photography capture social changes?

#literature
Where does a writer's inspiration come from?
How can literature be used to bring difficult times to light?

Lisez et écoutez de l'anglais en dehors de la salle de classe ! Voici quelques conseils en lien avec votre séquence.

SÉQUENCE 1

Books

Wall and Piece, Banksy, 2005

Street Art London, Frank "Steam 156" Malt, 2016

New Architecture London, Richard Schulman, Agnese Sanvito, 2017

Film

Websites

Upfest street art festival, Bristol
http://www.upfest.co.uk

UK street art
http://www.ukstreetart.co.uk

RIBA Stirling Prize
http://bit.ly/2tMNpD8

Videos

The World According to Anish Kapoor, dir. by Heinz Peter Schwerfel, 2011
http://bit.ly/2JVtkI2

Bristol's street art scene, BBC England, 2017
http://bit.ly/2utTzen

Street art in East London, Guglielmo Biason and Valentina Vitali, 2017
http://bit.ly/2TZrvi6

The old and new architecture of London, Colton Walter, 2017
http://bit.ly/2OxwsZk

The Upfest Movie, 2018
http://bit.ly/2U1t672

Articles

John Riddy's photos of London, Tate, 2016 http://bit.ly/2UWboya

Who are the best street artists working in Britain today, *Inspiring City*, August 27, 2017
http://bit.ly/2uzsKWe

A walking tour of the best contemporary landmarks in London, Ella Braidwood, January 16, 2018 http://bit.ly/2B2S4EN

SÉQUENCE 2

Novels and graphic novel

Of Mice and Men, John Steinbeck, 1937

To Kill a Mockingbird, Harper Lee, 1960

A Time of Troubles, Pieter Van Raven, 1990

Bud Not Buddy, Christopher Paul Curtis, 1999

The Storm in the Barn, Matt Phelan, 2009

Films

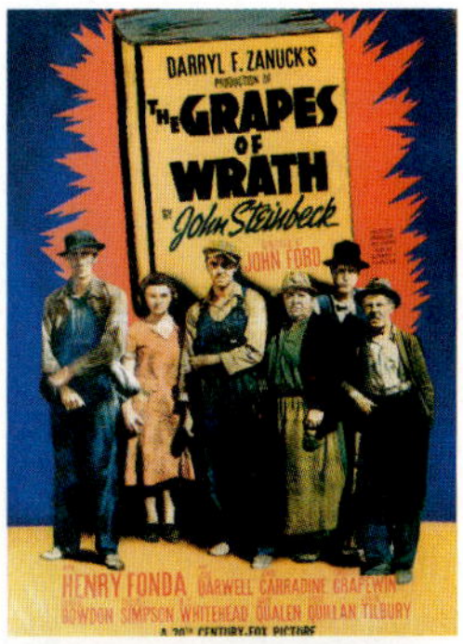

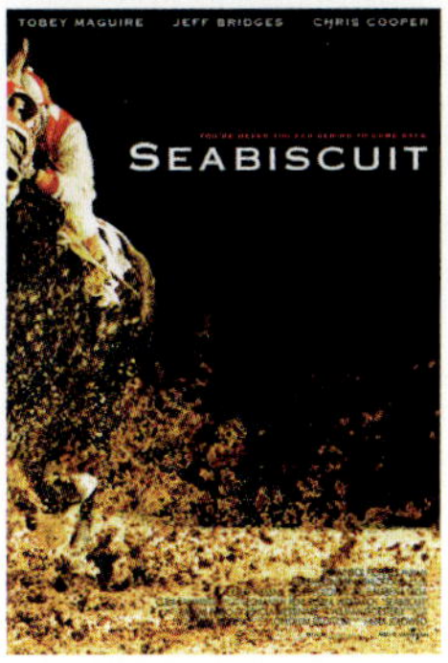

Songs

Brother Can You Spare a Dime?, Bing Crosby, 1932

Blowin' Down This Road, Woody Guthrie, 1940

Artists

Dorothea Lange
http://mo.ma/2HJhPla

Grant Wood
http://bit.ly/2FxRvqN

Edward Hopper
http://mo.ma/2CIUfBo

BAC in sight

ÉPREUVE 1

COMPRÉHENSION ORALE

Vidéo
hatier-clic.fr/lmu1059

BBC reports on a photography festival, open to amateurs, which celebrates the city of Hull.

✦ *The Hull Beermat Photography Festival*, BBC Look North, 2017

Tips
➤ Pay attention to the title of the video. Look out for clues.
➤ Leave space when taking notes (to fill in later).

➤ Fiche de méthodologie N°15 p. 290 Compréhension orale

EXPRESSION ÉCRITE

SUJET 1 You want to be part of the jury selecting the photographs. Write a letter showing your love of architecture and your motivation.

OU

SUJET 2 Why should art be brought to the masses?

Tip
➤ Think about the different art forms you have studied in the unit.

➤ Fiche de méthodologie N°20 p. 300 Expression écrite

Pour l'épreuve

Questions
Fiche modifiable
hatier-clic.fr/lmu1060

Évaluation
Grille à imprimer
hatier-clic.fr/lmu1061

ÉPREUVE 2

EXPRESSION ÉCRITE

SUJET 1 "The simple solution, Malthouse says, is 'putting beauty at the heart of our housing and communities policy'." Two friends discuss whether it is important to build beautiful homes or not. They disagree. Imagine the conversation.

OU

SUJET 2 Do you think art and architecture play an important part in cities?

✦ Mann Island apartments and Liver Building in Liverpool

Tips
➤ Identify the type of language you need to use (formal, informal...).
➤ Think of examples that you have seen in class.
➤ Pay attention to the layout (paragraphs, lines...), punctuation and spelling.

➤ Fiche de méthodologie N°20 p. 300 Expression écrite

COMPRÉHENSION ÉCRITE

Can we trust the government to judge what's beautiful?

The UK government has resolved to put beauty first to create better homes. Shame no one can agree on what that means

The UK government thinks it has got to the heart of the housing crisis: the problem is, new homes just aren't beautiful enough. "Build beautifully and get permission," says the housing minister, Kit Malthouse. "Build beautifully and communities will actually welcome developers, rather than drive them out of town at the tip of a pitchfork[1]."

If only housebuilders would make their product more visually appealing, the thinking goes, then opposition to them would fade away, more homes would be built, prices would drop and we would all live happily ever after. The simple solution, Malthouse says, is "putting beauty at the heart of our housing and communities policy".

Hence[2] the new Building Better, Building Beautiful commission, which was established in November to interrogate the question of beauty in the built environment and met with howls of outrage and derisive sneers. It's not hard to see why. A parliamentary debate that preceded the announcement played out like a parody of Victorian mores[3], as successive MPs lined up to lament the state of modern architecture. […]

Matters weren't helped when Malthouse tweeted a photo of a glazed commercial building on Oxford Street and a neo-classical stone courthouse in Alabama with the caption: "Both built in the last 10 years. One will stand for centuries, one won't." If the comment was intended to troll the architecture profession, it worked. The minister was slammed for being out of touch, anti-progress and "pandering to[4] rightwing populist nostalgia". […]

There is more to housing quality than beauty alone, but if there is indeed a gulf between what developers are building and what people want, then it makes sense to look at how this might be bridged. Are architects out of touch with popular taste? Is there an obsession with new development being "in keeping" at the expense of it being good? And is a planning system even capable of regulating beauty?

The government may be keen to put beauty at the top of the agenda, but whose idea of beauty are they talking about? […]

One person's masterpiece may be another's carbuncle[5]. But is there at least some public consensus on what is welcome and what constitutes blight? If so, how can we find out what it is?

Some campaign groups, such as Create Streets, swear by their methods of public polling, in which people are shown photographs of different kinds of urban environments and asked which they prefer. But such exercises are prone to distortion: do you prefer a tree-lined terraced street in sunshine or a tower block glowering[6] under leaden[7] skies?

✦ Oliver Wainwright, *The Guardian*, January 15, 2019

1. brutally 2. as a consequence 3. traditions and conventions 4. flattering 5. something horrible 6. grimacing 7. grey

✦ The former Pimlico School in London, now demolished

Tips

➤ Underline the key words when reading the text.
➤ Don't forget to look at the vocabulary footnotes.
➤ Don't panic if there are words you don't understand!

➤ Fiche de méthodologie N°16 p. 292 Compréhension écrite

Pour l'épreuve

Questions — Fiche modifiable — hatier-clic.fr/lmu1062

Évaluation — Grille à imprimer — hatier-clic.fr/lmu1063

BAC in sight

ÉPREUVE 1

COMPRÉHENSION ORALE

Vidéo
hatier-clic.fr/lmu1064

It is the opening of the exhibition entitled "America After the Fall: Painting in the 1930s" at the Royal Academy of Arts in London. The curator explains American artists' goals in a time of economic crisis.

Tips
➤ Be ready to take notes and focus on words that are repeated.
➤ Make a list of the people mentioned.

➤ Fiche de méthodologie N°15 p. 290 Compréhension orale

EXPRESSION ÉCRITE

SUJET 1 Imagine a dialogue between two visitors at this exhibition. They discuss the artworks but also the context in which they were created.

OU

SUJET 2 What can the role of artists be during times of crisis?

Tip
➤ Remember how you felt when you first looked at the artworks in this unit!

➤ Fiche de méthodologie N°20 p. 300 Expression écrite

✦ Alice Neel, *Pat Whalen*, 1935

Pour l'épreuve

Questions
Fiche modifiable
hatier-clic.fr/lmu1065

Évaluation
Grille à imprimer
hatier-clic.fr/lmu1066

ÉPREUVE 2

EXPRESSION ÉCRITE

SUJET 1 Write the page that comes just after this text. Include dialogues to explain the economic context and add testimonies to express the characters' feelings.

OU

SUJET 2 Do you think American artists provided a pessimistic testimony of the 1930s?

Tips
➤ Make a checklist of elements you will need in your production.
➤ Prepare a short recap of words and cultural facts you may need.
➤ Make an outline or a mind map to organise your ideas.

➤ Fiche de méthodologie N°20 p. 300 Expression écrite

✦ Unemployed worker selling apples outside of his "Hooverville" shanty home, 1930s

COMPRÉHENSION ÉCRITE

Bud, Not Buddy **tells the story of a 10-year old African American boy who embarks on a mission to find his father during the Great Depression. Bud and his friend Bugs want to catch a free ride on a train, and they are told to go to "Hooperville" to do so.**

We found out that we'd have to go to a city called Hooperville just outside of Flint. The only trouble was nobody knew exactly where Hooperville was. It was dark before we found out the right direction. I'd never heard of a city that was so doggone hard to find.

We walked on a trail through some woods that run right up against Thread Crick. We could tell we were getting close to Hooperville 'cause we heard somebody playing a mouth organ[1] and the smell of food cooking was getting stronger. We kept walking in the direction that the sky was glowing with a orangeish light.

When we could hear the music real clear, and folks talking to each other and the sound of sticks cracking in a fire, we started cutting through the trees. That way we could peek into Hooperville first.

We looked out from behind a big tree and saw that a big wind or even two or three big wolves huffing and puffing real hard could blow Hooperville into the next county. It was a bunch of huts and shacks thrown together out of pieces of boxes and wood and cloth. The Amoses' shed would've looked like a real fancy house here.

Right near our tree was the big fire that had been lighting up the sky. It looked like a hundred people were sitting around it, watching things burn or waiting for the food cooking in three big pots set up in the fire. There were two littler fires burning in Hooperville. One had a pot that was big enough to boil a whole person in it. A man was stirring things in the pot with a big stick and when he raised the stick up he'd pull some britches or a shirt out and pass it over to a white man who was hanging the clothes on a line to dry. There was a mountain of clothes on the ground next to him waiting on their turn.

The other fire in Hooperville was real small. It was off to the side, by itself. There were five white people sitting at this fire, two kids, a man, and a woman holding a little wrapped-up baby. The baby sounded like all those new sick babies at the Home, it was coughing[2] like it was a half-dead little animal.

Bugs whispered, "Shoot, this ain't no city, this is just another cardboard jungle[3]."

"A what?"

"A cardboard jungle, somewhere you can get off the train and clean up and get something to eat without the cops chasing you out of town."

I said, "Well, what're we going to do? We can't just go busting[4] into this city and expect someone to feed us, can we?"

Bugs said, "One of us has got to talk to them, let's flip for it."

"OK."

Bugs rumbled around in his pocket and found a penny. He rubbed it up against his britches[5] and said, "Heads I win, tails you lose."

"OK."

He flipped the penny up into the air and caught it, then slapped it down on the back of his left hand. He peeked underneath his right hand to see and a big smile cracked his face. Shucks!

Bugs said. "Tails. You lose."

"Dang! So what should I say?"

"Ask them if this is Hooperville, see if they got any extra food."

I moved out from behind our tree and walked over toward the biggest fire, I waited until some folks noticed me, then said, "Excuse me, is this here Hooperville?"

The man who was playing the mouth organ stopped and everyone else around the fire looked up at me. One of the white men said, "What is it you looking for?"

I said, "A city called Hooperville, sir."

They all laughed.

The mouth organ man said, "Naw, son, what you're looking for is Hooverville, with a v, like in President Herbert Hoover."

I said, "Oh, is this it, sir?"

The man said, "This is one of them."

✦ Christopher Paul Curtis, *Bud, Not Buddy*, 1999

1. harmonica 2. expulsing air when sick 3. city made of reused materials 4. arriving in a precipitated manner 5. trousers

Tips

➤ Read the introductory paragraph to understand the story.
➤ Find as much information as you can on each character.
➤ Focus on the adjectives used in the descriptions.

➤ Fiche de méthodologie N°16 p. 292 Compréhension écrite

Pour l'épreuve

Questions	Évaluation
Fiche modifiable	Grille à imprimer
hatier-clic.fr/lmu1067	hatier-clic.fr/lmu1068

AXE 4

Citizenship and virtual worlds

Citoyenneté et mondes virtuels

SÉQUENCE 1

What is the Americans' relationship to the media?

Projects

Project #1: Act out a discussion between a journalist and an expert about the evolution of the media and the dangers of fake news.

Project #2: Write a post about the changing face of the news on an online forum about journalism in the USA.

Tools

Grammaire	les quantifieurs (1), l'aspect *be* + V-*ing*
Phonologie	l'accentuation d'un mot et de ses dérivés
Écriture	l'apostrophe
Vocabulaire	les médias, l'information

SÉQUENCE 2

Is online activism effective in the USA?

Projects

Project #1: Live stream on Instagram to speak about your experience as an activist.

Project #2: Launch an online petition for a cause that matters to you.

Tools

Grammaire	les quantifieurs (2), les adjectifs en *-ed* et *-ing*
Phonologie	l'accent de phrase
Écriture	les faux amis
Vocabulaire	le militantisme, les actions

#fakenews #freedomofexpression #sharinginformation #medialiteracy #whistleblowers

CNN World Headquarters, Atlanta, Georgia

#onlineactivism #citizensandpower #participativedemocracy #freedomofspeech #clicktivism

Thousands of protesters took part in the "Justice For All" march, December 13, 2014

What is the Americans' relationship to the media?

A Real news vs fake news

The New York Times

VOL. CLXIV ... No. 56,604 — NEW YORK, SEPTEMBER 16, 2018 — $2.50

Before You Buy That Couch[1], an App Will Put it in Your Living Room

✦ *The New York Times*, Sept. 16, 2018

1. sofa

SCIENCE AND TECHNOLOGY

Mark Zuckerberg: America Will Elect Its Next President via Facebook

✦ *Real News Right Now*, Apr. 14, 2016

CityWorldNews

Woman Names Her Daughter After Superstore

✦ cityworldnews.com, Apr. 14, 2015,

NEWS PUNCH

Scientists Discover Mineral That Could Make Internet 1,000 Times Faster

✦ Newspunch.com, Nov. 29, 2017

FOX NEWS — AMPHIBIANS Published November 17

Bioreactor helps regrow legs on frogs

✦ *Fox News*, Nov. 17, 2018

NBC NEWS

Man survives bear attack and shark bite in one year

✦ *NBC News*, Apr. 23, 2018

1 ***PAIR WORK*** Read the headlines. Discuss to decide which are real and which are fake.

2 Explain why you didn't believe the fake news headlines.

3 Write a short paragraph on a forum warning people about fake news. Give examples.

B Think for yourself

Classe inversée

Vidéo
hatier-clic.fr/lmu1069

E-workbook
Classe inversée
hatier-clic.fr/lmu1070

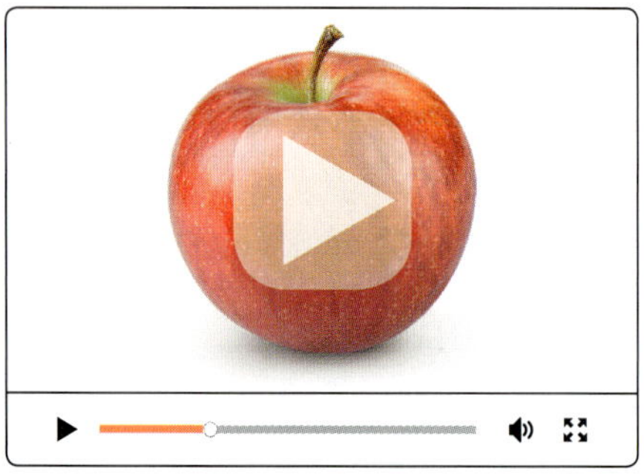

✦ *This is an Apple*, CNN, 2017

1 Identify the type of document.

2 Deduce who "some people" are and why they are criticised.

3 How does the tone of voice contrast with what is said? Guess the real message.

4 Write a tweet advising people to watch this video.

Word Spot

aim: objective, goal
objectivity ≠ subjectivity
manipulation /mənɪpjəleɪʃᵊn/
credible: convincing, believable
far-fetched: incredible, improbable
biased /baɪəst/: not objective
likely, probable ≠ unlikely, improbable
irrelevant ≠ pertinent
research: collect information about
look for: search for
look into: find out about
check: verify
question
go further: get more information
all around: everywhere

Grammar Spot

Quantifiers Tools → p. 92

"Some people might try to tell you that it's a banana."

C Become a media expert

GROUP WORK

✦ International Federation of Library Associations and Institutions (IFLA), 2018

1. proves it is true 2. appropriate 3. bizarre 4. personal opinions that influence your judgment

1 In groups, take notes to be ready to explain three of the symbols in your own words. Give the number of the guideline.

E-workbook
Fiche à imprimer
hatier-clic.fr/lmu1071

2 Hide the document and listen to the others explain a symbol in turn. Take notes.

3 Without looking at the document, use all of your notes to rewrite the eight guidelines together. Then compare them with the original document.

4 You want to post the guidelines in your school library. Explain to your librarian why it is important, in English or in French.

Prepare your project

You are a media expert speaking to a class of American teenagers. Define and give examples of fake news. Warn your audience and give them some tips so they avoid being fooled.

Grammar Tip Précis → p. 237
Use **should** to give advice.

Memory Challenge

How many pieces of advice about fake news can you write down in two minutes?

D Teens' views on the news

Trump Has Changed How Teens View the News

Since President Trump took office, he has relentlessly attacked the media. He's shunned[1] individual reporters, referred to the press as "the enemy of the American people," and popularized the term "fake news" to denigrate credible articles. Meanwhile, public trust in the press is at an all-time low. According to a recent Knight-Gallup report, only a third of Americans view the press positively.

There is increasing evidence that this skepticism, exacerbated by the president's relentless[2] attacks, is trickling down[3] to the next generation of voters.

A 2017 report on a series of focus groups with 52 people between the ages of 14 and 24 conducted by Data & Society and the Knight Foundation, found that many young Americans believe the news is biased[4] and are skeptical of its accuracy. [...]

Teenagers, in particular, appear to be increasingly questioning the credibility and value of traditional media organizations. In interviews with *The Atlantic*, teens expressed great skepticism about the accuracy of the mainstream media [and] reiterated Trump's biased characterization of many news sources. [...]

"I don't believe there [are] any neutral news organizations," said Emma Neely, a 19-year-old in Tennessee. "Each writer and editor has their own personal bias. What they write, even if it's a little biased, it's still biased."

Angie, a 16-year-old in New York, agreed. She contends that Trump's comments have revealed to people that the news media cannot be trusted. "I think this whole phenomenon has given teens awareness that bias exists and things are not what they seem," she said.

Sally, a 17-year-old in Puerto Rico, said she's learned not to trust the media [...]. "They say what they want to say, I don't feel they say the truth as it is."

Social media has given young people unprecedented access to real-time news. Many teens I spoke with follow the president, other politicians, journalists, and news outlets on Twitter. The ones who don't follow Trump directly all said they were aware of almost everything he tweets thanks to screenshots posted to Snapchat or Instagram.

✦ Taylor Lorenz, *The Atlantic*, August 29, 2018

1. rejected 2. continuous 3. passed on 4. not objective

Pédagogie différenciée

TRAIL A

1 Read lines 1 to 13. Describe President Trump's vision of the media.

2 Focus on the 2017 report and find out if American teenagers trust the media. Justify your answer with figures from the article.

3 Pick out the names of the teenagers interviewed. Note down the keywords that explain what they think about the media.

TRAIL B

1 Explain President Trump's attitude towards the press with examples of what he has done.

2 Find out what the two reports mentioned in the article show.

3 Identify the criticisms teenagers have against the media.

Meet up! For your presentation on American media in class, explain how American teenagers access information nowadays and what vision of the news they have.

Grammar Spot

be + V-*ing* aspect Tools → p. 92

"skepticism (...) is trickling down to the next generation of voters"

Word Spot

varied: diverse
aware /əweəʳ/ of
exposed to
informed
available: easy or possible to get
interested in
have faith in: trust
comment on
share
disclose: reveal, publish /pʌblɪʃ/
tweet
consult /kənsʌlt/
access: get
leak: give secret information
in touch with

E Who controls the media?

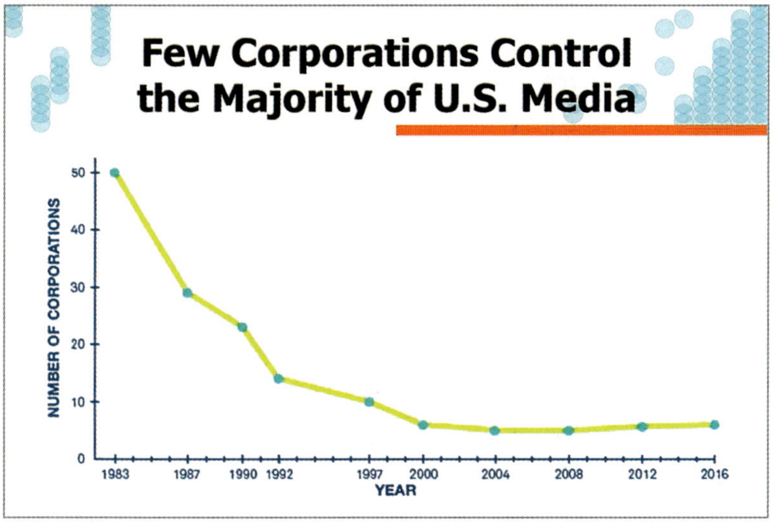

✦ Stephen Ansolabehere, Benjamin Ginsberg, Theodore J. Lowi, Kenneth A. Shepsle, *American Government: Power and Purpose*, 2017

In 1983, 50 corporations controlled most of the American media (magazines, books, music, news feeds, newspapers, movies, radio and television).
In 1992, that number had dropped by half.
In 2000, six corporations owned most of the media.
Over time many online news sites which used to be independent have also become properties of the small number of media corporations.
Today five corporations dominate the American media industry: Time Warner, Disney, Murdoch's News Corporation, Bertelsmann of Germany and Viacom.

1 Look at the graph and explain what has happened to the number of companies controlling American media since 1983.

2 Read the text and find information to develop your answer to question 1.

3 Find out in the text if online news is independent.

4 Explain the effect that this concentration of media ownership has on the news that is available. Use these words to write a few sentences.

power - control - decide - influence

F Whistleblowers

Vidéo
hatier-clic.fr/lmu1072

E-workbook
Fiche à imprimer
hatier-clic.fr/lmu1073

1 Identify people, places and news outlets.

2 Who and what are the American news presenters talking about and how do they sound? Take notes.

3 Find out what type of shocking information WikiLeaks published.

4 Explain this event to your friend and show why the American media and society were so perturbed by this event.

Culture Tip

The first three estates (powers) in the USA are the executive, the legislative and the judiciary. The media are commonly called **the fourth estate**. The internet media are considered to be **the fifth estate**.
WikiLeaks is an international, non-profit organisation that publishes secret information, classified documents and news leaks, from anonymous sources on its website. **Julian Assange**, an Australian internet activist, is considered to be its founder. The people who release secret information are called **whistleblowers**.

Prepare your project

Write a short article for your school newspaper with the following title: "What's new about the news in the USA?"

Grammar Tip

Précis → p. 241 and 239

Use the **preterite** to talk about how things were in the past and the **simple present** to talk about current habits and realities.

Memory Challenge

Make a list of 10 words that are indispensable when talking about the media. You have one minute! Compare your list with your classmates'.

Tools in the Spotlight

Practise your grammar

Précis grammatical, p. 216

Les quantifieurs (*some, any, no, not any*)

• Ils désignent une certaine quantité, **indéfinie**. Le nom qui les accompagne est soit indénombrable au singulier, soit dénombrable ou un nom collectif (par exemple, ***people***) au pluriel.

• On utilise ***some*** dans les phrases affirmatives ou pour faire une proposition ou une requête.

Some people might try to tell you that it's a banana.
*Would you like to read **some** newspapers?*

• On emploie ***any*** dans les phrases interrogatives.

*Did President Trump send **any** tweets last week?*

Dans une phrase affirmative, ***any*** veut dire « n'importe quel·le ».

Any journalist should respect people's privacy.

• On rencontre ***no*** ou ***not any*** dans les phrases négatives.

*There are **no / not any** neutral news organizations.*

1 Complétez les phrases suivantes avec *some, any, no, not any*.

a. According to the First Amendment, "Congress shall make ... law abridging the freedom of speech or of the press".
b. Have you bought ... quality newspapers today?
c. ... whistleblowers have contacted the main newspapers to reveal secrets to the public.
d. There are ... objective articles. They are all biased.
e. ... American reporters, like Bod Woodward and Carl Bernstein, became famous after revealing the Watergate scandal.
f. There is ... doubt that this is fake news! That's so astonishing!
g. Did you meet ... reporters at the Minneapolis Media Center?

L'aspect *be* + V-*ing*

• Le présent en ***be* + V-*ing*** indique que l'action est **en cours** au moment où l'on parle.

*The journalist **is talking** to this American senator at the moment.*

• On emploie aussi l'aspect en ***be* + V-*ing*** dans les **descriptions**, par exemple pour décrire une image.

*In this picture, American students **are reading** online news.*

• Avec un marqueur futur, l'aspect en ***be* + V-*ing*** désigne une **intention** ou un événement qui va avoir lieu dans un **avenir** relativement proche.

*The reporter **is interviewing** the American president tomorrow afternoon.*

• L'aspect ***be* + V-*ing*** peut également être associé à l'aspect ***have + en*** (participe passé) pour former le ***present perfect* en V-*ing***. Les deux aspects combinés indiquent la **durée** : un événement a commencé dans le **passé**, mais il est toujours **en cours** au moment où l'on parle.

*The press **has been publishing** a lot of articles about politicians' private lives for a long time.*

2 Indiquez la valeur de l'aspect *be* + V-*ing* :
(1) action en cours, (2) description, (3) futur proche, (4) expression de durée.

a. This columnist **has been writing** an article on *The Fourth Estate* for two hours.
b. She **is giving** a speech this afternoon on the unethical practices of investigative journalism.
c. He **is driving** to the media centre, where he **is doing** a three-week internship.
d. In this picture the presenter **is comparing** the various broadsheets and tabloids.

3 Utilisez l'aspect *be* + V-*ing* ou la forme simple.

a. The president (**critised / has been critising**) the media since he was elected.
b. The US mass media (**include / are including**) newspapers, radio, television, magazines... and social networks of course!
c. A lot of reporters (**come / are coming**) to the conference tomorrow evening.
d. Usually, efficient reporters (**spend / are spending**) little time writing their articles.

Improve your pronunciation

Précis de phonologie, p. 262

L'accentuation d'un mot et de ses dérivés

Audio
CD1 piste 34
MP3 n° 52

- L'**accent tonique** porte sur l'une des syllabes d'un mot. Lorsqu'on ajoute un préfixe (avant le nom) ou un suffixe (terminaison) à un mot, on parle de **mot dérivé**.
- L'ajout d'un **préfixe** ne change pas la place de l'accent tonique du mot dérivé.

in'form → *misin'form* *'comfortable* → *un'comfortable*
'active → *in'active* *'likely* → *un'likely*

- Mais l'ajout d'un **suffixe** peut changer la place de l'accent tonique du mot dérivé.

→ Il n'y a **pas de modification** de l'accentuation avec les suffixes : ***-ish***, ***-ism***, ***-ist***, ***-ize***, ***-ing***, ***-ly***, ***-er***, ***-ed***, ***-hood***, ***-ship***, ***-ment***, ***-ness***.

a'ware → *a'wareness* *'green* → *'greenish*
'national → *'nationalist* *misin'form* → *misin'formed*

→ L'accentuation est **modifiée** avec l'ajout des suffixes ***-ion***, ***-ual***, ***-ial***, ***-ious***, ***-ic***, ***-ity***. L'accent tonique porte sur la syllabe qui est placée **avant** ces suffixes.

in'form → *infor'mation* *ob'jective* → *objec'tivity*

4 **Écrivez les mots suivants et indiquez l'accent tonique, puis écoutez l'enregistrement pour confirmer vos réponses.**

Audio
CD1 piste 35
MP3 n° 53

nation • national • nationally • nationalist • nationalistic • friend • friendly • friendliness

5 **Écrivez les mots soulignés et indiquez l'accent tonique, puis écoutez l'enregistrement pour confirmer vos réponses.**

Audio
CD1 piste 36
MP3 n° 54

a. Communication and awareness are essential both in politics and in the media.
b. This is not a realistic achievement according to a famous journalist.
c. The printed press has dropped dramatically since the advent of the internet.
d. The Americanisation of European journalism has been studied recently.

Work on your writing skills

L'apostrophe

On utilise l'apostrophe en anglais pour contracter un mot ou pour former le génitif.

- La **contraction** d'un mot

Dans ce cas, l'apostrophe indique qu'une ou plusieurs lettres ont été supprimées.

I'm = I am *let's go = let us go*
I can't = I cannot *you've got = you have got*

- Le **génitif**

Dans ce cas, l'apostrophe + ***s*** indique la possession.

the journalist's questions (les questions **du** journaliste)

James's questions (les questions **de** James)

⚠ Les noms au pluriel prennent uniquement l'apostrophe.

the journalists' questions (les questions **des** journalistes)

6 **Contractez des mots lorsque c'est possible. Indiquez toutes les possibilités.**

a. I do not have an opinion.
b. They are going to write an article.
c. We are not listening to the radio.
d. He will not give any interviews.
e. They have not explained why.
f. I would like to read the newspaper.

7 **Traduisez les groupes nominaux suivants en employant le génitif. Veillez à bien placer l'apostrophe.**

a. la réponse du président
b. les opinions des journalistes
c. la voix du peuple
d. les choix de l'éditeur
e. la réaction des adolescents

Build up your vocabulary

Audio
CD1 piste 37

Media in the USA

Media literacy MP3 n°55

aim: objective, goal
bias /baɪəs/
judgement
guidelines: rules
go further: get more information
look for: search for
look into: find out about
question: have doubts about
research: collect information about
select
check: verify
discriminate: differentiate
avoid being fooled

Public opinion MP3 n°56

criticism
previous generations
scepticism
negative ≠ positive
aware /əweər/ (of): knowing
exposed to
informed ≠ misinformed
interested in
trickling down: impacting
in touch with

Social media MP3 n°57

social networks
the fifth estate
screenshot
privacy /prɪvəsi/
available: easy or possible to get
varied: diverse
comment on
tweet
follow
share
post

Whistleblowers MP3 n°58

activist
anonymous source
classified documents
WikiLeaks
phenomenon
truth
shocking information
secret information
inform
disclose: publish /pʌblɪʃ/
leak: give secret information
hack

Fake news MP3 n°59

danger
manipulation /mənɪpjəleɪʃən/
subjectivity ≠ objectivity
biased /baɪəst/: not objective
far-fetched /fɑːfetʃt/: incredible, improbable
irrelevant: not pertinent
all around: everywhere
unlikely: improbable

Real news MP3 n°60

the fourth estate: the press
corporations
mainstream / mass media
news outlets
real-time news
objectivity ≠ subjectivity
credible: convincing, believable
independent
neutral /njuːtrəl/
pertinent: relevant
likely: probable
control
access: get
consult /kənsʌlt/
have faith in: trust

Apprenez et révisez le vocabulaire !

Utilisez Quizlet pour vous entraîner en vous amusant.

Quizlet
hatier-clic.fr/lmu1074

Utilisez le vocabulaire en contexte.

1 Complétez les phrases suivantes avec des mots ou expressions de la carte mentale.

a. A lot of the news is … which means that it is not neutral.
b. You should always … the source of the information you read on the internet.
c. More and more people don't … the media nowadays.
d. It is important to be … … the fact that some media can manipulate us.
e. The press is called … … … . This means that it has considerable power.

2 Choisissez six mots ou expressions dans les catégories *Fake news* et *Media literacy* de la carte mentale. Écrivez un tweet sur les *fake news* comprenant ces mots.

AUTO évaluation

Faites le quiz interactif en ligne et suivez les conseils pour vous préparer à l'évaluation.

Quiz
hatier-clic.fr/lmu1075

Project #1

Act out a discussion between a journalist and an expert about the evolution of the media and the dangers of fake news.

1 **Start the radio show.**

Journalist: Mention the name of the show. Present the guest and the theme of discussion.

Media expert: Greet the journalist.

2 **Discuss the evolution of news sources and media control.**

Journalist: Make sure your questions are structured correctly: **Wh- / How + auxiliary + subject + verb + complement?**

Media expert: Use the preterite and the present perfect to show the evolution of the media over time.

3 **Discuss how people access the news.**

Journalist: Use the present tense to ask about current habits.

Media expert: Make comparisons between the different generations using **while** or **whereas**.

4 **Discuss the dangers of fake news and the importance of media literacy.**

Journalist: Ask about the dangers of fake news and the right attitude to adopt.

Media expert: Give advice and explain methods citizens can use to avoid being fooled.

➤ Fiche de méthodologie N°6 p. 278

Project #2

Write a post about the changing face of the news on an online forum about journalism in the USA.

1 **Introduce the subject with the evolution of news sources over the last century.**

- ✓ Write about traditional sources of news, then explain how the internet and social media have changed the way people can get information.
- ✓ Use the present perfect to explain changes: **The face of the media has changed...**

2 **Mention the control of the media.**

- ✓ Give information about the ownership of news sources and explain what this means about who decides what news is broadcast.
- ✓ Use **used to** + V and the preterite to write about the past. Compare with the present using **Nowadays** + present tense.

3 **Explain the problem with fake news.**

- ✓ Present the issue of media distrust and the problems regarding fake news.
- ✓ Say what people need to do to avoid being misinformed.

4 **Explain how new media forms have changed how people can access the news.**

- ✓ Write about social media and give examples of how people share information now compared with the past.
- ✓ Mention the WikiLeaks phenomenon.

➤ Fiche de méthodologie N°10 p. 282

SÉQUENCE 2

Is online activism effective in the USA?

A Changing the world with petitions

change.org Start a petition Browse Membership Log in

Starbucks, we know you can make a #BetterCup

Victory

This petition made change with 347,574 supporters!

Starbucks, we know you can #BreakFreeFromPlastic and make...

Share on Facebook

Send a Facebook message

Send an email to friends

Tweet to your followers

Copy link

Gina Ko started this petition to Starbucks and 1 other

Our names are Mya and Eve and we are 11-year old students in Grade 6 attending school in Calgary. **A science project of ours on single-use disposable cups revealed shocking facts and we think it's time to act.**

✦ Caption from *Change.org*, victory section

1. In a few words, explain what this petition and the #BetterCup are about.
2. Find elements in the screenshot and the paratext that indicate that this petition was a success.
3. ***PAIR WORK*** You are the two students in charge of the #BetterCup petition. Present your project to your classmates and be ready to answer their questions.

B The effects of #MeToo

Audio CD1 piste 38

E-workbook Fiche à imprimer hatier-clic.fr/lmu1076

1. Find elements about the beginning of the #MeToo movement.
2. Find out what impacts this movement has had.
3. In your own words, explain the movement and its consequences to your friends.

Grammar Spot

Quantifiers TOOLS → p. 100

"**many** influential figures and celebrities also took to social media to show their support for the movement."
"the #MarchforOurLives hashtag ignited a **much**-needed conversation"

Word Spot

activist
protest: strong complaint
criticism
advantage: benefit
distraught: upset: annoyed
involved: interested
recyclable /riːsaɪkləbᵊl/
environmentally-friendly
show support
march: demonstrate
stand up for a cause
raise awareness
create a hashtag
post / share on social media
impact
positively ≠ negatively

C Showing support on social media

✦ Emma González spoke at the March for Our Lives rally in Washington about Parkland shooting, one of the deadliest shootings at a high school in US history, that took place on February 14, 2018.

While thousands of protesters gathered today for the March for Our Lives — an anti-gun march held across the country following the school shooting in Parkland, Florida — many influential figures and celebrities also took to social media to show their support for the movement. After quickly becoming a trending topic on Twitter, the #MarchforOurLives hashtag ignited[1] much-needed conversation around America's lax[2] gun laws, where people sounded off[3] on the epidemic of gun violence and what needs to change.

Former President Barack Obama showed his support for the march and its inspiring student leaders, such as Parkland survivor Emma González, who delivered a powerful speech, which lasted just six minutes and 20 seconds — the length of the entire Parkland shooting spree[4]. Obama tweeted, "Michelle and I are so inspired by all the young people who made today's marches happen. Keep at it. You're leading us forward. Nothing can stand in the way of millions of voices calling for change."

Lady Gaga also documented the march via social media in Los Angeles, releasing a series of Instagram videos calling for action from politicians to enforce stricter gun laws. "School is not a place where kids should go to be afraid for their lives," she said in one video, where she holds a "Disarm Hate" sign.

Meanwhile, several people on Twitter, including comedian Kathy Griffin, were also quick to point out the successful turnout[5] of the march, comparing it to President Donald Trump's more, say, *lean*[6] inauguration. (Neither President Trump nor Vice President Mike Pence commented on the marches today.)

✦ Christian Allaire, *This Is What Social Media Had to Say About the March for Our Lives*, *Vogue US*, March 24, 2018

1. started 2. not strict 3. complained 4. murder frenzy
5. number of people who gathered 6. (*here*) insignificant

Culture Tip

The Second Amendment (*Bill of Rights*, 1791) guarantees the right to keep and bear arms. However, there have always been debates over gun control legislation in the USA. The NRA (National Rifle Association) sees these restrictions as a violation of the Second Amendment. The debate is revived after every mass shooting.

1 Explain the #MarchforOurLives movement.

2 Find who is supporting Emma González and clarify why.

3 Explain the role of social media in the March for Our Lives movement.

4 You want to show your support for March for Our Lives. Write a twitter-size post with the corresponding # (280 characters).

Prepare your project

PAIR WORK You want to launch an online petition: imagine the exchange with a successful online activist and ask him or her questions on how to do it.

Grammar Tip

Précis → p. 249

The online activist can give advice using: S + **should** + V.

Memory Challenge

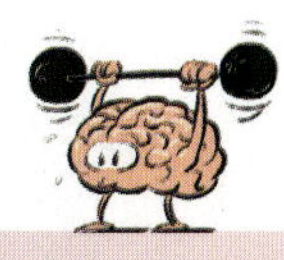

In groups, choose a document studied in class and play Chinese whispers. Think of one sentence about the document and whisper it to your neighbour. Your neighbour repeats your sentence and adds another one. The last student must repeat all the sentences!

D The limits of online activism

Vidéo DVD

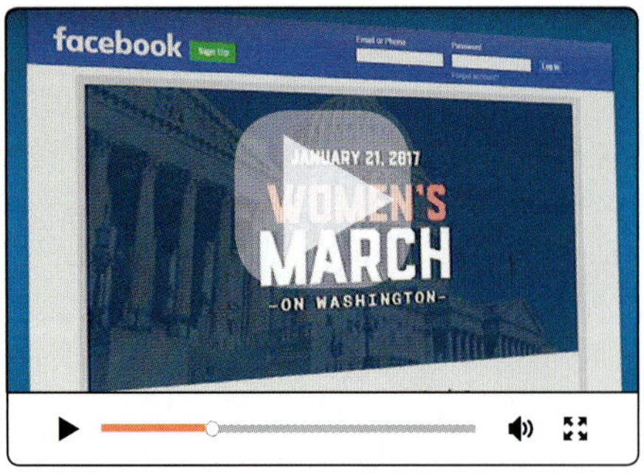

✦ *How online social movements become offline results*, PBS NewsHour, 2017

Culture Tip

The March on Washington for Jobs and Freedom was organised to advocate for the civil and economic rights of African Americans. It took place on August 28, 1963 when Martin Luther King Jr. delivered his famous speech "I have a dream".
The Women's March on Washington was first organised by women in 2017 to send a message to Trump's administration about issues such as women's rights, the healthcare system and immigration.

Pédagogie différenciée

TRAIL A

1 Watch the video, choose adjectives and use them to define the first example of activism.

empowering - useless - dangerous - powerful - long - large

2 Pick out words to describe what the impact of a march or an online campaign is.

3 Compare the second example of protest in the video with the first one using the following words.

organisation - easy - similar - long - crowded - process - unite - outcome

TRAIL B

1 Watch the video and define the first example of activism.

2 In your own words, explain the consequences a march or an online campaign can have.

3 Describe the second example of protest in the video and analyse its effects.

Meet up! ***PAIR WORK*** Discuss the advantages and limits of online activism.

E Online activism or slacktivism?

✦ *Slacktivism*, cartoon by Patrick LaMontagne

slacker (noun): sb who does not make much effort

1 Read the cartoon and explain the situation (feelings, faces).

2 Read the cartoon again. Using the definition of slacker, guess the meaning of slacktivism.

3 ***PAIR WORK*** Act out the scene using the right tone.

Grammar Spot

Adjectives in -ed and -ing Tools → p. 100

"The Power of **Networked** protest"
"Marches are great. They're really **empowering** to people."

Word Spot

- speech bubble: cartoon's dialogue
- sarcasm: irony /aɪrəni/
- investment: commitment
- militant: political activist
- ground activism ≠ online activism
- result: outcome
- effective ≠ ineffective
- dubious: questionable
- raise the question of sth
- make a difference
- take action: act
- gather sb: bring sb together
- threaten: make sb worry
- go viral: spread widely
- put together sth: assemble, organise
- join a cause
- go door to door

F Slacktivism: is it useful?

Classe inversée

E-workbook
Classe inversée
hatier-clic.fr/lmu1077

Activism is now a computer mouse away. With a click, one can register approval or disapproval of a cause, send money, alert Twitter followers and forward a conscience-stabbing video to hundreds of Facebook "friends."

The ungainly[1] word "clicktivism" emerged to describe this form of participation. So did an offshoot[2], "slacktivism," a portmanteau[3] of "slacker"[4] and "activism." By definition, it is not the highest compliment. Does a mouse click constitute true involvement? As Felix Salmon, a business journalist who has examined the issue, said, "If I retweet your video, is that going to make the world a better place?" [...]

In the Ice Bucket Challenge, the famous and the not-so-famous poured frigid water over their heads, and posted videos of their antics. The purpose was to promote awareness of — and to encourage donations for research in — amyotrophic lateral sclerosis, or A.L.S., the incurable neurodegenerative malady often referred to as Lou Gehrig's disease. The campaign was astonishingly successful. In a matter of weeks, more than $200 million was raised.

But, perhaps inevitably, questions arose.

For one thing, to what extent was anti-Kony[5] or the challenge a mere passing fancy? A measure of faddishness has long accompanied certain causes. [...]

In today's digital age, when Twitter hashtags come and go, the very nature of social consciousness has come under scrutiny. Raising broad awareness of an issue is surely important. But is retweeting #bringourgirlsback (to show solidarity with Boko Haram victims) or #NotOneMore (to deplore gun violence) really changing the world? The same might be said about shading one's Facebook photo in rainbow colors after terrorism at a gay nightclub in Florida or in the French tricolor after attacks in Paris. Skeptics have asked if the real motivation behind some of this is to feel good about oneself and impress one's cyberbuddies.

The best-selling author Malcolm Gladwell seems less than bowled[6] over by online activism. In a 2010 New Yorker article, he invoked the lunch counter sit-ins of the 1960s civil rights movement, when committed young men and women risked life and limb to fight enforced racial segregation. "Fifty years after one of the most extraordinary episodes of social upheaval in American history," Mr. Gladwell said, "we seem to have forgotten what activism is." He argued that, to be effective, movements require strict planning, strong personal connections and firm discipline; mouse clicks do not get the job done. Putting boots on the ground counts enormously, whether in the Arab Spring revolts or the Black Lives Matter protests.

There is, too, a crapshoot[7] quality to online involvement. The Ice Bucket Challenge is an example. Why A.L.S.? With 6,000 new cases a year in this country, it is far less common than, say, lung cancer, with 224,000 new cases a year, or H.I.V. infection, with 44,000 new cases. "One charity sort of won the lottery," Mr. Salmon said. [...]

But if the past is a guide, anything can happen. Even blowout[8] concerts may not be finished. That was shown four years ago when some of the biggest names in entertainment, including the seemingly eternal Rolling Stones, gathered at Madison Square Garden, performing for nearly six hours to help victims of superstorm Sandy. They raised millions.

✦ Clyde Haberman, *Philanthropy That Comes From a Click*, *The New York Times*, November 13, 2016

1. inelegant 2. descendant 3. word formed by combining two other words 4. lazy person 5. leader of a guerrilla group that formerly operated in Uganda 6. impressed 7. random 8. very successful

1 Use the first two paragraphs to give a definition for clicktivism then find some examples in the article.

2 Find what causes were brought to social media and whether it benefited them.

3 Compare online activism with ground activism as explained in the article.

4 Draw a grid of pros and cons of online activism. Write at least five arguments for each column.

Prepare your project

GROUP WORK You are taking part in a change.org meeting. Form groups and find six proposals for online and ground actions on: climate change, gender inequalities or racism. You have only up to 7 minutes! Then, debate!

Grammar Tip

Précis → p. 257

You can use **whereas**, **although** and **while** to contrast your partners' ideas.
Although organising a march can be a good idea, I think...

Memory Challenge

You have one minute to write or say all the words that come to your mind when you think about online activism. Have a competition with your classmates!

Tools in the Spotlight

Entraînez-vous sur la plateforme *Let's Meet Up!*
reussirenlangues.fr

Practise your grammar

Précis grammatical, p. 216

Les quantifieurs (*a lot of, much, many*)

- Les quantifieurs ***a lot of, much, many***, sont employés pour indiquer une **grande quantité**, et correspondent au français « beaucoup. »
- ***Much*** est suivi d'un nom au singulier, alors que ***many*** doit être suivi d'un nom au pluriel.

*There is **much** concern about gun control in the USA.*
***Many** influential figures and celebrities also took to social media.*

- ***A lof of*** peut s'employer indifféremment avec un singulier ou un pluriel.

*There is **a lot of** concern about gun control in the USA.*
***A lot of** influential figures and celebrities also took to social media.*

- De manière générale, ***a lot of*** sera employé davantage dans des phrases **affirmatives**, alors que l'on préférera plutôt ***much*** et ***many*** dans les phrases **négatives** et **interrogatives**.

*There is **a lot of** social activism online.*
*The march didn't cause **much** violence.*
*Did **many** people take part in March for Our Lives?*

1 Complétez les phrases par un élément entre parenthèses.

a. A lot of (**protester / protesters**) gathered in Florida for the March for Our Lives.
b. There is much (**concern / concerns**) about the effectiveness of online activism.
c. Did the Parkland shooting result in many (**reaction / reactions**) from politicians?
d. The Women's March on Washington gathered a lot of (**woman / women**) across the country.
e. A lot of (**activist / activists**) use inspiring hashtags.

2 Complétez par *a lot of*, *much* et *many*.

a. There were ... Instagram videos asking politicians to enforce stricter gun control.
b. Did ... people back up the march by making donations?
c. There wasn't ... money collected at the end of the protest.
d. Unfortunately, ... mass shootings in the US take place in schools.
e. The march didn't attract ... celebrities.

Les adjectifs en *-ed* et *-ing*

- Les adjectifs en ***-ing*** et ***-ed*** ont respectivement une forme de **participe présent** (par exemple, *empowering*) et de **participe passé** (*empowered*) : leur fonctionnement est donc différent.
- Les adjectifs en ***-ed*** ont un sens **passif**, et peuvent en général être paraphrasés par la voix passive.

*I felt **empowered** when I marched.*
→ Je me suis senti·e forte quand j'ai manifesté.

- Les adjectifs en ***-ing*** ont un sens **actif**, et on pourrait souvent traduire par « qui donne, qui amène, qui te fait sentir... ».

*Marches are great. They're really **empowering** to people.*
→ Les manifestations sont géniales. Elles donnent véritablement aux gens les moyens d'agir.

3 Complétez par un adjectif en *-ed* ou *-ing*.

a. The #MeToo movement has become (**inspired/inspiring**).
b. Guns have caused (**alarmed/alarming**) situations in the States.
c. Parkland survivor Emma González delivered a (**captivated/captivating**) speech.
d. Michelle Obama spoke in front of a (**committed/committing**) group of teenagers.
e. Activists usually stand up for (**endangering/endangered**) rights.

4 Transformez le verbe en adjectif en *-ed* ou *-ing*.

a. She was ... (delight) to join the march.
b. I found the speech very ... (interest).
c. They were ... (motivate) in raising funds.
d. An ... (estimate) 1 million people made a donation.

Improve your pronunciation

Précis de phonologie, p. 262

L'accent de phrase

Audio
CD1 piste 39
MP3 n° 61

- L'accent de phrase permet d'attirer l'attention de l'interlocuteur·rice sur une partie de la phrase. Il peut donc **se déplacer** sur les éléments de phrases **sur lesquels l'on souhaite insister**.

- Dans la phrase suivante, on peut **faire le choix** de porter l'accent de phrase sur *magic* si l'on veut insister sur ce mot.

*Marches are great, they're empowering to people, but the **magic** isn't really in the streets by itself or any online action.*

- En règle générale, l'accent de phrase va porter sur l'**information nouvelle**, celle qui est la plus intéressante.
Par exemple, il est souvent placé sur l'information nouvelle après ***but*** pour insister justement sur le contraste.

*You think that these marches are useless, but they **are** essential!*

Ici, la personne qui parle peut choisir de faire porter l'accent de phrase sur l'auxiliaire. La forme non contractée *are* doit donc être obligatoirement utilisée.

5 Écoutez les phrases suivantes et recopiez le mot qui porte l'accent de phrase.

Audio
CD1 piste 40
MP3 n° 62

a. Social activism not only fights against climate change but also against sweatshops.
b. Activists target politicians and citizens.
c. What is beneficial to improving working conditions is organising boycotts.
d. The voices of discontent have been broadcast via #MeToo and #BlackLivesMatter, but also via #NeverAgain.

6 Placez l'accent de phrase sur le mot qui vous semble devoir être le plus accentué en fonction du contexte. Comparez votre réponse avec un·e camarade, puis écoutez l'enregistrement pour vérifier votre réponse.

Audio
CD1 piste 41
MP3 n° 63

a. You don't need to send a membership letter. You can sign up directly online.
b. I didn't go to the March for Our Lives event, but I went to the #MeToo protest.
c. These activists didn't take to the streets for two hours. They demonstrated for two days!

Work on your writing skills

Les faux amis

- En anglais, il existe de nombreux mots qui ressemblent à des mots français, mais qui n'ont pas le même sens.
Nous serons par exemple tentés d'utiliser le mot *support* en anglais pour dire « un support » en français. Or, il s'agit d'un « soutien ». De la même façon, le mot *cry* ne se traduit pas par « crier » en français, mais par « pleurer ».

TIP Cherchez dans le dictionnaire la signification de ces quelques faux amis courants et complétez votre liste au fil de l'année : *actual, actually, agenda, arrive, comprehensive, deceive, demand, eventual, experience, location, pass an exam* ...

7 Complétez les phrases par un des faux amis proposés.

eventually • demanded • evidence • rendez-vous • agenda

a. Their appointment with the CEO of Starbucks was nothing like a ... .
b. They had to prepare today's meeting ... .
c. The two middle school pupils ... that he took action. He did not have a choice.
d. ..., the CEO of Starbucks agreed to invest millions into research.
e. It was obvious, there was ... against the company.

8 Associez ces mots à leur synonyme.

a. eventual b. ignore c. genial d. march
1. parade 2. final 3. cordial 4. disregard

Build up your vocabulary

Audio
CD1 piste 42

Activism

Limits — MP3 n°64

sarcasm: irony /aɪrəni/
dubious: questionable
effective ≠ ineffective
inelegant
useless
lazy ≠ active
be distraught: be upset: be annoyed
threaten: be likely to cause harm

Positive impact — MP3 n°65

result: outcome
benefit
visibility
effects: consequences
investment: commitment
positively ≠ negatively
advocate: recommend
make a difference
raise awareness
raise funds
take part in sth: participate in sth

Online activism — MP3 n°68

social network
clicktivism
slacktivism
go on the internet
launch an online petition
post / share on social media
create a hashtag
go viral: spread widely

Actions — MP3 n°66

criticism
protest
empowering
get involved: participate in sth
stand up for a cause
show support
impact
join a cause
denounce
raise the question of sth
be engaged in activism

Ground activism — MP3 n°67

militant: political activist
march: demonstration
gather sb: bring sb together
go door to door
march: demonstrate
put together sth: assemble, organise
take action: act

Apprenez et révisez le vocabulaire !

Utilisez Quizlet pour vous entraîner en vous amusant.

Quizlet
hatier-clic.fr/lmu1078

Utilisez le vocabulaire en contexte.

1 Complétez les phrases suivantes avec des mots de la carte mentale à la forme qui convient.

a. Emma González's speech at the March for Our Lives ... having the right to carry an arm.
b. You can ask for change by ... a petition on social media.
c. Last week, Beyoncé posted an image of Rosie the Riveter on Instagram and it ... ... in a few minutes.
d. Young people's ... is actively criticised today. They are said to be lazy activists.
e. Many people, women and men alike, ... in the Women's March on Washington.
f. The real motivation of people who share online petitions is ... .
g. It is a lot of work to ... a group of people who can fight for a common goal.

2 Remettez les lettres dans l'ordre pour trouver un mot provenant de la carte mentale et utilisez-les pour rédiger un court paragraphe sur le militantisme.

a. VDIOLNVE b. SIARE SASEWANER c. DNOTRMSTNEAOI d. SIAVTICT

AUTO évaluation

Faites le quiz interactif en ligne et suivez les conseils pour vous préparer à l'évaluation.

Quiz
hatier-clic.fr/lmu1079

Project #1

Live stream on Instagram to speak about your experience as an activist.

1 Gather information about ground and online activism.

- ✓ Find information on ground and online activism (effects in real life, clicktivism, power...).
- ✓ Use your notes to find examples of both forms of activism.

2 Prepare your arguments.

- ✓ Use the present perfect (**have + en**) to make an assessment.
  I have been an activist for a few years.
- ✓ Use the preterite (**V + -ed**) to speak about your past experiences.
  I took part in a lot of marches last year.
- ✓ Use comparatives to compare each form of activism.

3 Prepare your notes.

- ✓ Write the outline of your live stream: fill it with key words to organise your presentation.
- ✓ Use gap fillers if you need time to think.
  Well, ... Let me think... So...
- ✓ Rehearse your talk and try not to read.
- ✓ If you are unsure of the pronunciation, check it on the Cambridge online dictionary or wordreference.com.

4 Record your Instagram live or prepare to speak in front of the class.

- ✓ You may use notes but make sure you did not write complete sentences.
- ✓ Be convincing.
- ✓ Speak loudly and clearly!

Fiche de méthodologie N°18 p. 296

Project #2

Launch an online petition for a cause that is important to you.

1 Introduce your campaign.

- ✓ Identify the cause you want to defend.
- ✓ Choose your social media and a #word to share your petition.
- ✓ Research your cause and make sure you know what could be changed.

2 Prepare a draft version of your petition.

- ✓ Identify who your target is and what your goals are.
- ✓ Write down and organise your ideas.
- ✓ Prepare at least five arguments.

3 Convince people.

- ✓ Explain the reasons for putting your petition online.
- ✓ Use be + V-ing to describe ongoing situations.
- ✓ Use modals such as **should**, **have to** or **must** to persuade your readers.

4 Write your petition!

- ✓ Mention the number of signatures needed.
- ✓ Ask people to share your petition online.
- ✓ Proofread your article using an online dictionary.

Fiche de méthodologie N°20 p. 300

Let's RECAP

Lisez les questions-clés et complétez la fiche bilan avec des exemples et des documents que vous avez étudiés ou découverts.

AXE 4 | Citizenship and virtual worlds

SÉQUENCE 1 What is the Americans' relationship to the media?

Do Americans trust the media? How does the younger generation see the media? How has news consumption changed over the last few decades?

E-workbook
Bilan à compléter
hatier-clic.fr/lmu1080

#fakenews
How is fake news changing the way Americans view the media? How can we recognise fake news?

#sharinginformation
How does information circulate nowadays? What role do social media play in the way we consider news?

#freedomofexpression
How important is freedom of expression?

#whistleblowers
How have whistleblowers changed the face of the news? Should all information be freely available?

#medialiteracy
Why is it important to be media literate? How can we avoid being fooled by the media?

SÉQUENCE 2 Is online activism effective in the USA?

In which circumstances has online activism proved useful? To what extent can we say that ground activism is still relevant?

E-workbook
Bilan à compléter
hatier-clic.fr/lmu1081

#clicktivism
What are the limits to using online tools?

#freedomofspeech
How can planning a demonstration affect the political decisions of a country as big as the USA?

#participativedemocracy
Can online activism be part of participative democracy?

#citizensandpower
Does online activism give more power to American citizens? How does online activism help more American citizens to get involved?

#onlineactivism
What is the link between online activism and people's involvement on the ground?

GO4IT!

Lisez et écoutez de l'anglais en dehors de la salle de classe ! Voici quelques conseils en lien avec votre séquence.

SÉQUENCE 1

Books

Darnell Rock Reporting, WALTER DEAN MYERS, 1994

Muckrakers: How Ida Tarbell, Upton Sinclair, and Lincoln Steffens Helped Expose Scandal, Inspire Reform, and Invent Investigative Journalism, 2007

Yours for Justice, Ida B. Wells: The Daring Life of a Crusading Journalist, PHILIP DRAY, 2008

Ten Days a Madwoman: The Daring Life and Turbulent Times of the Original "Girl" Reporter Nellie Bly, DEBORAH NOYES, 2016

The Truth Matters: A Citizen's Guide to Separating Facts from Lies and Stopping Fake News in Its Track, BRUCE BARTLETT, 2017

Films

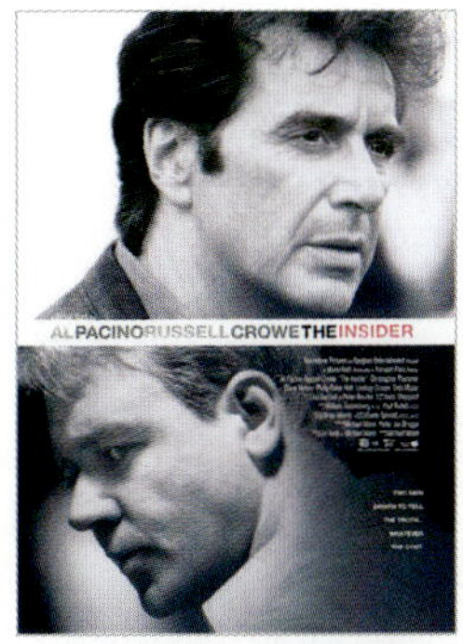

TV series

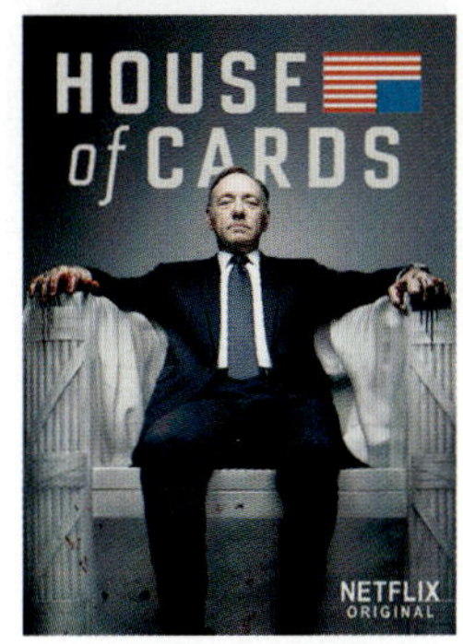

SÉQUENCE 2

Books

Yes You Can!: Your Guide to Becoming an Activist, JANE DRAKE, ANN LOVE, 2010

Digitally Enabled Social Change: Activism in the Internet Age, JENNIFER EARL AND KATRINA KIMPORT, 2011

On the Other Side of Freedom: The Case for Hope, DERAY MCKESSON, 2018

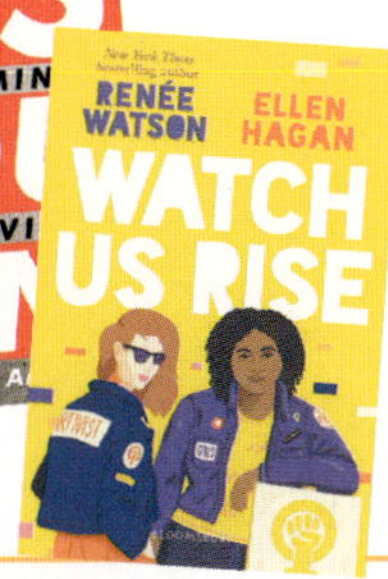

Putting Peace First: 7 Commitments to Change the World, ERIC DAWSON, 2018

Glimmer of Hope: How Tragedy Sparked a Movement, BY THE FOUNDERS OF MARCH FOR OUR LIVES, 2018

Watch Us Rise, RENEE WATSON, ELLEN HAGAN, 2019

Films

Videos

How the internet has made social change easy to organize, hard to win, TED Talk by ZEYNEP TUFEKCI, 2015 http://bit.ly/2WwsWkH

The power of online activism, THE PINK PROTEST, 2017 http://bit.ly/2CKhxGO

Social media activism and a call to action, TEDx Talk by ALEXA CHUKWUMAH, 2018 http://bit.ly/2HWTiIM

Articles

How the March For Our Lives Gen Z organizers changed the gun control conversation when no one else could, ZAMEENA MEJIA, CNBC, March 24, 2018 http://cnb.cx/2CHwrO1

Six activists who are using social media for change offline, UN WOMEN, June 29, 2018 http://bit.ly/2NtSZUL

'The beginning of great change': Greta Thunberg hails school climate strikes, JONATHAN WATTS, *The Guardian*, February 15, 2019 http://bit.ly/2BGfGIH

Websites

Avaaz http://avaaz.org

Change.org http://change.org

Black Lives Matter http://blacklivesmatter.com

Me Too Movement http://metoomvmt.org

He For She http://heforshe.org

Not One More http://notonemore.com

BAC in sight

ÉPREUVE 1

COMPRÉHENSION ORALE

Vidéo DVD This extract of PBS News Hour focuses on the importance of teaching children how to spot bias in the media.

✦ *How media literacy can help students discern fake news*, PBS NewsHour, Editorial Projects in Education, June 6, 2017

Tips

- Try to anticipate what you might hear as soon as you see the title.
- Use the images to make sense of the content of the video.

➤ Fiche de méthodologie N°15 p. 290 Compréhension orale

EXPRESSION ÉCRITE

SUJET 1 Write a letter to the pupils of the schools in the video where you list 10 rules to spot fake news. Explain each one to make it very concrete.

OU

SUJET 2 Should schools be the only ones in charge of helping students discern fake news?

Tip

- Use the imperative to give advice.

➤ Fiche de méthodologie N°20 p. 300 Expression écrite

Pour l'épreuve

Questions
Fiche modifiable
hatier-clic.fr/lmu1082

Évaluation
Grille à imprimer
hatier-clic.fr/lmu1083

ÉPREUVE 2

EXPRESSION ÉCRITE

SUJET 1 Imagine the editorial of *Forbes* following this survey, encouraging people to read newspapers first, online or not.

OU

SUJET 2 Why is it important to have media skills in today's society?

Tip

- Use the documents you have studied in this unit as well as your own experience to give examples supporting your arguments.

➤ Fiche de méthodologie N°20 p. 300 Expression écrite

COMPRÉHENSION ÉCRITE

How Social Media Has Changed How We Consume News

It's the age of "fake news" and gone are the days of waiting for the morning news for breaking stories or reading gossip magazines for the latest celebrity dirt[1]. We now have all the information we need at the touch of an app and most people now get their news information online, specifically from social media.

Social media has become the main source of news online with more than 2.4 billion internet users, nearly 64.5 percent receive breaking news from Facebook, Twitter, YouTube, Snapchat and Instagram instead of traditional media.

In a recent survey, 50 percent of Internet users surveyed said that they hear about the latest news via social media before ever hearing about it on a news station. Many internet users will see the breaking stories on their feed and go to the news sites to learn more. The survey found 57 percent increase in traffic to news sites referred from social media.

However, there has been a decrease in how much of an article that people read. Most people will just scroll through their newsfeed and stumble upon relevant news content but just read the headlines or a short video clip of the piece. An average[2] visitor will only read an article for 15 seconds or less and the average video watch time online is 10 seconds.

However, social platforms have a control over what news and information we see. Our social media friends have become the "managing editors" deciding what we see. An article needs to be "liked" and shared multiple times before many people see it in their feed. Therefore social media and your social friends have control over what news pieces you see and what you do not.

There are also many "fake news" websites that compete for attention with sensational headlines and ridiculous storylines that tend to get shared more often due to the lack of readers fact checking or reading more than the headline. That means that authentic content is hard to come by[3] now. In fact, fake news is actually more likely to spread than the truth.

"Falsehood diffused significantly farther, faster, deeper, and more broadly than the truth in all categories of information, and the effects were more pronounced for false political news than for false news about terrorism, natural disasters, science, urban legends, or financial information," the team, led by Sinan Aral of the Massachusetts Institute of Technology, wrote in the journal Science.

✦ Nicole Martin, *Forbes*, November 30, 2018

1. gossip 2. normal 3. get

Tips

➤ Focus on the title and pay particular attention to the first sentence of each paragraph.

➤ Link the numbers to what they refer to.

➤ Fiche de méthodologie N°16 p. 292 Compréhension écrite

Pour l'épreuve

Questions
Fiche modifiable
hatier-clic.fr/lmu1084

Évaluation
Grille à imprimer
hatier-clic.fr/lmu1085

BAC in sight

ÉPREUVE 1

COMPRÉHENSION ORALE

Audio
CD1 piste 43

Michel Martin, the host of this National Public Radio programme, asks Rashad Robinson about the importance of social media in uniting people around the same cause in 2012, after Trayvon Martin was shot to death by a neighbourhood watch coordinator in his gated community.

✦ New York City council speaker Christine Quinn puts on a hoodie during a press conference to call for justice in New York City, March 28, 2012.

Tips

➤ Pay attention to the different people in the recording.

➤ Take notes on all the actions taken by the people in the audio and connect them to social media.

➤ Fiche de méthodologie N°15 p. 290 Compréhension orale

EXPRESSION ÉCRITE

SUJET 1 Write a manifesto which was handed out on the day of the demonstration.

OU

SUJET 2 Is it the role of citizens or of the state to fight for people's rights?

Tip

➤ Use linking words to structure your arguments.

➤ Fiche de méthodologie N°20 p. 300 Expression écrite

Pour l'épreuve

Questions
Fiche modifiable
hatier-clic.fr/lmu1086

Évaluation
Grille à imprimer
hatier-clic.fr/lmu1087

ÉPREUVE 2

EXPRESSION ÉCRITE

SUJET 1 You participated in the #NeverAgain movement and are asked to write an article for *Time Magazine* about the place of social media in your online and ground actions.

OU

SUJET 2 To what extent is online activism effective?

Tips

➤ Make sure you know how to write an article or an essay.

➤ Use linking words to structure your arguments.

➤ Illustrate your written expression with precise examples that you can find in the text.

➤ Fiche de méthodologie N°20 p. 300 Expression écrite

COMPRÉHENSION ÉCRITE

Youth Activism and the #NeverAgain Movement

What ultimately drives young people to take a political stand? According to recent data from an MTV/PRRI survey of young people ages 15–24, we can get a sense of what doesn't. Young people report that feeling uninformed about an issue is by far the most discouraging factor when it comes to getting involved. But for a generation raised with regular active shooter drills[1] and the near-weekly experience of hearing about actual shootings at some school in the country, the issue of gun violence in school is far from abstract.

At Marjory Stoneman Douglas High School in Parkland, Florida, many students touched by the mass shooting that left 17 dead and at least 14 wounded have mobilized to call for changes to gun policy on a scale seen as unprecedented by many who have covered the aftermath of these tragedies for years. Social media has proven to be a critical tool both in helping to illustrate the impact of this reality for those who did not come of age post-Columbine, and in helping students organize for change. During the massacre itself, live video and images posted from inside the school coalesced[2] into a broad, literal and figurative cry for help from students trapped inside.

In the wake of the shootings, Parkland youth activists such as Emma González, Jaclyn Corin, David Hogg, and Cameron Kasky have adeptly deployed social media as a tool for their activism and an effective means of controlling their own narratives.

Many of today's young people have spent many of their formative years posting online about issues that matter to them. These conversations are translating into broader political activism for many young Americans (ages 15–24), especially online and among young women. Thirty-seven percent of young women and 30 percent of young men have volunteered for a group or cause they care about in the last year. Almost half (48 percent) of young women say they have signed an online petition, as have 39 percent of young men.

✦ March For Our Lives rally, Chicago, Illinois, March 24, 2018

Young people undeniably are paying attention to the current political climate. More than three-quarters (77 percent) of young people say the country is very divided by politics. Even so, they are hopeful and empowered. Fifty-nine percent of young people say that America's best days are ahead of us.

While pundits[3] often criticize millennials and those coming of age behind them as self-absorbed, growing evidence suggests that this is far from the case. On issues such as gun control and the Movement for Black Lives, this generation of emerging adults may continue the legacy of previous youth-led movements, such as the anti-war and civil rights movements.

It remains to be seen whether the growing #NeverAgain movement will find success in gun policy reform. Still, current lawmakers and future political candidates would be wise to consider how the synergy between a passion for change and a coming of age in the digital era is catalyzing a new moment in youth activism. Today's young student activists may not be able to vote in the 2018 midterm elections, but many of them will be eligible in 2020, when the stakes[4] will be even higher.

✦ Carolyn Davis, medium.com, February 21, 2018

1. training exercise 2. merged 3. experts 4. risks, interests

Tips

➤ Read the title to predict what you will be reading about.

➤ Pay attention to: the different figures, proper nouns, adjectives; it will help you understand the text!

➤ Fiche de méthodologie N°16 p. 292 Compréhension écrite

Pour l'épreuve

Questions — Fiche modifiable — hatier-clic.fr/lmu1088

Évaluation — Grille à imprimer — hatier-clic.fr/lmu1089

AXE 5

Fictions and realities

Fictions et réalités

SÉQUENCE 1 How close to reality can dystopia be?

Projects

Project #1: Audition for a role in a dystopian series. Deliver a speech explaining the problems in this society.

Project #2: Take part in a creative writing competition. Write the beginning of a dystopia.

Tools

Grammaire	la modalité, le passif
Phonologie	les diphtongues /əʊ/, /aʊ/ et /ɪə/
Écriture	le début d'une histoire
Vocabulaire	la surveillance, la manipulation

SÉQUENCE 2 How did British pirates inspire fiction?

Projects

Project #1: Show visitors around the Pirates of Nassau Museum and tell them about the lifestyles of pirates.

Project #2: Create a leaflet depicting a fictional pirate, to win the Cayman Islands Pirates Week Festival contest.

Tools

Grammaire	le prétérit, les adjectifs composés
Phonologie	la terminaison *-ed*
Écriture	l'utilisation du *y* et du *i*
Vocabulaire	les pirates, le commerce

#dystopia #reality #literature #denunciation
#fiction #imaginaryworlds

1984, film adaptation by Michael Anderson, 1956

#literature #culturalheritage
#questioningmyths
#legends #collectiveimaginary

The Capture of the Pirate Blackbeard, 1718, Jean Leon Gerome Ferris, 1920

SÉQUENCE 1

How close to reality can dystopia be?

A Dystopian book covers

GROUP WORK

GROUP A

✦ Aldous Huxley, *Brave New World*, 1932

GROUP B

✦ Ray Bradbury, *Fahrenheit 451*, 1954

GROUP C

✦ Sinclair Lewis, *It Can't Happen Here*, 1935

GROUP D

✦ George Orwell, *1984*, 1949

Culture Tip

The word **dystopia** comes from the word "utopia" — an ideal world — with the prefix *dys* meaning wrong or bad. So, it's an ideal world which has gone wrong. Dystopian fictions take place in the future. A dystopia can be seen as a warning about what might happen in the future if people allow technology, the government, etc. to manipulate their lives.

1 Describe your group's book cover (title, author, colours, layout).

2 With your group, guess what the story is about.

3 Imagine the first lines of the story of your book cover.

Word Spot

exhaustion of resources
dehumanising technology
totalitarian regime: dictatorship
society /səsaɪəti/
dictator
law /lɔː/: legal system
pessimistic
dysfunctional
frightening
mandatory: obligatory
grim: gloomy: without hope
be compelled to: be forced to
be allowed /əlaʊd/ to:
be permitted /pəmɪtɪd/ to:
be authorised to
be forbidden to

Grammar Spot

Passive Form TOOLS → p. 116

"orders **are being shouted** into telephones"
"it would **be punished** by death"

B 1984

❶ The Ministry of Truth — Minitrue, in Newspeak[1] — was startlingly different from any other object in sight. It was an enormous pyramidal structure of glittering white concrete, soaring up, terrace after terrace, 300 metres into the air. From where Winston stood it was just possible to read, picked out on its white face in elegant lettering, the three slogans of the Party:

WAR IS PEACE
FREEDOM IS SLAVERY
IGNORANCE IS STRENGTH

❷ The thing that he was about to do was to open a diary. This was not illegal (nothing was illegal, since there were no longer any laws), but if detected it was reasonably certain that it would be punished by death, or at least by twenty-five years in a forced-labour camp. Winston fitted a nib[2] into the penholder and sucked it to get the grease off. The pen was an archaic instrument, seldom used even for signatures, and he had procured one, furtively and with some difficulty, simply because of a feeling that the beautiful creamy paper deserved to be written on with a real nib instead of being scratched with an ink-pencil. Actually he was not used to writing by hand. Apart from very short notes, it was usual to dictate everything into the speak-write which was of course impossible for his present purpose. He dipped[3] the pen into the ink and then faltered for just a second. A tremor had gone through his bowels[4]. To mark the paper was the decisive act. In small clumsy[5] letters he wrote:

April 4th, 1984.

✦ George Orwell, *1984*, 1949

1. fictional language created by the government in *1984*. It uses limited vocabulary and grammar to limit freedom of thought. 2. pen point 3. immersed 4. intestine 5. awkward

Pédagogie différenciée

TRAIL A

1 Use the first excerpt to draw the Ministry of Truth and its environment in your notebook.

2 Read the second excerpt and pick out words describing how strict this society is.

3 Describe Winston's intention.

TRAIL B

1 Explain what the Ministry of Truth is.

2 Find information about the society Winston lives in.

3 Describe Winston's intention and the possible consequences he could face.

Meet up! Write the first five lines of Winston's diary, describing his feelings as he starts writing.

C Resisting the government

Vidéo hatier-clic.fr/lmu1090

E-workbook Fiche à imprimer hatier-clic.fr/lmu1091

In 2032, after a disease had devastated Great Britain 14 years back, Chancellor Sutler rose to power and created an oppressive government. V, who is wearing a Guy Fawkes mask, attempts to begin a revolution against the government.

1 Pick out key words in V's speech. Use them to explain his message.

2 Explain in your own words what V says about High Chancellor Adam Sutler and his relation with the people.

3 ***PAIR WORK*** Imagine the conversation between two Londoners who heard V's message.

Culture Tip

Guy Fawkes Night, also called Bonfire Night, is a British commemoration (November 5th). It commemorates the failure of the Gunpowder Plot, a plan to blow up the British Houses of Parliament and kill King James I, in 1605.

Prepare your project

At an annual meeting of young writers, you make a speech explaining what a dystopia is.

Grammar Tip

Précis → p. 255

Use **passive forms** to express the powerlessness of the people in a dystopian world.

Memory Challenge

In less than a minute, name as many characteristics of dystopian fictions as you can.

D Women with no rights

June Osborne, the main character, describes what happens in the United States after an imaginary American Civil War. On that particular day, her boss comes in to make an announcement to the women in his company.

I'm sorry, he said, but it's the law. I really am sorry.

For what? somebody said.

I have to let you go[1], he said. It's the law, I have to. I have to let you all go. He said this almost gently, as if we were wild animals, frogs he'd caught, in a jar, as if he were being humane.

We're being fired? I said. I stood up. But why?

Not fired, he said. Let go. You can't work here any more, it's the law. He ran his hands through his hair and I thought, he's gone crazy. The strain has been too much for him and he's blown his wiring[2].

You can't just *do* that, said the woman who sat next to me. This sounded false, improbable, like something you would say on television.

It isn't me, he said. You don't understand. Please go, now. His voice was rising. I don't want any trouble. If there's trouble the books might be lost, things will get broken … He looked over his shoulder. They're outside, he said, in my office. If you don't go now they'll come in themselves. They gave me ten minutes. By now he sounded crazier than ever.

He's loopy, someone said out loud; which we must all have thought.

But I could see out into the corridor, and there were two men standing there, in uniforms, with machine guns. This was too theatrical to be true, yet there they were: sudden apparitions, like Martians. There was a dreamlike quality to them; they were too vivid, too at odds with their surroundings. […]

✦ *The Handmaid's Tale*, TV series by Bruce Miller, 2017

I've been fired, I told Moira when I got her on the phone. She said she would come over. By that time she was working for a women's collective, the publishing division. They put out books on birth control and rape and things like that, though there wasn't as much demand for those things as there used to be.

I'll come over, she said. She must have been able to tell from my voice that this was what I wanted.

She got there after some time. So, she said. She threw off her jacket, sprawled into the oversized chair. Tell me. First we'll have a drink.

She got up and went to the kitchen and poured us a couple of Scotches, and came back and sat down and I tried to tell her what had happened to me. When I'd finished, she said, Tried getting anything on your Compucard today?

Yes, I said. I told her about that too.

They've frozen them, she said. Mine too. The collective's too. Any account with an F on it instead of an M. All they needed to do is push a few buttons. We're cut off.

But I've got over two thousand dollars in the bank, I said, as if my own account was the only one that mattered.

Women can't hold property any more, she said. It's a new law. Turned on the TV today?

✦ Margaret Atwood, *The Handmaid's Tale*, 1985

1. fire you 2. become crazy

1 Describe the picture and imagine the situation.

E-workbook
Fiche à imprimer
hatier-clic.fr/lmu1092

2 Explain the boss's announcement to the women and analyse their reactions.

3 Find out which problems Moira and June faced and explain why.

4 ***PAIR WORK*** Discuss what could have happened between the text and the situation shown in the picture.

Grammar Spot

Modals Tools → p. 116

"You **can't** work here any more, it's the law."
"Women **can't** hold property any more"

Word Spot

second-class citizen
drift: slow change
unfair: unjust
powerful ≠ powerless
useful ≠ useless
inhumane /ɪnhjuːmeɪn/
unjustified
awful
dreadful
helpless: defenceless
feel outraged /aʊtreɪdʒd/: feel indignant
feel sad, miserable, desperate
be treated as
be deprived of
be discriminated against
infringe the law ≠ abide /əbaɪd/ by the law
empower: give power to sb

E Black mirror of society

Classe inversée

✦ 'Nosedive', *Black Mirror*, Netflix, 2017

Vidéo hatier-clic.fr/lmu1093

E-workbook Classe inversée hatier-clic.fr/lmu1094

1 Pick out the words used by the creator of *Black Mirror* to describe the episode 'Nosedive'.

2 Find information about Bryce Dallas Howard and the character she portrays.

3 Explain Charlie Brooker's conclusion about 'Nosedive'.

4 Tell the story of the episode 'Nosedive' to a friend who has not seen the show. Explain how it may criticise our lives today.

Culture Tip

Black Mirror is a British dystopian science fiction television series created by Charlie Brooker. Each episode is unrelated and is set in an alternative present or near future. It explores humans' relationship with new technologies and the unanticipated consequences they could have on our lives. The series is called *Black Mirror* in reference to the black screens of TV, computers and mobile phones.

F From fiction to reality

Audio CD2 piste 01

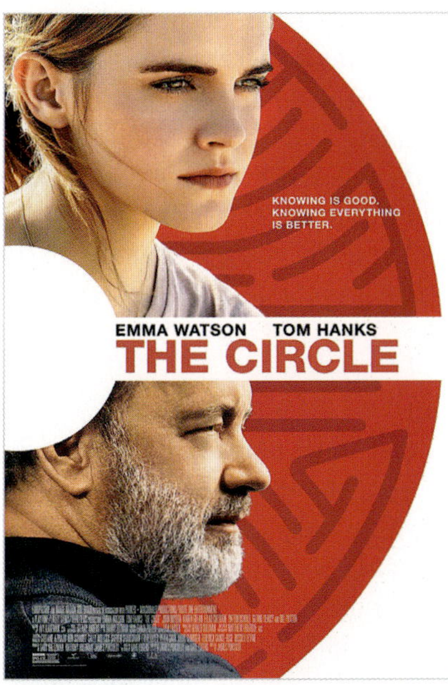

✦ *The Circle*, dir. by James Ponsoldt, 2017

Emma Watson is interviewed about *The Circle*, a dystopian film based on Daniel Eggers's book.

1 Listen to Emma Watson and explain the general subject of *The Circle*. Focus on dystopian elements (dates, themes...).

2 Find out Emma Watson's opinion about social media.

3 List the things she says about Tom Hanks's role.

4 Explain the consequences that technology may have on people's lives.

Prepare your project

You live in a dystopian society. Write a letter to a friend in Canada describing the situation and asking for help.

Grammar Tip

Précis → p. 236

Use **modals** like **can** and **can't** to express what people are allowed to do or not allowed to do in a dystopian society.

Memory Challenge

List all the dangers faced by the characters in the dystopian worlds shown p. 114-115.

Tools in the Spotlight

Entraînez-vous sur la plateforme ***Let's Meet Up!***
reussirenlangues.fr

Practise your grammar

précis grammatical, p. 216

La modalité

- La **possibilité** est exprimée par le modal ***can***. ***Cannot*** (forme contractée : ***can't***) traduit l'**impossibilité**.

*Women **can** vote in democracies.*

*Women **can't** hold property any more.*

Ici, la possibilité (***can***) ou l'impossibilité (***can't***) de faire quelque chose émanent des **circonstances**, de la situation due à un régime politique particulier.

On peut aussi trouver une possibilité ou impossibilité venant directement de **celui qui parle** :

*You **can** take my copy of* Animal Farm *if you haven't got yours. But you **can't** write on it of course! It's my book.*

- L'**obligation** est exprimée par le modal ***must*** + **base verbale**. L'obligation **vient de celui qui parle**.

*I **must** read* 1984*, by George Orwell because next week I'll be too busy.*

Si, au contraire, cette **nécessité** émane de la situation, des circonstances, on emploie ***have to*** ou ***need to***.

*It's the law, I **have to**. I **need to** let you all go.*

On emploie ***don't have to*** ou ***don't need to*** pour l'**absence de nécessité**.

*You **don't have to / don't need to** understand this story to know it's about a dystopian world.*

1 Exprimez la possibilité, l'impossibilité, ou l'obligation venant de celui qui parle : *can, can't* ou *must*.

a. You ... read any dystopian novel this term, but you ... write an in-depth analysis of one novel.

b. All the citizens ... obey Big Brother, otherwise they are sent to jail.

c. You ... take this copy of *Fahrenheit 451*. It's mine!

2 Exprimez la possibilité ou l'impossibilité émanant des circonstances : *can* ou *can't*.

a. You ... vote in a democracy, but you ... in a dictatorship.

b. She ... keep this meeting secret because there are CCTV cameras all over the place.

c. Eligible voters ... vote in democracies when they come of age.

3 Exprimez la nécessité ou l'absence de nécessité.

a. You ... stay if you don't want to. It's an informal meeting!

b. Everyone ... vote to decide which type of government they want. This is democracy.

c. But you ... be registered on the election lists to be allowed to vote, as you should know.

Le passif

- Le passif est formé de l'auxiliaire ***be***, accompagné du participe passé du verbe. Le complément d'agent, facultatif, est introduit par ***by***.

*It would **be punished by** Big Brother.*

- Il est également possible de construire la voix passive avec les **auxiliaires de modalité** : modal + ***be*** + participe passé (+ ***by*** + complément d'agent).

*She **will be rescued by** a masked man called V.*

*A dystopia **can** usually **be defined** as a totalitarian regime.*

- Pour les verbes prépositionnels, il faut garder la préposition **à la fin du verbe** au passif.

*People's houses **have been broken** into.*

*Children **were looked** after by authoritarian nurses.*

4 Mettez les phrases à la voix passive.

a. In *1984*, the Thought Police arrest those who are thinking of rebelling against the Party.

b. In *Fahrenheit 451* the fireman named Montag saves books.

c. A freedom fighter called V overthrew a future British tyranny in the film *V for Vendetta*.

d. In Aldous Huxley's *Brave New World* they create human beings in test tubes.

e. Big Brother can watch millions of people at the same time.

f. Rebels can overthrow an authoritarian regime.

g. You must read these three dystopian novels by the end of the academic year.

Improve your pronunciation

Précis de phonologie, p. 262

Les diphtongues /əʊ/, /aʊ/ et /ɪə/

Audio CD2 piste 02 MP3 n° 69

Les diphtongues sont des sons composés de deux sons voyelles. Le premier porte l'accentuation la plus forte.

- Le son /əʊ/ peut correspondre aux graphies :
  - *o* (*dystopia*, *note*, *over*, *nobody*)
  - *oa* (*coat*, *boat*, *float*)
  - *ou* (*soul*)
  - *ough* (*although*, *dough*)
  - *ow* (*own*, *know*)
- Le son /aʊ/ peut correspondre aux graphies :
  - *ou* (*out*, *loud*, *shout*, *thousand*)
  - *ow* (*allow*, *down*, *town*, *crowd*)
- Le son /ɪə/ peut correspondre aux graphies :
  - *e* (*here*, *hero*, *serious*)
  - *ea* (*hear*, *fear*, *near*, *theatre*)
  - *ee* (*career*)
  - *ei* (*weird*)
  - *ia* (*dystopia*)
  - *ie* (*cashier*)
  - *io* (*melodious*)

5 Écrivez les mots suivants et indiquez s'il s'agit du son /əʊ/, /aʊ/ ou /ɪə/, puis écoutez l'enregistrement pour confirmer vos réponses.

Audio CD2 piste 03 MP3 n° 70

• utopia • crowd • here • allow • pier • amount • fear • coast

6 Écrivez les quatre phrases suivantes et indiquez si la graphie soulignée correspond au son /əʊ/, /aʊ/ ou /ɪə/, puis écoutez l'enregistrement pour confirmer vos réponses.

Audio CD2 piste 04 MP3 n° 71

a. Here in this exercise, you are allowed to write a paragraph about your own dystopia.
b. As you know, you can note your own ideas, although they are more utopian than dystopian.
c. Thousands of people have expressed their ideas about the danger of totalitarian regimes.
d. Are characters in dystopian literature heroes or merely victims who fear authoritarian power?

Work on your writing skills

Le début d'une histoire

- Le début d'une histoire (incipit) sert à :
  - **créer votre monde fictif** : présenter les personnages (choisir le point de vue du récit), le lieu et le moment de votre histoire ainsi que le thème principal.
  → *who, when, where, what, why*
  - **définir le genre de narration** (récit dystopique...).
  - **attirer l'attention du ou de la lecteur·rice** et lui donner envie de poursuivre la lecture.

TIP Avant de rédiger, prenez des notes sur les éléments principaux que vous souhaitez faire ressortir dans votre incipit.

- Sélectionnez les outils linguistiques qui vous seront utiles :
  - **le lexique** pour décrire les personnages, les lieux et les actions.
  - **la grammaire** : les formes verbales liées au passé, au présent ou à l'avenir, des connecteurs chronologiques comme *first*, *then*, *after*, *until*...

7 Transformez les phrases suivantes.

Ex. The boss called all the women. He fired them.
→ The boss called the women. Then he fired them.
→ After calling all the women, he fired them.
→ As soon as he had called all the women, he fired them.

a. They attacked Congress. The dictatorship was established.
b. June was captured. She became a handmaid.

8 Utilisez les mots suivants pour écrire le début d'un roman dystopique.

revolution • technology • pollution • 2119 • dictatorship

Build up your vocabulary

Audio
CD2 piste 05

Resistance
MP3 n°72

message
plot
revolution
subversive
unequal /ʌniːkwəl/
indignant: outraged
blow up
empower: give power to sb
feel outraged /aʊtreɪʤd/
refuse /rɪfjuːz/ ≠ oppose
infringe the law ≠ abide /əbaɪd/ by the law

Women's oppression
MP3 n°73

awful: dreadful: appalling
helpless: defenceless: powerless ≠ powerful
unfair: unjust
be forced to: be compelled /kəmpeld/ to: be coerced into + V-ing
be treated as second-class citizen
be discriminated against
feel sad, miserable, desperate

Characteristics
MP3 n°77

denunciation
future
ideal world
reality
warning
frightening
grim: gloomy: without hope
pessimistic
useful ≠ useless

Dystopias

Manipulation
MP3 n°74

dysfunctional
inhumane /ɪnhjuːmeɪn/
dehumanising
restrict
censor
control
ban

Oppressive governments
MP3 n°76

dictator
law /lɔː/
legal system
society /səsaɪəti/
totalitarian regime: dictatorship
mandatory: obligatory
unjustified
be deprived of
be forbidden to ≠ be allowed to
be permitted to: be authorised to

Plots
MP3 n°75

overuse
fertility issues
pollution
consequences
drift: slow change
technology
exhaustion of resources /rɪzɔːsiz/

Apprenez et révisez le vocabulaire !

Utilisez Quizlet pour vous entraîner en vous amusant.

Quizlet
hatier-clic.fr/lmu1095

Utilisez le vocabulaire en contexte.

1 Complétez les phrases suivantes avec des mots de la carte mentale à la forme qui convient.

a. In *The Handmaid's Tale*, women ... ... their rights and are ... as second-class citizens. It think this is ... .
b. In dystopian fictions, people must ... by the law or they could be killed.
c. *Black Mirror* is the most ... series I have ever watched.
d. Dystopian fiction functions as a ... against our society. If we are not careful, dystopia could become ... .
e. In many dystopias, it is ... to read books.

2 Utilisez les mots de la carte mentale pour commenter l'image.

✦ *Equilibrium*, dir. by Kurt Wimmer, 2002

AUTO évaluation

Faites le quiz interactif en ligne et suivez les conseils pour vous préparer à l'évaluation.

Quiz
hatier-clic.fr/lmu1096

Project #1

Audition for a role in a dystopian series. Deliver a speech explaining the problems in this society.

1 Imagine elements about the society you live in.

- ✓ Choose an English-speaking country.
- ✓ Prepare your character: name, age, city, personality...

2 Invent details about the situation.

- ✓ Find examples of problems in this dystopian society and try to explain their origins.
- ✓ You can get inspiration from the dystopias you have studied in the unit or find other ones on the internet.
- ✓ Give details about the situation.

3 Prepare your speech.

- ✓ Create a mind map to remember all the important ideas.
- ✓ Make sure you use linking words to connect your ideas: **first**, **then**, **besides**, **in addition**, **moreover**...
- ✓ Check the pronunciation of the key words using the Cambridge online dictionary.

4 Give your speech!

- ✓ Make sure you are convincing by using the correct intonation.
- ✓ Watch the time: you have 1 minute 30 seconds.

Fiche de méthodologie N°18 p. 296

Project #2

Take part in a creative writing competition. Write the beginning of a dystopia.

1 Create your dystopia.

- ✓ You can focus on a theme of the unit (women's oppression, overuse of technology, etc.) or find another theme.
- ✓ Remember, a dystopia is set in the future.
- ✓ Use past tenses to talk about what the situation was like before it was a dystopia.

2 Imagine the setting of your story.

- ✓ Choose the main character(s), the place, the time of your story, the actions.
- ✓ Use adverbs and adjectives to describe the setting.

3 Organise your ideas in different paragraphs.

- ✓ To express a negative situation your characters are submitted to, use modals and passive forms.
  We are not allowed to... We cannot...
- ✓ Make sure your paragraph starts with a general idea and moves to focus on one main idea.

4 Write your story.

- ✓ Use linking words to connect your ideas: **at the beginning**, **then**, **finally**.
- ✓ Make sure you have left no spelling mistakes. Check your spelling with an online dictionary.

Fiche de méthodologie N°20 p. 300

SÉQUENCE 2

How did British pirates inspire fiction?

A Pirates at sea

Classe inversée

✦ *True Caribbean Pirates*, The History Channel, 2006

Vidéo
hatier-clic.fr/lmu1097

E-workbook
Classe inversée
hatier-clic.fr/lmu1098

1 Watch the video and say how pirates are represented.

2 Describe their lifestyle as precisely as possible.

3 In your own words, express the vision of pirates suggested in the video.

B The Golden Age of piracy

Audio
CD2 piste 06

✦ Pirates dividing the booty, National Geographic Creative

1 Listen and pick out information about the periods, places and nations mentioned.

2 Find information about their exchanges (places and goods). Draw a triangle to show the exchange between the continents.

3 Write the name and characteristics of the pirate described.

4 Write down the following summary and complete it in your copybook.

At that time, the Caribbean was the big ... area of the world economy. And so it became the ... place for ... .

Word Spot

trade route
triangular /traɪæŋgjələr/ trade
trade goods
hideout, haven /heɪvən/: refuge
thief: person who steals

booty: stolen goods
growth: expansion
safe: in security
lucrative: profitable
noble
heroic
plunder, loot: pillage

allow sb to
trade: buy and sell goods
make it easier for sb to
be described as
be regarded as: be considered as

Grammar Spot

The preterite Tools → p. 124

"They generally **limited** their attacks to the Spanish."

Improve your pronunciation

Précis de phonologie, p. 262

La terminaison -ed

Audio
CD2 piste 11
MP3 n°78

La prononciation de la terminaison ***-ed*** des verbes réguliers au prétérit ou au participe passé peut être différente. Elle peut se prononcer /d/, /t/ ou /ɪd/, selon le **son final** de la dernière syllabe du verbe.

- Si le son final de la dernière syllabe du verbe est /p/, /k/, /f/, /s/, /ʃ/ ou /tʃ/, la terminaison *-ed* se prononce /t/.
parked /t/, *washed* /t/, *watched* /t/, *fixed* /t/, *missed* /t/

- Si le son final est /d/ ou /t/, la terminaison *-ed* se prononce /ɪd/.
wanted /ɪd/, *decided* /ɪd/, *started* /ɪd/, *exhausted* /ɪd/

- La terminaison *-ed* se prononce /d/ dans tous les autres cas.
moved /d/, *arrived* /d/, *turned* /d/, *pulled* /d/

6 Écoutez les mots suivants et indiquez la bonne prononciation : /d/, /t/ ou /ɪd/. Puis vérfiez avec l'enregistrement.

Audio
CD2 piste 12
MP3 n°79

decided • shared • slipped • divided • changed • faced • captured • attacked • plundered • sailed • raided • terrorised • hopped

/t/	/ɪd/	/d/
...	...	...

7 Complétez les phrases suivantes.

La terminaison –*ed* des verbes au prétérit se prononce ... en règle générale.
Cependant, si le verbe se termine par le son /p/, /k/, /f/, /s/, /ʃ/, ou /ʧ/, cette terminaison se prononce ... et si le verbe se termine par le son /d/ ou /t/, elle se prononce ...

Work on your writing skills

L'utilisation du *y* et du *i*

L'orthographe de la lettre *y* à la fin d'un mot change en fonction de plusieurs critères.

	Type de modification
Nom	Un nom terminé par une consonne suivie d'un *y* se terminera par *-ies* au pluriel. *memory* → *memories* *story* → *stories* ⚠ Les noms propres ne suivent pas cette règle : *I have seen the Murphys today.*
Verbe	Un verbe terminé par une consonne suivie d'un *y* se terminera par : • ***-ies*** au présent simple à la 3e personne du singulier (*try* → *she tries*) ; • ***-ied*** au prétérit simple à la 3e personne du singulier (*cry* → *he cried*) ; • ***-ied*** au participe passé (*reply* → *they have replied*).
Adjectif	Les adjectifs dont la terminaison est un *y* comme *lazy* ou *funny* par exemple subissent une modification. • Au comparatif : *she is lazier than her friend.* • Au superlatif : *he is the funniest man I have ever met!*

8 Mettez les mots suivants au pluriel et placez-les au bon endroit dans ces phrases.

century • quantity • enemy • diary

a. Pirates plundered huge ... of goods.
b. For ... , pirates terrorised the high seas.
c. Pirates were cruel to their ... .
d. He is a famous expert who has read all the ... of the most famous pirates.

9 Écrivez un court paragraphe sur les pirates en utilisant les verbes et les adjectifs ci-dessous, au comparatif ou au superlatif.

Verbes : terrify • defy • try • carry.
Adjectifs : bloody • heavy • ugly • scary.

Build up your vocabulary

Audio
CD2 piste 13

Living conditions
MP3 n°80

hideout: haven /heɪvən/, refuge
crew: sailors
harsh: hard
crowded
safe: in security
endure: suffer sth difficult
allow sb to

Commerce
MP3 n°81

trade route
triangular /traɪæŋgjələr/ trade
growth: expansion
lucrative: profitable
trade: buy and sell goods
make it easier for sb to

Pirates

Characteristics
MP3 n°83

peg leg: wooden leg
fierce look: ferocious look
infamous: famous for a bad quality
larger than life: impressive
fearsome: terrifying
fearless: intrepid
brave: courageous
wild: ferocious
cold-blooded: callous, cruel
hard-hearted: merciless, pitiless
evil-looking: terrifying
noble
heroic
be described as
be regarded as: be considered as
be dressed up as: be disguised as
portray: illustrate

Crimes
MP3 n°82

thief: person who steals
booty: stolen goods
pistol holster
plunder, loot: pillage
commit a crime
set on fire: start a fire

Apprenez et révisez le vocabulaire !

Utilisez Quizlet pour vous entraîner en vous amusant.

Quizlet
hatier-clic.fr/lmu1103

Utilisez le vocabulaire en contexte.

1 Complétez les phrases suivantes avec des mots de la carte mentale.

Mary Read had just plundered a ship and was satisfied with her ... . She was walking back to the harbour, when suddenly she saw an ... pirate who was trying to ... her boat ... ... with a torch. She recognised him immediately, he was the ... Black Beard. She knew that he was ... , ... and ... . Mary Read was ... , but she had heard of all the ... Black Beard had committed. So she waited for her ... to fight against him.

2 Écrivez le début d'une histoire de pirates en utilisant la traduction en anglais de ces mots, que vous trouverez dans la carte mentale.

sans pitié — jambe de bois — se livrer au pillage

subir — refuge — en sécurité

AUTO évaluation

Faites le quiz interactif en ligne et suivez les conseils pour vous préparer à l'évaluation.

Quiz
hatier-clic.fr/lmu1104

Project #1

Show visitors around the Pirates of Nassau Museum and tell them about the lifestyles of pirates.

1 Welcome the visitors!

- Introduce yourself and explain what you will be doing during the tour.
- Tell the visitors they can ask questions at the end of your presentation.

2 Choose one or two pirates.

- Describe the pirates and their personalities.
- Say what they are famous (or infamous!) for.
- Use the **preterite** to talk about the past.

3 Describe the life of a pirate.

- Comment on their daily activities.
- Describe the risks they took.

4 Organise your ideas in a well-structured presentation.

- Don't forget your audience might not know anything about pirates, so be clear and precise.
- Use linking words to organise your ideas (**firstly**, **secondly**, **in the end**...).

5 Practise!

- Read your notes a few times but only use a list of 15 words for your presentation.
- Be natural when you speak!

Fiche de méthodologie N°18 p. 296

Project #2

Create a leaflet depicting a fictional pirate to win the Cayman Islands Pirates Week Festival contest.

1 Pick a character.

- Choose a pirate (female or male) and give her or him a name.
- Outline her or his physical characteristics, reputation and character.
- Use the **simple present** to make the description.

2 Create a storyline.

- Say where your pirate comes from and why she or he is well-known.
- Describe your character's major actions and adventures.

3 Add an extraordinary event and find pictures!

- Add a lot of details to make this event realistic and use **superlatives** and **adverbs** to make it spectacular.
- Use a few pictures or your own drawings to make your leaflet more attractive.

4 Be creative.

- Write a captivating slogan to catch people's attention and convince them that your pirate is unique.
- You can use online tools to create your leaflet.

Fiche de méthodologie N°12 p. 286

Let's RECAP

Lisez les questions-clés et complétez la fiche bilan avec des exemples et des documents que vous avez étudiés ou découverts.

AXE 5 | Fictions and realities

SÉQUENCE 1 — How close to reality can dystopia be?

E-workbook
Bilan à compléter
hatier-clic.fr/lmu1105

How can fiction warn us of real dangers?
What do dystopian novels teach us about the power of words?

#dystopia
How do historical and political context influence literature?

#literature
How can literature and artworks play an important role in society?

#reality
How is reality depicted in dystopian novels and films?

#fiction
How can fiction warn us about the consequences of societal issues?

#imaginaryworlds
How can imaginary world settings help denounce current issues?

#denunciation
How are reading and writing real weapons in dystopian books?

SÉQUENCE 2 — How did British pirates inspire fiction?

E-workbook
Bilan à compléter
hatier-clic.fr/lmu1106

What influence did real British pirates have on the creation of fictional ones?
What part of their story inspired artists?

#culturalheritage
To what extent are pirates a strong part of Britain's cultural heritage?

#collectiveimaginary
What vision do British people have of pirates?

#questioningmyths
Are pirates fictional heroes or real villains?

#literature
How popular are pirates in literature?

#legends
How did certain historical pirates become true legends?

GO4IT!

Lisez et écoutez de l'anglais en dehors de la salle de classe ! Voici quelques conseils en lien avec votre séquence.

SÉQUENCE 1

Novels

Animal Farm, George Orwell, 1945
1984, George Orwell, 1949
Fahrenheit 451, Ray Bradbury, 1953
A Clockwork Orange, Anthony Burgess, 1962
The Giver, Lois Lowry, 1993
The Hunger Games, Suzanne Collins, 2008

Comics

American Flagg!,
Howard Chaykin, 1983-1988
Transmetropolitan,
Darick Robertson, 1997-2002
Lazarus,
Greg Rucka and
Michael Lark, 2013

Songs

We Will Become Silhouettes,
The Postal Service, 2003
Intervention, Arcade Fire, 2007
Resistance, Muse, 2009

Films

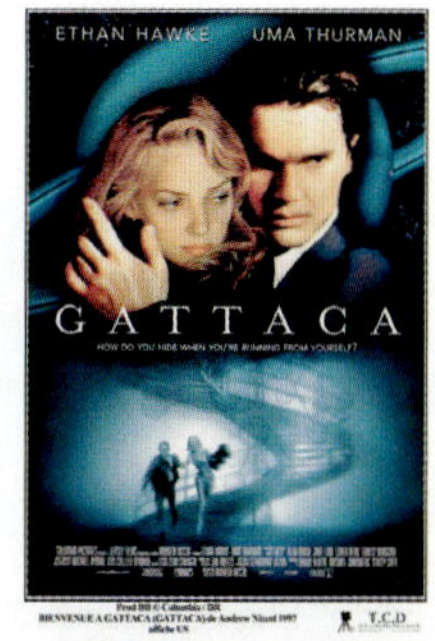

SÉQUENCE 2

Books, articles and comics

Treasure Island,
Robert Louis Stevenson, 1883
Peter Pan,
J. M. Barrie, 1911
Pirate Diary,
Richard Platt, 2001

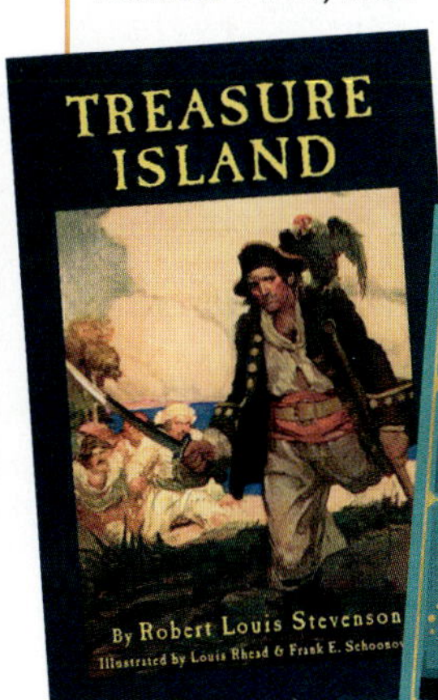

Film

Documentary

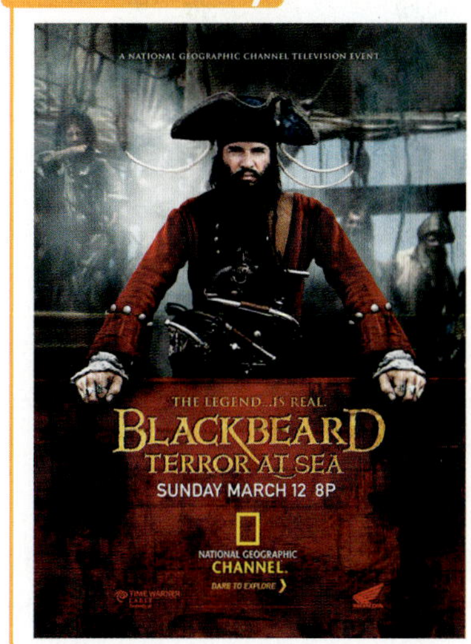

Songs

Jolly Roger, Roger McGuinn, 1976
The Ballad of Captain Kidd, Carl Peterson, 2003
The Derelict, The Saucy Rovers, 2016

BAC in sight

ÉPREUVE 1

COMPRÉHENSION ORALE

Audio
CD2 piste 14

Lois Lowry talks about her book *The Giver*. The novel follows a 12-year-old character named Jonas who lives in a society that has taken away pain and conflicts to promote "sameness". He is chosen to be the one who stores the past memory of the time before "sameness".

✦ Lois Lowry author of *The Giver* (1993)

Tips

➤ Focus on stressed words as they are important.
➤ Try to create a story based on your notes.

➤ Fiche de méthodologie N°15 p. 290 Compréhension orale

EXPRESSION ÉCRITE

SUJET 1 Imagine the first page of *The Giver*.

OU

SUJET 2 How realistic is dystopia?

Tip

➤ Find examples from the documents you have studied in class.

➤ Fiche de méthodologie N°20 p. 300 Expression écrite

Pour l'épreuve

Questions
Fiche modifiable
hatier-clic.fr/lmu1107

Évaluation
Grille à imprimer
hatier-clic.fr/lmu1108

ÉPREUVE 2

EXPRESSION ÉCRITE

SUJET 1 As a journalist, write an article to show that dystopian fictions (books, series, films) are inspired by previous works and real facts.

OU

SUJET 2 Write an exchange of messages between two characters from two dystopian worlds. They explain their situation and they support each other.

✦ *The Hunger Games: Catching Fire*, dir. by Francis Lawrence, 2013

Tips

➤ Underline or highlight the key words.
➤ Proofread your draft work twice before starting to copy it.

➤ Fiche de méthodologie N°20 p. 300 Expression écrite

COMPRÉHENSION ÉCRITE

Twentieth Century Dystopian Fiction

The term 'utopia', literally meaning 'no place', was coined by Thomas More in his book of the same title. *Utopia* (1516) describes a fictional island in the Atlantic ocean and is a satire on the state of England.

Dystopian fiction of the twentieth century has its beginnings in the utopian fiction of authors such as H.G. Wells and William Morris. Wells called himself a 'utopiographer' and believed that scientific advancements would outlaw war and poverty, as he fictionalised in his novel *Men Like Gods* (1923). [...]

Aldous Huxley, with his novel *Brave New World* (1932), started to criticise the utopian values of science and the domineering political ideals of novelists such as Wells and Morris. *Brave New World* is set in a future society, and takes Wells' idea that scientific advancement will improve every aspect of life as its foundation. In Huxley's vision, children are artificially bred[1] in test tubes, and are content to accept whatever the domineering State bestows[2] on them. [...]

Orwell's *Nineteen Eighty-Four* is perhaps the best-known dystopia of the twentieth century. The future world has been divided into three super-states, Oceania, Eurasia and Eastasia all of which are embroiled in a perpetual war. In Orwell's world, the governments use a manipulative form of language called 'Newspeak', which states 'War is Peace' and is able to convince anyone that '2 + 2 = 5'. Britain has been designated 'Airstrip One' and monitors its citizens for the Hitler-esque leader, Big Brother. The novel's protagonist, Winston Smith, is the last man to possess any concept of freedom and futilely attempts to rebel against Big Brother only to be arrested and 'rehabilitated' by the State. Orwell's novel inspired many other post-war dystopias, including Anthony Burgess's *1985* (1978).

[...]

In *The Wanting Seed*, Burgess tackles overpopulation. Set in a future London that sprawls from the south coast to Birmingham, the novel depicts a society in which reproduction is brutally policed by the Ministry of Infertility and homosexuality is actively encouraged by the State. The story follows the plight of teacher Tristram Foxe as he witnesses the dissolution of civilisation. With reports of mass famine, people begin turning to cannibalism, leading to chaos and war.

[...] Dystopian fiction is rarely about the future. It always reflects the time in which it is written. For the authors of Burgess's generation, their writing was connected with their experiences of military life and events surrounding the Second World War, but as the twentieth century progressed, grand political narratives such as fascism and communism ceased to be relevant. Dystopias began to reflect dominant concerns such as consumerism and equality, and the ever-present technological world.

More recently, literary dystopias have returned to the idea of the conflict between scientific advancement and human freedom. Kazuo Ishiguro's *Never Let Me Go* (2005) is about a near-future boarding school for clones that provide donations of vital organs for 'normals', or the regular population. Recent dystopias also deal with the idea of class and freedom. Suzanne Collins's *The Hunger Games* (2008), a novel for young adults, pitches teenagers against each other in a battle to the death in a futuristic arena, overseen by the elite sections of society. There has also been the development of technological dystopias, especially in film and television. Charlie Brooker's series *Black Mirror* (2011-2013) depict 'how we might live in ten minutes time if we are clumsy', and show the possible effects of smart phones, reality television and social networking.

✦ Anthony Burgess, www.anthonyburgess.org

1. created 2. (*here*) gives

Tips

➤ List the books mentioned and what they are about.

➤ Write down all the proper nouns and who or what they refer to.

➤ Fiche de méthodologie N°16 p. 292 Compréhension écrite

Pour l'épreuve

Questions — Fiche modifiable — hatier-clic.fr/lmu1109

Évaluation — Grille à imprimer — hatier-clic.fr/lmu1110

BAC in sight

ÉPREUVE 1

COMPRÉHENSION ORALE

Audio
CD2 piste 15

Learn more about two famous but different pirates who roamed the high seas in search of wealth in the Golden Age of piracy.

✦ Henry Every, also known as John Avery, Captain Bridgeman, or Long Ben

Tips
➤ Write down the words that are stressed.
➤ Link the people with their actions.

➤ Fiche de méthodologie N°15 p. 290 Compréhension orale

EXPRESSION ÉCRITE

SUJET 1 Create a fictional pirate character and write his or her biography.

OU

SUJET 2 Would you have liked to live like a pirate? Explain why or why not.

Tip
➤ Use past tenses when speaking about pirates' lives.

➤ Fiche de méthodologie N°20 p. 300 Expression écrite

Pour l'épreuve

Questions
Fiche modifiable
hatier-clic.fr/lmu1111

Évaluation
Grille à imprimer
hatier-clic.fr/lmu1112

ÉPREUVE 2

EXPRESSION ÉCRITE

SUJET 1 "Blackbeard didn't go quietly." Imagine the speech Blackbeard gave to his crew before boarding the ship where he would be killed.

OU

SUJET 2 In your opinion, what makes pirate fiction so popular?

✦ Captain Blackbeard and his crew

Tips
➤ Pay attention to the tenses.
➤ Find examples in the unit to support your arguments.

➤ Fiche de méthodologie N°20 p. 300 Expression écrite

COMPRÉHENSION ÉCRITE

More Than a Pirate, a Rebel With a Democratic Spirit

Decades before the American Revolution, Blackbeard and his pirates revolted against unjust conditions imposed by shipowners and captains.

BATH, N.C. — Three hundred years ago this week, a band of Royal Navy sailors killed Blackbeard, the most infamous pirate in history, putting a symbolic end to the golden age of piracy, a maritime rebellion that strangled trans-Atlantic commerce, terrified naval captains and colonial governors, and briefly gave hope to downtrodden[1] sailors, plantation slaves and even the House of Stuart, recently deposed from the British throne.

Blackbeard didn't go quietly. Surprised at his Outer Banks pirate's nest on the morning of Nov. 22, 1718 — his crew hung over from a night of revelry[2] — he blasted his opponents' vessels with broadsides and died in hand-to-hand combat, with five musket wounds "and 20 dismal cuts on several parts of his body."

He didn't live quietly, either. In a piracy career lasting no more than four years, Blackbeard helped his fellow pirates occupy war-torn Nassau in the Bahamas, where they restored the fort and strangled commerce making the obligatory passage out of the Caribbean via the nearby Florida Straits. He terrorized the approaches to New York, Philadelphia, the Chesapeake and Charleston, S.C., and cultivated so terrible a visage that merchant captains simply surrendered to him without a fight.

In the process, his deeds captivated the popular consciousness on both sides of the Atlantic and never let it go. "A General History of the Pyrates," a surprisingly sympathetic and often embellished account of their depredations[3], became a best seller in Britain and its colonies. The book, written by a pseudonymous author, informed the novels of Robert Louis Stevenson, the films of Walt Disney and most every fictional pirate from Captain Hook to Captain Jack Sparrow.

But why? The Bahamian pirates were unlike most other pirates who've come before or since in that they claimed to be engaged in more than simple banditry. Most, including Blackbeard, were former merchant and naval sailors who thought themselves engaged in a social revolt against shipowners and captains who'd made their lives miserable. The pirate Sam Bellamy's crew referred to themselves as Robin Hood's men. "They vilify us, the scoundrels[4] do, when there is only this difference," Bellamy told a captive. "They rob the poor under the cover of law" and "we plunder the rich under the cover of our own courage."

There was also a democratic spirit aboard the pirates' ships six decades before Lexington and Yorktown, more than seven ahead of the storming of the Bastille. Upon seizing a vessel, the pirates turned its government upside down. Instead of using whips and beatings to enforce a rigid, top-down hierarchy, they elected and deposed their captains by popular vote. They shared their treasure almost equally and on most ships didn't allow the captain his own cabin. The contracts some crews drew up and signed included disability benefits: payments for lost eyes and limbs taken from the shared plunder before it was divvied up.

✦ Colin Woodard, *The New York Times*, November 22, 2018

1. treated badly 2. festivities 3. acts causing damage or destruction 4. unscrupulous persons

Tips

➤ Read the title and the introduction carefully: it will help you understand the text!

➤ Identify the characters, the places and the period.

➤ Focus on verbs linked to the title.

➤ Fiche de méthodologie N°16 p. 292 Compréhension écrite

Pour l'épreuve

Questions — Fiche modifiable — hatier-clic.fr/lmu1113

Évaluation — Grille à imprimer — hatier-clic.fr/lmu1114

AXE 6

Scientific innovations and responsibility

Innovations scientifiques et responsabilité

SÉQUENCE 1 How far are Americans willing to let AI into their lives?

Projects

Project #1: Participate in a debate about the place artificial intelligence has and will have in our lives.

Project #2: Write an article for *Tech Insider* about what life will be like in 2050 thanks to AI and how to prepare for it.

Tools

Grammaire *should* et *would*, le futur
Phonologie les sons /ə/ et /ɜː/
Écriture les majuscules
Vocabulaire la technologie, l'éthique

SÉQUENCE 2 How important is the Space Race for the USA?

Projects

Project #1: Interview an American astronaut. Discuss the possibility and the consequences of sending humans to Mars.

Project #2: Write a speech about the Space Race for a conference at a famous US university.

Tools

Grammaire la capacité, la possibilité et l'obligation au futur, les verbes à particule
Phonologie les groupes de souffle
Écriture l'organisation d'un discours
Vocabulaire l'espace, les découvertes

#ethics #progress

#responsibility

#artificalintelligence #technology

Ava, a humanoid robot in the film *Ex Machina*, dir. by Alex Garland, 2015

#transportation #SpaceRace

#innovation

#spaceexploration #frontiers

The Martian, dir. by Ridley Scott, 2015

SÉQUENCE 1

How far are Americans willing to let AI into their lives?

A An AI amusement park

✦ *Westworld*, HBO, 2016

1 Describe the picture and imagine who the characters are.

2 Guess what happens in this lab.

3 **PAIR WORK** Read the Culture Tip and imagine a short dialogue between the two characters in this scene.

Culture Tip

Westworld is a TV series depicting a futuristic amusement park that recreates the Wild West. It is inhabited by very realistic androids called 'hosts', who are programmed to repeat the same actions every day without remembering the past. The rich visitors called 'guests' can do anything they want without any consequences. Things start to go wrong when some robots start remembering and begin to have a conscience.

B Meet Sophia the robot

Vidéo DVD

Culture Tip

Artificial intelligence (AI) is an area of computer science that creates machines or programs which can think and act like humans. This means that they can react to situations and learn from experience.

Pédagogie différenciée

TRAIL A

1 Listen and take notes about Sophia.

2 Explain what Sophia thinks about humans using the following words.

compatriots - close - knowledge

3 Focus on what Sophia says about the series *Westworld* and what it can teach us.

She believes the series can...

TRAIL B

1 Listen and take notes about Sophia and what she can do.

2 Explain what she thinks about humans and the relationship they can have with robots.

3 Find out if Sophia likes the series *Westworld* and why.

Meet up! After watching this video, write a text message to a friend to tell him or her about Sophia.

Grammar Spot

Should / Would TOOLS → p. 140

"*Westworld* is a warning of what we **should** not do to robots."

"Musk suggested that the first stage **would** be to learn as much as possible."

Word Spot

threat: menace
fear: worry
developments
helpful: useful
risky: dangerous
worrying: distressing
enact: make a law
avoid ≠ confront
imitate
prevent ≠ encourage
envisage: imagine
arise: happen
potentially: possibly
hopefully

C Regulate before it's too late

Tesla and SpaceX CEO says AI represents a 'fundamental risk to human civilisation' and that waiting for something bad to happen is not an option.

Tesla and Space X chief executive Elon Musk has pushed again for the proactive regulation of artificial intelligence because "by the time we are reactive in AI regulation, it's too late".

Speaking at the US National Governors Association summer meeting in Providence Rhode Island, Musk said: "Normally the way regulations are set up is when a bunch of bad things happen, there's a public outcry[1], and after many years a regulatory agency is set up to regulate that industry. "It takes forever. That, in the past, has been bad but not something which represented a fundamental risk to the existence of civilisation."

Musk has previously stated that AI is one of the most pressing threats to the survival of the human race, and that his investments into its development were made with the intention of keeping an eye on its development.

"AI is the rare case where I think we need to be proactive in regulation instead of reactive. Because I think by the time we are reactive in AI regulation, it'll be too late," Musk told the meeting. "AI is a fundamental risk to the existence of human civilisation."

While Musk has repeatedly shared his worries over AI and its development that is seen as inevitable in some regard, words appeared to hit home with multiple governors of the 32 taking part in the meeting, with follow-up questions looking for suggestions for how to go about regulating AI's development. Musk suggested that the first stage would be to "learn as much as possible" to better understand the problem.

Musk also talked about electric and self-driving cars, saying that at some stage having a non-autonomous vehicle intended for travel rather than recreation would be considered strange and that the biggest threat to autonomous cars would be a hack of the software to take control of a fleet of connected vehicles.

✦ Samuel Gibbs, *Elon Musk: regulate AI to combat 'existential threat' before it's too late*, *The Guardian*, July 17, 2017

1. reaction showing that people are angry or unhappy

1 Find out what Elon Musk is worried about.

2 Give information about how and when laws are normally made and how this procedure must change according to Elon Musk.

3 Explain what he fears regarding autonomous cars (l. 33 to the end).

4 Imagine the first five sentences of Elon Musk's speech at the meeting.

D Connecting AI and humans

Audio
CD2 piste 16

E-workbook
Fiche à imprimer
hatier-clic.fr/lmu1115

1 Find the name of Elon Musk's new company and what it is researching.

2 Rephrase in your own words Lynette Lopez's explanation of what this new technology is. Explain its aim.

3 Find out when and how this will be installed.

4 Write the title and the introduction to a news article about this new technology.

Prepare your project

PAIR WORK Act out a discussion on a US radio show between a caller who is worried about AI and a computer scientist who tries to be reassuring.

Grammar Tip Précis → p. 248

To make a hypothesis about the future use:
If + subject + **V** in the **present tense**, subject **will / won't** + **V**.

Memory Challenge

In pairs, challenge another team. You have 2 minutes to write down all the words that come to mind when you think about AI (one point per word). Which team has scored the most points?

E A mind of their own

✦ Jon Carter, KDNuggets.com

1 Explain the cartoonist's message.

2 Say if you find this cartoon funny and why.

3 Imagine the man's response.

F AI companion for seniors

Classe inversée

✦ *ElliQ - The Active Aging Companion*, Intuition Robotics, 2017

Vidéo
DVD
hatier-clic.fr/lmu1116

E-workbook
Classe inversée
hatier-clic.fr/lmu1117

1 Give the nature of this document and its goal.

2 Focus on verbs and find out what ElliQ can do.

3 Describe ElliQ in detail: her voice, attitude, role.

4 Create an advertising poster for elderly people and their families. Explain how ElliQ could change a person's life.

Grammar Spot

The future TOOLS → p. 140
"I **will not take** you to A-1 Steakhouse."

Word Spot

decision making
understanding: comprehension
partnership ≠ rivalry /raɪvəlri/
conflict: tension
near future ≠ distant future
reasoning: way of thinking
omnipresent
harmful ≠ harmless
inevitable
likely: probable
allow /əlaʊ/: permit
hand over: give
solve: find solutions
consider: envisage
be capable of: be able to

G AI for security

E-workbook
Fiche à imprimer
hatier-clic.fr/lmu1118

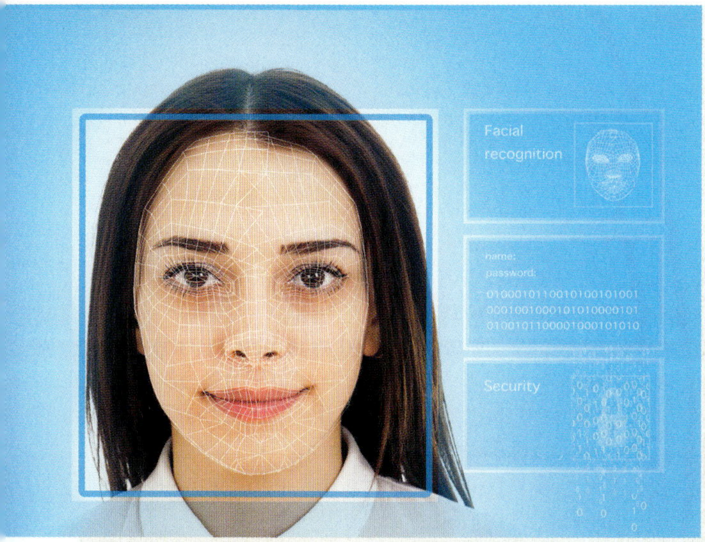

Facial recognition software that spots when someone is lying could help weed out[1] terrorists and drug smugglers at airports.

After analysing millions of frames of footage[2], researchers have discovered the giveaway facial expressions of untrustworthy individuals that could be utilised by smart surveillance cameras to assess boarding passengers.

The artificial intelligence would aid officers to decide whether a suspicious person in an immigration queue is telling the truth or just nervous. It could also minimise cases of racial profiling by airport staff.

In the study, computer scientists at the University of Rochester, in New York, created the largest public data resource of liars' facial expressions. In a few weeks, they amassed 1.3 million frames[3] from 151 pairs of individuals. To collect the footage they used a system like Skype "on steroids", where one participant played the interrogator and the other lied or told the truth whilst being filmed by their webcams.

Using a machine learning program that detects patterns in video footage, the researchers spotted new expressions that are associated with liars. Tay Sen, one of the scientists, explained: "It told us there were basically five kinds of smile-related 'faces' that people made when responding to questions."

They found an intense smile involving cheek, eye and mouth muscles, called the Duchenne smile, was one of the most frequently associated with not telling the truth. Liars appear to "smile with their eyes" in the expression, which Mr Sen said is consistent with the "duping delight[4]" theory that "when you're fooling[5] someone, you tend to take delight in it".

Strangely their researcher found honest participants would often contract their eyes, but not smile at all with their mouths. However they concluded these expressions were down to the person "concentrating and trying to recall honestly".

Seasoned[6] liars would apparently not be able to deceive trained officers who know how to spot untruthful expressions, because the Duchenne smile involves "a cheek muscle you cannot control".

Ehsan Hoque, a co-author of the research, said: "In the end, we still want humans to make the final decision. But as they are interrogating, it is important to provide them with some objective metrics that they could use to further inform their decisions."

✦ Joseph Archer, *Facial recognition software can spot liars and could help bust airport terrorists, The Telegraph*, May 24, 2018

1. find and exclude 2. filmed images 3. photos 4. satisfaction 5. tricking sb 6. experienced

1 Find out where this form of AI can be used and who it can assist.

2 Explain how this technology works and how it was developed.

3 Focus on the last paragraph. Find out whether artificial intelligence will take control.

4 Call a friend who is interested in AI and tell him or her about the advantages of this facial recognition software.

Prepare your project

Write the introduction to a newspaper article in *The New York Times* with the following title: *The growing importance of AI*. Sum up the pros and cons of AI in our lives today.

Grammar Tip Précis → p. 231

Use the **comparative** to explain differences: **faster, more intelligent**...

Memory Challenge

In pairs, say two things that are true and one thing that is false about an example of AI you have studied. Your partner has to find the lie.

Tools in the Spotlight

Entraînez-vous sur la plateforme *Let's Meet Up!*
reussirenlangues.fr

Practise your grammar

Précis grammatical, p. 216

Should et would

• Le modal ***should*** permet d'exprimer le **conseil**. Il est suivi de la base verbale. Le conseil peut porter sur une chose à faire (***should do***) ou sur une chose à ne pas faire (***should not do***). La négation, ***not***, se place alors entre le modal et la base verbale.

*Westworld is a warning of what we **should** not **do** to robots.*

• Le modal ***would*** est employé pour exprimer le conditionnel présent et désigne une **hypothèse** encore réalisable.

*If AI was taught in schools, a lot of students **would** choose this subject.*

Dans le cas du discours rapporté ou indirect introduit par un verbe au prétérit tel que *suggested*, ***would*** est la transposition de *will* au discours direct.

'The first stage will be to learn as much as possible,' Musk suggested. → discours direct

*Musk suggested that the first stage **would** be to learn as much as possible.* → discours indirect

1 Complétez les phrases suivantes par *should (not)* ou *would (not)*.

a. We ... be vigilant with AI as it may destroy our lives.

b. He said that Jill Watson, the first AI teacher, ... be there at the next exhibition.

c. If I were you, I ... attend this lecture on AI at the University of Georgia.

d. Robots ... be in charge of our health. It's too dangerous.

e. He ... say anything if he was questioned.

2 Reformulez les phrases avec *should* ou *shouldn't*.

a. I advise you to listen to Sophia. You ...

b. However, I advise you not to rely too much on robots. You ...

c. Musk advises us to learn as much as possible. We ...

d. The CEO of Tesla and SpaceX advises us not to take any risks. We ...

Le futur

• Il existe plusieurs façons de **parler de l'avenir** en anglais. On aura généralement recours au modal ***will***, suivi de la base verbale, pour exprimer une **prédiction**, voire une **quasi-certitude**.

*AI **will** be part of Americans' lives.*

*I **will not (won't)** use a self-driving car.*

• On exprime un futur plus ou moins proche par le **présent en *be* + V-*ing***, en particulier lorsque ce futur est planifié (*next year, for Christmas...*).

*I **am attending** an AI conference this afternoon.*

*What **is** this scientist **preparing** for next year's conference?*

• Pour une **intention**, on aura recours à ***be + going to***. La décision de faire ou de ne pas faire a été prise.

*She **is going to** attend this conference.*

• Pour un événement **programmé**, il est possible d'utiliser ***be to*** + V dans un registre plus **formel**.

*The scientist **is to** make a speech on AI in London.*

3 Indiquez quel type de futur serait la meilleure traduction: *will* ou *will not*, *be* + V-*ing*, *be to* ou *be going to*.

Ex. *Il a l'intention d'assister à cette conférence sur l'intelligence artificielle.* → **be + going to**

a. Le scientifique viendra faire un discours à la fin du mois. C'est au programme !

b. Les robots seront-ils utiles pour la génération de demain ?

c. Non, je ne ferai pas appel à un robot !

d. Que fais-tu l'été prochain ? As-tu l'intention d'assister à ce cours d'été sur l'intelligence artificielle ?

4 Complétez par *will* (*not*), *be* + V-*ing (to)* ou *be to*.

a. Scientists ... (improve) our daily lives by developing robots.

b. Elon Musk ... (launch) a new project. It's in today's newspaper.

c. They ... (weigh) the pros and cons of AI in the medical professions.

d. He ... (change) his mind about AI.

Improve your pronunciation

Précis de phonologie, p. 262

Les sons /ə/ et /ɜː/

Audio
CD2 piste 17
MP3 n° 84

• Le son /ə/ renvoie au **e** muet (appelé le *schwa*). Ce son voyelle neutre n'est jamais accentué. Il peut correspondre à plusieurs graphies différentes.

Le son /ə/ peut correspondre aux graphies :
- graphie ***a*** (*above*)
- graphie ***e*** (*brother, numerous, intelligence*)
- graphie ***ia*** (*nuptial, partial, artificial*)
- graphie ***o*** (*actor*)
- graphie ***ou*** (*meticulous, numerous*)

• Le son /ɜː/ est une voyelle longue. Ce son est toujours suivi par la graphie ***r***. En anglais britannique, ***r*** n'est cependant pas prononcé. Il convient de prononcer uniquement le son /ɜː/.

Le son /ɜː/ peut correspondre à plusieurs graphies.
- graphie ***ear*** (*earn, learn, early*)
- graphie ***er*** (*eternal*)
- graphie ***ir*** (*girl*)
- graphie ***or*** (*work*)
- graphie ***our*** (*journey*)
- graphie ***ur*** (*nurse, purse*)

5 Indiquez si les voyelles soulignées correspondent au son /ə/ ou /ɜː/, puis vérifiez avec l'enregistrement.

Audio
CD2 piste 18
MP3 n° 85

machine • mercy • memorable • driver • important • alive • earn

6 Indiquez si les syllabes soulignées correspondent au son /ə/ ou /ɜː/, puis vérifiez avec l'enregistrement.

Audio
CD2 piste 19
MP3 n° 86

a. Artificial intelligence will spell the end of humans.
b. It is important to be aware of the danger AI may cause.
c. Are we at the mercy of machines and robots?
d. We learn about new digital innovations everyday.

Work on your writing skills

Les majuscules

• En anglais, les mêmes règles qu'en français s'appliquent pour les majuscules de début de phrase, des noms propres, des noms de pays, villes, entreprises, acronymes, etc.

• Néanmoins, en anglais, on utilise également des majuscules pour :
- les langues et les adjectifs de nationalité.

*A lot of people can speak **English**. Elon Musk became an **American** citizen in 2002.*

- le pronom personnel ***I*** qui s'écrit toujours avec une majuscule, même à l'intérieur d'une phrase.

*Sophia said that **I** was her friend.*

- les jours de la semaine, les mois et les périodes de l'année.

*I was born on a **Monday**, the 24th of **December**, 2003. I was almost born on **Christmas** day!*

7 Recopiez les phrases suivantes en rajoutant les majuscules si nécessaire.

a. elon musk spoke at a conference in new york on tuesday.
b. space x is an american company.
c. my friend samuel told me that i should watch the british film about robots that was released in december.
d. the series *westworld* is very popular in the usa.

8 Écrivez une phrase avec les mots suivants en prenant soin de mettre les majuscules là où il faut.

us government • us citizens • protect • laws • i • dangers of ai

Build up your vocabulary

Audio
CD2 piste 20

AI

Regulation (MP3 n°87)

guideline: information to advise sb
proactive ≠ inactive
allow /əlaʊ/: permit
regulate: fix rules
enact: make a law
hand over: give
solve: find solutions
keep an eye on sth

Characteristics (MP3 n°91)

decision making
machine /məʃiːn/
program
software: computer program
reasoning: way of thinking
act like a human
imitate
learn from experience
be capable of: be able to
work out: understand how sth works

Risks (MP3 n°88)

developments
fear: worry
threat /θret/: menace
hopefully
potentially: possibly
risky: dangerous /deɪndʒərəs/
worrying: distressing
take over: take control
deceive: lie to

Relationship with humans (MP3 n°90)

conflict: tension
partnership ≠ rivalry /raɪvəlri/
understanding: comprehension
harmful ≠ harmless
helpful: useful
omnipresent
avoid ≠ confront
prevent ≠ encourage

Future (MP3 n°89)

near ≠ distant
inevitable
likely: probable
consider: envisage
envisage: imagine
arise /əraɪz/: happen
avoid: stop from happening
anticipate

Apprenez et révisez le vocabulaire !

Utilisez Quizlet pour vous entraîner en vous amusant.

Quizlet
hatier-clic.fr/lmu1119

Utilisez le vocabulaire en contexte.

1 **Complétez les phrases suivantes avec des mots de la carte mentale à la forme qui convient.**

a. Some robots are … … acting like humans.
b. We should not … dangerous robots to exist.
c. Some people have … about the potential threat posed by AI.
d. Governments need to … laws to make our future safe.
e. Computers and technology are … in our lives today.

2 **Écrivez une définition de l'intelligence artificielle pour un dictionnaire sur internet avec les mots suivants.**

programme | imitate | solve | learn from experience

AUTO évaluation

Faites le quiz interactif en ligne et suivez les conseils pour vous préparer à l'évaluation.

Quiz
hatier-clic.fr/lmu1120

Project #1

Participate in a debate about the place artificial intelligence has and will have in our lives.

1 **Choose which position you will adopt.**
Student A: You are the journalist and you want more information about AI.
Student B: You work for an AI company and want to promote AI.
Student C: You work for the US government and are worried about the potential risks of AI.
Student D: You are a satisfied user of AI.

- ✓ Note down some arguments and key words.
- ✓ Revise expressions to give your opinion: **to my mind, I disagree, I believe, for me...**
- ✓ Use the simple present. And don't forget to add an -s in the 3rd person singular.

2 **Anticipate what the other participants might say.**

- ✓ Anticipate the arguments of the opposite side and prepare counter-arguments.
- ✓ Use linking words like: **whereas, although, however, in addition, yet...**

3 **Make sure you speak correctly, clearly and sound realistic.**

- ✓ Think about the gap fillers you could use. **Er... Let me think... Well...**

4 **Start the debate!**

- ✓ Make sure you listen to what the other participants say and react in a logical way. You can also help each other if necessary.
I agree / disagree... **Could you explain why / how...** **That said...**

Fiche de méthodologie N°17 p. 294

Project #2

Write an article for *Tech Insider* about what life will be like in 2050 thanks to AI and how to prepare for it.

1 **Prepare the content of your article.**

- ✓ Note down all the things you already know about the subject.
- ✓ Do some research to add some new ideas.

2 **Think about how to express your ideas.**

- ✓ Check the grammatical structures you need to write about the future.
- ✓ Use adjectives and adverbs to enrich your expression.

3 **Write your article.**

- ✓ Structure your work into clear parts with an introduction and one paragraph per idea.
- ✓ Use linking words like: **however, although, besides, firstly, secondly, yet...**

4 **Make a conclusion.**

- ✓ Finish your article with a few lines that sum up your message. What do you want your readers to remember?
To conclude... All in all...

Fiche de méthodologie N°20 p. 300

SÉQUENCE 2

How important is the Space Race for the USA?

A Cross new frontiers

GROUP WORK

From March 22, 1952 to April 30, 1954, *Collier's* magazine published a series of articles that predicted some aspects of the future with disturbing precision. The articles were written by members of a panel of experts who offered a project for space exploration.

GROUP A Scientists and engineers working towards man's exploration of the great new frontier know now that they are going to send aloft[1] a robot laboratory as the first step – a ... which, for 60 days, will circle the earth at an altitude of 200 miles and a speed of 17,200 miles an hour, serving as scout for the human pioneers to follow. [...] Three more cameras, located inside the cone, will transmit equally exciting pictures: the first sustained view of life in space.

1. into space

GROUP B We will go to the ... in the next 25 years. We have the knowledge and the tools[1] to do it now, but years of preparation and detailed planning are needed first. What we can do now is get the project started. [...] Within the next 10 or 15 years, we can expect to see a permanent station erected[2] in space. [...] The station will be built of materials carried to the two-hour orbit by great rocket ships – called three-stage rockets because they will have three separate batteries of motors.

1. technology 2. built

1 Read the introductory paragraph on the left and observe the magazine covers.

2 Read your group's text and match it with the corresponding cover.

3 Fill in the gaps of the text with word(s) from the cover.

4 In groups, present your text and your cover to the class in your own words. Justify your choice.

Grammar Spot

Phrasal verbs TOOLS → p. 148

"The lunar module **touched down**."
"The astronauts **set up** several experiments."

Word Spot

- rocket: fast space vehicle
- spaceship: spacecraft
- aerial view: view from above
- technologically advanced equipment
- pioneer: a person who goes somewhere first
- milestone, breakthrough: major change, innovation
- achievement, accomplishment: success
- groundbreaking: very innovative
- remote: distant
- crowded /kraʊdɪd/, packed: with a lot of people
- daring: audacious
- momentous: significant
- forecast, foresee: predict, anticipate
- be determined /dɪtɜːmɪnd/ to do sth
- be confident: be self-assured, bold
- set a challenge: set a goal
- carry out a scientific experiment: try scientific procedures

B "We choose to go to the moon"

Audio CD2 piste 21

E-workbook Fiche à imprimer hatier-clic.fr/lmu1121

1 Listen to the beginning of President Kennedy's speech. Pick out the words he stresses and opposes. Say what it reveals about the world at the time.

2 Listen to the second part of his speech. He compares going to space with other accomplishments. Identify them.

3 Listen to the last part. Choose from the list what the aims of President Kennedy's speech were, then explain your choice.

criticise people – attract attention – convince people

4 Many students were in the stadium that day. Write the article that student reporters wrote for Rice University's newspaper.

Culture Tip

During the **Cold War**, the United States and the Soviet Union began the **Space Race** to make their nuclear weapons more powerful and demonstrate their power. In 1961, the USSR sent the first man in space, Yuri Gagarin, but the first men to walk on the moon in 1969, Neil Armstrong and Edwin "Buzz" Aldrin, were American.

C Apollo 11: the first men on the moon

The historic launch[1] of the Apollo 11 mission carried[2] three astronauts toward the moon. Two of them would set foot on the lunar surface for the first time in human history as millions of people around the world followed their steps on television. The crew of Apollo 11 were all experienced astronauts. All three had flown missions into space before. […]

Apollo 11 launched from Kennedy Space Center in Florida at 9:32 a.m. […] on July 16, 1969. While in flight, the crew made two televised broadcasts[3] from the interior of the ship, and a third transmission as they drew closer to the moon, revealing the lunar surface and the intended approach path.[4] […]

The lunar module touched down on the moon's Sea of Tranquility. […] A camera in the Eagle provided live coverage as Armstrong descended down a ladder[5] at 11:56 p.m. on July 20, 1969, and uttered the words, "That's one small step for man, one giant leap for mankind." Aldrin followed twenty minutes later […].

While on the surface, the astronauts set up several experiments, collected samples[6] of lunar soil and rock to bring home, erected a United States flag, and took core samples from the crust. They spoke with US President Richard Nixon, whose voice was transmitted from the White House.

✦ Nola Taylor Redd, www.space.com, December 19, 2017

1. departure 2. transported 3. television programmes 4. itinerary 5. object you use to go up and down 6. fragments

Pédagogie différenciée

TRAIL A

1 Explain what the text is about. Spot the names of the astronauts.

2 Pay attention to all the words linked to the media. Guess why so many are mentioned.

3 Focus on the last paragraph. Gather details about scientific experiments.

TRAIL B

1 Identify who the "first men on the moon" were.

2 Spot the references to the media and explain their presence.

3 Explain why this mission was important in terms of geology and communication.

Meet up! Explain the goals of the mission and why this was a "historic" mission.

Prepare your project

Imagine a conversation between an astronaut and a US president. They are communicating with an online instant message service. Imagine the questions the president would ask and the details the astronaut could provide.

Grammar Tip

Précis → p. 238

Use expressions like "**be able to**" or "**manage**" to express capacity.

Memory Challenge

Talk about the Space Race without saying the words moon, USA, astronaut, Apollo.

D The Red Planet

Classe inversée

✦ *Fascination for Mars*, National Geographic, 2016

Vidéo
hatier-clic.fr/lmu1122

E-workbook
Fiche à imprimer
hatier-clic.fr/lmu1123

1 ***PAIR WORK*** Watch the video. Describe what you saw or heard to your classmate. Together, write a short paragraph about the video.

2 Watch the first half again and match an action with the following words.

always ...
ancestors ...
as soon as ...
modern ...
shortly after ...

3 Watch the second half. Name the different forms of art used to talk about Mars in the past and the reason for this passion.

4 Use a list of ten words from the document to explain it to your physics teacher.

Culture Tip

The War of the Worlds is a well-known science fiction novel written between 1895 and 1897 by English author H.G. Wells. It is one of the first stories to depict a conflict between mankind and an extra-terrestrial race. It was dramatised on the radio in 1938 by the famous American director Orson Welles and was so convincing that some people thought the Martian invasion was real.

E Exploring the Red Planet

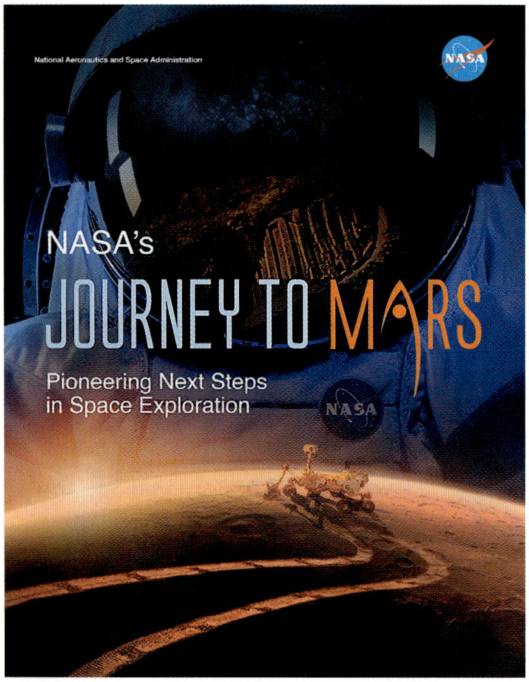

✦ *NASA's Journey to Mars: Pioneering Next Steps in Space Exploration*, 2015

1 Describe the cover image as precisely as possible.

2 Explain the vision of Mars that is depicted here using the colours used on the cover.

3 Comment on the title.

4 You are a spokesperson for NASA and you are presenting a new expedition to Mars. Defend your project in front of your class.

Grammar Spot

Capacity in the future → p. 148

"SpaceX **will be able to** establish a base on the moon."

Word Spot

ambition: drive
journey: long trip
asteroid /æstərɔɪd/
mankind: the totality of human beings
explorer
rover: vehicle exploring the surface of a planet
spokesperson: someone who speaks for another person or for a group
DNA: genetic information
thriving /θraɪvɪŋ/: successful
preposterous: absurd
launch: send

F We're going to Mars

Vidéo
hatier-clic.fr/lmu1124

1 Listen to the speech. Note down the predictions Petranek suggests.

2 Pick out the reasons why Petranek thinks we should go to Mars.

3 Petranek tells us about the history of mankind. Find out what his opinion is.

4 You are a reporter for space.com. Report on this speech and explain why you find it audacious, exciting or boring.

G Can humans travel to Mars?

Mars City: Human missions to space colony will start in 2024, Elon Musk says

Humans could travel to Mars as early as 2024 with the aim of building a colony on the red planet, Elon Musk has claimed.

Musk's space exploration company SpaceX has laid out[1] ambitious plans to establish a base on Mars after it unveiled a reusable rocket that it said could travel at speeds of up to 27,000 kilometres per hour.

SpaceX said it would be able to establish a base on the moon and fly two cargo missions to Mars in 2022 that would be able to find water and place power and life support infrastructure. The first human travellers would depart in 2024, where they would be able to set up a solar-powered plant[2] that would produce propellant[3] to return them to earth. Crucially, the rockets would land vertically, meaning they can be re-used for other missions. [...]

Over time a habitable space city would evolve on the planet, that would become "a really nice place to be", he said.

✦ James Titcomb, *The Telegraph*, September 29, 2017

1. explained 2. place where energy is produced 3. fuel

✦ Elon Musk, the billionaire and engineer who founded SpaceX in 2002.

Culture Tip

Elon Musk was born in 1971 and is South African, American and Canadian. He is an entrepeneur, investor and engineer and has co-founded very famous companies like PayPal, Tesla and SpaceX. His goal is to change the world by reducing global warming with sustainable energy, and reduce the risk of human extinction by establishing a human settlement on Mars.

1 Focus on the picture and the title of the text. Identify Musk's goals.

2 Read the text. "Would" and "could" are used several times. Make suppositions on what they indicate.

3 Draw a simple diagram. Specify the destinations, the dates, the vehicles and what they will transport.

4 In your opinion, say what SpaceX will be able to do. Explain what will be easy and what will be harder to accomplish.

Memory Challenge

Say two things that will be possible on Mars and one thing that will be impossible, based on the documents you studied in class. Your classmate has to find the lie. Take turns.

Prepare your project

Imagine you have just spent a day with your school at a space base and launch site for Mars. When you get home, write in your diary what you discovered about space, Mars and spacecrafts.

Grammar Tip Précis → p. 248

Use **will** to talk about the future.

Tools in the Spotlight

Practise your grammar

Précis grammatical, p. 216

La capacité, la possibilité et l'obligation au futur

• Lorsqu'on veut parler de la possibilité ou de la capacité de faire quelque chose dans l'avenir, on emploie ***will be able to*** + V.

SpaceX ***will be able to*** *establish a base on the moon.* (establish = verbe)

• La forme négative est soit ***will not be able to***, soit ***won't be able to*** (contractée).

Astronauts ***won't be able to*** *breathe on Mars.* (breathe = verbe)

• À la forme interrogative, il faut que l'auxiliaire précède le sujet et le verbe.

Will *NASA* ***be able*** *to do it?* (do = verbe)

• Pour exprimer l'obligation ou la contrainte au futur, on utilise ***will*** + ***have to*** + V.

The explorers ***will have to*** *live on the great red planet.* (live = verbe)
(= Ils n'auront pas le choix.)

Les verbes à particule

• Ces verbes sont suivis d'une particule adverbiale, appelée aussi « postposition », qui **modifie** le **sens initial** de ces verbes. La particule n'indique ni un lieu ni un moment.

The astronauts ***set up*** *several experiments.*

- *set : go down* (se coucher) ≠ *set up : install* (installer) ≠ *set off : start* (déclencher)
- *look : watch* (regarder) ≠ *look out : pay attention to* (faire attention à)
- *give : offer* (donner) ≠ *give up : stop doing* (renoncer)

• Contrairement aux verbes prépositionnels, les verbes à particule peuvent être **employés seuls**, sans nom après la particule.

He first wanted to take part in this mission. Then he ***gave up***.

⚠ Quand le verbe à particule est suivi d'un pronom, la particule doit se placer après le pronom.

He has discovered a problem on this spaceship, but can't ***sort*** *it* ***out*** *right now.*

1 Entraînez-vous : choisissez soit *will have to* soit *will be able to* pour compléter ces phrases.

a. Space travellers (not) ... watch meteors.
b. ... the crew ... wear oxygen masks?
c. Astronauts ... learn a lot about planets.
d. On Mars, ... they ... eat bad food?
e. The space crew ... watch TV during the flight.
f. The explorers ... remain on the great red planet for more than a year.
g. Then, they ... set foot back on earth again after an eight-month journey.
h. All astronauts ... prepare this expedition. It's compulsory.
i. SpaceX says that it ... establish a base on the moon by 2022.

2 Vous avez gagné un billet pour aller sur Mars. Faites une liste de ce que vous pourrez emporter et de ce dont vous ne pourrez pas vous encombrer. Utilisez la capacité, la possibilité et l'obligation au futur.

3 Dans un dictionnaire, vérifiez le sens des verbes à particule suivants, puis complétez les phrases ci-dessous au temps qui convient.

take off • blow up • set up • touch down • give up • lay out

a. They plan to ... a colony on Mars.
b. They ... this plan years ago, as it was too expensive.
c. In his speech, he ... what they will do in the years to come.
d. The rocket ... just before landing. It was a terrible accident.
e. When the capsule ..., the crowd was thrilled to see the crew get back safely.
f. When the spacecraft ..., there was a loud noise but everything went well.

Improve your pronunciation

Précis de phonologie, p. 262

Les groupes de souffle

Audio
CD2 piste 22
MP3 n° 92

- Un groupe de souffle est un groupe de mots prononcé dans un même souffle, c'est-à-dire sans faire de pause.

De manière générale, l'anglais regroupe les **mots ayant la même fonction dans un même souffle.**

- Par exemple :

This American science-fiction book / has been translated / into a lot of foreign languages.

Le sujet forme un groupe de souffle : il faut donc faire une légère pause après *book*.

Si une pause était faite après *American*, on comprendrait qu'*American* renvoie à une personne (= cet Américain). Il est donc difficile de se faire comprendre si les groupes de souffle ne sont pas marqués au bon endroit.

4 Prononcez les phrases suivantes en vous appuyant sur la ponctuation. Puis vérifiez avec l'enregistrement.

Audio
CD2 piste 23
MP3 n° 93

a. As soon as people understood what planets were, some of them said: "Wouldn't it be neat to go there?".
b. There it is! The red planet Mars. For over two thousand years, a symbol of war.

5 Découpez les phrases suivantes en groupes de souffle et prononcez-les. Écoutez l'enregistrement pour vérifier vos réponses.

Audio
CD2 piste 24
MP3 n° 94

a. All of this led to an early twentieth century sense that there's probably something out there.
b. The public perception of going to Mars and going to the moon is what pushed us to go there.

Work on your writing skills

L'organisation d'un discours

- **Identifiez le contexte.**
  - À quelle occasion ? Indiquez où l'on se trouve et ce qui a conduit à ce discours (*yesterday*, *last week*, *in recent months*).
  - Qui prend la parole ? Quel est son statut, son rôle par rapport à l'événement ?
  - Quel type d'événement ? Heureux ou triste ? (*We are happy* / *honoured* / *thankful* ≠ *sorry* / *sad*).
  - Pour quel public ? Proche (*Dear*) ou plus formel (*We are gathered here*) ?
- **Hiérarchisez les informations.** L'information principale doit apparaître clairement et se distinguer du reste. N'hésitez pas à la reformuler (*Don't forget that*, *not to mention*).
- **Intégrez des informations secondaires.** Comparez le fait principal à d'autres phénomènes similaires (*one of the most* / *best* ; *(not) as + adjective + as*).
- **Concluez.** On peut répéter l'idée cruciale, mais il faut surtout inclure des formules de remerciements (*thank you for listening* / *coming here* / *your attention*) et d'ouverture sur l'avenir (*let's hope that* / *hopefully* / *in years to come*).

6 Remettez ces phrases dans le bon ordre.

a. Good luck to our new team.
b. These daring predecessors have inspired our teams.
c. We hope that our shuttle will come back to earth safe and sound.
d. We will make them proud.
e. We are gathered here to celebrate the launch of our shuttle.
f. But we have successfully completed this project.
g. Twenty years ago, SpaceY's team paved the way for young astronauts.
h. Thank you for coming here today.
i. It has been a tough decade.

7 Rédigez un discours à partir des mots suivants.

a. After a successful landing, NASA thanks the team.
Congratulations on this landing • daring • achievement • launch • achieve • brave • dedicated • hope • (not) give up • keep + V-ing
b. After a long career, an astronaut retires.
My whole career, I've always • enjoy • confident • pioneer • breakthrough • thankful • exciting • rough times

Build up your vocabulary

Audio
CD2 piste 25

Space

Speeches and news — MP3 n°95

spokesperson: someone who speaks for another person or for a group
headline: title of an article
front page: cover
crowd: group of people
mankind: the totality of human beings
crowded /kraʊdɪd/, packed: with a lot of people
utter: pronounce

Danger — MP3 n°96

scary: frightening
threatening: menacing
far-fetched: exaggerated
daring: audacious
preposterous: absurd
forever
obliterate: remove all signs of sth
be determined /dɪtɜːmɪnd/ to do sth
be confident: be self-assured, bold

Discoveries and progress — MP3 n°97

ambition: drive
pioneer: a person who goes somewhere first
technologically advanced equipment
milestone, breakthrough: major change, innovation
achievement, accomplishment: success
groundbreaking: very innovative
thriving /θraɪvɪŋ/: successful
forecast, foresee: predict, anticipate
set a challenge: set a goal
momentous: significant

Space travel — MP3 n°98

journey: long trip
asteroid /æstərɔɪd/
explorer
rover: vehicle exploring the surface of a planet
rocket: fast space vehicle
spaceship: spacecraft
aerial view: view from above
remote: distant
carry out a scientific experiment: try scientific procedures
launch: send

Apprenez et révisez le vocabulaire !

Utilisez Quizlet pour vous entraîner en vous amusant.

Quizlet
hatier-clic.fr/lmu1125

Utilisez le vocabulaire en contexte.

1 Complétez les phrases suivantes avec des mots de la carte mentale à la forme qui convient.

a. The ... in newspapers were all about the moon landing.
b. This asteroid could kill ... and all living beings.
c. The ... Apollo 13 was launched successfully.
d. The satellite went very far and took pictures of ... planets.
e. The first walk on the moon was a ... in US history.
f. The ... to Mars was long but uneventful.
g. This lab ... ... plenty of experiments to allow men to live on Mars.
h. Lots of innovations were ... during the Space Race.

2 Après avoir atterri sur une planète éloignée, l'équipage d'un vaisseau spatial envoie un message à la Terre. Écrivez-le en utilisant ces mots.

journey — spacecraft — goal — significant — mankind — breakthrough

AUTO évaluation

Faites le quiz interactif en ligne et suivez les conseils pour vous préparer à l'évaluation.

Quiz
hatier-clic.fr/lmu1126

Project #1

Interview an American astronaut! Discuss the possibility and the consequences of sending humans to Mars.

1 Pick a role card.

- ✓ Now you know if you are a journalist or an astronaut.
- ✓ The astronaut can be real or fictional (from a movie or a TV series for example).

2 Get ready for the interview.

- ✓ Prepare questions and answers, depending on the role card you picked.
- ✓ Think about the words you will need.
- ✓ Don't forget to specify how the Space Race and the idea of new frontiers are important for mankind.

3 Nice to meet you!

- ✓ Use greetings as an introduction. It's the first time you have met each other! Use "**Good morning**", "**Nice to meet you**"...
- ✓ End on a polite note. Use "**Thank you** (**so much**)", "**Have a nice day**"...

4 Question time.

- ✓ Pay attention to your questions (**wh-words**, **verbs**, **yes/no questions**).
- ✓ Focus on stressed words.

➤ Fiche de méthodologie N°17 p. 294

Project #2

Write a speech about the Space Race for a conference at a famous US university.

1 Choose the American astronaut you would like to be.

- ✓ You can be a real astronaut or a fictional one (in a movie or a TV series for example).
- ✓ Look for information about her or him on the internet.

2 Select the most significant points in your speech.

- ✓ Talk about the main milestones in NASA history and the American Space Race.
- ✓ Write about the astronaut's past experiences and the difficulties she or he encountered.
- ✓ Use the **preterite** to talk about the past.

3 Explain how she or he overcame difficulties.

- ✓ Write about his or her personal accomplishments.
- ✓ Use the **present perfect** to show how it impacts her or his life today.

4 Be convincing!

- ✓ Show you are proud of what NASA has achieved.
- ✓ Use **superlatives** (**the most dangerous**, **the boldest**, **the most frightening**...).

➤ Fiches de méthodologie N°5 p. 276 N°20 p. 300

Let's RECAP

Lisez les questions-clés et complétez la fiche bilan avec des exemples et des documents que vous avez étudiés ou découverts.

AXE 6 | Scientific innovations and responsibility

SÉQUENCE 1 How far are Americans willing to let AI into their lives?

E-workbook
Bilan à compléter
hatier-clic.fr/lmu1127

To what extent will our lives change due to the development of AI?
What do we need to do to prepare for our future with AI?

#artificialintelligence
What recent evolution has AI undergone?
Do we all comprehend the possibilities offered by AI?

#technology
To what extent has technological progress made fiction become a reality?

#progress
To what extent is scientific progress a threat to Man?
Should we limit scientific progress?

#responsibility
Should we make laws to regulate AI?

#ethics
How should we behave towards AI?
Should limits be set regarding the fusion of man and machine?

SÉQUENCE 2 How important is the Space Race for the USA?

E-workbook
Bilan à compléter
hatier-clic.fr/lmu1128

Why is the USA interested in space exploration?
Have these reasons evolved through time?

#spaceexploration
What is the history of space exploration in the United States?
What role does it have today?

#frontiers
Is space the ultimate frontier?
Why is it important for Americans to conquer new frontiers?

#SpaceRace
What were the political implications of the Space Race?

#innovation
How can space innovation transform our lives?

#transportation
What type of transportation was created to go into space?
How was it imagined?

Lisez et écoutez de l'anglais en dehors de la salle de classe ! Voici quelques conseils en lien avec votre séquence.

SÉQUENCE 1

Films

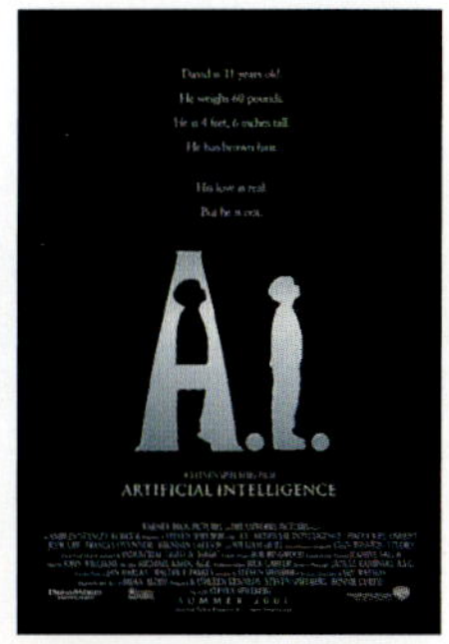

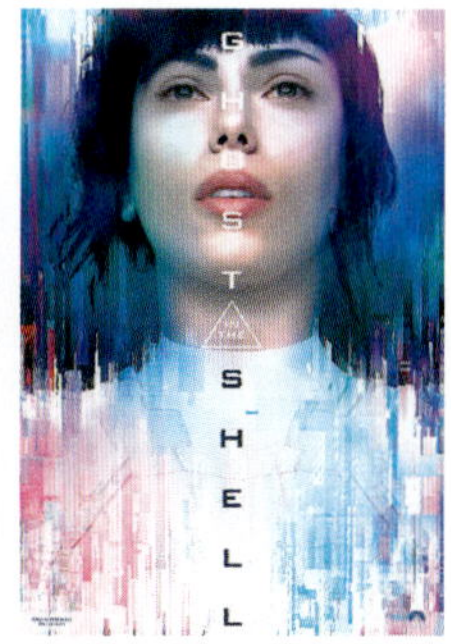

Books

Robbie,
Isaac Asimov, 1940

This Perfect Day,
Ira Levin, 1970

The Bicentennial Man,
Isaac Asimov, 1976

Caleb-Seven,
James Andrew Wilson, 2013

Articles

How AI-generated music is changing the way hits are made,
Dani Deahl,
The Verge, August 31, 2018
http://bit.ly/2ME035M

Essays reveal Stephen Hawking predicted race of 'superhumans',
Sarah Marsh,
The Guardian, October 14, 2018
http://bit.ly/2pZEgb3

TV series

SÉQUENCE 2

Films

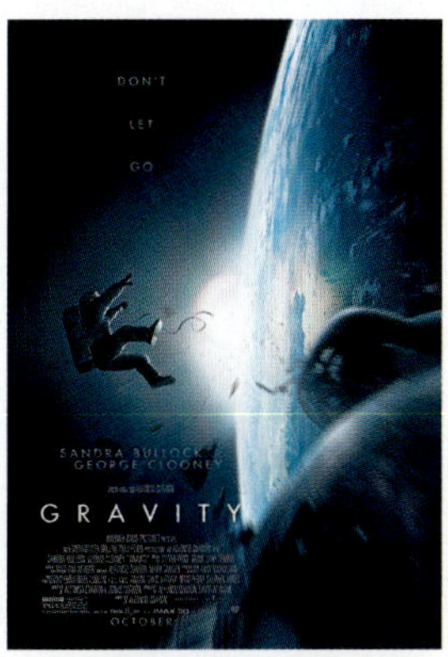

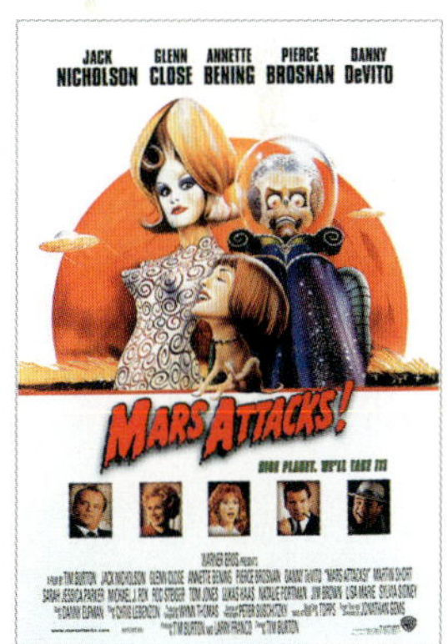

Novels and short stories

The Time Machine,
H.G. Wells, 1895

The War of the Worlds,
H.G. Wells, 1898

The Martian Chronicles,
Ray Bradbury, 1950

The Jaunt,
Stephen King, 1981

Videos

Space tourism, The Economist
http://bit.ly/2u8RUOo

Mars videos channel, National Geographic
http://bit.ly/2pta3kL

Recent interview with Michael Collins,
Smithsonian National Air and Space Museum
http://bit.ly/2FbIhCB

BAC in sight

ÉPREUVE 1

COMPRÉHENSION ORALE

Vidéo
hatier-clic.fr/lmu1129

AI expert Professor Toby Walsh gives a TED Talk on AI and ethics.

✦ Toby Walsh with Baxter the robot

Tip
➤ Read the caption to help you apprehend the document.

➤ Fiche de méthodologie N°15 p. 290 Compréhension orale

EXPRESSION ÉCRITE

SUJET 1 Write a letter to Toby Walsh explaining why you are both worried and excited about AI.

OU

SUJET 2 Do you think AI can be dangerous for humans?

Tips
➤ Use linking words to add information or contrast different views.

➤ Fiche de méthodologie N°20 p. 300 Expression écrite

Pour l'épreuve

Questions
Fiche modifiable
hatier-clic.fr/lmu1130

Évaluation
Grille à imprimer
hatier-clic.fr/lmu1131

ÉPREUVE 2

EXPRESSION ÉCRITE

SUJET 1 After this conversation, Grace goes to see a friend. She tells him or her about her conversation with her husband and explains how she feels.

OU

SUJET 2 Do you think we should let AI into our lives?

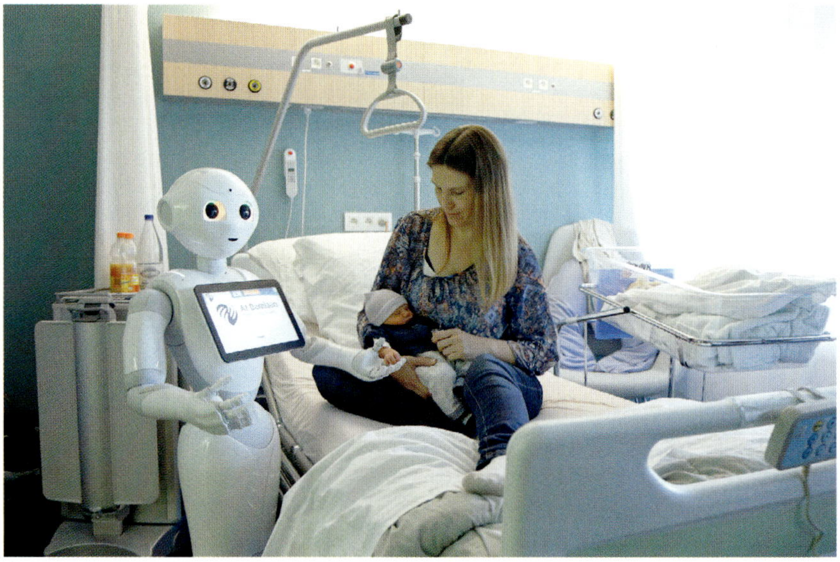

✦ Pepper the robot

Tips
➤ Don't forget to structure your text: introduction, part 1, part 2, part 3 (if necessary), conclusion.
➤ Use vocabulary you have learnt in this unit.
➤ Read the instructions carefully.

➤ Fiche de méthodologie N°20 p. 300 Expression écrite

COMPRÉHENSION ÉCRITE

"You listen to me, George. I won't have my daughter entrusted to a machine — and I don't care how clever it is. It has no soul, and no one knows what it may be thinking. A child just isn't made to be guarded by a thing of metal."

Weston frowned, "When did you decide this? He's been with Gloria two years now and I haven't seen you worry till now."

"It was different at first. It was a novelty; it took a load off me, and — and it was a fashionable thing to do. But now I don't know. The neighbors–"

"Well, what have the neighbors to do with it? Now, look. A robot is infinitely more to be trusted than a human nursemaid[1]. Robbie was constructed for only one purpose really — to be the companion of a little child. His entire 'mentality' has been created for the purpose. He just can't help being faithful[2] and loving and kind. He's a machine-made so. That's more than you can say for humans."

"But something might go wrong. Some- some-" Mrs. Weston was a bit hazy about the insides of a robot, "some little jigger will come loose and the awful thing will go berserk[3] and- and-" She couldn't bring herself to complete the quite obvious thought.

"Nonsense," Weston denied, with an involuntary nervous shiver. "That's completely ridiculous. We had a long discussion at the time we bought Robbie about the First Law of Robotics. You know that it is impossible for a robot to harm a human being; that long before enough can go wrong to alter that First Law, a robot would be completely inoperable. It's a mathematical impossibility. Besides I have an engineer from U. S. Robots here twice a year to give the poor gadget a complete overhaul. Why, there's no more chance of anything at all going wrong with Robbie than there is of you or I suddenly going loony[4] — considerably less, in fact. Besides, how are you going to take him away from Gloria?"

He made another futile stab at the paper and his wife tossed it angrily into the next room.

✦ Author and Scientist Isaac Asimov

"That's just it, George! She won't play with anyone else. There are dozens of little boys and girls that she should make friends with, but she won't. She won't go near them unless I make her. That's no way for a little girl to grow up. You want her to be normal, don't you? You want her to be able to take her part in society."

"You're jumping at shadows, Grace. Pretend Robbie's a dog. I've seen hundreds of children who would rather have their dog than their father."

"A dog is different, George. We must get rid of that horrible thing. You can sell it back to the company. I've asked, and you can."

"You've asked? Now look here, Grace, let's not go off the deep end. We're keeping the robot until Gloria is older and I don't want the subject brought up again." And with that he walked out of the room in a huff[5].

✦ Isaac Asimov, *Robbie*, 1940

1. nanny 2. loyal 3. crazy 4. crazy 5. angry

Tips

➤ Focus on the characters: look for names, relationships, opinions...

➤ Make sure you know who is speaking for each quote ("...").

➤ Analyse the types of emotion expressed.

➤ Fiche de méthodologie N°16 p. 292 Compréhension écrite

Pour l'épreuve

Questions — Fiche modifiable — hatier-clic.fr/lmu1132

Évaluation — Grille à imprimer — hatier-clic.fr/lmu1133

BAC in sight

ÉPREUVE 1

COMPRÉHENSION ORALE

Audio
CD2 piste 26

On NPR, various NASA scientists talk about NASA's next big step in search of Earth's twin.

✦ NASA logo at the Kennedy Space Center, Florida

Tips

- Be ready and organised to note down the details about all the planets.
- Try to spot clues about the astronomers' goals, expectations and past achievements.

Fiche de méthodologie N°15 p. 290 Compréhension orale

EXPRESSION ÉCRITE

SUJET 1 Do you think mankind will ever live on another planet?

OU

SUJET 2 Should we keep exploring space or is it a waste of time and money? Two experts argue in an interview.

Tips

- Making suppositions about the future: imagine possible positive or negative outcomes.
- Use nuanced intensifiers like rather, very, quite or adverbs such as incredibly, dreadfully or unusually.

Fiche de méthodologie N°20 p. 300 Expression écrite

Pour l'épreuve

Questions
Fiche modifiable
hatier-clic.fr/lmu1134

Évaluation
Grille à imprimer
hatier-clic.fr/lmu1135

ÉPREUVE 2

EXPRESSION ÉCRITE

SUJET 1 How would you answer Eric Anderson's last question: "Will the Earth be so ravaged by war, or catastrophic climate change, or whatever else, that people will want to leave?"

OU

SUJET 2 Should humans explore the universe instead of focusing on Earth?

✦ 3D Illustration, Mars colony

Tips

- Use examples from the unit and your personal knowledge to support your arguments.

Fiche de méthodologie N°20 p. 300 Expression écrite

COMPRÉHENSION ÉCRITE

Mars, Our First Outpost on the Final Frontier

In 1998, two years after graduating from college, Eric Anderson co-founded Space Adventures, which, for ticket prices of $20 million, sold seats aboard Russian space flights. Today, he also heads a programming company, Intentional Software, and a third company called Planetary Resources, which plans to extract minerals from near-Earth asteroids.

James Fallows: Space exploration seems to have lost its hold on the public imagination, compared with a generation ago. Why should people be excited about what lies ahead?

Eric Anderson: In the next generation or two—say the next 30 to 60 years— there will be an irreversible human migration to a permanent space colony. Some people will tell you that this new colony will be on the moon, or an asteroid. In my opinion asteroids are a great place to go, but mostly for mining. I think the location is likely to be Mars. This Mars colony will start off with a few thousand people, and then it may grow over 100 years to a few million people, but it will be there permanently. That should be really exciting, to be alive during that stage of humanity's history.

JF: I have to ask—really? This will really happen?

EA: I really do believe it will. First of all, the key to making it happen is to reduce the cost of transportation into space. My colleague Elon Musk is aiming to get the cost of a flight to Mars down to half a million dollars a person. I think that even if it costs maybe a few million dollars a person to launch to Mars, a colony could be feasible[1]. To me the question is, does it happen in the next 30 years, or does it happen in the next 60 to 70 years? There's no question it's going to happen in this century, and that's a pretty exciting thing.

JF: Apart from the cost of transport, what are the challenges in making that a reality? Are they cost and engineering challenges, or are they basic science problems?

EA: I think it's all about the economics. There is no technological or engineering challenge. One key to making all this happen is that we need to use the resources of space to help us colonize space. It would have been pretty tough for the settlers who went to California if they'd had to bring every supply they would ever need along with them from the East Coast. That's why Planetary Resources exists. The near-Earth asteroids, which are very, very close to the Earth, are filled with resources that would be useful for people wanting to go to Mars, or anywhere else in the solar system. They contain precious resources like water, rocket fuel, strategic metals. So first there needs to be a reduction in the cost of getting off the Earth's surface, and then there needs to be the ability to "live off [2] the land" by using the resources in space. […]

JF: Apart from the practicalities of asteroid mining, what is it going to mean in spiritual and philosophical ways for people to leave the Earth? I guess this is taking us back to the science fiction of the '50s and '60s, but what do you think?

EA: I've thought a lot about that. The interesting thing will be to see why the people who go to Mars, or to a colony on the moon, or to an asteroid, decide to go there. Will they go there because they're escaping something? Will they go there because they're curious? Will they go to make money?

Throughout history, most of the frontiers that we have had on the Earth have been opened up because people were seeking land—new hunting grounds, or fertile locations for cattle [3]—or mining for gold or precious metals. But occasionally they would go somewhere new because they were seeking religious freedom or some other kind of freedom.

So I don't actually know why people will go. Will the Earth be so ravaged by war, or catastrophic climate change, or whatever else, that people will want to leave?

✦ James Fallows, *The Atlantic*, April, 2013

1. possible 2. survive 3. cows

Tips

➤ Read the introduction carefully. Identify categories of information you will probably find in this interview.

➤ Draw a table or diagram to link these ideas.

➤ Focus on words expressing probability, hopes or doubts like will, may or could.

➤ Fiche de méthodologie N°16 p. 292 Compréhension écrite

Pour l'épreuve

Questions — Fiche modifiable — hatier-clic.fr/lmu1136

Évaluation — Grille à imprimer — hatier-clic.fr/lmu1137

AXE 7

Diversity and inclusion

Diversité et inclusion

SÉQUENCE 1 How far is the USA from Martin Luther King Jr.'s dream?

Projects

Project #1: Deliver a speech on the situation of black Americans since the Civil Rights Movement to celebrate Black History Month.

Project #2: Create a poster on an inspiring black American figure to celebrate Black History Month.

Tools

Grammaire *for*, *since*, *ago*, les questions
Phonologie la prononciation du *a*
Écriture l'écriture des nombres
Vocabulaire le racisme, la lutte pour les droits

SÉQUENCE 2 How do social realist films question British society?

Projects

Project #1: Act out an interview between a film student and the director of a social realist film. They discuss the director's vision of British society.

Project #2: Write the review of a British social realist film for a film magazine.

Tools

Grammaire les articles, le contraste et la concession
Phonologie les sons /s/, /z/ et /ʒ/
Écriture les homophones
Vocabulaire le cinéma, la société

#minorities #discrimination
#emancipation
#equality #representation

People marching for Black Lives Matter in Manhattan, New York, 2016

#integration #emancipation
#minorities
#socialcategories #discriminations

This is England, dir. by Shane Meadows, 2006

SÉQUENCE 1

How far is the USA from MLK Jr.'s dream?

A Fighting for equality

Classe inversée

✦ *I Am Not Your Negro*, dir. by Raoul Peck, 2016

Vidéo
hatier-clic.fr/lmu1138

E-workbook
Classe inversée
hatier-clic.fr/lmu1139

1 Say what kind of document this is and what it is about.

2 Identify the two periods of time shown in the film and comment on the situation of black Americans then.

3 Comment on James Baldwin's tone.

4 Summarise what you understood.

Culture Tip

The African-American **Civil Rights Movement** was a fight for racial equality that took place mainly in the 1950s and 1960s, as several major events happened and racial acts were outlawed. Political figures like Martin Luther King Jr., Malcolm X and writers like James Baldwin were emblematic figures of the movement.

B An eloquent silence

PAIR WORK

✦ Eric Reid and Colin Kaepernick of the San Francisco 49ers kneel during the anthem, prior to the game against the San Diego Chargers on September 1, 2016

1 **Student A** Focus on the background (place, people, attitudes). Present the situation.

Student B Focus on the foreground. Describe the two players' attitudes.

2 Read the Culture Tip and discuss what is happening. Give your opinion on the action of the two kneeling players.

Culture Tip

Following Colin Kaepernick, other athletes have decided to **take a knee** when the national anthem is sung. Most of them are black American athletes protesting against racism, police brutality and social injustice. This has resulted in a controversy as it is seen by some as unpatriotic behaviour and a sign of disrespect for the national anthem.

Grammar Spot

For, since, ago TOOLS → p. 164

"Back then, a half century **ago**"

Word Spot

leader
first/second-class citizen
opportunity: chance
equality ≠ inequality
protection
disadvantage
segregation
issue: problem
challenge
biased: partial
decry: denounce
discriminate against: show prejudice against
improve: progress
protest: oppose
threaten sb /θretən/

C Black Americans mostly left behind?

On Apr. 4, 1968, Dr. Martin Luther King Jr. was assassinated in Memphis, Tennessee, while assisting striking[1] sanitation workers.

Back then, a half century ago, the wholesale racial integration required by the 1964 Civil Rights Act was just beginning to chip away at[2] discrimination in education, jobs and public facilities. Black voters had only obtained legal protections two years earlier, and the 1968 Fair Housing Act was about to become law. African-Americans were only beginning to move into neighborhoods, colleges and careers once reserved for whites only.

I'm too young to remember those days. But hearing my parents talk about the late 1960s, it sounds in some ways like another world. Numerous African-Americans now hold positions of power, from mayor to governor to corporate chief executive — and, yes, once upon a time, president. The U.S. is a very different place than it was in 1968.

Or is it? As a scholar[3] of minority politics, I know that while some things have improved markedly for black Americans in the 50 years, today we are still fighting many of the same battles as Dr. King did in his day.

The 1960s were tumultuous years indeed. During the long, hot summers from 1965 to 1968, American cities saw approximately 150 race riots[4] and other uprisings. The protests were a sign of profound citizen anger about a nation that was, according to the National Advisory Commission on Civil Disorders, "moving toward two societies, one black, one white — separate and unequal." [...]

In some ways, we've barely budged[5] as a people. Poverty is still too common in the U.S. In 1968, 25 million Americans — roughly 13 percent of the population — lived below poverty level. In 2016, 43.1 million — or more than 12.7 percent — do.

Today's black poverty rate of 22 percent is almost three times that of whites. Compared to the 1968 rate of 32 percent, there's not been a huge improvement. [...]

There are, of course, positive trends. Today, far more African-Americans graduate from college — 38 percent — than they did 50 years ago.

Our incomes are also way up. Black adults experienced a more significant income increase from 1980 to 2016 — from $28,667 to $39,490 — than any other U.S. demographic group. This, in part, is why there's now a significant black middle class. [...] Progress has been made. Just not as much as many of us would like.

✦ Sharon Austin, *Black Americans mostly left behind by progress since Dr. King's death*, *The Conversation*, February 7, 2018

1. protesting 2. make sth gradually weaker 3. person who has studied 4. social unrest/disorder 5. moved slightly

Pédagogie différenciée

TRAIL A

1 Say what happened during the following dates or periods.

1964 - 1968 - from 1965 to 1968 - from 1980 to 2016

2 Draw two columns and find elements describing the economic situation of black Americans in the 1960s and today.

3 Use the following key words to explain the quote "moving toward two societies, one black, one white — separate and unequal." (l. 29-31)

inequality - separate - colour line - riots

TRAIL B

1 Use the dates to explain the situation in the 60s for black Americans.

2 Compare the economic situation of black Americans in the past and today.

3 Describe the "two societies" (l. 30) mentioned in the article.

Meet up! Create a mind map to explain the situation of black Americans since Dr. King's assassination.

Prepare your project

Write the editorial of a special issue of *Time Magazine* about how life has changed for black Americans since 1960.

Grammar Tip Précis → p. 244

Use the **present perfect**: **have + past participle** to explain what has changed for black Americans since 1960.

Memory Challenge

Choose a date or a past event concerning black Americans and be ready to say what it corresponds to.

D Black Lives Matter

Audio
CD2 piste 27

E-workbook
Fiche à imprimer
hatier-clic.fr/lmu1140

1 Identify the situation (people talking, place, time, general message) and the context.

2 Find the movement's demands.

3 Explain why the interviewee refutes the idea of a post-racial American society.

4 Imagine the interviewee's answer to this question: "So if you had to present the movement to American society, what would you say in a few words?"

Culture Tip

The terms **"Black"** and **"African American"** are often used interchangeably but they have different origins and connotations. "Black" came into use in the late 1960s at the end of the Civil Rights Movement to replace the word "Negro" and showcase black culture. "African American" became popular with the speech of Reverend Jesse Jackson in 1988 to insist on the African ancestry of black Americans.

✦ Patrisse Cullors, Alicia Garza, Opal Tometi, Founders of Black Lives Matter

E The rise of new superheroes

✦ *Black Panther*, dir. by Ryan Coogler, with Chadwick Boseman and Lupita Nyong'o, 2018

Culture Tip

The character **Black Panther**, co-created by Jack Kirby and Stan Lee, first appeared in 1966 in the comic book *Fantastic Four #52*, in the context of the Civil Rights and Black Power movements. He is the first ever black superhero in mainstream American comics. In 2016, the character entered the Marvel Cinematic Universe (MCU) with the film *Captain America: Civil War*. *Black Panther* set a record by earning $292 million in North America in its first week.

1 Look at the colours, the accessories and the type of characters in the poster. What kind of film is this poster for?

2 Read the Culture Tip, then focus on the designs, the buildings and the heroes. Explain what is original about the film.

3 You are the producer of *Black Panther*. Present your approach and choices to the film's fans.

Grammar Spot

Questions Tools → p. 164

"Is part of the goal to shape electoral politics and what the candidates are saying?"

Word Spot

- responsibility
- role model: example
- sword /sɔːd/
- gloves
- experience: encounter
- courageous: brave
- grateful
- high-tech
- successful: triumphant
- potent: powerful
- overcome: defeat
- stand for: represent: symbolise
- stand one's ground: resist
- thank: show gratitude
- acknowledge: recognise
- maintain hope
- take sth for granted: think that sth is normal and will always be that way

F An inspiring woman

Vidéo
hatier-clic.fr/lmu1141

1 Pick out the two dates Oprah Winfrey is recalling and explain why those moments were important.

2 Comment on Oprah Winfrey's childhood and how she talks about it at the ceremony.

3 Record a story on Snapchat to give your opinion on Oprah's speech and why she is an inspiring woman.

G A museum to reconcile America

Susan Goldberg. The museum has been an overwhelming[1] success; visitors have to order tickets months in advance. To what do you attribute that passionate interest?

Lonnie Bunch. I think part of it is that so many people really wanted to understand the full history of the United States. A lot of people find this a pilgrimage[2]. The most amazing thing is to watch grandparents talk to grandchildren about an event they lived through or to see people cross racial lines to find common ground over[3] things that once divided us. It really has become a place whose time is now and whose story is so important to all of us. [...]

SG. The discussions about race in the United States right now have taken on a hard edge[4], a pointed edge. Do you think that this museum is helpful in allowing people to have a place to talk?

LB. We are in a divided America, where race and issues of white supremacy are at the forefront of our conversations. I think the museum is a place that helps us explore things that are difficult, helps us explore where race matters and how it's divided us. I also think people come because they believe that by looking at the history of America through an African-American lens, they're finding moments of optimism, moments to believe that no matter how bad things are, you can effect change if you're willing to struggle and to demand America live up to its stated ideals.

SG. April is the 50th anniversary of the assassination of Martin Luther King, Jr. If Dr. King could come back, what would he think about things now?

LB. Dr. King would feel that there has been great progress. We had an African-American president. You have people like me running[5] museums. But I think he also would be saddened by the fact that we've not found what he called "the beloved community." We've not found the community where there is economic justice. We've not found the community where race matters, but matters less.

I think he would be impressed by the growth of a black middle class and also the growth in the number of African Americans going through college and being educated. He'd be pleased to see that there are better notions of integration in certain areas.

I think he'd be disappointed in that we're still so segregated in our schools, that the cities are places where often the American dream doesn't exist for many people.

✦ Susan Goldberg, *A place to come together on matters that divide us*, *National Geographic Magazine*, April, 2018

1. huge 2. visit to a special place to pay homage 3. agree on 4. side of a blade that cuts 5. managing

1 Give the reasons for the great success of the museum.

2 Show the role the museum plays in reconciliating America.

3 Explain what Martin Luther King Jr. would think about the situation of black Americans today.

4 Write a short review on TripAdvisor® to encourage people to visit this museum.

Prepare your project

PAIR WORK Imagine the interview between a journalist and a celebrity discussing inspiring people and positive events in black history.

Grammar Tip Précis → p. 241

Use the **preterite** to talk about past events.

Memory Challenge

Play the Jeopardy game. In groups of four, write five questions on the topics of p. 162 and 163 with their detailed answers. Read each answer. Your classmates must guess the question.

Tools in the Spotlight

Entraînez-vous sur la plateforme *Let's Meet Up!*
reussirenlangues.fr

Practise your grammar

Précis grammatical, p. 216

For, since, ago

• ***For*** et ***since***, accompagnés de l'aspect ***have + en*** (*present perfect* ou *past perfect*) signifient « **depuis** ».

– ***For*** est utilisé avec une expression de **durée** : *for ten minutes, for two weeks*…

*Black Lives Matter has been campaigning against racism towards black people **for** six years.*

⚠ Avec un prétérit, ***for*** veut dire « **pendant** ».

*Rosa Parks sat on the bus **for** a while and refused to give up her seat to a white man.*

– ***Since*** est employé pour le **point de départ d'une durée** : *since last year, since he took a knee*…

*So, how far has the situation of black Americans progressed **since** 1968?*

• ***Ago*** est uniquement accompagné du **prétérit**. Il se place après un complément de temps et correspond à « **il y a** + complément de temps » : *ten minutes ago, three years ago*…

*That was 50 years **ago**.*

Les questions

Il existe deux types de questions :

• les **questions directes**, auxquelles on peut répondre par *yes* ou *no*. Elles se forment en plaçant l'auxiliaire comme *be*, *have* ou *do* en tête de phrase.

***Was** Colin Kaepernick the only player who took a knee during the football match?*

Have** you **read** James Baldwin's novel?* (ici, auxiliaire ***have du *present perfect*)

***Did** the Civil Rights **attract** many people in the 1960s?*

***Wasn't** it dangerous?* (question interro-négative)

• les **questions en *Wh-* ou *How***, qui sont introduites par un mot interrogatif (*who, whose, where, when, why, what, how, how long, how much, how many, how often*, etc.). Elles se construisent sur ces modèles :

– ***Wh- / How*** + **auxiliaire + sujet + verbe (+ complément) + ?**

*How many times **did** Colin Kaepernick **take** a knee?*

– ***Wh-*** **(sujet) + verbe (+ complément) + ?**

*Who **watched** the film last night?*

1 Complétez les phrases suivantes par *for*, *since* ou *ago*.

a. Rosa Parks was arrested on December 1, 1955. It was 65 years … .

b. The public has been familiar with Black Lives Matter … 2013.

c. The documentary *I Am Not Your Negro* was released a couple of years … .

d. After the Civil War and the Jim Crow laws, African Americans fought for equality … over 100 years.

2 Complétez par le verbe proposé au prétérit ou au *present perfect*.

a. The Civil Rights Movement (start) in 1954 and (last) for more than 10 years.

b. Human rights activists (fight) for a better world and more justice for a long time.

c. James Arthur Baldwin (die) in France in 1987. It (be) over 30 years ago.

d. Black Lives Matter (organise) demonstrations in the USA since 2013.

3 Reconstituez la question en mettant les éléments dans l'ordre.

a. the / where / place / did / bus boycott / ? / take

b. president / ? / be / who / black / to / the / elected / first / was

c. is / ? / goal / what / 's / Black Lives Matter

d. industry / ? / in / wasn't / successful / Will Smith / the / music

4 Complétez par le mot interrogatif qui convient.

a. … was Martin Luther King assassinated?

b. … was Malcolm X?

c. … did these two figures of the Civil Rights Movement want?

d. … did Rosa Parks refuse to give up her seat to a white passenger?

e. … does the Black Lives Matter movement take to the streets?

Improve your pronunciation

Précis de phonologie, p. 262

La prononciation du *a*

Audio
CD2 piste 28
MP3 n° 99

- En général, la voyelle ***a*** peut se prononcer au moins de **sept** façons différentes :
  - prononciation /ə/ si elle est **inaccentuée** (*African, America*). On l'appelle *schwa* (e muet).
  - prononciation /æ/ si elle est **accentuée** (*African*) ou suivie de ***-ck*** (*black*).
  - prononciation /ɑː/ si elle est **suivie** de la consonne ***r*** ou de ***-lm*** (*arm, calm*).
  - prononciation /eɪ/ si elle est suivie d'une **consonne** elle-même suivie de la voyelle ***e*** (*female, cake, age*) ou s'il s'agit d'un mot dérivé se terminant par ***-ation*** (*discrimination*).
  - prononciation /ɪ/ dans la terminaison ***-age*** (*pilgrimage, encourage*).
  - prononciation /iː/ si elle est **précédée** de la voyelle ***e*** (*team, teach*).
  - prononciation /ɔː/ si elle est suivie de ***ll*** (*call, hall*), de ***-w*** (*draw*), de ***-lk*** (*walk*), de ***-rm*** (*warm*) ou de ***-u*** (*cause, caution*).

5 Écrivez les mots suivants et indiquez à quel son correspond la graphie *a*, puis écoutez l'enregistrement pour confirmer vos réponses.

Audio
CD2 piste 29
MP3 n° 100

nation • arduous • equal • manage • dream • state • matter • call

6 Écrivez les phrases suivantes et indiquez le son correspondant à la voyelle a soulignée, puis écoutez l'enregistrement pour confirmer vos réponses.

Audio
CD2 piste 30
MP3 n° 101

a. Oprah Winfrey has always acted against discrimination.
b. In Washington Martin Luther King Jr. made a speech called 'I have a dream.'
c. The situation of black Americans has improved dramatically since the Civil Rights Movement.
d. San Francisco quarterback Colin Kaepernick took a knee while the national anthem was being sung.

Work on your writing skills

L'écriture des nombres

- Pour écrire les nombres de 21 à 99, on met toujours un trait d'union entre les dizaines et les unités.
  55: fifty-five
- Le mot *hundred* est toujours suivi de ***and***.
  152: one hundred and fifty-two
- ***Hundred, thousand, million*** et ***billion*** sont séparés par des **virgules** lorsqu'ils sont écrits en chiffres. Ils sont invariables sauf quand ils sont suivis de *of*.
  5,500: five thousand five hundred
  *millions **of** people*
- Les nombres ordinaux sont précédés de ***the*** et terminés par ***-th*** sauf *1st, 2nd* et *3rd*.
  *the 25th: **the** twenty-fifth*
- Pour les décimaux, on utilise un point (***point*** à l'oral) entre la partie entière et la partie décimale.
  *12.72 % : twelve **point** seven two percent*
- Pour un prix, le symbole de la devise s'écrit avant le montant en chiffres ou après le montant en lettres.
  $29: twenty-nine dollars

7 Écrivez les chiffres et données en lettres.

a. 1956 b. 63.5 % c. 534 d. 22nd e. $15,952 f. 30,234 g. 37,648,921

8 Réécrivez chaque phrase en écrivant en toutes lettres les chiffres ou données entre parenthèses.

a. The Montgomery bus boycott lasted (1) year and (15) days.
b. The (14th) Amendment grants American citizenship to former slaves.
c. Barack Obama was the (44th) American president.
d. According to the (2017) US Census, there are (47,411,470) African Americans, that is to say (14.6%) of the total American population.
e. On (26.02.2012) George Zimmerman shot a (17) year-old African-American man called Trayvon Martin.

Build up your vocabulary

Audio
CD2 piste 31

Being Black in the USA

Reconciliation MP3 n°102

common ground
unity
museum
hope
historic
inspiring
peaceful
successful: triumphant
maintain hope
thank: show gratitude
acknowledge: recognise

Role model MP3 n°103

representation: visibility
celebrity
black community
positive image
leader
role model
protection
potent: powerful
experience: encounter /ɪnkaʊntə^{r}/
stand for: represent: symbolise
stand out

History MP3 n°107

civil war
slavery
emblematic figures
civil rights
segregation
discriminate against: show prejudice against
fight for equality
have a dream

Protesting MP3 n°104

activist
(citizen) anger
social movements
courageous: brave
fight
oppose: protest
overcome: defeat
demonstrate
take a knee

Current issues MP3 n°105

challenge
equality ≠ inequality
disadvantage
first/second-class citizen
issue: problem
opportunity: chance
police brutality
responsibility
social injustice
economic situation
biased /baɪəst/: partial

Racism MP3 n°106

minority politics
positions of power
poverty
post-racial society
white supremacy
decry: denounce
threaten sb /θretən/
improve: progress
take sth for granted: think that sth is normal and will always be that way

Apprenez et révisez le vocabulaire !

Utilisez Quizlet pour vous entraîner en vous amusant.

Quizlet
hatier-clic.fr/lmu1142

Utilisez le vocabulaire en contexte.

1 Complétez les phrases suivantes avec des mots de la carte mentale à la forme qui convient.

a. One of the most famous speeches delivered by Martin Luther King Jr. is called I … … … .
b. The Civil Rights Movement aimed at reaching … .
c. Black people are still … … today due to racial prejudice.
d. The Museum of African American History and Culture explores … in the US.
e. The Black Lives Matter movement reveals the … of the black community.

2 Utilisez chacun des mots suivants dans des phrases décrivant la situation des Noir·e·s américain·e·s depuis la mort de Martin Luther King Jr.

fight for equality | peaceful | overcome | role model | biased | post-racial society

AUTO évaluation

Faites le quiz interactif en ligne et suivez les conseils pour vous préparer à l'évaluation.

Quiz
hatier-clic.fr/lmu1143

Project #1

Deliver a speech on the situation of black Americans since the Civils Rights Movement to celebrate Black History Month.

1 Take notes about what you have learned about the situation of black Americans.

- ✓ Think about past and current issues:
  - inspirational figures,
  - economic situation,
  - education,
  - racial tensions,
  - progress since the Civil Rights Movement.
- ✓ List your ideas and add facts and figures for each issue.

2 Think about the structure of your speech.

- ✓ Make notes for each step of your speech (greeting the audience, explaining the situation, giving examples, thanking your audience).
- ✓ Write words, not full sentences.
- ✓ Order your ideas in a logical way.

3 Practise your speech.

- ✓ Check how to pronounce key words on the Cambridge online dictionary.
- ✓ Highlight the words that you need to stress: nouns, verbs, adjectives and adverbs.

4 Give your speech.

- ✓ Remember to greet your audience and introduce yourself.
  Welcome everyone... My name is...
  I am delighted to see all here today to...
- ✓ Be aware of your body language! Think about your voice, your posture, your hands...
- ✓ Maintain eye contact with your audience.

➤ Fiche de méthodologie N°18 p. 296

Project #2

Create a poster on an inspiring black American figure to celebrate Black History Month.

1 Choose an inspiring black American figure who contributed or has been contributing to black history.

- ✓ Make a brief internet research about black Americans who made or are still making black history - from major ones to hidden ones.
- ✓ Select the person that inspires you the most.

2 Collect information about his or her contribution.

- ✓ Focus on acts, speeches, opinions, roles and key events, and explain why he or she is inspiring.
- ✓ Use adjectives to describe him or her.
- ✓ Find arguments to support your opinion.

3 Find effective visuals and create your poster.

- ✓ Select relevant pictures illustrating why you chose this person.
- ✓ Add detailed captions.
- ✓ Put all the elements in the poster. The way you organise them matters.

4 Put together a hall of fame with your classmates.

- ✓ Decide on a specific order for the posters (chronological or thematic).
- ✓ Vote for the best poster!

➤ Fiche de méthodologie N°12 p. 286

SÉQUENCE 2

How do social realist films question British society?

A Portrait of an anti-hero

Classe inversée

Vidéo
DVD
hatier-clic.fr/lmu1144

E-workbook
Classe inversée
hatier-clic.fr/lmu1145

1 Describe the scene and choose two words to define the atmosphere.

2 Say what 954 and 14.3 refer to. Explain how Arthur feels about his work.

3 Pick out words describing Mr. Robboe, Jack and Fred. Say which colleague Arthur identifies with and why.

4 You are the film's director. Give stage directions to the actor who plays the role of Arthur.

B A new British cinema genre

Between the late 50s and the early 70s, a swathe[1] of films were released that changed the face and course of British cinema forever. Synonymous with but not confined to the British New Wave[2], the so-called 'kitchen sink' dramas that emerged in all their unvarnished, provocative glory presented cinemagoers with an unfettered[3], authentic realism that had largely been missing from British films up until that point.

Predominantly focused on the lives of the working classes, with broad regional accents thankfully intact, the kitchen sink films had no time for traditional, rose-tinted celluloid visions of England's supposedly green and pleasant land. Instead, these raw human stories revolved around crumbling marriages, the drudgery[4] of unskilled work, sexual orientation, stymied[5] aspirations, backstreet abortions, disenfranchised[6] youth, homelessness and gender, class and race discrimination. [...]

If you're unfamiliar with these films, and the stage plays and novels many of them were adapted or took their cue from[7], they may at first appear as the antithesis of big screen 'entertainment'. To be put off[8] by the uncomfortable themes, unglamorous urban locations and prevailing sense of gloom that, inherently, permeates kitchen sink films would, however, be a big mistake. These dramas crackle with angry energy, and reflect how grim[9] life really was and, unfortunately, still can be for large parts of the population.

✦ Neil Mitchell, *Where to begin with kitchen sink drama*, bfi.org, August 4, 2016

1. series 2. a style of films released in the UK between 1959 and 1963 3. unrestricted 4. hard boring work 5. blocked 6. excluded 7. were inspired by 8. discouraged 9. without hope

Culture Tip

Kitchen-sink realism is a British art movement from the 50s and 60s focusing on the everyday lives of poor and working-class communities, and often criticising modern society.

1 Read from line 1 to line 8. Use dates and adjectives to define kitchen-sink films.

E-workbook
Fiche à imprimer
hatier-clic.fr/lmu1146

2 Read from line 9 to line 17 and spot words linked to society and social issues. Show how these films gave a new and different image of England.

3 Focus on negative words from line 18 to line 27. Explain why these films may be considered "not entertaining".

4 Write a short article to present kitchen-sink films for your cinema club website.

Grammar Spot

Articles TOOLS → p. 172
"a group of Ø local skinheads in the 1980s"

Word Spot

assembly line work
working class
social progress
moral values
role model
issues: problems
conventional ≠ unconventional
rebellious ≠ obedient
belong to
depict: portray
criticise: denounce

C England in the 80s

GROUP WORK

GROUP A

✦ *This is England*, dir. by Shane Meadows, 2006

Vidéo
DVD

GROUP B

Shane Meadows' semi-autobiographical portrait of a 12-year-old boy who finds a sense of belonging with a group of local skinheads in the 1980s remains a masterpiece of working-class storytelling.

Twelve-year-old Shaun (Thomas Turgoose) lives with his mother in a shabby[1] council flat in a bleak[2] northern town and is lacking direction after losing his father in the Falklands War. After standing up to teasing at school he earns the respect of a group of kindly[3], multiracial skinheads, the leader of which Woody (Joseph Gilgun) takes him under his wing. Part of the gang and enjoying hanging out with his new friends, Shaun begins to question his identity when the gang splits into two factions after the arrival of Combo (Stephen Graham), a racist ex-convict[4], whom unfortunately the young Shaun begins to look upon[5] as a father figure.

Meadows' human drama captures a real sense of authenticity in the greasy-spoon cafes and at rowdy[6] house parties its colourful characters inhabit, and with superb performances from its largely young working-class cast[7], brilliantly evokes the working-class despair of the Thatcher era.

✦ watershed.co.uk

1. miserable 2. depressing 3. kind and generous 4. former criminal 5. consider 6. noisy and disorderly 7. actors

Culture Tip

From 1979 until 1990, **Margaret Thatcher** served as Prime Minister of the UK. She belonged to the Conservative Party. She believed the state's role should be restricted. She privatised most nationalised industries and encouraged a flexible labour market.

Pédagogie différenciée GROUP WORK

1 Identify the historical context and present Shaun, the main character.

2 Show how he is influenced by his new friends.

3 Say what social issues are covered in the film.

4 Use your group's document and the Culture Tip to explain how the film depicts England in the 1980s.

E-workbook
Fiche à imprimer
hatier-clic.fr/lmu1147

Prepare your project

You have just watched a social realist film. Convince your friend to go and watch it.

Grammar Tip

Précis → p. 236

Remember to use the verb without **to** after a modal: **must / can + verb**.

Memory Challenge

Ask three yes / no questions about social realist cinema to your partner, who must justify each answer.

D A realistic look on society

✦ *A Way of Life*, dir. by Amma Asante, 2004

Culture Tip

Amma Asante is a British filmmaker and screenwriter. She began her career as a child actress and turned to screenwriting in her late teens. Her debut film, *A Way of Life*, won multiple international awards including a BAFTA Award (British Academy of Film and Television Arts Award).

Released in 2004, *A Way of Life* is bleak[1] and at times difficult to watch. The film tells the story of a gobby[2], racist, single mum who joins a throng[3] of teens as they kick a Turkish Muslim man to death. It won Asante a BAFTA Carl Foreman Award for Special Achievement and changed her career trajectory. More than a decade since its release, the film seems depressingly contemporary — the Home Office recently reported a sharp rise in hate crimes motivated by race or religion in the wake of the referendum to leave the European Union. While Asante had never experienced violent racism personally, she says she wanted to understand what would motivate murderous hatred[4]. "I come from a belief that if we think we can exclude any portion of society… and say, 'You don't have any value, you don't have any voice, you have no right to contribute to the mainstream[5] world that the rest of us are going to live in' — if you think the only people we're going to hurt and harm[6] is that excluded group, we're nuts[7]." Racism is treated as a symptom rather than the cause in the film. "The cause is class inequality, exclusion," she says, adding: "If all parts of society had felt heard… I don't believe we'd have had a [vote for] Brexit."

✦ Emma Jacobs, *Filmmaker Amma Asante on race, Brexit and meeting Prince*, *The Financial Times*, November 10, 2016

1. depressing 2. rude and offensive 3. group 4. hate 5. conventional 6. damage 7. (*slang*) crazy

Pédagogie différenciée

TRAIL A

1 Identify expressions of violence in the poster and the text. Say what makes this film dramatic.

2 Read from line 1 to line 6. Explain the story of the film and say why it is still "contemporary".

3 Use the following words from the text to describe the director's motivation.

exclude - society - value - racism - class inequality - cause

TRAIL B

1 Use elements from the text to describe the poster. Demonstrate that the film is a drama.

2 Explain the parallel between the film and reality at the time.

3 Explain the aim and message of the film.

Meet up! Show that the film helps understand the vote for Brexit.

Grammar Spot

Contrast and concession TOOLS → p. 172

"**Although** the film is a piece of fiction, for some, the life in *I, Daniel Blake* is a grim reality."

Word Spot

spokesperson
illegal workers
human rights
racism
immigration
globalisation
exploitation
frustration
precariousness: lack of security
bureaucracy
capitalism ≠ anti-capitalism
political
socially engaged
involve: engage
integrate ≠ exclude
struggle: progress with difficulty

E A cinema of social engagement

Vidéo
hatier-clic.fr/lmu1148

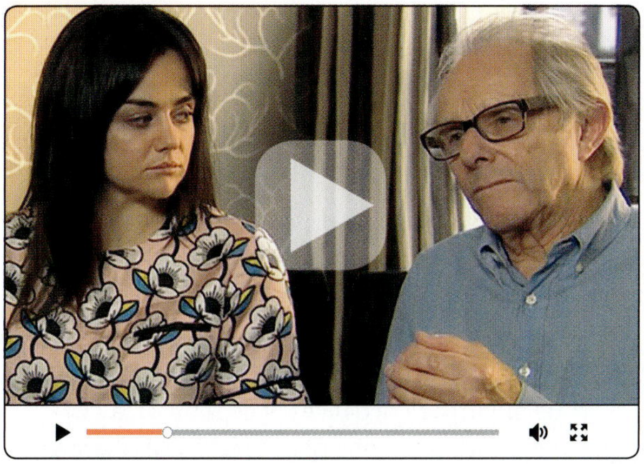

✦ *"I, Daniel Blake" is very real, The Economist*, 2017

✦ *I, Daniel Blake*, dir. by Ken Loach, 2016

1 Describe the difficult situation Daniel Blake is facing in the film.

2 Compare Stuart's situation to Daniel Blake's.

3 Explain what Paul Laverty and Ken Loach wanted to show about the British system.

4 You want *I, Daniel Blake* to be selected for a film festival in your school. Explain why to the president of the jury.

Culture Tip

Ken Loach is a British independent film director. He has strong socialist ideals which are reflected in his films. He believes that the benefits system in the UK is inefficient and cruel.

F A political film

Vidéo
DVD

E-workbook
Fiche à imprimer
hatier-clic.fr/lmu1149

✦ *It's a Free World...*, dir. by Ken Loach, 2007

***It's a Free World...* follows Angie, a 33-year-old working-class single mother. After being fired from a recruiting agency, she starts her own employment firm, with the help of her flatmate, Rose.**

1 Say why Angie and Rose disagree.

2 Find at least one argument Angie uses to convince Rose.

3 List the conditions she gives when she hands in their passports to the illegal immigrants.

4 Explain, in French or in English, what Ken Loach wants to show in this scene to someone who hasn't seen it.

Prepare your project

Share your opinion on an online forum about British cinema. Write a short post about *A Way of Life*, *I, Daniel Blake* or *It's a Free World...*

Grammar Tip

Précis → p. 223

Use **adjectives** to make your post more personal. Remember they are always invariable.

Memory Challenge

Give two words defining one of the films on p. 170-171. Your partner has to guess which film it is!

Tools in the Spotlight

Entraînez-vous sur la plateforme *Let's Meet Up!*
reussirenlangues.fr

Practise your grammar

Précis grammatical, p. 216

Les articles

• L'absence d'article (Ø) est possible pour parler de généralités.
Instead, these raw human stories revolved around Ø crumbling marriages, Ø sexual orientation, Ø stymied aspirations, Ø abortions, Ø disenfranchised youth, Ø homelessness and Ø gender.

• L'article indéfini ***a*** s'emploie devant un nom dénombrable au singulier.
***a** group of local skinheads in the 1980s*

⚠ Si le mot commence par un son voyelle, on utilise ***an***.
*British filmmakers developed **an** obsession with the everyday frustrations of the working class.*

• L'article défini ***the*** s'emploie dans des contextes spécifiques, où le mot est défini par une situation précise. Il ne s'agit pas de généralités.
*Between **the** late 50s and **the** early 70s, a swathe of films were released that changed **the** face and course of British cinema forever.*

L'article ***the*** s'utilise aussi avec les adjectifs substantivés.
***the** unemployed, **the** jobless, **the** poor, **the** homeless*

Le contraste et la concession

• La conjonction de subordination ***whereas***, « tandis que » en français, permet de comparer deux situations opposées afin de souligner un **contraste**.
Saturday Night and Sunday Morning *deals with the working class in Nottingham in 1960, **whereas*** This is England *is about young skinheads in 1983.*

• Le **contraste** peut aussi être exprimé par la conjonction de subordination ***while***, « alors que » en français.
***While** Asante had never experienced violent racism personally, she says she wanted to understand what would motivate murderous hatred.*

• La **concession** s'exprime en général à l'aide de la conjonction de subordination ***although*** ou ***though***, qui signifie « bien que » en français.
***Although** the film is a piece of fiction, for some, the life in* I, Daniel Blake *is a grim reality.*

1 Indiquez la bonne réponse.

a. Most of **(the / a)** cinemagoers who live in London enjoy **(a / an)** wide range of **(the / Ø)** choices.
b. He buys **(the / a)** packet of crisps and **(a / Ø)** popcorn whenever he goes to **(the / Ø)** cinema.
c. Now, if you want to watch **(a / an)** film or **(an / a)** interesting play about **(the / Ø)** lives of **(an / the)** underprivileged, you can find **(a / the)** great variety of **(the / Ø)** films.
d. Ken Loach is **(a / an)** famous British film director, who has dealt with **(the / Ø)** issues like **(the / Ø)** poverty, **(the / Ø)** homelessness and **(the / Ø)** labour rights.

2 Complétez par les articles : Ø, *a, an* ou *the*.

a. ... ingredients that make ... kitchen-sink drama are ... factories and ... working-class people.
b. ... British filmmakers embraced ... social realism.
c. They wanted to show ... everyday frustrations of ... poor.
d. ... urban proletariat was interested not only in ... economic growth but also in ... happiness.
e. For ... long time, ... working class had been neglected in ... films.

3 Complétez par *whereas, while* ou *although*.

a. Ken Loach's *Kes* is based on Barry Hines's novel *A Kestrel for a Knave*, ... *I, Daniel Blake* is inspired by true stories of unemployed people.
b. As a matter of fact, ... Daniel Blake has suffered from a heart attack, he is denied unemployment benefits and is expected to find another job.
c. In *It's a Free World...*, ... Angie was fired by her employer, she managed to set up a recruitment agency of her own.
d. Maisie is watching Stephen Frears's *My Beautiful Laundrette*, ... she should be very busy revising at the moment.
e. In *A Way of Life*, Leigh-Anne has made quite a few enemies on a poor Cardiff council estate, ... she gets on well with her brother Gavin.

Improve your pronunciation

Précis de phonologie, p. 262

Les sons /s/, /z/ et /ʒ/

Audio
CD2 piste 32
MP3 n° 108

• Le son /s/ correspond, en général, aux graphies **s, ss, c** ou **sc.**

s : *society, social, realist* — **ss** : *association, class*

c : *cinema, embrace, racist* — **sc** : *scientist*

Il correspond aussi à la marque du **pluriel** après un son **sourd** comme /p/, /t/, /k/, /f/ ou /θ/ : *lots*

• Le son /z/ correspond aux graphies **z, zz, s** ou **ss.**

z : *zoo, crazy* — **zz** : *buzz, puzzle*

s : *realism, visit* — **ss** : *dessert, possess*

Il correspond aussi à la marque du **pluriel** après un son **sonore** comme /a/, /e/, /i/, /o/, /u/, /b/, /d/, /g/, /v/, /ð/, /l/, /m/, /n/ ou /r/ : *sorrows, pubs, makers*

Et il correspond à la marque du pluriel ***es*** ou ***ies*** prononcée /iz/ : *boxes, factories*

• Le son /ʒ/ correspond, en général, à la graphie ***g*** en position initiale ou finale suivie de la voyelle ***e*** (***ge***).

g- initial : *genre* — ***-ge*** final : *sabotage, espionage*

Il correspond aussi aux graphies ***si***, ou ***s*** suivi de ***u*** (essentiellement en milieu de mot).

-si- : *decision* — ***-su-*** : *leisure, pleasure*

4 Indiquez s'il s'agit du son /s/, /z/ ou /ʒ/, puis vérifiez avec l'enregistrement.

Audio
CD2 piste 33
MP3 n° 109

realistic • realism • packs • measure • genre • producers • filmmakers • pits

5 Indiquez la prononciation des graphies soulignées dans les phrases suivantes, puis vérifiez avec l'enregistrement.

Audio
CD2 piste 34
MP3 n° 110

a. Leisure activities in the working class in the Sixties included going to pubs and watching movies.
b. Social realist films are my favourite TV programmes.
c. These films are similar to documentaries about a specific time in history.
d. You can discover the true lives of authentic working-class characters.
e. The ingredients included in kitchen-sink realism are factories, pregnancies, and pints.
f. Ken Loach's films always focus on the difficulties of the working class in Britain.

Work on your writing skills

Les homophones

• Les homophones sont des mots qui ont la **même prononciation** mais qui n'ont **pas le même sens.**

*They're going to **watch** a Ken Loach film with **their** grandparents. Last week Neil forgot his **watch there**.*

• Certains, comme ***they're***, ***their*** et ***there***, ont la même prononciation mais n'ont pas la même orthographe.

he's ≠ his — *whose ≠ who's* — *I ≠ eye*

ate ≠ eight — *hear ≠ here* — *buy ≠ by ≠ bye*

• D'autres en revanche, comme ***watch*** (regarder) et ***watch*** (montre), ont la même prononciation et la même orthographe.

bear (porter) ≠ *bear* (ours)

lie (être couché·e) ≠ *lie* (mentir)

ring (bague) ≠ *ring* (sonner)

6 Choisissez le mot qui convient.

a. You have to watch so many ... before the film starts playing! **(adds / ads)**
b. I ... a very good film review about *I, Daniel Blake*. **(read / red)**
c. The students must ... a short article about British society. **(right / write)**
d. Have you ever taken ... children to the cinema? **(you're / your)**
e. Let's ... two tickets for the new Mike Leigh film. **(by / buy)**

7 Utilisez les mots suivants dans des phrases qui explicitent leur sens.

a. know • no
b. weak • week
c. hear • here
d. knew • new
e. piece • peace
f. too • to

Build up your vocabulary

Audio
CD2 piste 35

Social realist cinema

Questioning society (MP3 n°111)

- spokesperson
- issues: problems
- political
- socially engaged
- modern: contemporary
- depict: portray
- criticise: denounce
- change
- involve: engage
- realistic ≠ unrealistic
- rebellious ≠ obedient
- conventional ≠ unconventional

Politics (MP3 n°116)

- basic human rights
- the Establishment: the institutional authority
- Conservative Party
- globalisation
- capitalism ≠ anti-capitalism
- nationalise ≠ privatise

Filmmaking (MP3 n°112)

- masterpiece: classic
- box-office hit
- documentary
- filmmaker
- director
- cast: actors and actresses of a film
- screenplay: scenario
- stage directions
- character
- antihero /æntihɪərəʊ/
- kitchen-sink drama: social realist film
- released
- shoot a scene

Economic situation (MP3 n°115)

- assembly line work
- illegal workers
- immigration
- economic growth
- exploitation
- labour /leɪbəʳ/ market
- unemployment
- benefits: financial help from the government
- precariousness: lack of security
- industrial
- bureaucracy
- fill in a form
- lose your job

Social issues (MP3 n°114)

- working class
- single mother
- father figure
- frustration
- despair /dɪspeəʳ/
- moral values
- social progress
- cross-generation
- struggle: progress with difficulty

Integration (MP3 n°113)

- community
- diversity
- racism
- injustice
- skinhead
- exclusion
- sense of belonging
- social cohesion /kəʊhiːʒᵊn/
- belong to
- integrate ≠ exclude

Apprenez et révisez le vocabulaire !

Utilisez Quizlet pour vous entraîner en vous amusant.

Quizlet
hatier-clic.fr/lmu1150

Utilisez le vocabulaire en contexte.

1 Complétez les phrases suivantes avec des mots de la carte mentale.

a. In social realist films the leading characters are from the … … .
b. Have you ever heard of *A Taste of Honey*? It is a kitchen-sink … .
c. The film was … in 1963, during the Swinging Sixties.
d. Ken Loach's films explore contemporary social … in Britain.
e. The filmmaker wants to … the realities of life in his country.
f. In the UK … … … are protected by the Human Rights Act 1998.
g. According to recent statistics more and more British people are in a situation of social and economic … .

2 Écrivez un paragraphe pour présenter le cinéma social réaliste britannique en utilisant au moins un mot de chaque catégorie de la carte mentale.

AUTO évaluation

Faites le quiz interactif en ligne et suivez les conseils pour vous préparer à l'évaluation.

Quiz
hatier-clic.fr/lmu1151

Project #1

Act out an interview between a film student and the director of a social realist film. They discuss the director's vision of British society.

1 Decide on a British social realist film director.

- ✓ In pairs, find films in the unit or on the internet.
- ✓ Select a film director you find interesting.

2 Find information on the director's films.

- ✓ Watch extracts, trailers or even full-length films of his or her major works.
- ✓ Take notes: film plots, characters, places, issues related to British society.

3 Choose your role and get ready to speak.

- ✓ **Student:** Be ready to ask the director questions about his or her films and motivations. Remember how to ask questions:
  Wh- / How + auxiliary + subject + verb (+ object)? or
  Auxiliary + subject + verb (+ object)?
- ✓ **Director:** Be ready to describe your film plots and characters and explain your choices. Use adjectives and quantifiers to be precise.

4 Act out the interview.

Student:

- ✓ Put the correct intonation for yes / no questions (↘) and Wh- questions (↗).
- ✓ Use the director's answers to ask new questions.

Director:

- ✓ To give examples, use: **For instance, this scene shows...**
- ✓ Use adverbs to show your personal views: **sincerely**, **maybe**, **certainly**, **absolutely**...

➤ Fiche de méthodologie N°17 p. 294

Project #2

Write the review of a British social realist film for a film magazine.

1 Choose a British social realist film you find interesting.

- ✓ Watch several trailers, extracts or full-length films if possible.
- ✓ Draw a grid and compare the films you have selected in order to pick one.

2 Draft the outline of your article.

- ✓ Note key information about the film: title, director, date of release, main actors and actresses.
- ✓ Think about facts to support your arguments: actors' and actresses' performances, issues, tone, filmmaking, comparisons with reality...

3 Write the film review.

- ✓ Mix information about the film and your opinion to write a dynamic and personal review.
- ✓ Use expressions to give your views: **from my point of view**; to link your ideas: **first**, **then**, **finally**; to introduce examples: **for instance**.

4 Polish your review.

- ✓ Check the spelling and the grammatical structures of your sentences. Avoid repetitions.
- ✓ Illustrate and personalise your review with a film poster, a screenshot or an extract from a dialogue.

➤ Fiche de méthodologie N°20 p. 300

Let's RECAP

Lisez les questions-clés et complétez la fiche bilan avec des exemples et des documents que vous avez étudiés ou découverts.

AXE 7 | Diversity and inclusion

SÉQUENCE 1 How far is the USA from Martin Luther King Jr.'s dream?

E-workbook
Bilan à compléter
hatier-clic.fr/lmu1152

Has the situation of black Americans improved?
Has MLK Jr's dream been fulfilled?

#minorities
What are the problems faced by minorities in the USA?

#equality
Will full equality be reached one day for black Americans?

#emancipation
To what extent is emancipation successful in the USA?

#discrimination
Are black Americans still discriminated against?

#representation
What are the role models for the black community? Are there new role models today?

SÉQUENCE 2 How do social realist films question British society?

E-workbook
Bilan à compléter
hatier-clic.fr/lmu1153

How is British society portrayed in social realist films?
How do social realist films reflect social issues in Britain?

#discriminations
How do social realist films denounce discriminations?

#emancipation
To what extent are social realist films a means of emancipation?

#minorities
How are minorities depicted in social realist films?

#integration
To what extent do social realist films encourage integration in the British society?

#socialcategories
How do social realist films question social categories?

GO4IT!

Lisez et écoutez de l'anglais en dehors de la salle de classe ! Voici quelques conseils en lien avec votre séquence.

SÉQUENCE 1

Novels and graphic novels

- *Black No More*, George S. Schuyler, 1931
- *The Fire Next Time*, James Baldwin, 1963
- *I Know Why the Caged Bird Sings*, Maya Angelou, 1969
- *Muhammad Ali: The King of the Ring*, Lewis Helfand and Lalit Kumar Sharma, 2012
- *March (Trilogy)*, John Lewis, Andrew Aydin and Nate Powell, 2013
- *X: A Novel*, Ilyasah Shabazz and Kekla Magoon, 2015

Films

Songs

- *Say It Loud - I'm Black And I'm Proud*, James Brown, 1968
- *What's Going On?*, Marvin Gaye, 1971
- *Baltimore*, Nina Simone, 1978
- *Formation*, Beyoncé, 2016
- *A Change Is Gonna Come*, Sam Cooke, 2016
- *This is America*, Childish Gambino, 2018

TV series

SÉQUENCE 2

Books

- *Room at the Top*, John Braine, 1957
- *Saturday Night and Sunday Morning*, Allan Sillitoe, 1958
- *The Loneliness of the Long-Distance Runner*, Allan Sillitoe, 1959
- *The Buddha of Suburbia*, Hanif Kureishi, 1990

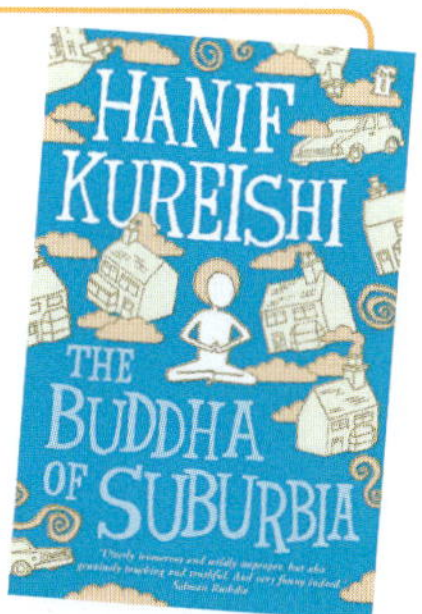

Plays

- *Look Back in Anger*, John Osborne, 1956
- *A Taste of Honey*, Shelagh Delaney, 1958

Songs

- *Sunny Afternoon*, The Kinks, 1966
- *Working Class Hero*, John Lennon, 1970
- *Career Opportunities*, The Clash, 1977
- *Parklife*, Blur, 1994

Films

- *Look Back in Anger*, dir. by Tony Richardson, 1959
- *Room at the Top*, dir. by Jack Clayton, 1959
- *A Taste of Honey*, dir. by Tony Richardson, 1961
- *Kes*, dir. by Ken Loach, 1969
- *My Beautiful Laundrette*, dir. by Stephen Frears, 1985
- *High Hopes*, dir. by Mike Leigh, 1988
- *Life is Sweet*, dir. by Mike Leigh, 1990
- *The Full Monty*, dir. by Peter Cattaneo, 1997

TV series

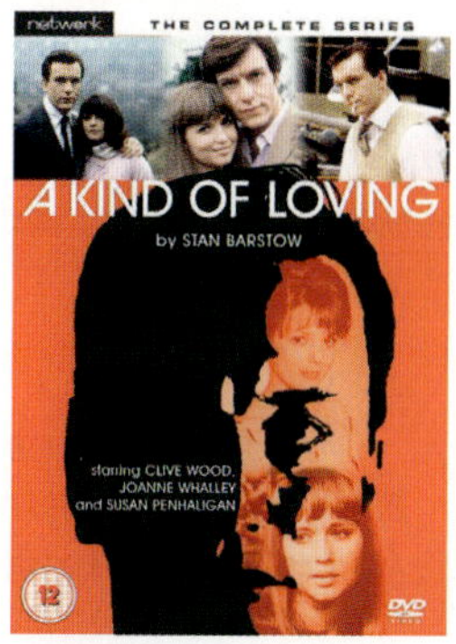

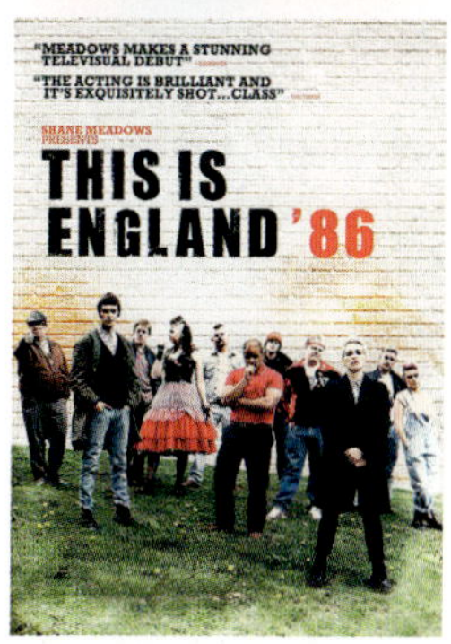

BAC in sight

ÉPREUVE 1

COMPRÉHENSION ORALE

Vidéo DVD Reniqua Allen, the author of *It Was All a Dream: A New Generation Confronts the Broken Promise to Black America* (2019), is discussing why so many young black Americans feel disillusioned today.

✦ *Reniqua Allen on the Struggles of Young Black Americans*, CNN, 2019

Tips

➤ Identify the key words in the journalist's questions.

➤ Write down the words stressed and repeated by the author.

➤ Fiche de méthodologie N°15 p. 290 Compréhension orale

EXPRESSION ÉCRITE

SUJET 1 Continue this interview. Imagine other questions and answers.

OU

SUJET 2 Why do some black American millennials feel disillusioned today?

Tip

➤ Think about the documents you have seen in this unit (texts, videos, images...).

➤ Fiche de méthodologie N°20 p. 300 Expression écrite

Pour l'épreuve

Questions	Évaluation
Fiche modifiable	Grille à imprimer
hatier-clic.fr/lmu1154	hatier-clic.fr/lmu1155

ÉPREUVE 2

EXPRESSION ÉCRITE

SUJET 1 Write an open letter to the NYPD denouncing the situation of black Americans and explaining the Black Lives Matter movement.

OU

SUJET 2 Do you think Martin Luther King Jr.'s dream is still possible today in America?

✦ Drinking fountain in use in the south of the USA before the end of segregation.

Tips

➤ Highlight the key words in the instructions.

➤ Read the unit again and complete your notes about the situation of black Americans in the USA and the Black Lives Matter movement.

➤ Fiche de méthodologie N°20 p. 300 Expression écrite

COMPRÉHENSION ÉCRITE

The #BlackLivesMatter Movement: Marches And Tweets For Healing[1]

In 2013, after George Zimmerman was acquitted for killing 17-year-old Trayvon Martin, a young woman in California named Alicia Garza wrote an emotional Facebook post that ended with the words "Our Lives Matter, Black Lives Matter." Her friend, Patrisse Cullors, turned that into a hashtag.

"I was devastated," Cullors says. "Honestly I think it was my naivete, but I really believed that George Zimmerman was going to be found guilty of something." She turned to social media to try to understand what was happening, and found Garza's "love note to black people." The three words 'Black Lives Matter' "hit me in the gut," she remembers. "I put a hashtag on it because it just felt so necessary to archive it." That developed into street protests and online organizing. As Cullors told her friend they should use it "to develop a new narrative around what it means to believe and fight for black life in this moment."

"Black Lives Matter reminds people that black people are human, but more importantly, it reminds black people that we are human," she says.

On becoming an activist

By the time I was 23, my brother and my father that raised me had spent most of their life in prison or jail because of the war on drugs. And I knew that the system didn't actually care to rehabilitate black communities, but rather the use of jail was really what Michelle Alexander calls it: "The New Jim Crow[2]." So for me, I had no choice but to be an organizer. I had no choice but to be an activist. It was the only way I could feel some resolve. For me, the choice is about either turning my eyes towards the violence happening in my community, turning my eyes away from it, or dealing with it head on. And people who know me well know that I deal with issues head on. And so that's why I say I didn't have a choice.

On whether #BlackLivesMatter has been healing

I appreciate you using the word healing, because I think sometimes that word is overused. But I think healing is actually an important piece of this conversation because what...black communities go through — especially poor black communities and poor communities in general — is a significant amount of trauma. To not be able to feed your children is traumatic. To witness people being kidnapped from their community, put in cars and handcuffed, you know, at 12, 13-years-old is traumatic. To witness people receive life sentences in prison is traumatic. And so if there's no sense of healing, if there's no way out of that, I think that leads to a significant amount of apathy in our communities, and so Black Lives Matter has created a track towards healing.

On what success might look like

I think the victory that people are actually looking at police killing black people is huge. Fifteen years ago, no one cared if police were killing black people. I mean that just wasn't newsworthy[3]... The media wasn't making this an issue, and the fact that it's now a real live conversation is a huge success. At some point there may be some national legislative goals. Right now, that's not where we're at but that's okay to me. Because right now Black Lives Matter has 26 chapters across the country, and two chapters outside of our country — one in Ghana, one in Toronto. People are organizing, and any good organizer understands that organizing takes years to develop someone, to develop thought leadership.

On being a "leader-full" — not a leaderless — movement

It's important to us in the Black Lives Matter movement that... we're not following an individual, right? This is a leader-full movement. I don't believe you can do anything without leadership. I don't believe that at all. I think there are many people leading this conversation, advancing this conversation...There [are] groups on the ground that have been doing this work, and I think we stand on the shoulders of those folks[4].

✦ *The #BlackLivesMatter Movement: Marches And Tweets For Healing*, *NPR*, June 9, 2015

1. recover 2. For author Michelle Alexander, systemic discrimination still continues in a hidden way depriving black Americans of their rights as the Jim Crow Laws. 3. important enough to be on the news / media 4. people

Tips

➤ Make sure you know who is quoted ("...").
➤ Underline key words using different colours.

➤ Fiche de méthodologie N°16 p. 292 Compréhension écrite

Pour l'épreuve

Questions — Fiche modifiable — hatier-clic.fr/lmu1156

Évaluation — Grille à imprimer — hatier-clic.fr/lmu1157

BAC in sight

ÉPREUVE 1

COMPRÉHENSION ORALE

Audio
CD2 piste 36

Listen to experts in British cinema discuss kitchen-sink realism.

✦ *My Beautiful Laundrette*, dir. by Stephen Frears, 1985

Tips
- ➤ Read the introduction and look at the film poster to guess what the recording will be about.
- ➤ Note down when someone is speaking (man #1, man #2).

➤ **Fiche de méthodologie N°15 p. 290** Compréhension orale

EXPRESSION ÉCRITE

SUJET 1 Write an article explaining the role of social realist cinema in the UK and what its limits could be.

OU

SUJET 2 Can social realist cinema change society for the better?

Tips
- ➤ Find examples and arguments in the documents you have studied in class.
- ➤ Use particular scenes to make your point.

➤ **Fiche de méthodologie N°20 p. 300** Expression écrite

Pour l'épreuve

Questions
Fiche modifiable
hatier-clic.fr/lmu1158

Évaluation
Grille à imprimer
hatier-clic.fr/lmu1159

ÉPREUVE 2

EXPRESSION ÉCRITE

SUJET 1 You are interviewing one of the directors mentioned in the article. Imagine the questions and answers about how their films reflect British society, about their inspiration and motivation.

OU

SUJET 2 According to you, what are the aims of British social realist films? Can they change British society for the better?

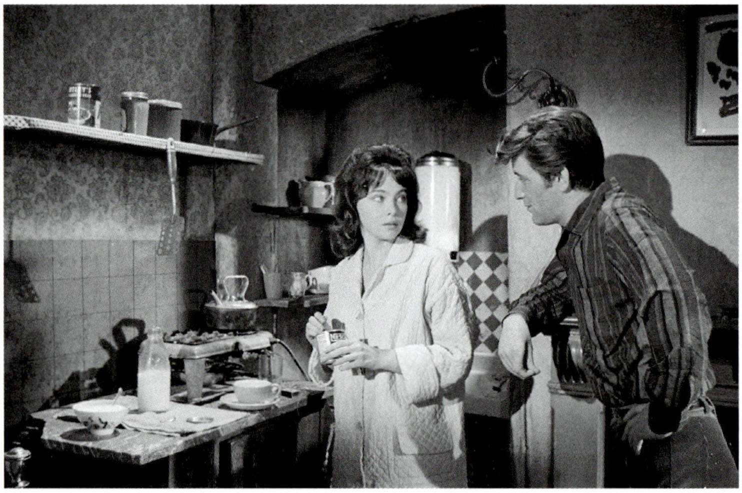
✦ *The L-Shaped Room*, dir. by Bryan Forbes, 1962

Tips
- ➤ Make sure your questions have an auxiliary verb.
- ➤ Use examples taken from kitchen-sink films.

➤ **Fiche de méthodologie N°20 p. 300** Expression écrite

COMPRÉHENSION ÉCRITE

An Introduction To British Social Realist Directors

Socially driven British directors are renowned for their interrogation of issues of poverty, race, and class in the UK's divided society. Ken Loach, Stephen Frears, and Shane Meadows are among the directors who have relentlessly examined injustice and inequality in their films.

The 2013 Venice Film Festival saw the Best Screenplay prize awarded to *Philomena*, the most recent work from lauded[1] British director Stephen Frears. It tells the true story of Philomena Lee, an unmarried woman in Ireland whose baby the Catholic Church sold for adoption in the 1950s. [...]

British cinema is well known for revealing the ugly underbelly[2] of society and being unafraid to criticise it. Such films are offered as a counterintuitive brand of Made in Britain patriotism. A combination of pride and shame, they champion the extraordinariness of ordinary people struggling in impossible circumstances. Character-driven and unpolished, they are a project in the humanisation of those individuals whose faces have been obscured by prejudice in contemporary Britain.

The young working class feature prominently in the narratives of many of these films, led by Ken Loach's example in the iconic *Kes*, a film that won critical acclaim at the time of its release in 1969 and exerts its influence on the British cinema scene to this day. [...] Whilst being sympathetic to his characters, Loach does not skirt around[3] the very real problem of violence in their communities — indeed, his depictions of this violence are brutal and unflinching[4]. Nor does he claim his protagonists' innocence. Rather, he places them, and by proxy[5] their actions, in the context of a particular social and political environment, in which the cycles of violence and poverty are a fact of everyday life.

In 2006, director Shane Meadows released what would become compulsory viewing for anyone looking to better understand the cultural history of modern-day England. *This is England* takes place in the early 1980s, in the midst of rapid deindustrialisation and in the aftermath of the Falklands War. [...] Indeed, for Meadows, *This is England* is a form of historical documentation, a means of capturing the country at a particularly tumultuous moment, according not to those who write history, but those who experienced it.

✦ *Kes*, dir. by Ken Loach, 1969

Britain's struggles with change and difference have also been well-documented by Stephen Frears in his earlier films. *My Beautiful Laundrette*, released in 1985, is the tale of Omar, a young, second-generation Pakistani man, navigating the new economic landscape of Thatcher's reforms, clashing with the growing resentment of British nationalists and discovering what it means to be gay in 1980s Britain. Frears also seems to ask the question: what does it mean to be English? He holds that it is not as simple as residing on one side of an ethnic rift[6].

[...] Here, Frears depicts the complexity at the root of British society in the 1980s, elucidating the divide not only between colour, but also between class.

The cultural touchstones[7] of British cinema rarely paint a pretty picture. They are political statements and artistic renderings of a country still struggling with class inequality and racial tension. [...]

✦ theculturetrip.com, January 7, 2017

1. acclaimed 2. hidden side of something 3. avoid 4. uncompromising 5. by extension 6. gap 7. standards

Tips

➤ Link the dates to particular events.

➤ List the film titles mentioned in the article.

➤ Fiche de méthodologie N°16 p. 292 Compréhension écrite

Pour l'épreuve

Questions — Fiche modifiable — hatier-clic.fr/lmu1160

Évaluation — Grille à imprimer — hatier-clic.fr/lmu1161

AXE 8

Territory and memory

Territoire et mémoire

SÉQUENCE 1

How strong is the UK's link with its overseas territories?

Projects

Project #1: Make a video promoting one of the BOTs to win a competition set up by the tourism agency VisitBritain.

Project #2: Following an article on BBC News, exchange a few tweets about the independence of British Overseas Territories.

Tools

Grammaire	le présent, le *present perfect*
Phonologie	la prononciation du *o*
Écriture	l'écriture sur les réseaux sociaux
Vocabulaire	les atouts, les relations

SÉQUENCE 2

How is slavery commemorated in the English-speaking world?

Projects

Project #1: Give a speech to convince the citizens of Liverpool to place a monument commemorating slavery in the main square.

Project #2: Songwriting contest: write the lyrics of a new song commemorating slavery.

Tools

Grammaire	les verbes d'état, les auxiliaires contractés
Phonologie	les préfixes et suffixes prononcés /ə/
Écriture	le doublement des consonnes
Vocabulaire	l'esclavage, les commémorations

#geography #nationalterritory

#history

#collectiveheritage #frontier

Port Lockroy on Wiencke Island, part of the British Antarctic Territory

#commemoration #placesofmemory

#history

#collectiveheritage #emblematiccharacters

Legacy, mural created by Josh Sarantitis and Eric Okdeh with the collaboration of school students, Philadelphia, Pennsylvania, 2016

SÉQUENCE 1

How strong is the UK's link with its overseas territories?

A The end of the British Empire

The rise and fall of the British Empire

Queen Elizabeth will officially become the longest serving monarch in British history this week, beating out her great-great-grandmother Queen Victoria to take the title. During her almost 64-year-long reign, the queen has seen a remarkable amount of change in the world, but perhaps no change has greater affected her life than the remarkable decline of the British Empire.

When Elizabeth was crowned in 1952, Britain still had a real empire, with more than 70 overseas[1] territories. Even then, however, it was clear that the situation could not last. India, often declared "the jewel[2] in the crown" for the Empire, had won its independence just five years before. In 1952, British troops were fighting independence movements in Egypt and Kenya. They would go on to lose both, and many others.

By 1979, the British Empire was reduced to a few pockets around the world. The shrinking[3] didn't stop, however. When Hong Kong was transferred to China in 1997, Queen Elizabeth's son Prince Charles himself dubbed[4] it the "end of the Empire." In 2015, Britain has 14 overseas territories left. Outside of Britain's land in the Antarctic, which is vast but mostly unpopulated, the largest remaining British overseas territory is the Falkland Islands. At 4,700 square miles, the islands are a little smaller than Connecticut.

It's a far cry from[5] the days when the sun never set[6] on the Empire: In 1921, at the empire's peak, the British ruled around a quarter of the land on Earth.

✦ Adam Taylor, *The rise and fall of the British Empire*, *The Washington Post*, September 8, 2015

1. across an ocean 2. ornament 3. reduction 4. called 5. a big difference 6. went down

✦ The Queen visiting Bermuda in 2009

1 Using the caption, comment on the photograph.

2 Read the text. Pick out information about Queen Elizabeth and Queen Victoria.

3 Draw a timeline with the following dates and note down what each date corresponds to.

1921 - 1947 - 1952 - 1979 - 1997 - 2015

4 Write an entry about the evolution of the British Empire for the encyclopedia published on your school's intranet.

Word Spot

wildlife /waɪldlaɪf/
destination
tax evasion
oil /ɔɪl/ : (*here*) petrol
asset: sth valuable
located: situated
scattered: disseminated
renowned for: famous for
strategic
belong to: be included in
possess: own
gain independence from
remain: subsist
enable to: allow to
under the sovereignty: under the domination

Grammar Spot

Present perfect Tools → p. 188

"the queen **has seen** a remarkable amount of change in the world."

B A trip to the BOTs

Classe inversée

✦ *Overwiew of Britain's Treasure Islands*, Warehouse Productions 51, 2016

Vidéo
DVD
hatier-clic.fr/lmu1162

E-workbook
Classe inversée
hatier-clic.fr/lmu1163

1 Pick out the places mentioned. Which adjective is repeated several times?

2 List all the unique characteristics of those territories. Use them to write a short description of those places.

3 Tell a friend what you have discovered about the BOTs and convince him or her to visit one of those territories.

C Major assets

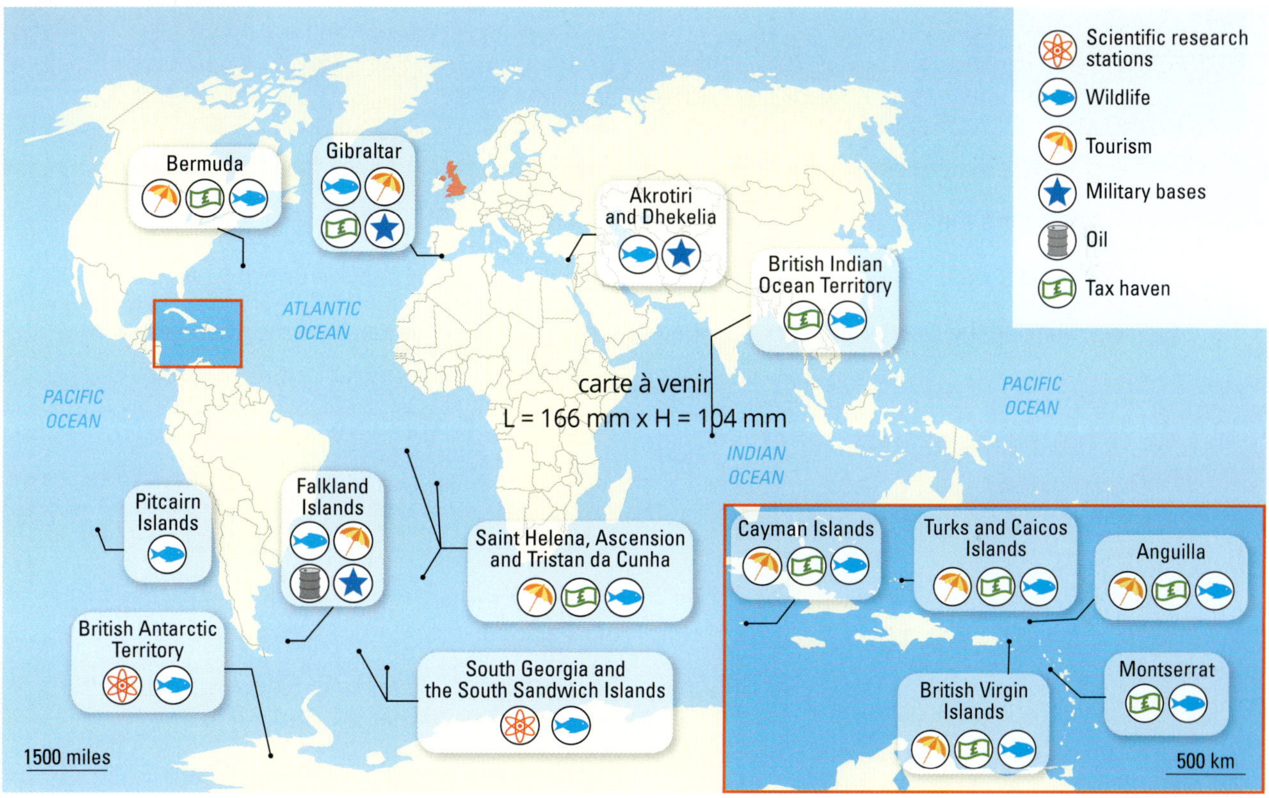

✦ The 14 overseas territories that are still British.

1 Read the map. Find out which characteristic is common to all the British Overseas Territories and explain how it is linked to two other categories.

2 Pick out the three characteristics that make some BOTs economic assets for the UK.

3 Find out which BOTs are military bases and imagine how this can be an asset for the UK.

4 Tell your geography teacher what you have learned about BOTs and explain how they are assets for the UK.

Prepare your project

Make a one-minute podcast about some British Overseas Territories.

Grammar Tip Précis → p. 225

To refer to the territories, use **quantifiers**: **a few**, **some**, **many**, **most**...

Memory Challenge

In 10 seconds, name five British Overseas Territories.

D A complex relationship

✦ "Decision March" against a law imposed by the UK to fight tax evasion, British Virgin Islands, May 24, 2018.

1 Read the caption, then describe and comment on the photograph.

2 Explain what it shows about the relationship between the UK and the British Virgin Islands.

3 Imagine the tweet written by the photographer when he or she posted the photograph.

E The Falklands War

Vidéo DVD

E-workbook Fiche à imprimer hatier-clic.fr/lmu1164

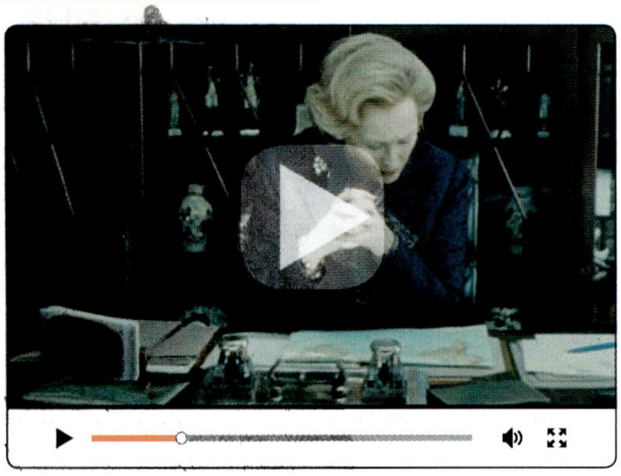

✦ *The Iron Lady*, dir. by Phyllida Lloyd, 2011

1 Watch the video and read the Culture Tip. Explain the situation.

2 Describe Prime Minister Margaret Thatcher's reaction. Sum up what she decided to do.

3 Try to explain to your classmates why Margaret Thatcher was called the "Iron Lady".

Culture Tip

The **Falklands Islands** have been British since 1833, but Argentina claims them as part of its territory. This led to the Falklands War in 1982.

Grammar Spot

Present simple TOOLS → p. 188

"The Falklands **belong** to Britain."

Word Spot

supplies /səplaɪz/
shelter: safe place
iron: (hard) metal
idyllic /ɪdɪlɪk/, perfect
inconceivable: unthinkable
diplomatic
stubborn: opposed to change or suggestion
firm
regret: deplore
warn sb: alert sb
respond to
devastate
rescue: aid: provide assistance
demonstrate: protest
blame sb for sth: accuse
resent: be angry for sth unfair
refuse /rɪfjuːz/
take action: take measures
order sb to + V
sever /sevəʳ/ ties with: end a connection with

F Blaming mainland Britain

The UK Government's response to Hurricane Irma in British overseas territories has been branded[1] "absolutely pathetic."

Dorothea Hodge, the former UK EU representative for the government of the Caribbean island of Anguilla, said the UK should invest in long-term reconstruction to help the island community.

She told *The Guardian*: "It's absolutely disgraceful that it has taken the whole day for Priti Patel to respond to the worst hurricane we have seen in a British territory since the 1920s."

Ms Patel said she had deployed three UK humanitarian experts and a British naval vessel with 40 Royal Marines and army engineers to the region.

Ms Hodge added: "Anguillans are all British nationals, as British as the Falklands or Gibraltar.

"In comparison to the French president who has set up an emergency fund, an emergency hotline and a reconstruction fund, her response after the storm has passed is absolutely pathetic."

Her comments were echoed by Anguilla resident Josephine Gumbs-Connor, a barrister[2], who was also critical of the UK's response to the hurricane.

Ms Gumbs-Connor told BBC Radio 4's *Today* programme: "I anticipated really that, given our relationship with the UK, they would have done in a similar fashion[3] to our French neighbours on St Martin, where the French made sure they had military on the ground so the response given is timely, which makes it effective, which makes it helpful to our people.

"That is sorely[4] lacking in this case. There was no echoing of chainsaws[5] in Anguilla. We have huge trees and some of our oldest trees are still lying across the roads, roads are remaining impassable.

"While we understand that these things take time, I am very disappointed. We are supposed to have a relationship - we are overseas territories, we are supposed to be of the same type of people as Gibraltar or the Falkland Islands."

She said: "I am truly disappointed because we should not be in this position. If we are indeed supposed to be in a partnership, it should work very much more effectively than it is now." [...] [Ms Hodge] told *The Guardian*: "What is needed now is a commitment to an immediate effective humanitarian, response, food, water, shelter, emergency health care, and a long-term reconstruction fund to get the island back on its feet after this battering."

1. judged 2. lawyer 3. the same 4. badly 5. used for cutting trees

✦ Samuel Osborne, *Irma: Caribbean overseas territories condemn UK Government's 'disgraceful' lack of help as Hurricane wreaks devastation, The Independent*, Sept 7, 2017

Pédagogie différenciée

TRAIL A

1 Find out what the UK did to help Anguilla and what France did for St Martin. Conclude who provided better help.

2 Pick out the two adjectives Anguillans used to qualify both the UK's response to the hurricane and how they felt.

3 Study Ms Hodge and Ms Gumbs-Connor's quotes. Pick out words that express what Anguillans are expecting from the UK.

TRAIL B

1 Compare the way the UK and France helped their overseas territories.

2 Describe the Anguillan population's feeling toward the UK's response to the hurricane.

3 Explain what the Anguillans would like to have from the UK in terms of relationship and direct aids.

Meet up! Ms Gumbs-Connor phones her niece to enquire about the situation in St Martin and they talk about the aid each island received.

Prepare your project

PAIR WORK A BOT has just been victim of a natural disaster. Two friends exchange short messages on WhatsApp.

Student A You live in this BOT and you are disappointed with the reaction of the British government.

Student B You are his or her best friend living in Liverpool.

Grammar Tip Précis → p. 236

To express your disappointment, use **modals** like: **should have + past participle, could have + past participle**.

Memory Challenge

You have 30 seconds to list three things that people from the British Overseas Territories could reproach the UK government with.

Entraînez-vous sur la plateforme *Let's Meet Up!*
reussirenlangues.fr

Practise your grammar

Précis grammatical, p. 216

Le présent simple

• Le présent simple est formé à partir de la base verbale, à laquelle on ajoute ***s*** à la 3e personne du singulier. Il correspond à une **habitude**, une **situation permanente** ou à une **vérité générale**.

*He **works** in Bermuda, but his parents **live** in Britain.*

*The Falklands **belong** to Britain.*

• Étant donné que le présent simple est employé pour des **événements** ou des **faits généraux**, on trouve souvent le présent simple avec des marqueurs temporels génériques tels que ***usually, generally*** ou les marqueurs de fréquence tels que ***sometimes, often, always*** ou ***hardely ever***.

*Queen Elizabeth II often **visits** the British Overseas Territories.*

• À la forme négative et interrogative, on a recours à l'auxiliaire ***do / does*** au présent simple.

*They **don't work** in Montreal.*

***Does** this history professor **teach** the decolonisation of the British Empire?*

1 Choisissez le bon adverbe de fréquence ou groupe adverbial.

a. All the British Overseas Territories ... offer a great variety of wildlife. (**always / currently**)

b. They are building a hotel on the Cayman Islands ... . (**often / at the moment**)

c. The Cayman Islands ... represent a tax haven for multinationals. (**often / now**)

d. These four British tourists are ... visiting Montserrat's Soufrière Hills volcano. (**regularly / currently**)

2 Complétez par le présent simple ou le présent en *be* + V-*ing*.

a. The Falkland Islands ... (consist) of two main islands off the east coast of southern South America.

b. She ... (do) a safari in Kenya at the moment.

c. Unfortunately, Queen Elizabeth ... (address) the issues of the British Overseas Territories quickly enough.

d. They ... (teach) the lives of the two longest serving queens in British history every year.

e. ... Hong Kong (belong) to the United Kingdom?

Le *present perfect*

• Le ***present perfect*** est composé de l'auxiliaire ***have***, suivi du participe passé du verbe. ***Has*** correspond à la forme de la 3e personne au singulier.

• Le présent est un temps chronologique, alors que le ***present perfect*** est un **aspect**, c'est-à-dire un point de vue sur un événement. Il correspond à un **bilan** d'une action passée fait par la personne qui s'exprime dans le présent.
Le ***present perfect*** est donc à cheval entre le passé et le présent, et souligne que l'action passée a des **conséquences** dans le présent : c'est pourquoi le ***present perfect*** est parfaitement adapté pour parler d'**expériences vécues** jusqu' ici.

*The queen **has seen** a remarkable amount of change in the world, but perhaps no change **has** greater **affected** her life than the remarkable decline of the British Empire.*

3 Indiquez la bonne réponse.

a. The British Virgin Islands (**have always been / were always**) famous for their splendid sandy beaches.

b. In 2018, she (**has conducted / conducted**) some research into the Pitcairn Islands in the Pacific Ocean.

c. India, the jewel in the crown, (**has become / became**) independent in 1947.

d. Queen Elizabeth II (**has seen / saw**) the decline of the British Empire.

e. She (**has come / came**) to the throne back in 1952.

4 Complétez par le *present perfect* ou le prétérit.

a. Queen Victoria ... (be) Queen of the United Kingdom of Great Britain and Ireland from 1837 to 1901, so for 64 years!

b. Queen Elizabeth II ... (be) Britain's Queen since 1952.

c. The Falkland Islands ... (belong) to Britain since 1833.

d. She ... (take) advantage of her trip to Saint Martin to go to Anguilla.

Improve your pronunciation

Précis de phonologie, p. 262

La prononciation du *o*

Audio
CD2 piste 37
MP3 n° 117

La voyelle ***o*** peut correspondre à plusieurs sons différents.

- /ə/ : *pension, territory, colony*
- /ʌ/ : *son, coming, encouraged, government*
- /uː/ : *soon*
- /ɔː/ : *door, thought, Georgia*
- /ɒ/ : *not, monarchy, Montserrat, volcano, colony*
- /ɜː/ : *world*
- /əʊ/ : *know, go, ocean, volcano, overseas*
- /aʊ/ : *crown, power*

5 **Écoutez les mots suivants et classez-les en fonction de la prononciation de la voyelle *o*, puis vérifiez avec l'enregistrement.**

Audio
CD2 piste 38
MP3 n° 118

London • monarch • remote • Victoria • world • sovereign • colonialism • lose • government

6 **Indiquez le son correspondant à la graphie *o* des phrases suivantes, puis répétez après l'enregistrement pour vérifier.**

Audio
CD2 piste 39
MP3 n° 119

a. Some territories of the British Crown are quite remote.
b. Victoria Station in London pays tribute to Queen Victoria.
c. Can the world get rid of colonialism?
d. The government has lost too much of its power.

Work on your writing skills

L'écriture sur les réseaux sociaux

Écrire en ligne pour communiquer des informations importantes, échanger des points de vue, apporter sa contribution à un groupe requiert certaines règles.

TIP Pensez : BEP ! Brièveté - Essentiel - Pertinence !

Chaque réseau social présente ses propres règles d'usage.

- Pour **Twitter**, il faut écrire 280 caractères maximum, utiliser un hashtag (#) significatif pour les mots-clés, @ pour mentionner un·e utilisateur·rice et ajouter éventuellement une photo. Après # et @, on ne met pas d'espace entre les mots.

JEFF DO
@jeffdo
#IsupportBritishGibraltar! Join us!
♥ 10 8:25 PM - November 7, 2002

- Pour **Instagram**, choisissez bien vos mots-clés et utilisez **#**. Publiez votre contenu sans dépasser 2200 caractères et postez vos photos, vidéos, ou stories. Attention, les hashtags rendent la photo publique même si le compte est privé !

- Pour **YouTube**, avant de poster votre vidéo, écrivez une description pour résumer et ajoutez des **tags**, c'est-à-dire des mots-clés, pour qu'elle soit bien répertoriée sur YouTube ou les moteurs de recherche. Par exemple : « BOT », « British », « territories ».

7 **Hillary ne sait pas bien tweeter, aidez-la à corriger son tweet et à le rendre plus efficace.**

HILLARY
@hillarysmithy
Dear followers,
Fancy a once-in-a-lifetime experience?
Go swimming or snorkelling with stingrays, observe turtles, exotic tropical species ...
Enjoy the rich marine environment of @ British Overseas Territories!
#Hillary Smithy
♥ 0 9:55 PM - March 22, 2019

8 **Vous postez une photo de vos vacances en Territoire antarctique britannique (p. 183) sur Instagram. Écrivez la légende de la photo en respectant les codes d'Instagram.**

Build up your vocabulary

Audio
CD2 piste 40

British Overseas Territories

Negative feelings MP3 n°120

resentment: anger for sth unfair
disappointment
unthinkable
disgraceful
blame sb for sth: accuse, criticise
regret: deplore
resent: be angry for sth unfair

Overseas territories MP3 n°124

resources
colony
idyllic /ɪdɪlɪk/: perfect
located: situated
scattered: disseminated
belong to: be included in
possess: own
remain: subsist
rule over
gain independence from
under the sovereignty: under the domination

Support MP3 n°121

reconstruction
hurricane /hʌrɪkeɪn/
supplies /səplaɪz/
pathetic
effective ≠ ineffective
late ≠ timely
appropriate
helpful
deploy
devastate
order sb to + V
rescue /reskjuː/: aid: provide assistance
take measures: take action: take steps

Assets MP3 n°123

destination
military base
power
oil /ɔɪl/: (*here*) petrol
scientific research stations
tax evasion
tourism
wildlife /waɪldlaɪf/
strategic
renowned for: famous for
enable to: allow /əlaʊ/ to

Relationship MP3 n°122

war
island community
trust
commitment
partnership
demonstrate
protest
refuse /rɪfjuːz/
respond to
sever /sevəʳ/ ties with: end a connection with
warn sb: alert sb

Apprenez et révisez le vocabulaire !

Utilisez Quizlet pour vous entraîner en vous amusant.

Quizlet
hatier-clic.fr/lmu1165

Utilisez le vocabulaire en contexte.

1 Complétez les phrases suivantes avec des mots de la carte mentale.

a. British Overseas Territories are territories ... ... of the UK and are ... all over the globe.
b. They are ... ... their remarkable ... and biodiversity.
c. Anguillans ... the British government ... its pathetic response to Hurricane Irma.
d. Some inhabitants in the British Virgin Islands want to ... ... the UK.
e. The British have established ... ... and ... ... in some of their overseas territories.

2 Écrivez un post sur Instagram avec les traductions anglaises des mots suivants pour convaincre vos abonné·e·s de visiter les territoires britanniques d'outre-mer.

appartenir à | tourisme | base scientifique | être connu pour | idyllique | permettre de

AUTO évaluation

Faites le quiz interactif en ligne et suivez les conseils pour vous préparer à l'évaluation.

Quiz
hatier-clic.fr/lmu1166

Project #1

Make a video promoting one of the BOTs to win a competition set up by the tourism agency VisitBritain.

1 **Prepare the introduction of your video.**
- ✓ Choose a territory.
- ✓ Explain why you have chosen to promote this territory.

2 **Find at least four arguments to show why people should go and visit your territory.**
- ✓ Look for information in the unit or on the internet.
- ✓ Take notes about all the arguments you could use (about five words for each argument).
- ✓ Select your four best arguments.
- ✓ Use expressions to convince or to give advice.
  You should + V…
  Why not + V…
  I advise you to + V…
  If I were you, I would + V…

3 **Prepare your speech.**
- ✓ Organise your ideas using linking words: **firstly, secondly, in addition, similarly, moreover, that's why, as a result…**
- ✓ Give examples: **for example, for instance…**

4 **Think about a good conclusion.**
- ✓ Conclude explaining why, as a British citizen, you are proud of the Overseas Territories.
- ✓ Start your conclusion with: **Finally… In conclusion… To conclude…**

5 **Practise and record your video!**
- ✓ Check the pronunciation of difficult words on an online dictionary.
- ✓ Speak from your notes with enthusiasm.

Fiche de méthodologie N°11 p. 284

Project #2

Following an article on BBC news, exchange tweets about the independence of British Overseas Territories.

1 **Choose which role you want.**
- ✓ **Student A:** You support independence and you want the British government to stop legislating for your island.
- ✓ **Student B:** You are British and proud of your heritage and you think that the UK territories should remain British.

2 **Think about the arguments you will use.**
- ✓ Go through the unit and take notes about all the arguments you could use to defend your point of view (heritage, asset, diversity, end of colonialism…).

3 **Try to guess what the arguments of your opponent could be to prepare your next post.**
- ✓ Prepare expressions of agreement, disagreement and opinion.
  Quite right, but… You may be right but… I don't agree… I strongly believe that…

4 **Write your tweets!**
- ✓ Read your arguments again to be reactive to your opponent's message.
- ✓ Adapt your tweets to his or her messages.
- ✓ Use short sentences and words with hashtags.

Fiche de méthodologie N°19 p. 298

SÉQUENCE 2

How is slavery commemo-rated in the world?

A What's Juneteenth?

As the Civil War came to a close in 1865, a number of people remained enslaved, especially in remote areas. Word of slavery's end traveled slowly[1], and for those who were largely isolated from Union armies, life continued as if freedom did not exist. This was especially the case in Texas, where thousands of slaves were not made aware of freedom until June 19, 1865, when Union Gen. Gordon Granger arrived in Galveston and issued an order officially freeing them. Their celebration would serve as the basis of June 19 — or Juneteenth — a holiday celebrating emancipation in the US.

Ironically, while Juneteenth has become the most prominent Emancipation Day holiday in the US, it commemorates a smaller moment that remains relatively obscure. It doesn't mark the signing of the 1863 Emancipation Proclamation, which technically freed slaves in the rebelling Confederate States, nor does it commemorate the December 1865 ratification of the 13th Amendment, which enshrined[2] the end of slavery into the Constitution. Instead, it marks the moment when emancipation finally reached those in the deepest parts of the former Confederacy.

In many ways, Juneteenth represents how freedom and justice in the US has always been delayed for black people. [...]

"There are those in this society that still hold on to[3] the idea that the Civil War wasn't about slavery, it was about states' rights or Northern aggression against slavery," says Karlos Hill, a professor of African and African-American studies at the University of Oklahoma and the author of *Beyond the Rope: The Impact of Lynching on Black Culture and Memory*. "Juneteenth is a moment where we step back[4] and try to understand the Civil War through the eyes of enslaved people."

I spoke with Hill recently about the history of Juneteenth, why the push[5] to make it a national holiday matters, and how commemorating the holiday could bring America closer to truly embracing its ideals of freedom and equality for all.

✦ P.R. Lockhart, *Why celebrating Juneteenth is more important now than ever, Vox*, June 19, 2018

1. It took Southerners a long time to know slavery was over.
2. enclosed 3. continue to believe 4. stop and think 5. effort

1 Draw a timeline showing these three dates and write a legend for each date.

1863 - June 19th 1865 - December 1865

2 Explain why the commemoration of Juneteenth is important for Americans.

3 Record a short presentation of Juneteenth for a museum audioguide.

Culture Tip

1861-1865: The American Civil War opposed the United States to 11 southern states that seceded from the Union and formed the Confederate States of America, also known as "the Confederacy".
January 1, 1863: President Lincoln issued the Emancipation Proclamation. More than 3.5 million enslaved African Americans were freed.
December 6, 1865: The 13th Amendment to the Constitution abolished slavery and involuntary servitude.

Word Spot

transatlantic slave trade
ordeal: misery
emancipation
remembrance
commemoration
state holiday
legacy: heritage
worthy of: deserving
honoured: recognised
enslave: enchain
abolish: stop
celebrate
commemorate: pay tribute to
honour /ɒnə^{r}/ sb's memory
gather: bring together
transmit: pass on

Grammar Spot

State verbs TOOLS → p. 196
"a number of people **remained** enslaved"

B Celebrating Juneteenth

Classe inversée

✦ A Juneteenth parade in Harlem, New York City, June 19, 2010

Vidéo hatier-clic.fr/lmu1167

E-workbook Classe inversée hatier-clic.fr/lmu1168

1 Explain what event is taking place in the photo above.

2 Watch the video. Pick out the name of the city, the event and the number of people.

3 Find keywords and use them to explain how the African American community celebrates this event.

4 You are a journalist. Write a tweet to describe the event.

C A symbolic memorial

Vidéo hatier-clic.fr/lmu1169

E-workbook Fiche à imprimer hatier-clic.fr/lmu1170

✦ Rodney Leon, *The Ark of Return*, New York City, 2015

1 Find out what *The Ark of Return* represents.

2 Say where the architect drew his inspiration from.

3 Explain the meaning of this memorial to a group of tourists.

Prepare your project

Deliver a short speech on Juneteenth about the importance of commemorating slavery. Give examples of what can be done to remember the past.

Grammar Tip Précis → p. 237

Use **must**, and its equivalent **have to**, to express obligation.
Use **should** to give advice.

Memory Challenge

In groups, find words relating to Juneteenth. The first group to reach 10 words wins.

D Slavery Remembrance Day

Audio
CD2 piste 41

In this recording, a few students from Liverpool are speaking about Slavery Remembrance Day. They are visiting the International Slavery Museum in Liverpool.

Pédagogie différenciée

TRAIL A

1 Using the following words, say why Slavery Remembrance Day is important to the students interviewed.

benefit - trade - tragedy

2 Explain why the fact they are Liverpudlians makes them feel especially concerned.

3 Sum up the main lesson of this visit for the students.

Meet up! Write a five-line commentary on the visitors' book of the museum.

TRAIL B

1 Explain why Slavery Remembrance Day is important to the students interviewed.

2 Explain why they feel especially concerned.

3 Explain how the students link the past to the future.

Culture Tip

Slavery Remembrance Day is an international celebration held every year on August 23rd. It memorialises the transatlantic slave trade, which used the **triangular trade route** to transport enslaved African people to the Americas.

E Redemption Song

Old pirates, yes, they rob[1] I[2]
Sold I to the merchant ships
Minutes after they took I
From the bottomless pit[3]
But my hand was made strong
By the hand of the Almighty[4]
We forward in this generation
Triumphantly
Won't you help to sing
These songs of freedom?
'Cause all I ever have
Redemption songs
Redemption songs
Emancipate yourselves from mental slavery
None but ourselves can free our minds [...]
Redemption songs
These songs of freedom
Songs of freedom

✦ Bob Marley, *Redemption Song*, 1980

1. steal 2. me 3. hole 4. God

1 Pick out elements linked to the slave trade.

2 Sum up the main message of the singer in this extract.

3 Imagine an alternative title to the song and explain your choice.

Grammar Spot

Short forms of auxiliaries Tool S → p. 196

"But it **isn't** just about the past, **it's** about the present."

Word Spot

duty of memory
testimony
abolitionist
redemption: reparation
unfair
emancipate ≠ imprison
realise
raise sb's awareness: make sb aware of
remind sbdy of: recall
immortalise
erect a statue
in memory of
formerly: in the past

F Memory for the slaves

✦ Clara Sornas, *Memory for the Slaves*, Stone Town, Zanzibar, United Republic of Tanzania

Culture Tip

Zanzibar is an archipelago situated in the Indian Ocean, off the coast of East Africa. It was one of the largest slave ports in the Indian Ocean. It gained independence from Britain in 1963.

1. Describe this document and explain why the statues have no lower parts.
2. Read the Culture Tip and explain why the artist chose to build this memorial in Zanzibar.
3. ***PAIR WORK*** Act out a short interview between a journalist and the artist about this memorial.

G A film about the abolition of slavery

Vidéo
DVD

Culture Tip

William Wilberforce (1759-1833) was a British politician who fought for the abolition of slavery until the Slavery Abolition Act was passed in 1833.

✦ *Amazing Grace*, dir. by Michael Apted, 2006

1. Pick out the figures and places given to explain where the Madagascar is back from.
2. Explain why the Members of Parliament stop enjoying the party.
3. ***PAIR WORK*** With your partner, discuss the message of the film on an online forum about British cinema.

Prepare your project

Write a four-line poem about the commemoration of slavery. Two lines must end in *-ion* and two lines must end in *-y*.

Grammar Tip Précis → p. 257

Use **to + V**, **in order to + V** or **so as to + V** to express your main objective

Memory Challenge

Use all the following words to explain how slavery is commemorated in the English-speaking world.

museum - song - memorial - film

Tools in the Spotlight

Entraînez-vous sur la plateforme ***Let's Meet Up!***
reussirenlangues.fr

Practise your grammar

Précis grammatical, p. 216

Les verbes d'état

- Ils expriment généralement :
  - une **opinion** : *think, believe, understand, know*
  - un **sentiment** : *like, dislike, hate, prefer*
  - l'**existence** : *exist, remain, be, seem, look*
- Les verbes d'état se conjuguent en général aux **temps simples** (présent ou prétérit simple).

*The mayor **seemed** to agree with Martin Luther King's non-violent methods.*

*A number of people **remained** enslaved.*

⚠ Certains verbes d'état peuvent se conjuguer au **présent** ou au **prétérit en** ***be*** **+ V-*ing***, s'il s'agit d'une perception volontaire ou d'un fait envisagé.

*She's **thinking** of creating a monument to commemorate slavery.*

- Certains verbes de **perception involontaire**, tels que *see, hear, smell* ou *taste*, font partie des verbes d'état.

*I **see** what you mean, but I prefer this painting.*

1 Indiquez la bonne réponse.

a. I (**imagine / am imagining**) that you will go to the exhibition on slavery.
b. The museums (**are seeming / seem**) to agree to give students a 20% discount.
c. Abraham Lincoln (**remained / was remaining**) famous worldwide, didn't he?
d. I (**am thinking / think**) of visiting the former slavery states in the south.

2 Complétez les phrases suivantes par les verbes *dislike*, *prefer*, *seem*, *smell* et *hear*.

a. I ... to visit the Deep South first if you don't mind.
b. The cellar ... bad because the museum guide has forgotten to open the door.
c. I can ... a noise over there. I'm so scared!
d. This commemoration site ... interesting.
e. They ... their trip to that place, so they decided to come back earlier than planned.

Les auxiliaires contractés

- À l'oral, et à l'écrit dans des textes informels, il est courant de contracter les auxiliaires *be*, *have* et *do*.

*But it **isn't** just about the past, **it's** about the present.*

- ***Be***

Au présent à la forme affirmative et négative :

is → ***'s***	*is not* → ***isn't***
are → ***'re***	*are not* → ***aren't***

Au passé à la forme négative : *was not* → ***wasn't***
were not → ***weren't***

- ***Have***

Au présent à la forme affirmative et négative :

has → ***'s***	*has not* → ***hasn't***
have → ***'ve***	*have not* → ***haven't***

Au passé à la forme affirmative et négative :

had → ***'d***	*had not* → ***hadn't***

- ***Do*** ne se contracte qu'à la forme négative.

Au présent : *does not* → ***doesn't*** *do not* → ***don't***
Au passé : *did not* → ***didn't***

3 Remplacez les auxiliaires *be*, *have* et *do* par des formes contractées.

a. It has become the most prominent Emancipation Day holiday in the USA.
b. Thousands of slaves were not made aware of freedom until June 19th 1865.
c. I was sure you did not remember the day when slavery was abolished.
d. The civil rights movement was not violent.
e. It is not urgent but you still have not booked the tickets for the exhibition!
f. He has not had good marks in history this semester so he does not want to become a historian anymore.

4 Écrivez les phrases suivantes avec la forme complète des auxiliaires.

a. It's been said that the end of slavery changed the situation of black people.
b. She isn't working on slavery, she's studying the civil rights movement.
c. They've forgotten the day when slavery was abolished.
d. There's a mistake in the TV programme — it's "Don't forget the past!" tonight.

Improve your pronunciation

Précis de phonologie, p. 262

Les préfixes et suffixes prononcés /ə/

Audio
CD2 piste 42
MP3 n° 125

• Un **préfixe** se place avant un mot pour former un mot de la même catégorie grammaticale. Certains préfixes sont des syllabes inaccentuées et comportent le **e muet**, /ə/ (le ***schwa***).

com- : *commemorate* /kə'mem.ə.reɪt/, *compress* /kəm'pres/

a- : *alike* /ə'laɪk/, *alive* /ə'laɪv/

• Un **suffixe** se place après un mot pour former un autre mot de la même famille. En règle générale, les suffixes ne sont pas accentués. Certains suffixes comportent le **e muet**.

-ion : *emancipation* /iˌmæn.sɪ'peɪ.ʃən/

-ial : *partial* /'pɑː.ʃəl/, *essential* /ɪ'sen.ʃəl/

-cian : *politician* /ˌpɒl.ɪ'tɪʃ.ən/, *musician* /mjuː'zɪʃ.ən/

-ous : *marvellous* /'mɑː.vəl.əs/

-ious : *gracious* /'greɪ.ʃəs/

-er : *driver* /'draɪ.vər/, *reporter* /rɪ'pɔː.tər/

-or : *instructor* /ɪn'strʌk.tər/, *conductor* /kən'dʌk.tər/

-less : *homeless* /'həʊm.ləs/, *hopeless* /'həʊp.ləs/

5 **Indiquez le son /ə/ correspondant aux préfixes ou suffixes des mots suivants, puis vérifiez avec l'enregistrement.**

Audio
CD2 piste 43
MP3 n° 126

childless • baker • magician • awake • communicate • debtor • cautious • impartial

6 **Indiquez le son /ə/ dans les phrases suivantes, puis vérifiez avec l'enregistrement.**

Audio
CD2 piste 44
MP3 n° 127

a. A lot of reporters have denounced slavery.
b. The mayor will commemorate the end of slavery next weekend.
c. Politicians need to take actions with regard to the commemoration of slavery.
d. However, the case of homeless people is hopeless as well, isn't it?

Work on your writing skills

Le doublement des consonnes

En anglais, lorsqu'un verbe ou un adjectif se termine par **consonne - voyelle - consonne**, on double la consonne finale si la syllabe est accentuée.

• **Verbes d'une syllabe** : *run* → *running*

The little boy was running with his dog, when he fell down.

• **Adjectifs d'une syllabe** : *hot* → *hotter*

It was getting hotter and hotter, which made it very difficult to work in the fields.

• **Verbes de deux syllabes ou plus** : *begin* → *beginning*

It was beginning to be difficult for slaves to remain hopeful.

• **Verbes terminés par une voyelle + la lettre *l*** :

En anglais britannique, lorsque le verbe se termine par une voyelle + la lettre *l*, on double le *l* : *travel* → *travelling.*

At that time, merchants kept travelling all around the world.

⚠ En anglais américain, on ne double pas le *l*.
Word of slavery's end traveled slowly.

7 **Complétez les phrases avec les verbes à la forme qui convient.**

a. The museum should commemorate slavery to prevent younger generations from (**forget**).
b. The transatlantic trade only (**stop**) with the end of slavery.
c. Singing and dancing used to be (**ban**) for slaves.
d. After (**travel**) to Africa, the teacher and his class understood the history of slavery more clearly.

8 **Rédigez un court discours prononcé lors de l'inauguration d'un mémorial de l'esclavage. Utilisez les verbes suivants, que vous conjuguerez au passé.**

stop • admit • prefer • plan • occur

Build up your vocabulary

Audio
CD2 piste 45

Slavery

Places of memory (MP3 n°128)

- architecture /ɑːkɪtektʃəʳ/
- monument
- museum
- sculpture
- mural /mjʊərəl/
- history memorial
- emblematic characters
- collective heritage
- inauguration
- historic
- symbolic
- be named after sb or sth
- erect a statue: build a statue /stætʃuː/
- in memory of

Celebrations (MP3 n°133)

- Juneteenth
- Slavery Remembrance Day
- day of remembrance
- state holiday
- celebrate

Commemoration (MP3 n°129)

- legacy: heritage
- duty of memory
- testimony
- honoured: recognised
- commemorate
- remember
- denounce /dɪnaʊns/
- gather: bring together
- pay tribute to: honour /ɒnər/
- honour sb's memory
- raise sb's awareness: make sb aware of sth
- realise
- remind sb of: recall
- transmit: pass on
- immortalise

The Confederacy (MP3 n°132)

- Civil /sɪvəl/ War
- Confederate States: the Confederacy
- Deep South
- emancipation
- involuntary servitude
- Union /juːnjən/ armies
- 13th Amendment
- former: previous
- enshrined /ɪnʃraɪnd/: preserved

Slave trade (MP3 n°131)

- Africa
- America
- Middle East
- the Caribbean
- Zanzibar
- archipelago /ɑːkɪpeləgəʊ/
- triangular trade route
- captor ≠ captive
- slave market
- slave port
- merchant ship
- ordeal: misery
- scourge: curse
- unfair
- rob: steal
- enslave: enchain

Abolition (MP3 n°130)

- abolitionist: person opposed to slavery
- Members of Parliament
- Slavery Abolition Act
- freedom ≠ servitude
- redemption: reparation
- free ≠ enslaved
- emancipate ≠ imprison
- abolish: stop

Apprenez et révisez le vocabulaire !

Utilisez Quizlet pour vous entraîner en vous amusant.

Quizlet
hatier-clic.fr/lmu1171

Utilisez le vocabulaire en contexte.

1 Complétez les phrases suivantes avec des mots de la carte mentale à la forme qui convient.

a. ... is the day that commemorates the emancipation of African American slaves in the Confederate States of America.
b. In the 19th century, many ... fought to end slavery.
c. It is important to ... the history of their country, so that they don't forget about it.
d. One of the largest ... ... in the Indian Ocean was Zanzibar.
e. The ... ... to the United States Constitution was ratified in 1865. It abolished slavery.
f. Many ... ... sailed from Liverpool and were used to carry slaves across the Atlantic.

2 Écrivez quelques phrases pour présenter les différentes façons de commémorer l'esclavage. Utilisez cinq mots de la catégorie *Places of memory* et cinq mots de la catégorie *Commemoration* de la carte mentale.

AUTO évaluation

Faites le quiz interactif en ligne et suivez les conseils pour vous préparer à l'évaluation.

Quiz
hatier-clic.fr/lmu1172

Project #1

Give a speech to convince the citizens of Liverpool to place a monument commemorating slavery in the main square.

1 Imagine the monument you have designed.

- ✓ Draw a sketch of your project or use the internet to find one with the following keywords: **commemorative + monument + slavery**.
- ✓ Find a name for your monument.

2 Prepare what you are going to say to convince your audience.

- ✓ Think about the symbolic meaning of your monument (shape, material, colour, symbols).
- ✓ List three arguments about the importance of having a memorial dedicated to slavery in Liverpool.

3 Organise your speech.

- ✓ Get ready to introduce yourself, show your sketch and describe your monument.
- ✓ Use linking words to present your arguments: **first**, **then**, **finally**...
- ✓ Make your speech convincing using expressions like: **I am certain that**, **surely**, **obviously**...

4 Practise and deliver your speech!

- ✓ Use wordreference.com to check the pronunciation of the words you don't know.
- ✓ Practise your speech in front of a friend.
- ✓ To be convincing, try not to read your notes and make eye contact with the audience.

Fiche de méthodologie N°18 p. 296

Project #2

Songwriting contest: write the lyrics of a new song commemorating slavery.

1 Think about what you want to say about slavery.

- ✓ Review the documents of the unit and search the internet if you need more ideas. You can check these websites for example: http://bit.ly/1L7LtsS, http://bit.ly/UtgPoU.
- ✓ Organise all the words and ideas you will use in your song. You can make a mind map.

2 Choose a song structure.

- ✓ You can write two verses and one chorus and organise them the following way:

  VERSE - CHORUS - VERSE - CHORUS
- ✓ If you want to use rhymes, decide how to place them: **A - B - A - B** or **A - A - B - B** or **A - B - B - A**.

3 Write the lyrics.

- ✓ Select the ideas you want to highlight: one in the chorus and one in each verse. They can express emotions, feelings, actions, a particular event...
- ✓ If you want to use rhymes you can use this website to find words: rhymezone.com.
- ✓ Don't forget to read your lyrics aloud to check their rhythm.

4 Find a title for your song.

- ✓ Choose a title that sums up the message of your song.
- ✓ Make your title catchy! It needs to be clear and contain no more than six words.

Fiche de méthodologie N°20 p. 300

Let's RECAP

Lisez les questions-clés et complétez la fiche bilan avec des exemples et des documents que vous avez étudiés ou découverts.

AXE 8 | Territory and memory

SÉQUENCE 1 How strong is the UK's link with its overseas territories?

E-workbook
Bilan à compléter
hatier-clic.fr/lmu1173

How has the relationship evolved in time? What does it reflect?

#history
What link and influence did the UK use to have on its overseas territories?

#collectiveheritage
What do the UK and its overseas territories still have in common?

#geography
What are the geographical locations and characteristics of the BOTs?

#nationalterritory
What makes the BOTs culturally, politically and economically linked to the UK?

#frontier
How was pushing back the frontier of the British Empire of any use to the UK?

SÉQUENCE 2 How is slavery commemorated in the English-speaking world?

E-workbook
Bilan à compléter
hatier-clic.fr/lmu1174

How do people pay tribute to the victims of slavery in English-speaking countries?

#emblematiccharacters
How do symbols and icons contribute to remembering the past?

#collectiveheritage
How are English-speaking countries building a collective memory of slavery?

#placesofmemory
How important are art and architecture to create places of memory?

#history
How is the memory of the past passed on to younger generations?

#commemoration
How do people celebrate the end of slavery?

GO4IT!

Lisez et écoutez de l'anglais en dehors de la salle de classe ! Voici quelques conseils en lien avec votre séquence.

SÉQUENCE 1

Books

The Battle for the Falklands, Max Hastings, Simon Jenkins, 1984

A Trip to the Beach: Living on Island Time in the Caribbean, Melinda Blanchard, Robert Blanchard, 2001

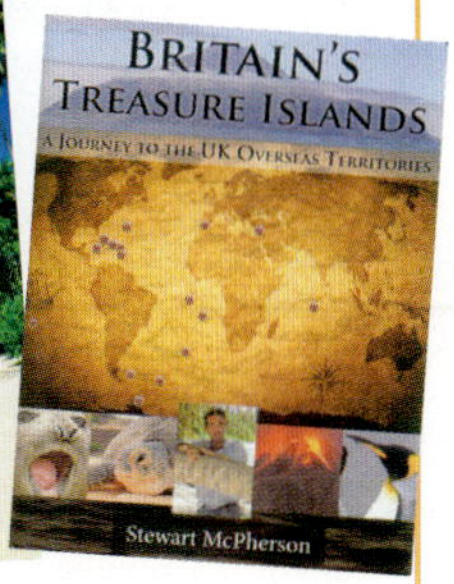

Britain's Treasure Islands: A Journey to the UK Overseas Territories, Stewart McPherson, 2016

Poem

Heritage, Linda Banks, 2013
http://bbc.in/2CHt21r

Film

Documentary

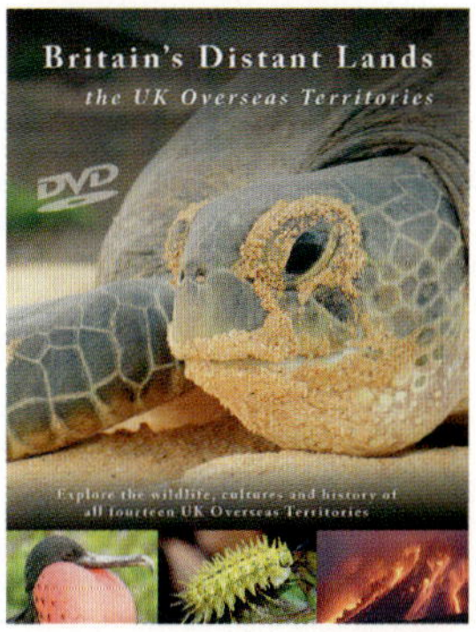

Websites

UK Overseas Territories Association
https://ukota.org

BBC News about British Overseas Territories
http://bbc.in/2U26zHe

Britain's Treasure Islands, BBC Four
http://bbc.in/2WrVcVJ

Britain's Treasure Islands mini-documentaries, Redfern Natural History Productions
http://bit.ly/2VoTk61

Songs

General Election, Lord Beginner, 1950

Sunset in Bermuda, The Talbot Brothers, 1958

Brothers in Arms, Dire Straits, 1985

Como Estais Amigos, Iron Maiden, 1998

SÉQUENCE 2

Novels and graphic novel

Roots: The Saga of an American Family, Alex Haley, 1976

Beloved, Toni Morrison, 1987

Amistad, Joyce Annette Barnes, 1997

Cane River, Lalita Tademy, 2001

The Known World, Edward P. Jones, 2003

Kindred, Octavia E. Butler, Damian Duffy and John Jennings, 2016

Songs

Long John, Lightning, 1934

Go Down Moses, Louis Armstrong, 1958

Slavery Days, Burning Spear, 1975

Slave Song, Sade, 2000

Films

TV series

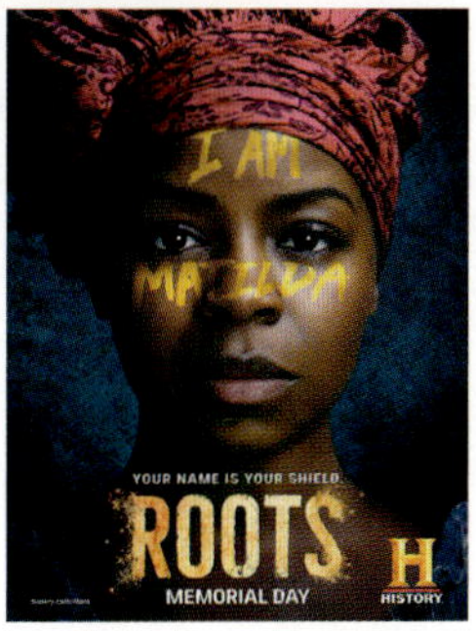

Museums

Liverpool International Slavery Museum
http://bit.ly/2uzakEY

Whitney Plantation Museum, Louisiana
http://bit.ly/2RXIE9X

Island of Gorée, Senegal
http://bit.ly/2UeSoOs

BAC in sight

ÉPREUVE 1

COMPRÉHENSION ORALE

Vidéo DVD This is a documentary about the last Royal Mail Ship stopping at the remote island of St Helena.

✦ *St. Helena – a remote island in the Atlantic*, SWR, 2017

Tips

- Focus on the title.
- Note down the words that are stressed.
- Make up a story with the words you have written.

Fiche de méthodologie N°15 p. 290 Compréhension orale

EXPRESSION ÉCRITE

SUJET 1 Write the letter sent by an inhabitant of St Helena to a friend telling him or her about life on the remote island.

OU

SUJET 2 Should all the British Overseas Territories become independent?

Tips

- Use the methodology of the letter p. 301.
- Give details to make your essay or letter more realistic.

Fiche de méthodologie N°20 p. 300 Expression écrite

Pour l'épreuve

Questions
Fiche modifiable
hatier-clic.fr/lmu1175

Évaluation
Grille à imprimer
hatier-clic.fr/lmu1176

ÉPREUVE 2

EXPRESSION ÉCRITE

SUJET 1 During their first meeting, the man representing the New Zealand construction consortium asks Mayor Steven Christian, a descendant of chief mutineer Fletcher Christian, about the legend of Pitcairn. Write the interview.

OU

SUJET 2 Do you think that "a volcanic outcrop" like Pitcairn Island has enough assets to become a popular tourist destination?

✦ Pacific Island, Pitcairn Island

Tips

- Read the instructions carefully.
- Don't forget to structure your text: introduction, part 1, part 2, part 3 (if necessary), conclusion.
- Use vocabulary you have learnt in this unit.

Fiche de méthodologie N°20 p. 300 Expression écrite

COMPRÉHENSION ÉCRITE

TEXTE 1

His Majesty's Armed Vessel Bounty set sail from England in December of 1787, under the command of 33-year old lieutenant William Bligh. The destination was Tahiti, and the mission was to obtain saplings[1] of the breadfruit[2] tree, and to convey these safely to various stations in the West Indies, where they would be propagated as a source of cheap, fast-growing food for slaves.

The Bounty arrived in Tahiti, the plants were duly collected, the arduous return voyage was begun. But in the early hours of 28 April 1789, some two weeks out from Tahiti, Bligh was awoken by the weight of hands pressed upon his chest and opened his eyes to see members of his crew under arms, led by 23-year old Master's Mate Fletcher Christian.

Bligh was hustled on deck at musket[3] point where he discovered that the mutineers had segregated the ship's company. Those who were loyal to Bligh and those whom they simply did not like, 18 souls in all, were forced off the ship into the Bounty's 23-foot long launch.

[...] Those who remained on the Bounty, under command of Christian, sailed first to Tahiti, then to the island of Tubuai, where they came to blows[4] with the islanders and with each other. They sailed back to Tahiti where the majority chose to remain, some with the hope of building new lives.

However, many of these men were eventually captured on the island and brought back to England where they were found guilty of mutiny and hanged from the yardarms of the HMS Brunswick in Portsmouth Harbour. Eight hard-core mutineers, however, escaped this fate after departing with Christian, along with 20 Tahitian men and women — the latter against their will — for parts unknown, eventually stumbling upon and settling the island of Pitcairn*, where their descendants live today.

✦ Caroline Alexander, *Mutiny on the Bounty: The true story of Captain Bligh's mutineers*, *The Telegraph*, March 12, 2017

**Pitcairn* Islands: a British Overseas Territory.

1. young trees 2. tropical fruit 3. type of gun 4. started fighting

TEXTE 2

First Mate Fletcher Christian led his rebels to isolated Pitcairn Island in 1790. Two centuries later their children hope to rejoin the world.

For more than 200 years it has been famed as one of the most remote communities in the world. Its legendary history has inspired several films. Its population of 42, all descendants of the mutineers of the Bounty, only have contact with the outside world through the occasional passing ship, mail that comes once every two months and a single satellite telephone.

There is no harbour, no landing strip[1], and their nearest neighbours are almost 1,300 miles to the east. It has a courthouse that has never seen a trial and a prison that is used for storing three life jackets. But now Pitcairn Island, a volcanic outcrop[2] girdled[3] by crashing cliffs and surrounded by untouched coral atolls has voted to end its isolation and join the outside world. Its people have agreed to let a New Zealand construction consortium turn it into a major tourist destination, with two airports, its own airline, a four-star hotel and two lodges.

Tourists will be tempted by the empty beaches on the uninhabited atolls, lagoons, scuba diving, the Unesco world heritage site of the nearby bird sanctuary island of Henderson, and the rusty anchor of HMS Bounty in the capital Adamstown. But most will probably come just to gawp[4] at the locals and soak up[5] the legend.

Though welcomed by most islanders, environmentalists warn the development could devastate the island's unique plant and animal life. Mayor Steven Christian, a descendant of chief mutineer Fletcher Christian (played by Mel Gibson in the latest film version of the story), told The Observer: 'The community decided to go ahead and see what happens. It shows that someone out there is thinking of us, and giving us a hand along in the world. We hope something good comes out of it.' [...]

✦ Anthony Browne, *Ahoy there! Mutiny island grabs tourist bounty lifeline*, *The Guardian*, March 25, 2001

1. long road used by planes when arriving 2. large rock 3. surrounded by 4. look in great surprise at sb 5. listen with great attention

Tips

➤ Read the two captions and the introduction carefully.
➤ Find out what the two texts have in common.

➤ Fiche de méthodologie N°16 p. 292 Compréhension écrite

Pour l'épreuve

Questions — Fiche modifiable — hatier-clic.fr/lmu1177

Évaluation — Grille à imprimer — hatier-clic.fr/lmu1178

BAC in sight

ÉPREUVE 1

COMPRÉHENSION ORALE

Vidéo
hatier-clic.fr/lmu1179

In this report, Victor Mooney calls for a stone plaque to be mounted at Brooklyn Bridge Park to commemorate the 400th anniversary of the first enslaved Africans' arrival in the English colonies in 1619.

✦ *Victor Mooney calls for tribute to slaves to be added at Brooklyn Bridge Park*, News12 Brooklyn, March 5, 2019

Tips

- Be active and take notes right from the start of the first viewing.
- The images can help you understand the video!

Fiche de méthodologie N°15 p. 290 Compréhension orale

EXPRESSION ÉCRITE

SUJET 1 Write a petition for the campaign for a memorial plaque to be placed at Brooklyn Bridge Park.

OU

SUJET 2 How should the USA commemorate its past with regard to slavery?

Tips

- Find inspiration in the documents you have studied.
- Write about the future as well as the past.

Fiche de méthodologie N°20 p. 300 Expression écrite

Pour l'épreuve

Questions
Fiche modifiable
hatier-clic.fr/lmu1180

Évaluation
Grille à imprimer
hatier-clic.fr/lmu1181

ÉPREUVE 2

EXPRESSION ÉCRITE

SUJET 1 Imagine the speech given by Rodney Leon during the ceremony of the unveiling of a slavery memorial at the United Nations' headquarters.

OU

SUJET 2 In your opinion, are memorials necessary to celebrate history? Give precise examples.

✦ Kwarme Akoto-Bamfo's sculpture *Nkyinkim*, National Memorial for Peace and Justice, Montgomery, Alabama

Tips

- Address the audience directly in your speech to catch their attention.
- Choose the right tense: past (what happened) or present (the situation nowadays).

Fiche de méthodologie N°20 p. 300 Expression écrite

COMPRÉHENSION ÉCRITE

United Nations unveils slavery memorial

The United Nations on Wednesday remembered the millions of victims of the largest forced migration in history with the unveiling of a slavery memorial on its visitors plaza before global ambassadors and Jamaica Prime Minister Portia Simpson Miller.

Designed by Haitian-American architect Rodney Leon, *The Ark of Return* memorializes the estimated 15 million African men, women, and children who died during the transatlantic slave trade and the millions of others forced into plantation slavery in the Americas. Leon beat out 310 architects and designers for the chance to design the permanent structure at the U.N.'s New York headquarters.

Leon said the triangle-shaped marble structure was inspired by the theme, "acknowledge the tragedy, consider the tragedy, lest we forget." He and his team drew inspiration from the maps of the triangular slave trade, which are etched[1] in the structure; the ships that ferried Africans to Europe and the Americas, and the experiences people underwent[2] through the "door of no return" — a door at a castle on Gorée Island in Senegal where many slaves were kept before they were shipped to the Americas.

"We felt it was very important for us to counteract that experience and pay homage to their legacy," Leon said.

U.N. Secretary General Ban Ki-moon said the memorial stands as a reminder of not just the brutal crossing across the Atlantic Ocean but also recognizes "the significant contributions that slaves and their descendants have made."

"This poignant and powerful memorial helps us to acknowledge the collective tragedy that befell[3] millions of people," he said during the outdoor ceremony. "It encourages us to consider the historical legacy of slavery and above all, it ensures that we never forget."

The U.N. has declared 2015-2024 as the International Decade for People of African Descent. Ban called slavery "a stain on human history," and the monument allows all a chance to reflect on the causes and consequences of racism "so we may eradicate prejudice and intolerance."

✦ Sam Kutesa, Minister for Foreign Affairs of Uganda and President of the United Nations General Assembly, New York City, March 25, 2015

"I hope *The Ark of Return* will also serve as a call to action against the many contemporary manifestations of slavery, from human trafficking and sexual enslavement to debt bondage[4]," he said.

The memorial project was conceived more than five years ago and led by African and Caribbean nations. The Permanent Representative of Jamaica, Courtenay Rattray, served as chair of the Permanent Memorial Committee and noted that several nations, along with UNESCO, helped raise more than $1.7 million for it.

Jamaica is a member of the 15-member Caribbean Community, which is currently pursuing reparations claims against European nations that engaged in the slave trade.

Simpson Miller did not raise the reparations issue in her remarks but spoke of slavery's enduring legacy. She noted that even after Britain passed a law on March 25, 1807, abolishing the slave trade, slavery continued.

"For us freedom came after a long journey," she said. "Freedom was not gifted to us but rather earned by the sweat, blood, and tears of millions of our forebears[5] on whose back the economic foundations of the New World was built."

✦ Jacqueline Charles, *Miami Herald*, March 25, 2015

1. engraved 2. suffered 3. happened to 4. servitude 5. ancestors

Tips

➤ Focus on words with capital letters and on numbers. Find out what they refer to.

➤ Make sure you know who is speaking.

➤ Fiche de méthodologie N°16 p. 292 Compréhension écrite

Pour l'épreuve

Questions — Fiche modifiable — hatier-clic.fr/lmu1182

Évaluation — Grille à imprimer — hatier-clic.fr/lmu1183

Annexes

Pour vous donner des repères culturels

Pour travailler la langue

Pour acquérir des savoir-faire

L'histoire de l'anglais

L'histoire de la Grande-Bretagne vous permettra de mieux comprendre l'évolution de la langue.

Voici un schéma qui montre les différentes périodes d'invasion et l'impact des langues importées sur l'anglais.

N'oubliez pas : la langue continue d'évoluer et de s'imprégner des influences d'autres langues. Par exemple, ***pasta***, ***violin*** viennent d'Italie, ***potato***, ***cigar*** viennent d'Espagne et ***waltz***, ***rucksack*** d'Allemagne.

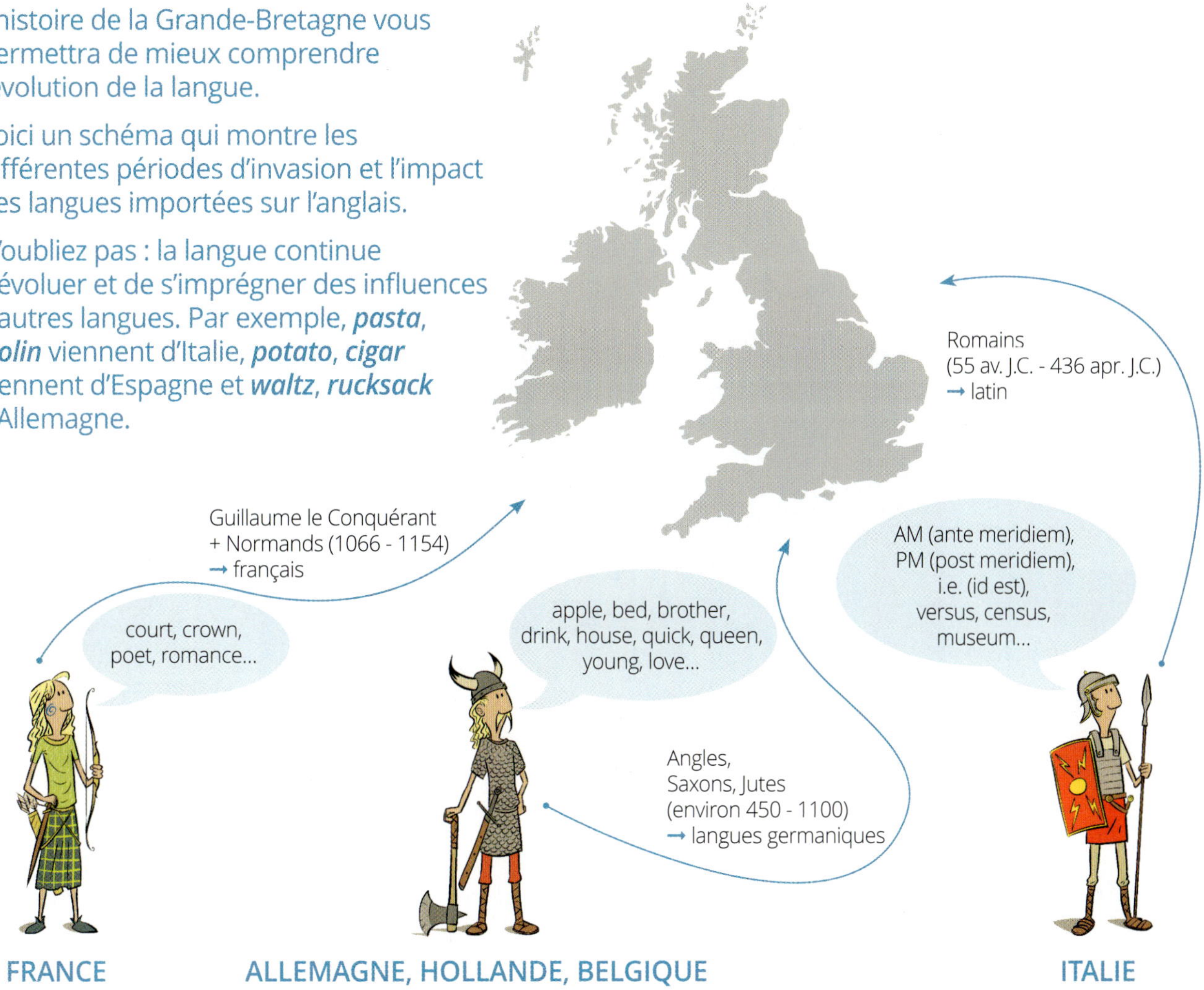

Le français, la langue de la cour

Sous le règne des Normands, le français était parlé à la cour.
Par conséquent, les mots d'origine française appartiennent à un niveau de langue plus recherché.
Les mots anglo-saxons, souvent plus courts, étaient plutôt utilisés dans le langage de tous les jours.

Si vous avez le choix entre un mot d'origine anglo-saxonne et un mot d'origine française, prenez plutôt le premier.
Ex :
brotherhood plutôt que *fraternity* ;
hunt plutôt que *chase* ;
freedom plutôt que *liberty* ;
meet plutôt que *encounter* ;
go on plutôt que *continue*.

Anglais britannique ou anglais américain ?

Choisissez en fonction de l'accent que vous commencez à avoir, puis tenez-vous-en à cet accent en utilisant les mots et l'orthographe appropriés. Les différences entre l'anglais britannique et l'anglais américain sont nombreuses et principalement de trois types.

- **L'ORTHOGRAPHE peut être différente.** Par exemple, le « L » est doublé en fin de verbe devant une terminaison *–ed* ou *–ing* en anglais britannique :
  travelling (UK) → *traveling* (US),
  counselling (UK) → *counseling* (US)
- **Certains MOTS sont différents.** Par exemple :
  ascenseur : *lift* (UK) → *elevator* (US)
  trottoir : *pavement* (UK) → *sidewalk* (US)
  frites : *chips* (UK) → *French fries* (US)
  appartement : *flat* (UK) → *apartment* (US)
- **L'ACCENT DE MOT** est parfois placé sur une syllabe différente en anglais britannique et en anglais américain.
  laboratory : (UK) /lə'bɒr.ə.tər.i/ (US) /'læb.rə.tɔːr.i/
  advertisement : (UK) /əd'vɜː.tɪs.mənt/ (US) /æd.vɝː'taɪz.mənt/

La géographie de l'anglais

Au Royaume-Uni

L'accent est un marqueur géographique, social et ethnique. Il y a une grande diversité d'accents au Royaume-Uni.

Parmi tous ces accents, la *Received Pronunciation*, RP, aussi appelée « anglais de la Reine » ou « anglais de la BBC », a longtemps été considérée comme une référence.

Voici quelques exemples d'accents.

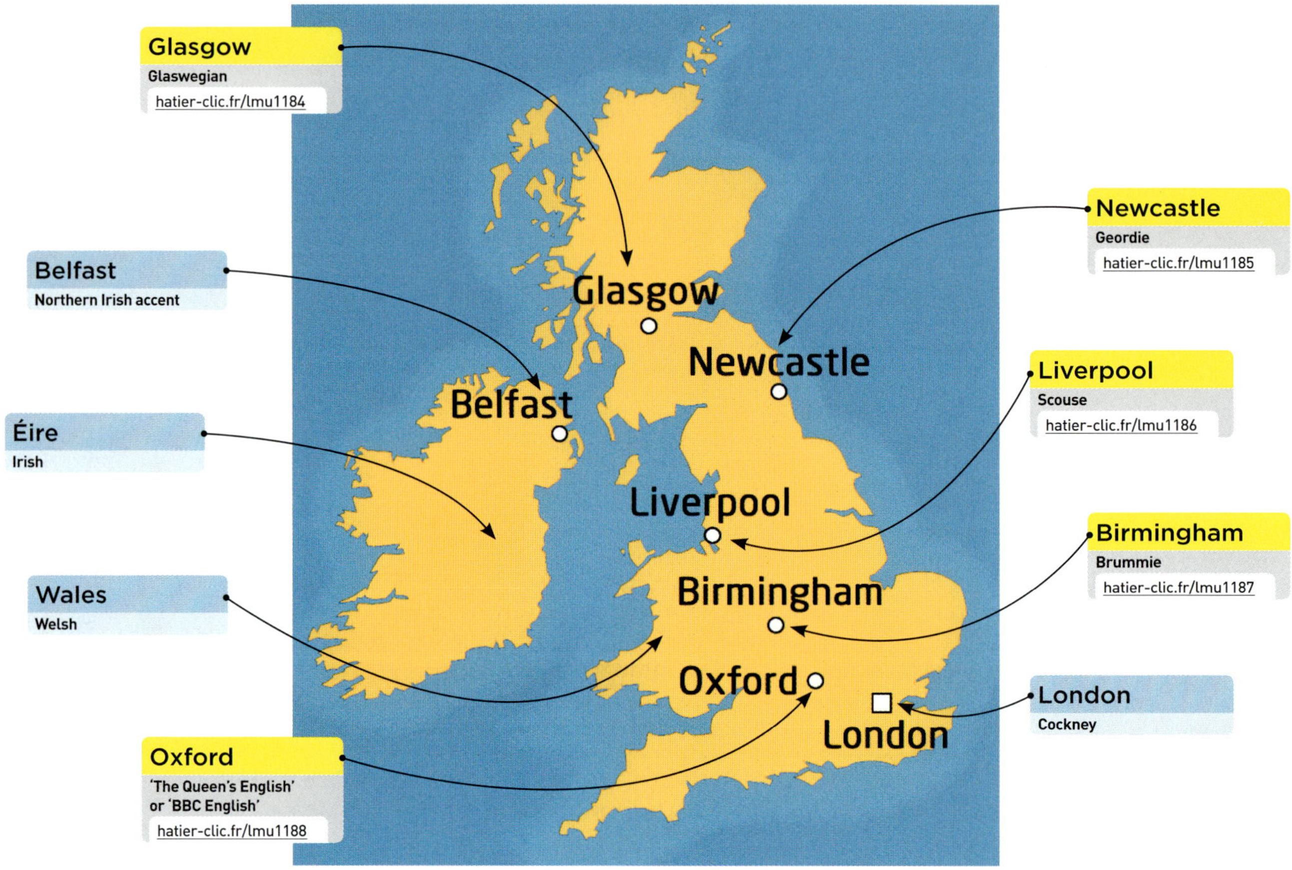

Aux États-Unis

Les régions influent aussi sur l'accent comme par exemple le *Southern drawl*, accent traînant sur les voyelles, dans de nombreux états du sud des États-Unis. Par ailleurs, l'origine ethnique influence la langue.

Voici une animation montrant les différents dialectes et accents aux États-Unis :

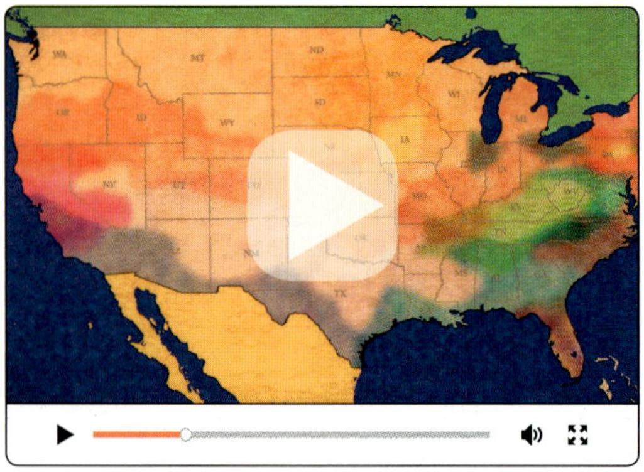

Vidéo
hatier-clic.fr/lmu1189

En Australie, l'anglais parlé se rapproche davantage de l'anglais britannique.

Au Canada, l'anglais parlé tend à se rapprocher de l'anglais américain.

Vous pouvez utiliser *WordReference* pour entendre le même mot avec différents accents.

Institutions - UK & USA

The United Kingdom

is a constitutional monarchy.

The UK does not have a written, codified constitution but a set of rules and regulations constituted by jurisprudence and laws.

Monarch
= Head of State (representative role)

✦ The Queen's speech, opening the parliamentary year in the House of Lords

Legislative power
(makes laws)

Parliament

House of Commons
= 650 Members of Parliament (MPs) elected every 5 years

House of Lords
= more than 700 unelected members

✦ The Palace of Westminster: the Houses of Parliament

Executive power
(puts laws into practice)

Prime Minister
= Head of Government, the leader of the majority party

Cabinet
= other ministers

✦ 10 Downing Street, official residence of the Prime Minister and headquarters of the Government

The United States of America

is a federal republic of 50 states.

Constitution
= ratified in 1788, providing a separation of powers

Legislative power
(makes laws)

Congress

House of Representatives
= 435 representatives according to each state's population

Senate
= 100 senators, two from each state

✦ The Capitol, meeting place of the Congress, Washington, D.C.

Executive power
(puts laws into practice)

President
= Head of Government, elected every 4 years

Vice President

Cabinet
= other ministers

Judicial power
(interprets laws)

Supreme Court
= nine justices nominated for life by the president with the consent of the Senate

Lower courts

The president is elected indirectly, by an electoral college of 538 electors. Americans vote for their state's electors according to which president and vice president they promise to elect.

✦ The White House, official residence and workplace of the president, Washington, D.C.

Timelines - UK

History/Society

1605
A group of English Catholics attempted but failed to assassinate King James I. Among them was **Guy Fawkes**.

1807
The **Slave Trade Act** abolished the slave trade in the British Empire.

1833
The **Slavery Abolition Act** abolished slavery throughout the British Empire except the territories in the possession of the East India Company, Ceylon (Sri Lanka today) and Saint Helena and it was extended to these territories in 1843. It freed 800,000 Africans who were then the legal property of Britain's slave owners.

1838-1901
Queen Victoria's coronation took place on June 28, 1838 in Westminster.
She later became Empress of India (1876). She reigned for 63 years and during that period, the UK underwent changes in several fields: industry, politics, culture... This is called the Victorian Era.

1920
The **Unemployment Insurance Act** created the dole system which was a system of payments to unemployed workers on a weekly basis.

1928
British women received the right to vote on the same terms as men.

1940-1941
Great Britain was bombed by Nazi Germany during the Second World War. This mass air attacks period is also called **"The Blitz"**.

Arts

1920
Agatha Christie wrote her first detective story entitled *The Mysterious Affair at Styles*, first appearance of Detective Hercule Poirot.

1930
The first time Miss Marple, an amateur detective written by **Agatha Christie**, appeared in a novel entitled *The Murder at the Vicarage*.

1931
Brave New World by **Aldous Huxley**

1948
Nineteen Eighty Four by **George Orwell**

May 8, 1956
The British realist play *Look Back in Anger* premiered at the Royal Court Theatre in London.

1958
The British writer **Alan Sillitoe**, known as part of the "Angry Young Men", wrote his first novel *Saturday Night & Sunday Morning*.

Science & technology

1599
The **Globe Theatre** was built by Shakespeare's playing company called the Lord Chamberlain's Men. It was destroyed by fire in 1613.

1776
James Watt invented his **Watt steam engine** which was one of the driving forces of the Industrial Revolution.

1816
George Stephenson known as a "The Father of Railways", built with his son's company the **1st steam locomotive** for passengers.

1894
The **Tower Bridge** located close to the Tower of London was completed.

1950
Alan Turing published a landmark paper in which he speculated about the possibility of creating **machines that think**.

1959
Antarctic Treaty which provides an internationally agreed regime for the governance of the continent. For just over 50 years now, it has preserved Antarctica for peace and science and is arguably one of the world's most successful international agreements.

June 2, 1953
Coronation of Elizabeth II in Westminster Abbey

1966
The **first Notting Hill Carnival** was held over two days at the end of August. It is a street festival to highlight Caribbean and black diasporic cultures.

May 4, 1979
Margaret Thatcher became the first female British Prime Minister (Conservative Party).

1982
The **Falklands War** opposed Argentina to the UK concerning two BOTs among which were the Falkland Islands. It lasted a few months and diplomatic relations were restored between the two countries in 1989.

1997
Tony Blair (Labour party) won a landslide victory after more than 15 years of Conservative PMs.

Summer 2012
The UK hosted the **Summer Olympics and Paralympics** in order to gain international acclaim.

September 9, 2015
Elizabeth became the longest reigning monarch in British history.

July 13, 2016
After David Cameron's resignation, **Theresa May** became the British Prime Minister (Conservative Party).

1970
Kes directed by the British filmmaker **Ken Loach** was awarded Best Film at the BAFTA.

June 19, 2002
The first exhibition in Los Angeles of the British artist called **Banksy**, from Bristol entitled *Existencilism*. He has gained international acclaim. He is seen as an iconic street artist and has always remained anonymous.

2004
Opening of the Gherkin (30 St Mary Axe) designed by **Norman Foster** and Arup Group. It is located in the financial district, the City of London. It is 180 metres high and there are 41 floors.

August 23, 2007
The **International Slavery Museum** located in Liverpool opened, commemorating slavery and slave trade.

July 5, 2012
The Shard was inaugurated in London. It is a 95-storey skyscraper located in Soutwark, London. It is the tallest building in the UK and the European Union (architect: **Renzo Piano**).

1989
The English scientist Tim Berners-Lee invented the **World Wide Web**.

1994
The **Channel Tunnel** which links London to Paris was inaugurated.

July 5, 1996
Dolly, a sheep, was the **first mammal cloned**.

1997
The Shakespeare Globe's theatre was built as a modern reconstruction of **the Globe**.

1997
The English anonymous street art artist **Banksy** painted his first mural *The Mild Mild West* in Bristol. He is known for his stencil technique and his anti-war and anti-capitalist positions.

2000
The London Eye opened to the public and was, at that time, the world's tallest Ferris wheel.

Timelines - USA

History / Society

1620
Pilgrim Fathers sailed to America on the Mayflower.

1775
American War of Independence

July 4, 1776
Declaration of Independence. American people declared their independence from the British crown to form a new country: the USA.

1789
US Constitution.
1st Amendment: freedom of speech. George Washington became the 1st American president.

1830
Indian Removal Act.
The US government was allowed to relocate Native American tribes west of the Mississippi River.

1838
Underground Railroad

1845
Journalist John L. O'Sullivan mentioned for the first time the expression '**Manifest Destiny**' meaning that the settlers were meant to go West. The US frontier was modified anytime a new territory was integrated as an American state.

December 7, 1941
The US base Pearl Harbor was attacked by Japanese airplanes and submarines which led the country to enter **World War II**.

1947-1991
The Cold War was a non-armed conflict opposing the Eastern Bloc (the USSR and other Communist countries) to the Western Bloc (the US and its allies).

1955-1975
Vietnam War. The conflict opposed North Vietnam backed by Communist countries and South Vietnam backed by the US and other non-communist allies.

August 28, 1963
Martin Luther King Jr. delivered his famous speech **"I have a dream"** completing the **March on Washington** for Jobs and Freedom.

1960's-1970's
Black Power Movement. It emerged from the Civil Rights Movement which aimed at spreading racial pride, creating political and cultural institutions for black Americans.

April 4, 1968
Martin Luther King Jr was assassinated in Memphis, TN.

June 17, 1972
The Watergate Scandal. Five people broke into the Democratic National Committee offices in the Watergate hotel in Washington D.C. President Nixon's administration tried to cover up its involvement. There was an investigation led by the Congress which ended in the president's resignation (August 9, 1974).

Arts / Science & technology

1876
Graham Bell invented the **telephone**.

1885
The Home Insurance Building was the **first skyscraper built in Chicago**.

1890's
George Washington Ferris who was a civil engineer from Illinois, invented **the Ferris Wheel** which was built for the 1893 Chicago World's Fair.

1910s-1930s
This period was known as the **Harlem Renaissance**. The neighbourhood in NYC teemed with black artists and intellectuals. It was considered to be a rebirth of African American arts.

1927
1st **sound movie** produced in Hollywood *The Jazz Singer*.

1937
John Steinbeck wrote *Of Mice and Men*.

1939
John Steinbeck wrote *The Grapes of Wrath*.

1940s
Abstract expressionism is a post-WWII art movement with painters such as **Jackson Pollock**.

1942
Edward Hopper painted *Nighthawks*.

1861-1865
American Civil War, mainly over the question of slavery

1865
Slavery was abolished. End of the American Civil War.

1866
The **National Labour Union**. It was the first national labor federation which was dissolved in 1873.

1882
Chinese Exclusion Act. It prohibited all immigration of Chinese workers. It was the first law which prevented a national group from immigrating.

April 6, 1917
The US waged war on Germany because German U-boats started sinking American merchant ships.

1920
The Nineteenth Amendment granted **women** with the **right to vote**.

1930's
Great Depression. A huge fall in stock prices (September 4, 1929) led to unemployment for many Americans (25% in 1933). Because of poverty and a persistant drought, hundreds of thousands of people found themselves homeless, and began gathering in shanty towns – dubbed "Hoovervilles".

1990-1991
Gulf War. A coalition of 35 countries led by the US, waged war on Iraq after it invaded and annexed Kuwait over the question of oil.

2001
Terrorist attacks on the World Trade Center and the Pentagon. 2,996 people were killed and over 6,000 people were injured.

2008
Barack Obama became the 1st Black politician to be elected president of the United States. He was re-elected in 2012 for a second and last term.

September 17, 2011
Occupy Wall Street. Left-wing protesters demonstrated in Zuccotti Park (NYC) in the financial district of Wall Street, in order to denounce economic inequality. They were forced out of the park two months later and they decided to occupy banks, university campuses...

2013
Alicia Garza and Patrisse Cullors founded the **Black Lives Matter** as a reaction to the acquittal of George Zimmerman in the murder of Trayvon Martin.

June 26, 2015
Same-sex marriage became legal in the whole country.

November 2016
Election of President **Donald Trump**

Feb 14, 2018
Parkland Shooting one of the deadliest shootings at a high school in US history.

1950s
The Pop Art movement emerged in the UK and the US, mixing painting and what is seen as popular culture: advertising, comic books. Artists such as **Andy Warhol** used mechanical means of reproduction.

1951
Ray Bradbury wrote *Fahrenheit 451*

1958
NASA was created as a result of the **space race** between the USA and the Soviet Union.

July 1969
Neil Armstrong along with Buzz Aldrin became the **first men to land on the moon**. "A small step for man, one giant leap for mankind".

1974
If Beale Street Could Talk by **James Baldwin**

1976
Steve Jobs along with Steve Wozniak and Ronald Wayne founded **Apple Computer** now called Apple Inc.

May 28, 2002
Change.org was created, allowing people to launch petitions online.

2004
Launching of **Facebook** by **Mark Zuckerberg** along with fellow students.

July 2016
Twitter was launched.

Let's watch history!

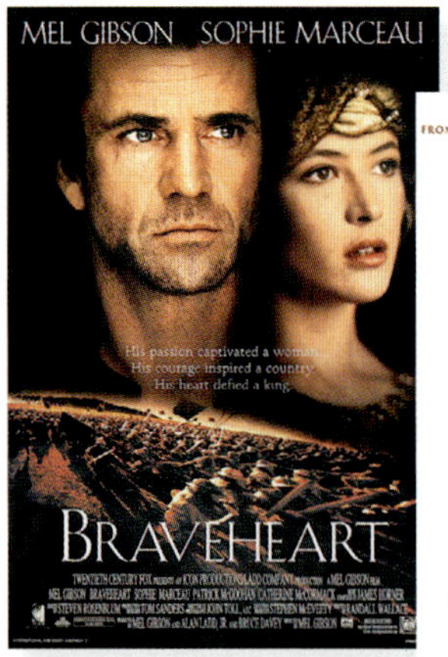

UK

866 The Vikings invade Britain with a large army.
- *The Last Kingdom*, Stephen Butchard, 2015

1066 The Norman Conquest occurs. William of Normandy becomes king.
- *A Year to Conquer England*, drama documentary series, 2017

1297 William Wallace leads the Scotts against the English. He is defeated a year later.
- *Braveheart*, Mel Gibson, 1995

1337-1453 The Hundred Years' War with France
- *Henry V*, Kenneth Branagh, 1989

1558 Elizabeth I becomes Queen.
- *Elizabeth: The Golden Age*, Shekhar Kapur, 2007
- *Mary Queen of Scots*, Josie Rourke, 2018

1605 Guy Fawkes attempts to blow up the Parliament.
- *Gunpowder*, TV series, 2017

1620 The Pilgrims set sail from Plymouth for America aboard the Mayflower.

1770s The Industrial Revolution begins in England.
- *Oliver Twist*, Roman Polanski, 2005

1776 The American colonies declare their independence from Britain.

1833 Slavery Abolition Act
- *Amazing Grace*, Michael Apted, 2006

1837 Queen Victoria is crowned queen. The Victorian Era begins.
- *Victoria & Abdul*, Stephen Frears, 2017

1845 Irish Potato Famine and immigration to the USA
- *Black '47*, Lance Daly, 2018

From 40, 000 BC	15th-16th century	17th century	18th century	19th century

USA

From 40, 000 BC Native American settlements (from Asia)
- *The New World*, Terence Malick, 2005

1492 Christopher Columbus discovers America.
- *1492*, Ridley Scott, 1992

1607 First English settlement in Virginia
- *Jamestown*, TV series, 2017

1620 The Pilgrim Fathers arrive in Plymouth on board the Mayflower.
- *Saints & Strangers*, Netflix series, 2015

1692 Salem Witch-hunt
- *The Scarlet Letter*, Roland Joffé, 1995
- *The Crucible*, Arthur Miller, 1996

18th -19th centuries Slave Trade
- *Amistad*, Steven Spielberg, 1997
- *12 Years a Slave*, Steve McQueen, 2013
- *Roots*, TV mini-series, 2016
- *The Birth of a Nation*, Nate Parker, 2016

1775-1783 War of Independence
- *Sons of Liberty*, mini-series, 2015

1789 First president, George Washington, elected and the American Constitution enforced
- *We Fight to Be Free*, Kees Von Oostrum, 2006

18th - 19th centuries Indian wars
- *Dances with Wolves*, Kevin Costner, 1990
- *The Last of the Mohicans*, Michael Mann, 1992

1804-1806 Lewis and Clark's expedition. The Frontier starts moving westward.
- *Lewis & Clark: Great Journey West*, documentary film by National Geographic, 2002

1848 The Gold Rush starts.
- *The Gold Rush*, Charlie Chaplin, 1925
- *Heaven's Gate*, Michael Cimino, 1980

1861-1865 The Civil War
- *Gone with the Wind*, Victor Fleming, 1939
- *Free State of Jones*, Gary Ross, 2016

1865 Abolition of slavery by President Abraham Lincoln
- *Lincoln*, Steven Spielberg, 2012

1914-1918 World War I. The United Kingdom fights with the Allies against the Central Powers led by Germany.
- *Testament of Youth*, James Kent, 2014

1921 Ireland is granted independence.
- *The Wind That Shakes the Barley*, Ken Loach, 2006

1928 The right to vote is granted to women.
- *Suffragette*, Sarah Gavron, 2015

1939-1945 World War II. The United Kingdom joins the Allies against the Axis Powers.
- *Hope and Glory*, John Boorman, 1987
- *The King's Speech*, Tom Hooper, 2010
- *Churchill*, Jonathan Teplitzky, 2017
- *Dunkirk*, Christopher Nolan, 2017

1947 India becomes independent from the UK.
- *Gandhi*, Richard Attenborough, 1982
- *Viceroy's House*, Gurinder Chadha, 2017

1953 Elizabeth II is crowned Queen.
- *The Queen*, Stephen Frears, 2006
- *The Crown*, Netflix series, 2016

1979 Margaret Thatcher becomes the first female Prime Minister of the United Kingdom.
- *The Iron Lady*, Phyllida Lloyd, 2012

2016 Brexit Referendum
- *Brexit: The Uncivil War*, TV movie, 2019

20th century

1892-1954 Ellis Island is used as an immigration center.
- *America America*, Elia Kazan, 1963
- *The Immigrant*, James Gray, 2013

1917 The US enters WW1.
- *The Lost Battalion*, Russell Mulcahy, 2001

1920 The right to vote is granted to women.
- *Iron Jawed Angels*, Katja von Garnier, 2004

1920-1933 Prohibition
- *Boardwalk Empire*, TV series, 2009

1929-1939 Great Depression
- *Modern times*, Charlie Chaplin, 1936
- *The Grapes of Wrath*, John Ford, 1940

1941 Attack on Pearl Harbor. The US enters WW2.
- *Saving Private Ryan*, Steven Spielberg, 1998
- *Pearl Harbor*, Michael Bay, 2001

1946-1991 Cold War
- *Three Days of the Condor*, Sydney Pollack, 1975
- *Thirteen Days*, Roger Donaldson, 2000

1950s The Space Race begins.
- *Hidden Figures*, Theodore Melfi, 2016

1955-1975 Vietnam War
- *Apocalypse Now*, Francis Ford Coppola, 1979
- *Platoon*, Oliver Stone, 1986
- *Born on the Fourth of July*, Oliver Stone, 1989

1963 President Kennedy dies.
- *JFK*, Oliver Stone, 1991
- *Jackie*, Pablo Larrain, 2016

1954-1968 Civil Rights movement led by Martin Luther King Jr.
- *Mississippi Burning*, Alan Parker, 1988
- *Malcom X*, Spike Lee, 1992
- *The Butler*, Lee Daniels, 2013
- *Selma*, Ava DuVernay, 2014
- *Greenbook*, Peter Farrelly, 2018

1969 First man on the moon
- *First Man*, Damien Chazelle, 2018

1990-1991 Gulf War
- *Jarhead*, Sam Mendes, 2005

21th century

Jan 20, 2001 George W.Bush becomes the 43rd American president.
- *Vice*, Adam McKay, 2018

Nov 9, 2001 Terrorist attack on the World Trade Center
- *9/11*, Martin Guigui, 2017

2003-2011 Iraq war
- *American Sniper*, Clint Eastwood, 2014

2008 Barack Obama, first African-American President
- *By the People: The Election of Barack Obama*, documentary film, 2009

Le groupe nominal

1. Les articles

→ L'article zéro (Ø) ou l'absence d'article

On emploie l'article zéro pour désigner les choses **de manière générale**, et essentiellement pour des **noms indénombrables**, c'est-à-dire qu'on ne peut pas compter.

Ø Butter contains a lot of Ø fat.

Ø Unemployment has become a plague in several countries.

Les noms dénombrables (*car, pen, boat...*) ne peuvent apparaître sans article, sauf dans certaines expressions de lieu, souvent accompagnées du verbe *go* ou d'une préposition pour certains noms comptables (*jail, school...*) :

Go to Ø jail, Ø school

Be at Ø school, in Ø jail

Dans tous les autres cas, les noms dénombrables doivent donc obligatoirement avoir un article.

L'article zéro est également utilisé dans les cas suivants :

- devant les dénombrables pluriels

  Ø Schools are Ø places where Ø children are taught Ø essential subjects.

- devant les noms de pays

  Ø England, Ø Scoland, Ø Wales, Ø Canada, Ø France

- devant les noms propres

  Ø Michelle Obama, Ø Theresa May

- devant les titres suivis du nom propre

  Ø Prime Minister Theresa May, Ø President Donald Trump, Ø Queen Elizabeth II

→ L'article indéfini *a / an*

L'article indéfini ***a / an*** est employé devant les noms dénombrables pour désigner un élément parmi d'autres. Cela permet de référer à un seul élément, d'extraire un élément d'un ensemble.

I need a pen to write and an eraser in case I make a mistake.
J'ai besoin d'**un** stylo pour écrire et d'**une** gomme si je fais **une** erreur.

What is a college in English-speaking countries?
Qu'est-ce qu'un « college » dans les pays anglophones ?

On emploie l'article indéfini *a / an* :

- pour désigner un seul élément d'un nom dénombrable :

  She has bought a detective book from a bookshop in the city.

- devant les noms de métier :

  Miss Marple is a detective. Miss Marple est détective.

  Sherlock Holmes, a famous detective, is a character created by Arthur Conan Doyle.
  Sherlock Holmes, détective célèbre, est un personnage inventé par Arthur Conan Doyle.

  She is a civil servant. Elle est fonctionnaire.

Attention, on note la présence de l'article *a* en anglais, mais l'absence d'article dans la traduction en français.

- après *as* pour désigner une fonction :

  As a member of this organization… En tant que membre de cette association…

- pour référer à une fréquence :

  Three times a day… trois fois par jour…

- pour indiquer une mesure ou un prix :

  £ 5 a kilo 5 £ le kilo

  £ 10 a metre 10 £ le mètre

- après *without* :

  Without a noise sans bruit

→ L'article défini *the*

Comme l'appellation de l'adjectif « défini » le souligne, l'article ***the*** renvoie à un nom ou à un élément facilement identifiables par le locuteur, celui qui parle, et son interlocuteur.

- Soit parce qu'il s'agit d'une reprise d'un élément déjà posé en amont :

  There was an accident in Cardiff yesterday. The accident caused a lot of traffic jams.

  (L'accident d'hier à Cardiff, je l'ai annoncé par *an accident*, avant de le reprendre par l'article défini *the*. L'accident / Cet accident a causé beaucoup d'embouteillages.)

- Soit parce que l'on a affaire à un nom dont l'identification ne pose aucune difficulté entre les deux personnes dans la situation :

  Could you pass me the salt, please?

  (si je suis à table, mon interlocuteur comprend immédiatement qu'il s'agit du sel qui se trouve près de lui.)

Autres cas où il faut employer l'article défini *the* :

- pour parler de quelque chose qui est défini par une proposition relative :

  I like the book that she gave me for my birthday. (La proposition relative soulignée définit le livre en question.)

- Pour les noms de pays et d'îles au pluriel :

  The United States, the Netherlands, the Canaries, the Philippines, the UK (le Royaume-Uni = l'Angleterre, l'Ecosse, le Pays de Galles et l'Irlande du Nord)

- Pour les noms de fleuves :

  The Seine, the Thames, the Hudson, the Nile, the Rhine

- Pour parler des astres :

  The sun, the earth, the moon

- Pour parler des instruments de musique :

  Play the piano, the guitar, the trumpet

- Pour les adjectifs substantivés :

  The blind les aveugles the unemployed les chômeurs

- On dit aussi : ***the environment*** et ***the internet.***

Your turn!

1 Complétez les phrases suivantes avec l'article *Ø, a, an* ou *the*.

a. Do you know that ... United States is 17 times as big as ... France?
b. She studies history at ... University of Edinburgh. She wants to become ... historian.
c. ... tuition fees can be very expensive. ... university course costs quite a lot a money in ... Britain and in ... English-speaking countries in general.
d. Paul bought ... new car two weeks ago in Manchester. When he drove to ... London, ... car broke down on ... motorway.
e. Could you pass me ... gravy, please! I would like some with my Yorkshire pudding.
f. He came back home with ... enormous cheesecake to celebrate his birthday.

2. Les noms dénombrables et indénombrables

→ Formation

Les **noms dénombrables** peuvent être quantifiés et donc être précédés de l'article ***a.*** Ils peuvent aussi prendre la marque du pluriel : par exemple, on dira *a car* au singulier, et *cars* au pluriel.

À l'inverse, les **noms indénombrables** ne peuvent en aucun cas accepter l'article indéfini *a.* Ils ne portent pas non plus la marque du pluriel *s.* Ils sont donc invariables.

→ Emploi

Your turn!

2 Recopiez les phrases et soulignez les indénombrables dans les phrases suivantes.

a. As the saying goes, no news is good news!
b. The information is as alarming today as it was last week, because all the evidence is against him. This thief is about to be arrested by the policeman.
c. Your luggage is too heavy. You have got too many bags. You should take a taxi.
d. The good news is that this student has made a lot of progress this semester. He has improved all his grades.

3. Le pluriel des noms

→ Formation

Le pluriel régulier des noms se construit en ajoutant **s** au nom au singulier : *a bag* → Ø *bag**s***.

Certains noms voient leur terminaison modifiée au pluriel. Il s'agit des noms se terminant par *-ch, -x, -ss, -sh, -f* et *-fe*. Voici un tableau qui indique les modifications orthographiques pour ces terminaisons.

Singulier se terminant par :	Modification orthographique au pluriel
ch : breach	breach**es** /iz/
x : box	box**es** /iz/
ss : mass	mass**es** /iz/
sh : bush	bush**es** /iz/
f / fe : leaf / wife	leav**es** / wiv**es** /z/ /z/

Il existe aussi des noms qui ont un pluriel irrégulier :

a child → children
man → men
woman → women
foot → feet
mouse → mice
tooth → teeth
phenomenon → phenomena
criterion → criteria
medium → media

Certains noms ont une forme invariable au pluriel : aucune modification orthographique par rapport au singulier.

an aircraft (un avion) : two aircraft (deux avions)
sheep → sheep
deer → deer

! Attention, en anglais, les noms de famille prennent la marque **s** au pluriel, contrairement au français : les Martin = the Martins

Your turn!

3 **Mettez les noms soulignés au pluriel, en faisant les modifications nécessaires.**

a. A mouse is a frightening animal.
b. Boeing has built an aircraft that flies much quicker.
c. Is there a criterion that is more important than the other ones?
d. A woman and a man should be on an equal footing.
e. The dentist has pulled out one tooth.

4. Les noms composés

→ Formation

Un mot peut s'associer avec un autre mot pour former un mot composé : mot 1 + mot 2 = mot composé. Les quatre catégories grammaticales – nom, adjectif, verbe et adverbe – peuvent se combiner dans la formation des noms composés.

Dans un nom composé, c'est **toujours le deuxième mot** qui est le nom **central**, celui qui porte donc l'**identification**, c'est-à-dire le sens principal. Le premier mot, lui, qualifie le second, en indiquant le type d'objet ou de personne, voire la fonction dont il s'agit. Ce mot composé peut s'écrire en un seul mot (*policeman*), en deux mots (*washing machine*) ou avec un trait d'union (*savings-bank*).

Qualifiant ou fonction	Indentification	Nom composé	Sens
police	man	policeman	**a man** who works for the police un policier
washing	machine	washing machine	**a machine** that washes une machine à laver
savings	bank	savings-bank	**a bank** where your savings are une caisse d'épargne

→ Formation avec les combinaisons de mots possibles

Mot 1 et mot 2	Nom composé	Sens
nom bank + nom account	bank account	compte en banque
nom hair + verbe cut	haircut	coupe de cheveux
nom hand + adverbe out	handout	prospectus
verbe driving + nom licence	driving licence	permis de conduire
verbe take + adverbe off	take-off	décollage
adjectif dry + verbe cleaning	dry-cleaning	nettoyage à sec
adjectif green + nom house	greenhouse	serre
adverbe over + nom time	overtime	heures supplémentaires
adverbe over + verbe flow	overflow	débordement

La traduction en français montre bien que c'est le deuxième mot qui doit être porteur du sens principal, le premier mot qualifiant ce mot principal.

Your turn!

4 Complétez les phrases avec le mot composé qui convient.

Exemple : Susan has just bought a new fitted kitchen. She wants to buy some new ... (*you drink tea in these cups*) too = Susan has just bought a new fitted kitchen. She wants to buy some new teacups too.

a. In most modern kitchens, you will find ... and ... (*a machine to wash clothes and a machine to wash dishes*).

b. The secretary needs a ... software (*to process words*).

c. Please ask the ... (*officer at the customs*) if this item is allowed on board.

d. Queen Elizabeth II is fond of ... (*horses used for racing*). She often attends ... (*races where you watch horses running*).

5. Le génitif

Le génitif établit une relation entre deux noms, souvent un lien de possession.

→ Formation

Nom singulier = 'S	The neighbour's bike The driver's car	le vélo du·de la voisin·e la voiture du·de la conducteur·trice
Non singulier se terminant par un s = 'S	James's car Thomas's suitcase	la voiture de James la valise de Thomas
Nom pluriel se terminant par un s = '	His parents' home Her sons' clothes	la maison de ses parents les vêtements de ses fils
Nom pluriel irrégulier = 'S	women's clothes men's shoes	des vêtements pour femmes des chaussures pour hommes

→ Emplois

On note que le premier nom est, en général, une personne, et non pas un objet.

On peut aussi employer le génitif avec :

- les noms d'animaux

  The dog's bowl la gamelle du chien

- les institutions

  The Supreme Court's decision la décision de la Cour Suprême

- les pays

  Britain's new legislation la nouvelle législation de la Grande-Bretagne

- avec les expressions de temps : *yesterday, today, tomorrow, last week...*

  Yesterday's article l'article d'hier

  Tomorrow's weather forecast la météo pour demain

  Last week's strike la grève de la semaine dernière

- pour des lieux (chez le coiffeur, à la boulangerie, boucherie, etc.), avec souvent l'ellipse du mot ***shop***, qui est sous-entendu :

  At the baker's (shop) à la boulangerie

  At the hairdresser's chez le coiffeur

  At the chemist's à la pharmacie

Your turn!

5 Mettez au génitif quand cette construction est possible.

Exemple : This house belongs to the gardener.
It is the gardener's house.

a. The door of the café was painted green for St Patrick's Day.
b. Look! Kate has just bought new glasses.
c. They read the newspaper dated 22nd September. But, today, it is 23rd September!
d. The measures taken by the government have been criticised.
e. This brand-new computer belongs to Thomas.

6. Les adjectifs et noms de nationalité

→ Formation

On peut classer quatre grands groupes d'adjectifs et de noms de nationalité, selon leur terminaison :

- Ceux qui se terminent par ***-sh*** ou ***-ch***

Pays	Adjectif	Un·e habitant·e	Quelques habitant·e·s	Tou·te·s
Britain	British	a British person	some British people	the British
France	French	a Frenchman/woman	some French people	the French
Ireland	Irish	an Irishman/woman	some Irish people	the Irish
Wales	Welsh	a Welshman/woman	some Welsh people	the Welsh

- Ceux dont la terminaison est ***-ese***

Pays	Adjectif	Un·e habitant·e	Quelques habitant·e·s	Tou·te·s
China	Chinese	a Chinese	some Chinese people	the Chinese
Japan	Japanese	a Japanese	some Japanese people	the Japanese
Portugal	Portuguese	a Portuguese	some Portuguese people	the Portuguese
Vietnam	Vietnamese	a Vietnamese	some Vietnamese people	the Vietnamese

- Ceux dont la terminaison est ***-an***

Continent	Adjectif	Un·e habitant·e	Quelques habitant·e·s	Tou·te·s
America	American	an American	some Americans	the Americans
Africa	African	an African	some Africans	the Africans
Asia	Asian	an Asian	some Asians	the Asians
Australia	Australian	an Australian	some Australians	the Australians

- Ceux qui **diffèrent** selon qu'ils sont adjectifs ou noms

Pays	Adjectif	Un·e habitant·e	Quelques habitant·e·s	Tou·te·s
Finland	Finnish	a Finn	some Finns	the Finns
Greece	Greek	a Greek	some Greeks	the Greeks
Poland	Polish	a Pole	some Poles	the Poles
Spain	Spanish	a Spaniard	some Spaniards	the Spaniards / the Spanish

Your turn!

6 À partir du pays suivant, indiquez l'adjectif dans le groupe nominal, puis le nom de tou·te·s les habitant·e·s.

Exemple : England = car / inhabitants?
= an English car / the English

a. Finland = meal / inhabitants?
b. Spain = festival / inhabitants?
c. Greece = theatre / inhabitants?
d. Germany = building / inhabitants?

7. L'ordre des adjectifs

→ Emploi

Lorsque l'on a affaire à une suite d'adjectifs qualificatifs, il convient de se souvenir de l'ordre **Otafcom = O-T-A-F-C-O-M** du tableau ci-dessous, afin de ne pas se tromper dans la place que doivent occuper les différents adjectifs épithètes, qui se placent devant le nom auquel ils se rapportent.

Opinion	Taille	Age	Forme	Couleur	Origine	Matière	NOM
wonderful				brown		leather	shoes
		old		red	British		bus
splendid	large		round			oak	table
gorgeous				black	German		car
				yellow		wicker	chair

wonderful brown leather shoes de magnifiques chaussures marron en cuir
an old red British bus un vieux bus britannique de couleur rouge
a gorgeous black German car une magnifique voiture allemande de couleur noire

Your turn!

7 Mettez les adjectifs dans le bon ordre.

a. The mayor had a (large – round – glass) stadium roof built.
b. The burglars broke into an (English – splendid – large) mansion.
c. The coach has found a (plastic – yellow – big) bag in the cloakroom.
d. The detective has discovered a clue: an (old – leather – cigarette – black – English) case!

8. Les adjectifs en *-ing* et *-ed*

→ Formation

Les adjectifs en ***-ing*** et ***-ed*** ont respectivement une forme de participe présent (par exemple, *astonishing*) et de participe passé (*astonished*). Leur sens est donc différent :

He is **astonished** by this **astonishing** present. Il est **surpris** par ce cadeau **surprenant**.
She was **alarmed** by this **alarming** noise. Elle a été **alarmée** par ce bruit **alarmant**.

Your turn!

8 Complétez les phrases suivantes à l'aide d'un adjectif en *-ed* ou *-ing*.

a. She passed her A-levels with 3 As, so she was very delight... .
b. When he came up to the cashier, he noticed that he had forgotten his wallet, so he was very embarrass... . What an embarrass... situation!
c. You should roll up your sleeves and start working harder if you don't want to be disappoint... . This is a very competitive exam!
d. What a tir... day! I've been travelling all day!

9. Les quantifieurs : *some*, *any*, *no* ou *not any*

→ Emploi

Les quantifieurs *some, any, no ou not any* désignent une certaine quantité, indéfinie.

Pour affirmer	There is some milk in the fridge. Il y a du lait dans le réfrigérateur.
Pour proposer	Would you like some pancakes? Voudrais-tu / Voudriez-vous des pancakes ?
Pour interroger	Is there any milk left in the fridge? Est-ce qu'il reste du lait dans le réfrigérateur ?
Pour nier	Négation en *not any* : There aren't any pancakes left in the cupboard. Il ne reste plus de pancakes dans le placard. Négation pleine en *no* : There is no milk left. Il ne reste plus de lait.

Your turn!

9 Complétez les phrases suivantes par *some*, *any*, *no*, ou *not any*.

a. I'm sorry, but I cannot wait ... longer. I have ... time left. I must go now!

b. Would you like ... Dutch cheese? I've just come back from the Netherlands and I've brought ... .

c. Is there ... tea left in the pot? I would like ... please!

d. ... students take a gap year after graduating from school. They want ... free time for themselves as they usually don't have ... time when they prepare for their exams.

10. Les quantifieurs : *a lot of*, *much*, *many*

→ Emplois

Ces trois quantifieurs sont employés pour exprimer une grande quantité et veulent dire « beaucoup », cependant leur emploi peut varier selon le contexte.

De manière générale, on emploie ***a lot of*** pour les phrases affirmatives, et ***much*** et ***many*** pour les phrases négatives ou interrogatives. ***A lot of*** s'emploie indifféremment avec un nom au singulier ou pluriel, alors que ***much*** doit être suivi uniquement d'un singulier et ***many*** d'un pluriel.

! Attention, ***a lot of*** est parfois remplacé, dans un registre familier, par ***lots of*** ou ***loads of.***

	Indénombrable (singulier)	Dénombrable (pluriel)
Phrase affirmative *A lot of*	There is a lot of butter. Il y a beaucoup de beurre.	There are a lot of oranges. Il y a beaucoup d'oranges.
Phrase négative *Much, many*	There isn't much butter. Il n'y a pas beaucoup de beurre.	There aren't many oranges. Il n'y a pas beaucoup d'oranges.
Phrase interrogative *Much, many*	Is there much butter left? Est-ce qu'il reste beaucoup de beurre ?	Are there many oranges left? Est-ce qu'il reste beaucoup d'oranges ?

	Indénombrable (singulier)	Dénombrable (pluriel)
Quantité excessive : trop de *Too much, too many*	There is too much butter in my sandwich. Il y a trop de beurre dans mon sandwich.	There are too many oranges left. What about making some marmalade? Il reste trop d'oranges. Et si on faisait de la confiture ?
Quantité identique, au comparatif *As much as, as many as*	There is as much milk in my coffee as in your tea. Il y a autant de lait dans mon café que dans ton / votre thé.	There are as many bikes as cars in Berlin. Il y a autant de vélos que de voitures à Berlin.
Équivalents de ***a lot of / much / many*** *A great deal of, plenty of, a large number of*	***a great deal of* + *singulier*** ***plenty of*** a great deal of / plenty of work beaucoup de travail	***a large number of* + pluriel** ***plenty of*** a large number of / plenty of people beaucoup de gens
How much et ***how many?*** pour traduire « combien » ? *How much, how many*	How much is this bag? Combien coûte ce sac ?	How many cars can be parked in this car park? Combien de voitures peut-on garer dans ce parc de stationnement ?

Your turn!

10 Complétez ce texte sur William Shakespeare à l'aide de *a lot of*, *much* ou *many*.

... people know that Shakespeare is the most famous British playwright, who was born in 1564 in Stratford-upon-Avon and who died at the age of 52. There are not ... authors who wrote as ... masterpieces as he did. Some of them are very long plays, such as *Hamlet*, but others are shorter and don't take ... time to read. You can always borrow them from ... libraries, too, if you don't have ... money!

11. Les quantifieurs : *a little*, *a few*, *little*, *few*, *several*

→ Emplois

Les quantifieurs ***little, a little*** s'emploient devant un nom **au singulier** et expriment une quantité insuffisante (***little***) ou une petite quantité (***a little***).

Les quantifieurs ***few, a few, several*** sont utilisés devant un nom **au pluriel** et indiquent une quantité insuffisante (***few***), quelques éléments (***a few***) ou plusieurs éléments (***several***).

Quantifieur	Indénombrable (singulier)	Dénombrable (pluriel)
Little: une quantité insuffisante + suivi d'un nom au singulier	little milk peu de lait	
A little: une petite quantité + suivi d'un nom au singulier	a little milk un peu de lait Would you like a little milk in your tea? Voudrais-tu / voudriez-vous un peu de lait dans ton / votre thé ?	

Few: une quantité insuffisante + suivi d'un nom au pluriel		few cars peu de voitures There were few cars on the motorway. Il y avait peu de voitures sur l'autoroute.
A few: un certain nombre + suivi d'un nom au pluriel		a few cars quelques voitures There were a few cars outside the police station. Il y avait quelques voitures devant le commissariat.
Several: plusieurs éléments + suivi d'un nom au pluriel		several cars plusieurs voitures. There were several cars near the stadium. Il y avait plusieurs voitures près du stade.

Your turn!

11 Complétez les phrases à l'aide de *little, a little, few, a few* ou *several*.

a. If I have ... time this afternoon, I would like to go to the library because I would like to borrow ... books.

b. ... causes may account for the difficulties the country is facing – unemployment, higher and higher tuition fees, the drastic drop in people's purchasing power, truancy, and so on.

c. I've just come back from the United States. I have ... coins left, but ... banknotes, as usual. I actually spent most of my pocket money when I was there.

d. Very ... people know that this product is dangerous, which is why they keep using it.

12. Les pronoms personnels : *I, we, they... me, us, them...*

Un pronom s'emploie à la place d'un nom, notamment pour éviter de le répéter. Le pronom suit souvent le nom. On peut donc l'identifier, c'est-à-dire savoir de qui on parle.

Helen met John at the library yesterday. Helen a rencontré John à la bibliothèque hier.

She met him at the library yesterday. Elle l'a rencontré à la bibliothèque hier.

Le pronom sujet ***She*** remplace ***Helen*** et le pronom complément ***him*** remplace ***John.***

Whose house is this? It is big. (*it* = *house* = inanimé)

À qui appartient cette maison ? Elle est grande.

→ Formes

Personne	Au singulier		Au pluriel	
	Fonction sujet	complément	sujet	complément
1re personne	I	me	we	us
2e personne	you	you	you	you
3e personne	he-she-it	him-her-it	they	them

→ Emplois

Les pronoms personnels, fonction **sujet**, doivent être placés **avant le verbe ou l'auxiliaire** à la forme affirmative ou négative, mais ils se placent après l'auxiliaire dans les phrases interrogatives.

He came back from New Zealand two days ago. Il est rentré de Nouvelle-Zélande il y a deux jours.

She isn't planning to visit Ireland. Elle n'envisage pas de visiter l'Irlande.

Have you understood that you need to wait longer than expected?
As-tu / Avez-vous compris qu'il faut attendre plus longtemps que prévu ?

En fonction **complément**, direct ou indirect, le pronom se place toujours **après le verbe.**

They contacted him five minutes ago. Ils l'ont contacté il y a cinq minutes. (complément d'objet direct)

He didn't invite them. Il ne les a pas invité·e·s.

Did she call you yesterday? Est-ce qu'elle t'a appelé·e hier ?

He has brought her some gorgeous daffodils for her birthday.
Il lui a rapporté de magnifiques jonquilles pour son anniversaire. (complément d'objet indirect)

She brought us a cheesecake. Elle nous a apporté un cheesecake.

I saw them at the shopping centre. Je les ai vu·e·s au centre commercial.

Your turn!

12 Complétez le courriel suivant à l'aide d'un pronom, sujet ou complément.

Hello Abigail,
... hope all is well with ... . am fine, but ... have been so busy over the last few weeks, that's why ... didn't write to ... earlier ... mother has recently spent four days at the Prince Hospital. ... doctor told ... that ... needed to check if everything was fine after ... latest operation. So ... needed to stay with mum as much as possible.
As ... told ... the last time ... met in Leeds, Tom and Ben, ... two 18-year-old sons, had to take ... A level exams last week. ... worked hard throughout the year, so ... hope that ... will pass ... exams with distinction! And Sarah, ... youngest daughter, has just taken ... GCSE exams!
... am looking forward to hearing from ...
Love,
Sue X X

13. Les déterminants (*my*, *their*...) et les pronoms (*mine*, *theirs*...) possessifs

Le déterminant possessif se place avant le nom, comme un article, et indique à qui appartient la chose désignée : It's my pen. C'est mon stylo.

Le pronom possessif permet de remplacer le nom : It's mine. C'est le mien.

→ Formes

Personne	Au singulier		Au pluriel	
	Déterminant possessif	Pronom possessif	Déterminant possessif	Pronom possessif
1re personne	my	mine	our	ours
2e personne	your	yours	your	yours
3e personne	his-her-its	his-hers	their	theirs

→ Emplois

Les déterminants et les pronoms possessifs répondent à la question ***Whose... ?*** (À qui appartient .... ?) qui porte donc sur l'identité de la personne qui possède l'objet, par exemple :

Question en *Whose?*	Nom	Déterminant possessif	Pronom possessif
Whose bike is it? À qui appartient ce vélo ?	It's Mary's bike. C'est le vélo de Mary.	It's her bike. C'est son vélo.	It's hers. C'est le sien.

! Attention, les pronoms indéfinis *someone, everyone, nobody*..., bien qu'ils s'accordent au singulier, correspondent au déterminant possessif pluriel, ***their***.

Everyone has got their dictionary. Tout le monde a son dictionnaire.

Les **déterminants possessifs** (*my, your*, etc.) se placent devant un nom et indiquent à qui appartient l'objet en question.

My pen Mon stylo

Her book Son livre (à elle)

Les **pronoms possessifs** (*mine, yours*, etc.), quant à eux, ont deux emplois essentiels :

- Pour reprendre un nom déjà défini :

  Whose pen is it? It's yours. À qui est ce stylo ? C'est le tien.

- Dans les constructions nom + *of* + pronom possessif.

  A friend of mine Un·e de mes ami·e·s

  A friend of hers Un·e de ses ami·e·s (à elle)

  A friend of ours Un·e de nos ami·e·s

Your turn!

13 Transformez les phrases suivantes selon le modèle :

Exemples : Whose bag is it? (James) = It's James's bag. It's his bag. It's his.
One of my friends has just arrived = A friend of mine has just arrived.

a. Whose books are these? (Caroline and Jane).
b. Whose laptop computer is it? (Christopher).
c. One of his neighbours invited him.
d. Whose files are these? (I).
e. Whose flash drive is it? (You).

14. Les pronoms réfléchis (*myself*, *ourselves*…) et réciproques (*each other*, *one another*)

→ Formation

Personne	Au singulier		Au pluriel	
	Formé sur	Pronom réfléchi	Formé sur	Pronom réfléchi
1re personne	Déterminant possessif	myself	Déterminant possessif	ourselves
2e personne	Déterminant possessif	yourself	Déterminant possessif	yourselves
3e personne	Pronom personnel complément	himself-herself-itself	Pronom personnel complément	themselves

→ Emploi

Le pronom réfléchi reprend le sujet et il est employé comme forme d'insistance. Il doit correspondre en genre et en nombre au nom auquel il se rapporte.

You are talking to yourself. Tu parles tout·e seul·e.

! **Attention**, le sens de la phrase peut changer selon la place du pronom réfléchi.

She has cut herself. There is some blood. Elle s'est coupée. Il y a un peu de sang.
She has cut herself a slice of ham. Elle s'est coupé une tranche de jambon.
She has cut her hair herself. Elle s'est coupé les cheveux elle-même.

Cependant, même si « se couper » se dit *cut oneself*, certains verbes ne sont pas réflexifs en anglais, alors qu'ils le sont en français.

s'attendre à = *expect*
s'évanouir = *faint*
s'excuser = *apologise*
se laver = *wash*
se lever = *stand up*
se disputer = *quarrel*
se raser = *shave*
se rencontrer = *meet*
se réveiller = *wake up*
se sentir = *feel*
s'entraîner = *train*
s'arrêter = *stop*

They met yesterday. Ils·Elles se sont rencontré·e·s hier.
She trains twice a day. Elle s'entraîne deux fois par jour.

→ Formes et emplois des pronoms réciproques

Les pronoms réciproques ***each other*** et ***one another*** signifient *l'un l'autre, les uns les autres*. Ils indiquent que deux personnes font la même chose, l'une envers l'autre.

Nombre de personnes	Pour 2 personnes	+ de 2 personnes
Pronom réciproque	Each other	One another

Donovan and Jennifer are going to get married. They love each other.
Donovan et Jennifer vont se marier. Ils s'aiment.

The 10 students talked to one another in English during the oral exercise.
Les 10 étudiant·e·s se sont parlé en anglais pendant l'exercice oral.

Your turn!

14 Complétez avec le pronom qui convient.

Janet has invited her new neighbour Elizabeth for a cup of tea.
Elizabeth: Have you made these delicious flapjacks ... ?
Janet: Yes, I have. I did it ... this morning! And, you will be surprised to learn that, last month, the children made some ... !
Elizabeth: Wow ! You should be proud of ... ! Where are your two children by the way?
Janet: They're up there in the studyroom. They're talking to ... in Chinese! They've been learning Mandarin for three years now, so they're practising!

15. Le comparatif et le superlatif

→ Formation

	Comparatif	Superlatif
de supériorité	Adjectif court big = bigger than plus grand·e que	Adjectif court big = the biggest le·la plus grand·e
	Adjectif long comfortable = more comfortable than plus confortable que	Adjectif long comfortable = the most comfortable le·la plus confortable
d'égalité	Adjectif court big = as big as aussi grand·e que	
	Adjectif long comfortable = as comfortable as aussi confortable que	
d'infériorité	Adjectif court big = less big than moins grand·e que	Adjectif court big = the least big le·la moins grand·e
	Adjectif long comfortable = less comfortable than moins confortable que	Adjectif long comfortable = the least comfortable le·la moins confortable

→ Quelques formes irrégulières

Good et ***well*** : comparatif = better than (meilleur·e que), et superlatif = the best (le·la meilleur·e)

Bad = comparatif = worse than (pire que), et superlatif = the worst (le·la pire)

Far = comparatif = farther than (plus éloigné·e que – distance) / further than (sens figuré) further education (enseignement supérieur), et superlatif = the farthest (le·la plus éloigné·e)

Les adjectifs se terminant en ***-y*** forment leur comparatiif en ***-ier*** et leur superlatif en ***-iest.***

She is prettier than her sister. Elle est plus belle que sa sœur.

It's the prettiest dress I've ever seen. C'est la plus belle robe que j'aie jamais vue.

→ Emplois

Les adjectifs au comparatif ou au superlatif permettent d'effectuer des comparaisons et d'évaluer deux éléments, l'un par rapport à l'autre.

The more he works at school, the better his grades are. Plus il travaille à l'école, meilleures sont ses notes.

Your turn!

15 Faites des phrases en comparant la Tour CN, la Statue de la Liberté, ainsi que Big Ben et la Tour Elizabeth. Utilisez des comparatifs et des superlatifs à partir des renseignements sur chaque monument.

CN Tower, Toronto, Canada	The Statue of Liberty, New York Harbour, USA	Big Ben and the Elizabeth Tower, London, England

HEIGHT: 553 metres (1,815 feet)	**HEIGHT:** - height of copper statue to torch: 46 metres (151 feet 1 inch) - height from ground level to torch: 305 feet 1 inch (93 meters)	**HEIGHT:** 96m (315 feet)
Completed: 1976 **Visitors:** 1. 5 million	**Donated:** October 28, 1886 **Visitors:** 4. 5 million	**Completed:** May 31, 1859 **Visitors:** more than 20 million

16. *Not any more, no more, none, never*

→ Formation

no more	There is no more mineral water in the fridge. Il n'y a plus d'eau minérale dans le réfrigérateur.
not any more	There isn't any more pepper. Il n'y a plus de poivre.
none	Is there any sugar in this yoghurt? No, there is none. Y a-t-il du sucre dans ce yaourt ? Non, il n'y en a pas.
never	He has never eaten kangaroo. Il n'a jamais mangé de kangourou. Mais pour une question : Have you ever been to Australia? Es-tu / Êtes-vous déjà allé·e·s en Australie ?

→ Emploi

Not any more, no more, none et ***never*** sont employés dans des phrases négatives.
No more est l'équivalent de ***not any more.***
None est un pronom et, de ce fait, ne peut être suivi d'un nom.
Never est employé dans les phrases déclaratives négatives.
Pour poser une question, on aura recours à ***ever.***

! Attention, il faut éviter la double négation.

There is no more sugar in the cupboard. There isn't any more sugar in the cupboard.

Il n'y a plus de sucre dans le placard.

→ Mais on ne pourra pas dire *isn't no more.*

Your turn!

16 **Complétez les phrases suivantes par *not anymore, no more, none* ou *never*.**

a. She has ... been to New Zealand, but she is planning to visit this country in two years' time.
b. Is there any milk left? I think there is ... . I need to go to the supermarket.
c. You should go to the greengrocer's. There are ... vegetables left.
d. There is ... sugar. Would you like some sweetener instead?

Le groupe verbal

Le verbe est l'élément central d'une phrase : c'est lui qui va mettre en relation le sujet et, dans le cas des verbes transitifs (verbes qui peuvent être suivis d'un complément), le complément d'objet direct. Le verbe est donc porteur du message principal :

He / books ➛ mise en relation par le verbe *BUY* = *He* ***bought*** *some books.*

Comme on le voit, le verbe *BUY* a permis de construire la phrase, en mettant en relation le sujet *he* et le complément d'objet direct *books*.

Temps et aspects

En anglais, il y a deux **temps** (*tenses*), c'est-à-dire la valeur temporelle d'un verbe qui indique le moment où un événement se produit : **le présent et le passé.** Il n'existe pas de temps futur en anglais. On a recours au modal *will* ou au présent en *be* + V-*ing* pour parler de l'avenir.

L'aspect, quant à lui, indique comment cet événement a lieu à travers le temps : cet aspect peut être permanent (*simple*), progressif (*progressive*), parfait (*perfect*) ou encore parfait progressif (*perfect progressive*).

1. Les auxiliaires

Qu'appelle-t-on un auxiliaire ?

L'auxiliaire se différencie d'un verbe lexical (comme *eat, buy, sell, run*...) . Il est vide de sens à lui seul et a donc besoin, pour être conjugué, d'un verbe lexical. Un verbe lexical est un verbe ordinaire porteur de sens, comme *run, eat, sleep, decide.*

Il existe trois auxiliaires en anglais : ***be***, ***have*** et ***do.***

L'auxiliaire remplit trois principales fonctions :

a. Il permet de former la phrase déclarative, en présence d'aspect.

He is reading a book. (Aspect *be* + V-*ing*)

She has bought a bag. (Aspect *have* + V-*en*)

They did send their applications to the manager. (pour l'insistance, énoncé emphatique)

b. Il apparait dans la phrase négative et porte la négation.

He isn't reading a book.

She hasn't bought a bag.

They didn't send their applications to the manager.

c. Il se place en tête dans la phrase interrogative.

Is he reading a book?

Has she bought a bag?

Did they send their applications to the manager?

Ci-dessous le traitement de *be, have,* et *do* uniquement en tant qu'**auxiliaire**.

→ Emplois de *BE* auxiliaire

BE, en tant qu'auxiliaire, est accompagné d'un verbe lexical, comme dans *she is dancing. BE* auxiliaire est employé pour former le présent et le prétérit en *be* + V-*ing*, ainsi que la voix passive.

Présent en *be* + V-*ing*	She is learning Mandarin in China. Elle apprend le mandarin en Chine.
Prétérit en *be* + V-*ing*	He was mowing the lawn when his sister phoned him. Il tondait la pelouse lorsque sa sœur l'a appelé.
Voix passive au présent	This firm is being taken over by a foreign investor. Cette entreprise est rachetée par un·e investisseur·se étranger·ère.
Voix passive au passé	This castle was built in the 18th century by a Welsh architect. Ce château a été construit au dix-huitième siècle par un·e architecte gallois·e.

→ Emplois de *HAVE* auxiliaire

HAVE auxiliaire est utilisé pour former le *present perfect* simple et le *present perfect* en *-ing*, ainsi que le *past perfect* (plus-que-parfait) simple et le *past perfect* en *-ing*.

***Present perfect* simple**	They have settled down in Texas. Ils·Elles se sont installé·e·s au Texas.
Present perfect* en *be* + V-*ing	She has been working in this South-African firm for three years. Elle travaille pour cette entreprise sud-africaine depuis trois ans.
***Past perfect* simple**	He had forgotten to take his passport. Il avait oublié de prendre son passeport.
Past perfect* en *be* + V-*ing	She had been waiting for the bus for 20 minutes. Elle attendait le bus depuis 20 minutes.

→ Emplois de *DO* auxiliaire

DO auxiliaire est employé pour construire la forme emphatique, c'est-à-dire pour insister sur quelque chose, pour les phrases négatives et interrogatives.

- insistance, phrase emphatique :

  She does work for the BBC, no doubt about that!
  Elle travaille bien à la BBC, aucun doute là-dessus !

  He did send the letter yesterday. I took him to the post office.
  Il a bien envoyé cette lettre hier. C'est moi-même qui l'ai conduit à la poste.

- phrase négative :

  They don't understand why they have been punished.
  Ils·Elles ne comprennent pas pourquoi ils·elles ont été puni·e·s.

- phrase interrogative :

  Do you want to go to the cinema tonight?
  Est-ce que tu veux aller au cinéma ce soir ?

Your turn!

1 Complétez le dialogue par *BE* au temps et à la forme (affirmative, négative ou interrogative) qui conviennent.

A. Hello Peter! How ... you? I haven't seen you for ages!

B. I ... fine, thank you! I've been to France. The last time we met, I did tell you I ... leaving England for a couple of months, didn't I? Never mind, because of the Brexit vote, I ... planning to settle down in the South of France!

A. Wow! That ... unexpected! So, finally, you don't want to finish your studies in Birmingham, do you? You've had the opportunity of getting a scholarship at Birmingham University, haven't you?

B. Yes, I have, but that ... before Brexit! At the time I didn't know that Britain ... going to leave the European Union. Now that Brexit has become a reality, I've changed my mind!

2 Complétez par *HAVE* au temps et à la forme (affirmative, négative ou interrogative) qui conviennent.

a. ... you ever been to London?

b. Yes, I ... ! I went on a school trip to England last year and we visited London.

c. ... you already finished your homework?

d. No, I ... I need some more time.

3 Complétez par *DO* au temps et à la forme (affirmative, négative ou interrogative) qui conviennent.

a. ... you need this English dictionary? I would like to translate this text.

b. No, I ... . You can take it if you want.

c. ... you visit Buckingham Palace when you went to London two years ago?

d. No, I ... , unfortunately! It was a very short stay, so I ... have the time!

2. Les auxiliaires de modalité

Caractéristiques générales des modaux :

Les auxiliaires de modalité, ou les modaux, sont **invariables** :

- Ils ne s'accordent pas à la troisième personne du singulier (donc absence de -s).
- Ils ne sont jamais suivis de *to* de l'infinitif.
- En qualité d'auxiliaire, ils fonctionnent donc sans *do*.
- Deux modaux ne peuvent pas se suivre.

→ Formes simples : modal + base verbale

Modal	Valeurs exprimées	Exemple	Traduction
Can	a. Demande b. Permission c. Capacité	a. Can you help me please? b. Can I borrow your car? c. She can speak four languages.	a. Peux-tu m'aider s'il te plait ? b. Puis-je emprunter ta voiture ? c. Elle sait parler quatre langues.
Could	a. Hypothèse b. Pouvoir au passé	a. I could take the bus if you showed me the bus stop. b. They could not stay another year abroad.	a. Je pourrais prendre le bus si tu me montrais l'arrêt de bus. b. Ils·Elles ne pouvaient pas rester une année supplémentaire à l'étranger.
May	a. Permission b. Possibilité	a. You may use your dictionary. b. He may be late.	a. Tu peux utiliser mon dictionnaire. b. Il se peut qu'il soit en retard / Il est peut-être en retard.
Might	a. Incertitude	a. It might rain this afternoon.	a. Il pourrait pleuvoir cet après-midi / Il se pourrait qu'il pleuve…

Modal	Valeurs exprimées	Exemple	Traduction
Must	a. Obligation b. Quasi-certitude	a. She must study this chapter for her exam. b. She must be her sister.	a. Elle doit étudier ce chapitre pour son examen. b. Elle doit être sa sœur.
Shall	a. Promesse b. Loi c. Suggestion	a. I shall send you some news from Britain, don't worry! b. You shall obey your parents. c. Shall we go for a walk?	a. Promis, je t'enverrai des nouvelles de Grande-Bretagne, ne t'inquiète pas ! b. Tu obéiras à tes parents. c. Et si on allait se promener ?
Should	a. Conseil b. Vraisemblance	a. You should fill in this form if you want to get this scholarship. b. There's less traffic today. I should be home earlier tonight.	a. Tu devrais remplir ce formulaire si tu veux obtenir cette bourse. b. Il y a moins de circulation aujourd'hui. Je devrais être à la maison plus tôt ce soir.
Will	a. Avenir b. Fatalité	a. I will visit the United States next year. b. As the saying goes, boys will be boys!	a. Je visiterai les Etats-Unis l'année prochaine. b. Selon le dicton, les garçons resteront toujours des garçons !
Would	a. Conditionnel b. Répétition dans le passé	a. I would stay another night at the hotel if it snowed again. b. He would go fishing every week when he was a child.	a. Je resterais une autre nuit à l'hôtel s'il neigeait de nouveau. b. Enfant, il allait à la pêche toutes les semaines.

→ Formation formes complexes : modal + *have* + participe passé

Modal	Valeurs exprimées	Exemple	Traduction
Can	Impossibilité	He can't have missed the train. He always arrives early at the station.	Il est impossible qu'il ait raté le train. Il arrive toujours tôt à la gare.
Could	Possibilité	He could have lost his bag if he had not doublechecked everything.	Il aurait pu perdre son sac s'il n'avait pas tout re-vérifié.
May	Probabilité	She may have waited outside the bookshop.	Il est possible qu'elle ait attendu devant la librairie / Elle a peut-être attendu devant la librairie.
Might	Vraisemblance	He might have phoned her, but that would be surprising.	Il se pourrait qu'il l'ait appelée, mais ce serait surprenant.
Must	Quasi-certitude	She must have forgotten that she left her bag at the left-luggage office.	Elle a sûrement dû oublier qu'elle a laissé son sac à la consigne.
Shall	Promesse	I shall have sent you my report by Friday, trust me!	Fais-moi confiance, d'ici vendredi, je t'aurai envoyé mon rapport !
Should	Reproche	You should have worked more.	Tu aurais dû travailler davantage.
Will	Avenir	I will have done my homework by Saturday evening.	J'aurai terminé mes devoirs d'ici samedi soir.
Would	Conditionnel passé	They would have waited for her if they had known that she was also invited to the party.	Ils·Elles l'auraient attendue s'ils·elles avaient su qu'elle était aussi invitée à cette soirée.

→ Emploi

Le **modal + *have* + participe passé** s'emploie pour évaluer, porter un jugement, un point de vue sur une action passée. La valeur de ce point de vue va dépendre du modal employé.

She may have missed his bus. Il se peut qu'elle ait raté son bus. Elle a peut-être raté son bus.

They must have sent a message. Please check your mobile phone.
Ils·Elles ont certainement dû envoyer un message. Vérifie sur ton téléphone portable, s'il te plaît.

Your turn!

4 Reformulez en employant le modal proposé entre parenthèses. (formes simples)

Exemple : He is allowed to walk into this private room. (may)
He **may** walk into this private room.

a. She is able to speak four foreign languages. (can)
b. They have to wait in the terminal because the plane to Chicago has not landed yet. (must)
c. I advise you to resit this exam. It will be your second chance! (should)
d. Take your umbrella with you if you want. But I don't think it's going to rain today. (might)
e. I don't know anything about today's weather forecast, so take your raincoat. Rainy weather? (may)

5 Reformulez en employant le modal proposé. (formes complexes)

Exemple : John has not forgotten his passport. He is always so cautious. (can) =
John can't have forgotten his passport.

a. Perhaps he has put his passport somewhere else if it is not in his rucksack. (may)
b. I wish you had invited your new friend. (should)
c. Kate was certainly disappointed. (must)
d. I'm almost sure that he has forgotten his bag in the car. (must)

3. Modalité : équivalents des modaux

→ Formation

Il faut bien comprendre qu'un modal, aussi appelé « auxiliaire de modalité » fonctionne comme un auxiliaire. De ce fait, il est **impossible** de rencontrer deux modaux à la suite. Il convient donc d'avoir recours à des équivalents de modaux si l'on souhaite construire une phrase au **passé**, ou **référer à l'avenir** avec *must* et *can* ou *may*.

→ Emplois

Modal	Équivalent du modal	Au passé	Pour exprimer l'avenir
Can Capacité	*Be able to*	I was able to get in touch with my bank yesterday when my credit card was stolen Hier, j'ai pu contacter ma banque quand ma carte de crédit a été volée.	The strikers will be able to get a pay rise after the negotiations. Les grévistes pourront obtenir une augmentation de salaire après les négociations.

On peut aussi rencontrer *to be able to* au présent :

This secretary is able to type letters on her keyboard without looking at it.
Ce·tte secrétaire est capable de taper des lettres sur son clavier sans le regarder.

Modal	Équivalent du modal	Au passé	Pour exprimer l'avenir
May Permission	*Be allowed to*	Brigitta was allowed to vote in England when she became a British citizen. Brigitta a pu voter / a été autorisée à voter quand elle est devenue citoyenne britannique.	The Scots will be allowed to choose to become independent if there is a second referendum. Les Écossais·es pourront / auront la permission de choisir de devenir indépendant·e·s s'il y a un deuxième référendum.

Modal	Équivalent du modal	Au passé	Pour exprimer l'avenir
Must Obligation	*Have to*	I had to wait three hours at the station because of the train strike. J'ai dû attendre trois heures à la gare à cause de la grève des trains. She didn't have to resit her exams because that course was optional. Elle n'était pas obligée de repasser ses examens car ce cours était facultatif. (absence d'obligation)	They will have to apply for the job. Ils·Elles devront envoyer leur candidature pour ce poste.

Your turn!

6 **Reformulez les phrases en utilisant les consignes entre parenthèses.**
Exemple : You must decide before it is too late (mettre au futur) =
You will have to decide before it is too late.

a. You may borrow my car, but please be careful! (mettre au futur)
b. I was forced to spend two hours at the police station in Bath. (équivalence)
c. She can send her application after her A-levels. (mettre au futur)
d. The London train left immediately. I didn't wait long. (équivalence).

4. Le présent simple

→ Formation

Forme affirmative	I / you / we / they work… He / she / it works… (+ *s* à la 3ème personne du singulier)
Forme négative	I / you / we / they do not work (forme contractée = don't) He / she / it does not work (forme contractée = doesn't)
Forme interrogative	Do I / you / we / they work…? Does he / she / it work…?

Le présent simple a recours à l'auxiliaire *do / does*, à la forme négative et interrogative pour les verbes lexicaux.

→ Emplois

Le présent simple est employé pour parler de généralités, des caractéristiques du sujet. On l'associe donc à des habitudes, et aussi à une information donnée de façon objective.

Voici les adverbes de fréquence ou les expressions qui indiquent une **habitude** :

never
always
often
sometimes
usually
on Mondays...
every week...

Quelques exemples :

Peter is a waiter. He works in this Japanese restaurant : il s'agit de son emploi habituel.

She always goes to the library on Friday afternoons : c'est ce qu'elle a l'habitude de faire le vendredi après-midi (aller à la bibliothèque).

Dogs bark and cats mew : ce sont des vérités.

James doesn't like tea. He prefers coffee : c'est ce qu'il aime ou n'aime pas, d'habitude, ce qui le caractérise.

Your turn!

7 Reformulez les phrases en employant le présent simple et l'élément entre parenthèses.

a. Listen! Robert is playing the piano in the living room. (every afternoon)
b. Watch out! The children are crossing the street opposite the stadium. (whenever they do sport)
c. I am working at Bristol Library at the moment. (sometimes)
d. Look! She is not using her new laptop. (often)

5. Le présent en *be* + V-*ing*

→ Formation

Auxiliaire *be* au présent suivi du verbe en *-ing*

Forme affirmative	I am driving. (forme contractée = 'm) You / we / they are driving. (forme contractée = 're) He / she / it is driving. (forme contractée = 's)
Forme négative	I am not driving. (forme contractée = 'm not) You / we / they are not driving. (forme contractée = aren't) He / she / it is not driving. (forme contractée = isn't)
Forme interrogative	Am I driving...? Are you / we / they driving...? Is he / she / it driving...?

→ Emplois

Le présent en *be* + V-*ing* s'emploie pour décrire des activités en cours, qui ont donc lieu au moment où l'on parle. Compte tenu que le présent en ***be* + V-*ing*** indique qu'un événement est en déroulement, il est souvent accompagné d'adverbes ou de locutions adverbiales indiquant ce moment présent, en cours de réalisation :

now
at the moment
currently
for the time being

Le contexte peut aider à choisir le temps.

Listen! He is playing the guitar.

Écoute ! Il joue de la guitare. (l'action a lieu en ce moment-même, il est en train de jouer).

De plus, employé avec *always* fortement accentué, le présent en *-ing*, indiquera l'agacement ou l'irritation du locuteur :

He is always making mistakes! This is incredible!

Il fait toujours des erreurs ! C'est incroyable !

Your turn!

8 Mettez les verbes au présent simple ou au présent en *be* + V-*ing*.

a. My mother (take) the cat to the vet (this afternoon).
b. Her neighbour (mow) the lawn (every four weeks).
c. I'm just sick and tired of those people's behaviour! They (complain) (always).
d. She (get up) at six, (have) breakfast at seven and (go) to work at eight o'clock (every morning). But, (today), she (not • have) to get up at six because she (be) on leave.

6. Le prétérit simple

→ Formation

Les verbes réguliers comme *decide, dance, work*… forment leur prétérit simple, dans une phrase déclarative affirmative, par l'ajout de *-ed*. Et il existe bien entendu toute une liste de verbes irréguliers, qu'il faut donc savoir par cœur ! (Voir les verbes irréguliers, p. 259.)

	Verbes réguliers	Verbes irréguliers (exemple = go)
Forme affirmative	I / you / he / she / it / we / they decided.	I / you / he / she / it / we / they went…
Forme négative	I / you / he / she / it / we / they did not decide. (forme contractée : didn't)	I did not go…(forme contractée = didn't go)
Forme interrogative	Did I / you / he / she / it / we / they decide…?	Did I / you / he / she / it / we / they go…?

→ Emploi

Le prétérit simple est l'un des deux temps (*tenses*) grammaticaux de l'anglais et il est employé pour parler d'événements au passé, sans lien direct avec le présent.

Le prétérit simple est associé à une rupture par rapport au présent, c'est-à-dire à un passé sans rapport avec le présent.

Compte tenu que le prétérit indique qu'un événement est passé, sans lien avec le présent, il est souvent accompagné d'adverbes, de locutions adverbiales, de dates indiquant le passé :

yesterday
last month
three days **ago**
in 2017

The British decided to leave the European Union in 2016.
Les Britanniques ont décidé de quitter l'Union Européenne en 2016.

Le passé composé français se traduit par un prétérit en anglais lorsqu'il y a une date mentionnée (*in 2016*).

Your turn!

9 Mettez les verbes entre parenthèses au prétérit simple.

a. Last week the manager (make) up his mind to postpone the meeting. He (not • want) to negotiate with the strikers straight away because he (think) that they (be) wrong.
b. Jane (go) to Thailand two weeks ago. She (visit) the floating markets, as well as the numerous temples. Then, she (come) back to Europe.
c. His parents (forgive) him because he (not to do) that on purpose.
d. I (not • know) that they (be) Americans. I (think) they (come) from Britain!

7. Le prétérit modal

→ Formation

Construire d'une hypothèse	**If** you found a wallet, what would you do? Si tu trouvais un porte-monnaie, que ferais-tu ?
Emettre une supposition	**Suppose / Imagine** she accepted your proposal, what would you do? Imagine qu'elle accepte ta proposition, que ferais-tu ?
Formuler un souhait	**I wish** they came earlier tonight. Je souhaite qu'ils·elles viennent plus tôt ce soir.
Exprimer la préférence	**I'd rather** she went to the United States. Je préférerais qu'elle aille aux États-Unis.
Après certaines expressions	**It is (high) time** the government took a decision. Il est (grand) temps que le gouvernement prenne une décision. It **was as if** she had trouble deciding between accepting and refusing the offer. C'était comme si elle avait du mal à prendre une décision entre accepter et refuser cette offre.

→ Emploi

Contrairement au prétérit temporel qui renvoie au passé, le prétérit modal permet d'exprimer **l'irréel du présent**, c'est-à-dire de formuler une condition (hypothèse ou supposition), notamment dans les phrases en *if*, mais aussi le souhait, par exemple après *I wish*.

Your turn!

10 Indiquez, pour chaque prétérit des phrases suivantes, s'il s'agit d'un prétérit modal ou d'un prétérit temporel.

Exemple : It is time they decided. = prétérit modal

a. She settled down in Kent when she moved to England.
b. If she went to Wales, she would choose to live in Swansea.
c. His neighbour claimed that his ex-wife turned the children against him when he got divorced in 2018.
d. Imagine you won two million euros, what would you do?

8. Le prétérit en *be* + V-*ing*

→ Formation

Le prétérit en *be* + V-*ing* est composé de l'auxiliaire *be* au prétérit, suivi du verbe en *-ing* : par exemple, *he was playing.* Quelle différence avec le prétérit simple ?

Le prétérit en *be* + V-*ing* est utilisé pour indiquer qu'une action était en cours au moment où un événement ponctuel (au prétérit simple) a eu lieu dans le passé :

He was playing the guitar when the phone rang.

Il jouait de la guitare lorque le téléphone a sonné.

Notez que le **prétérit en *be* + V-*ing*** renvoie à **un seul événement** – jouer de la guitare. Le prétérit en *be* + V-*ing* convient à la description d'un événement unique qui était en cours.

Your turn!

11 Conjuguez les verbes au prétérit simple ou au prétérit en *be* + V-*ing* selon le contexte.

A. 'Hello Peter, what (do) last July?'
B. 'I (go) to the Bristol Harbour Festival, which (take) place at the end of July. My girlfriend (meet) me in Bath last winter (come) too. We (celebrate) Bristol's maritime heritage, by drinking pints of beer at the Watershed when I (bump) into an old friend of mine. He (drink) a pint of lager just behind us!'
A. 'Wow! That sounds terrific! And you (visit) any sights?'
B. 'Well, the next day, we actually (decide) to go to Bath because we (want) to visit the famous Roman Baths. And while we (wait) outside the Baths, we just (meet) an old friend of my girlfriend's this time! It's a small world indeed, isn't it? She (stroll) along the main street, while my girlfriend and I (have) lunch on the terrace of a posh restaurant!'

9. Le *present perfect*

→ Formation

Le *present perfect* est formé à l'aide de l'auxiliaire ***have*** et du participe passé du verbe. Par exemple pour ***forget***, on aura ***have + forgotten.***

Phrase affirmative	Phrase négative	Phrase interrogative
I have forgotten. (forme contractée = I've)	I have not forgotten. (forme contractée = I haven't)	Have I forgotten…?
He / she / it has forgotten. (forme contractée = he / she / it's)	He / she / it has not forgotten. (forme contractée = he / she / it hasn't)	Has he / she / it forgotten…?
You / we / they have forgotten. (forme contractée = I've)	You / we / they have not forgotten. (forme contractée = you / we / they haven't)	Have you / we / they forgotten…?

→ Emplois

Contrairement au présent ou au prétérit qui sont des temps chronologiques, le ***present perfect*** est **un aspect**. Il indique le point de vue de celui qui parle sur l'événement en question. Le *present perfect* est à cheval entre le passé et le présent. Il indique qu'une action passée a une conséquence dans le présent, en établissant un **bilan** dans le présent.

T-1 (Elodie forgot to take her wallet when she left home.)
T-0 Now, she can't pay because **she has forgotten** it!

On dira par exemple :

I'm sorry, but I have forgotten my wallet. Je suis désolé·e, mais j'ai oublié mon porte-monnaie.

Le porte-monnaie a été oublié (dans le passé), et le résultat (dans le présent), c'est que la personne se retrouve sans argent pour payer ce qu'elle doit.

Compte tenu du lien entre le passé et le présent que souligne le *present perfect*, il est souvent accompagné d'adverbes ou de locutions adverbiales indiquant eux-mêmes que le locuteur effectue un bilan :

Never
Already
Not… yet

Just
Since / for
Ever
Lately

On utilise le ***present perfect*** aussi après *It's the first / second... etc. time,* car **on effectue un bilan.**

It's the first / second… time I have visited this museum.

C'est la première / deuxième… fois que je visite ce musée.

10. Le *present perfect* en *be* + V-*ing*

→ Formation

Le *present perfect* en *be* + V-*ing* est composé du double aspect, apporté à la fois par le *present perfect simple* auquel on associe *be* + V-*ing* : ***has / have been* + V-*ing***.

Par exemple :

Wait / She has waited = *present perfect simple*

/ She is waiting = *présent* en *be* + V-*ing*

= **She has been waiting** = *present perfect* en *be* + V-*ing* = *has been* + V-*ing*

9 am. She is waiting.

11 am. She is still waiting!

She has been waiting since 9 o'clock this morning.

→ Emploi

On emploie le ***present perfect*** en *be* + V-*ing* pour des événements qui ont commencé dans le passé et qui continuent dans le présent (en français = présent + depuis), ou qui viennent de se terminer dans le présent mais dont les conséquences restent visibles (français = passé composé).

On insiste sur l'activité elle-même : *present perfect* en *be* + V-*ing* car valeur appréciative apportée par le *be* + V-*ing*.

I'm exhausted. I've been working all day. (résultat de cette lourde journée de travail = je suis fatigué·e maintenant !) Je suis épuisé·e. J'ai travaillé toute la journée.

Look! It has been raining. The pavements are wet. (les traces de la pluie sont encore visibles, même s'il ne pleut plus : les trottoirs sont mouillés). Regarde ! Il a plu. Les trottoirs sont mouillés.

→ Comparaison *present perfect simple* et *present perfect* en *be* + V-*ing*

On insiste sur le résultat (chiffré ou quantifié) : *present perfect simple*

It has rained a lot. Il a beaucoup plu.

Ce qui importe ici, c'est le **résultat.** Et ce résultat peut être chiffré ou quantifié (deux bouteilles, cinq fois, beaucoup...).

La durée : *present perfect* en *be* + V-*ing* avec *for / since*

! Attention, **en français** ici, le verbe est au **présent**, avec **depuis** !

For indique la durée de l'action, alors que ***since*** souligne son point de départ. En cas de doute entre ***for*** et ***since***, testez votre phrase : si vous pouvez dire en français, « cela dure + le complément », alors c'est ***for*** que vous devez employer.

Exemple : depuis deux heures = on peut dire « cela dure deux heures », donc c'est ***for two hours*** en anglais.

This Canadian architect has been working on this project for three weeks.

He started on 1st March 2019 and he is still working on this project

T-1 T-0 Now (21st March 2019)

At *Art and Tech's*, London (1st March 2019)

At *Art and Tech's*, London (21st March 2019)

This Canadian architect has been working on this project for three weeks.

Cet architecte canadien travaille sur ce projet depuis trois semaines.

Your turn!

12 Formulez les phrases avec un *present perfect* en *be* + V-*ing*.

a. How long (you / wait) for the bus?
b. I (be) here at the bus stop since this morning. I (wait) for almost two hours!
c. Look! It (snow) ! The path is covered with snow. It's gorgeous, isn't it?
d. Jamie! You (play) computer games again! And you have forgotten to log off again!

13 Mettez les verbes au *present perfect simple* ou au *present perfect* au *be* + V-*ing*.

a. It ... (rain) for three days! That's unusual at this time of the year, isn't it?
b. Three Australian backpackers ... (wait) outside the youth hostel for two hours.
c. I ... just (come) across a very interesting detective novel by Wilkie Collins entitled *The Moonstone*. I ... already (read) the first 20 pages.
d. Since the September 11 attacks in 2001 on the Twin Towers, New York's local authorities ... (work) to redevelop the Manhattan site.

11. Le *past perfect*

Le ***past perfect***, aussi appelé ***pluperfect***, est un temps du passé, qui est lui-même antérieur à un autre passé. Il correspond, en général, au plus-que-parfait français.

→ Formation

Il est formé de l'auxiliaire ***have*** au passé, accompagné du participe passé du verbe : ***had*** **+ participe passé du verbe.**

→ Emploi

She passed all her exams with honours because she had worked so hard.

→ 1 (to work) ....→ 2 (to pass) ....→ Now

T-2 T-1 T-0

→ Autres emplois

Avec **depuis**, on aura aussi recours au *past perfect* pour traduire l'imparfait français :

They had been working for three hours.

Ils travaillaient depuis trois heures. (verbe d'activité ***work*** au *past perfect* en *be* + V-*ing*)

They started at 2pm. They are still working at 5pm

T-2 T-1 T-0 Now

........→ 2pm 5pm

Your turn!

13 Mettez les verbes au prétérit ou au *past perfect*.

a. The Gibsons ... (go) to Ireland last summer. They ... (visit) the United States three years before.
b. They ... (be) in Chicago for four days when they ... (decide) to drive to Lake Michigan.
c. I ... (send) a complaint letter last month because I ... (not • receive) the parcel yet.
d. Nina ... (wait) for the bus for half an hour when a friend of hers ... (drive) past the post office and ... (give) her a lift.

12. *For/since/ago*

→ Emploi

Test	*For* ou *since* ?	Si vous pouvez dire « cela dure + le complément de temps » en français, il faut employer « *for* ».
FOR	+ *present perfect* « depuis »	• placé avant le complément de temps She has been learning Chinese for three years. Elle **apprend** le chinois **depuis** trois ans.

Test	*For* ou *since* ?	Si vous pouvez dire « cela dure + le complément de temps » en français, il faut employer « *for* ».
FOR	+ prétérit « pendant »	• placé avant le complément de temps He lived in England for four years. Il **a habité** en Angleterre **pendant** quatre ans.
SINCE	+ *present perfect* « depuis »	• placé avant le complément de temps, ***since*** indique le point de départ. Janet has been in the South of France since she moved to France. Janet est dans le Midi depuis qu'elle s'est installée en France.
AGO	+ prétérit « il y a… »	• placé après le complément de temps, il correspond à « il y a + complément de temps » en français. They went to Spain two years ago. Ils·Elles sont allé·e·s en Espagne il y a deux ans.

Your turn!

14 Traduisez les phrases suivantes en utilisant *for, since, ago*.

a. Ma famille s'est installée à la Nouvelle-Orléans il y a quatre ans.
b. Juliet vit en Louisiane depuis quatre ans.
c. Mes frères apprennent l'américain depuis qu'ils sont arrivés aux Etats-Unis.
d. Ils ont emménagé dans leur nouvelle maison il y a deux mois.

13. L'expression du futur

→ Emploi

En anglais, il n'existe pas de temps (*tense*) futur, mais l'anglais dispose de plusieurs façons de référer à l'avenir, que ce soit un futur plus ou moins proche ou éloigné.

Parler du futur avec :	Exemples	Valeur
Will	We will visit Sydney and Perth one day. We've always been interested in Australia! Un jour, nous visiterons Sydney et Perth. L'Australie nous a toujours intéressé·e·s !	Prédiction, quasi-certitude
Shall	We shall visit Cardiff Castle first. (prédiction) Nous commencerons par la visite du château de Cardiff. Don't worry, I shall bring you your flash drive this afternoon. (promesse) Ne t'inquiète pas. Je t'apporterai ta clé USB cette après-midi, promis !	Prédiction / promesse
Will be* + *V-ing	I am looking forward to the holidays! I will be skiing in the Swiss mountains in two weeks' time. Je suis pressé·e d'être en vacances ! Dans deux semaines, je serai en train de skier dans les montagnes suisses.	Anticipation
Présent* en *be* + *V-ing	I am taking the eight o'clock train from Bristol tomorrow. Demain, je prendrai le train de huit heures en provenance de Bristol.	Organisation datée
Be going to	We are going to visit the Norman Rockwell exhibition this afternoon. Cet après-midi, nous allons visiter l'exposition sur Norman Rockwell.	Futur proche

Parler du futur avec :	Exemples	Valeur
Be to	According to the official programme, the Queen is to go directly to the White House as soon as she arrives in Washington. Selon le programme officiel, la Reine doit se rendre directement à la Maison Blanche dès son arrivée à Washington.	Programme prévu
Be about to	Hurry up! The commencement ceremony is about to start. Dépêche-toi ! La cérémonie de remise des diplômes est sur le point de commencer.	Futur imminent

Subordonnées de temps en *when* (*as soon as*...) et futur

Les subordonnées de temps introduites par *when, as soon as, until, before, while,* ainsi que la subordonnée d'hypothèse introduite par *if* ne peuvent pas être suivies de *will* : elles sont suivies du présent ou du present perfect.

	Phrase principale	Phrase subordonnée au présent ou *present perfect*
***When* + présent**	I will send you a text message, Je t'enverrai un texto,	when I am in the international arrivals hall. quand je **serai** dans le hall d'arrivée des vols internationaux.
When* + *present perfect	I have already got the freshmen's list. I will keep you posted again, J'ai déjà la liste des étudiant·e·s de première année. Je te tiendrai à nouveau informé·e.	when I have received the sophomore students' list. quand **j'aurai reçu** la liste des étudiant·e·s de deuxième année.

Your turn!

15 Exprimez le futur dans les phrases suivantes.

a. New York City has decided to redevelop the Manhattan site where the Twin Towers stood. Three towers and a church ... (be built) soon.
b. Hurry up! The soccer match ... (start).
c. When she ... (be) older, she ... (study) economics at the London School of Economics.
d. Next July, I ... (visit) Yosemite Park in California. I am looking forward to it!

14. *Should*

→ Formation

Conseil = *should* + base verbale	Reproche = *should* + *have* + participe passé
You should apply for more Ivy League universities – and not just one! Tu **devrais** envoyer ta candidature à davantage d'universités de la Ivy League – et non pas à une seule !	With three As at your A-levels from a British public school, you should have applied for Oxbridge. Avec trois A au A-level réussi dans une école privée britannique, tu **aurais dû postuler** pour l'université d'Oxford ou de Cambridge.

→ Emploi

Pour formuler un conseil, on emploie le modal ***should*** suivi de la base verbale.

You should go now. Tu devrais partir maintenant.

Pour exprimer le reproche, on emploie ***should*** + ***have*** + participe passé.

You should have left earlier. Tu aurais dû partir plus tôt.

Your turn!

16 Exprimez le conseil ou le reproche selon le contexte.

a. I arrived late this morning at my job interview because of the bus strike.
You ... (take) a taxi!

b. I would like to pass my exams with distinction.
You ... (work) much more!

c. Abigail has been ill for the last few days.
She ... (go) to the doctor's.

d. Claire is planning to work as an air hostess.
She ... (improve) her foreign languages.

15. Le conditionnel : *would*

→ Formation

La valeur du conditionnel est formée du modal ***would*** suivi de la base verbale.

→ Emploi

Pour formuler une hypothèse en *-**if***, l'anglais a recours à ***would*** + base verbale dans la phrase principale pour l'irréel du présent, c'est-à-dire encore réalisable. Pour l'irréel du passé (ce n'est plus réalisable), l'anglais utilise ***would have***, suivi du participe passé du verbe dans la phrase principale.

Irréel du présent = *would* + base verbale	**Irréel du passé = *would* + *have* + participe passé.**
If Oliver arrived from Oxford early this afternoon, we would go to the Comic Relief tea. Si Oliver arrivait d'Oxford tôt cet après-midi, nous **irions** au goûter organisé par Comic Relief.	If I had known that there was a National Express coach from London Victoria all the way to Edinburgh, I wouldn't have taken the train. Si j'avais su qu'il y avait un bus National Express au départ de la gare Victoria à Londres jusqu'à Edimbourg, je **n'aurais pas pris** le train.
If + prétérit	Verbe de la proposition principale en ***would*** + base verbale
If + *past perfect* (***had*** + participe passé)	Verbe de la proposition principale en ***would*** + ***have*** + participe passé

Your turn!

17 Complétez les phrases suivantes par le conditionnel présent ou le conditionnel passé.

a. If I had known that he was so late, I ... (wait) for him!

b. He ... (apply) for another job if he was fired.

c. She ... (pass) all her exams if she had worked harder.

d. If I were you, I ... (give) him a ring this afternoon.

16. La formation des questions

→ Formation

Les questions directes, en *yes / no*, se forment en plaçant l'auxiliaire *be / have* en tête de phrase.

Question avec auxiliaire en tête de phrase	Is Charlotte coming with us to the flea market? Est-ce que Charlotte nous accompagne au marché aux puces ?

Question avec verbe lexical – *Do* en tête de phrase	Did she go to the car boot sale yesterday? Est-elle allée à la brocante hier ?

En revanche, les questions comportant des verbes lexicaux se forment à l'aide de l'auxiliaire *do / does / did* en tête de phrase. Il faut aussi bien distinguer le sens des mots interrogatifs dans les questions en ***Wh-*** (*what, which, who, whose, when*) et en ***How*** (*how long, how many times, how often*), toujours en tête de phrase avant les auxiliaires, selon le schéma :

Wh- / How	Aux.	Sujet	Verbe	(+ Complément)	?
Where	did	you	buy	this smartphone	?

What do you want for breakfast?
Que veux-tu / voulez-vous pour le petit-déjeuner ?

How many times did you go to London?
Combien de fois es-tu allé·e / êtes-vous allé·e·s à Londres ?

Your turn!

18 Mettez les éléments dans l'ordre pour trouver la question qui convient.

a. have – long – you been – how – waiting?
b. did – you – when – visit – Madame Tussaud's, that – museum – well-known – wax – London – in?
c. laptop – many – computers – how – did – the – buy – firm?
d. did – how – you – pay for – this laundry service – much?

17. La concordance des temps

→ Emploi

La concordance des temps est le rapport entre le temps employé dans la **proposition principale** et celui de la **proposition subordonnée.** La subordonnée complète la principale, elle dépend de celle-ci. La subordonnée est donc secondaire et peut être supprimée.

Le temps utilisé dans la proposition subordonnée va dépendre du temps employé dans la proposition principale.

She will come to your birthday party, if you invite her.
Proposition principale — Proposition subordonnée

Le tableau suivant indique les règles de concordance des temps pour les subordonnées de condition.

La concordance des temps des phrases en - *if*

Proposition principale	Proposition subordonnée
Principale en ***will*** He will prepare some lemon meringue cupcakes, Il préparera des cupcakes au citron meringués,	Subordonnée au présent if they come on Sunday s'ils·si elles viennent dimanche.
Principale en ***would*** He would prepare some lemon meringue cupcakes, Il préparerait des cupcakes au citron meringués,	Subordonnée au prétérit if they came on Sunday s'ils·si elles venaient dimanche.
Principale en ***would + have*** + participe passé He would have prepared some lemon meringue cupcakes, Il aurait préparé des cupcakes au citron meringués,	Subordonnée au *past perfect* if they had come last Sunday s'ils·si elles étaient venu·e·s dimanche dernier.

! **Attention** à la concordance des temps dans les subordonnées de temps en ***when***.
Les subordonnées de temps comportant un futur ou un conditionnel en français ne correspondent pas aux mêmes temps en anglais, car dans ces cas précis, ***when***, ainsi que ***as soon as, till*** et ***while***, ne pourront pas être suivis de ***will*** ni de ***would.*** Il convient donc de noter les ajustements à opérer en anglais.

Subordonnées de temps en français	Correspondance en anglais
quand + futur …, quand / dès que tu rentreras de ton cours de cricket.	*when* + présent …, when / as soon as you come back from your cricket coaching class.
quand + futur antérieur …, quand / dès que tu seras rentré·e de ton cours de cricket	*when* + *present perfect* …, when / as soon as you have come back from your cricket coaching class.
quand + conditionnel présent …, quand / dès que tu rentrerais de ton cours de cricket.	*when* + prétérit …, when / as soon as you came back from your cricket coaching class.
quand + conditionnel passé …, quand / dès que tu serais rentré·e de ton cours de cricket.	*when* + *pluperfect* …, when / as soon as you had come back from your cricket coaching class.

Your turn!

20 **Complétez par le temps qui convient.**

a. I will give you a ring as soon as I … (finish) my homework.
b. If she … (come) to the community centre today, I would break the news to her.
c. If Peter … (arrive) at the station earlier, he wouldn't have missed his train to Reading.
d. When … (be) at the Millennium Stadium, ask the coach to teach you how to play cricket!

18. Le discours direct et indirect

→ Emploi

Le discours indirect obéit à des règles de concordance de temps, ainsi qu'à des ajustements syntaxiques lors du passage du discours direct au discours indirect.

Concordance des temps lors du passage du discours indirect.

Si le verbe qui introduit le discours indirect est **au présent**, les temps ne sont pas modifiés.

Si le verbe qui introduit le discours indirect est au prétérit, ***s/he said, ou s/he told*** **+** personne à qui l'on s'adresse pour l'impératif, voici les correspondances :

Discours direct > devient >	Discours indirect
Présent : 'I am reading history at Durham University.'	prétérit : S/he said that s/he was reading history at Durham University.
Present perfect : 'I have booked two rooms. '	*pluperfect* : S/he said that s/he had booked two rooms.
Will : 'I will visit India.'	*would* : S/he said that s/he would visit India.
Prétérit : 'I met him at the Principality Stadium in Cardiff.'	*pluperfect* : S/he said that s/he had met him at the Principality Stadium in Cardiff.'
Impératif : 'Stop watering this plant too much!'	*tell someone* + infinitive en *to* : S/he told him/her/them to stop watering that plant too much.

Quelques ajustements syntaxiques lors du passage au discours indirect.

Lors du passage au discours indirect, certains éléments sont modifiés (pronoms, adverbes de temps, etc.) lorsque le verbe qui introduit le discours indirect est au prétérit (*said*).

Exemple : 'I will go to Cambridge tomorrow,' she said.
She said that **she would** go to Cambridge **the following day**.

Discours direct	Discours indirect
I, my, mine	he or she, his or her, his or hers
here	there
today	that day
now	then
tomorrow	the next (following) day
yesterday	the day before or the previous day
three days ago	three days before
last night	the night before

Your turn!

21 Mettez au discours indirect.

a. 'I'm flying to San Diego next week,' she said.
b. 'I moved to Worthing two weeks ago,' she said.
c. 'We will visit our relatives in San Francisco next year,' they said.
d. 'They phoned us last night,' they said.

19. Infinitif et gérondif

→ Emploi

Verbes suivis de l'infinitif

Après des verbes qui expriment un but, quelque chose que l'on cherche à atteindre comme *want, plan, mean, expect, decide, manage, tend, promise, ask*…, on emploie l'infinitif en *to* + verbe.

I want to translate this letter into English. Je veux traduire cette lettre en anglais.

Verbes ou prépositions suivis du gérondif

Le gérondif est la forme du verbe + *-ing*. Il apparaît là où l'on peut aussi trouver un nom ou un groupe nominal, que ce soit en tant que sujet du verbe ou après une préposition.

Eating vegetables is good for your health. Manger des légumes est bon pour la santé.

She is interested in driving this gorgeous sports car. Conduire cette magnifique voiture de sports l'intéresse.

On l'utilise aussi après les verbes tels que *like, prefer, regret, love*… pour exprimer des événements déjà expérimentés.

I like swimming. J'aime nager.

I regret buying this dictionary. Je regrette d'avoir acheté ce dictionnaire.

Your turn!

23 Utilisez l'infinitif ou le gérondif.

a. You must remember … (hand) in your keys at reception when you check-out.
b. I remember … (meet) such nice people at this housewarming party.
c. I regret … (tell) you that I won't able to come next week.
d. She doesn't like … (drink) hot beverages, but she likes … (drink) a nice cup of tea whenever she visits England.

20. *Used to* + Verbe

→ Emploi

Used to + verbe exprime un passé qui indique que la situation présente est différente, contrairement au prétérit simple qui ne fait que parler d'un fait au passé sans donner d'indication sur la situation présente.

Comparez :

There was a fish and chip shop opposite my high school.
Il y avait un *fish and chip* face à mon lycée (sous-entendu : je ne sais pas s'il existe encore).

There used to be a fish and chip shop opposite my high school.
Autrefois, il y avait un *fish and chip* face à mon lycée (sous-entendu : il n'existe plus maintenant).

Your turn!

24 Exprimez le révolu (avec *used to* + V).

a. I lived in the UK.
b. There was a wonderful roundabout at the end of Park Street.
c. He smoked 10 cigarettes a day.
d. The tax office had paper records.

21. Formuler des hypothèses

→ Formation

On peut formuler une hypothèse à l'aide d'une subordonnée introduite par ***if.***

→ Emploi

Hypothèse possible au présent	***If*** **+ présent /** ***will*** If you arrive at the train station at 3:55, I will pick you up at 4 p.m. Si tu / vous arrives / arrivez à la gare à 15h55, je passerai te / vous prendre à 16h.
Hypothèse portant sur le présent	**If + prétérit / would** If you missed this exam, you would not be shortlisted. Si tu / vous ratais / ratiez cet examen, tu / vous ne serais / seriez pas sélectionné·e·s.
Hypothèse portant sur le passé	***If*** **+** ***had been / would have*** **+ participe passé** If she had taken a taxi, she would have arrived on time for the graduation ceremony. Si elle avait pris un taxi, elle serait arrivée à l'heure pour la cérémonie de remise des diplômes.

Your turn!

25 Exprimez l'hypothèse.

a. If you have some free time this afternoon, we ... (go) to the second-hand shop.
b. I ... (be) delighted if I were invited.
c. I ... (make) some mince pies if you come to my place.
d. The postman would have delivered the registered letter, if he ... (receive) it.

22. La voix passive

→ Formation

Le passif est formé de l'auxiliaire ***be***, suivi du participe passé du verbe. Le complément d'agent, facultatif, est introduit par ***by.***

Construction à la voix active	Construction à la voix passive
They are driving the injured to the Royal Liverpool University Hospital. Ils·Elles conduisent les blessé·e·s au Centre Hospitalier Universitaire (CHU) Royal de Liverpool.	The injured are being driven to the Royal Liverpool university hospital. Les blessé·e·s sont conduit·e·s au Centre Hospitalier Universitaire (CHU) Royal de Liverpool.

→ Emplois

La forme passive s'emploie quand on ne souhaite pas ou quand on ne peut pas indiquer l'identité de la personne qui commet l'action.

This terraced house has been broken into.

Cette maison mitoyenne a été cambriolée. (sous-entendu : on ne sait pas qui est le·la coupable).

The patients are very carefully looked after in this new hospital.

On prend très bien soin des patient·e·s dans ce nouvel hôpital. (traduction par "on" – le complément d'agent est superflu, on comprend qu'il s'agit du personnel hospitalier)

Your turn!

26 Mettez à la voix passive.

a. The new nurses looked after the elderly people in York.
b. They are building an arts centre in Philadelphia.
c. Bristol has extended the Broadmead Shopping Centre.
d. They will send the invoice next week.

23. La subordonnée relative

Les pronoms relatifs ***who***, ***which***, ***that*** et ***whose*** permettent d'introduire une proposition subordonnée relative. Le choix du pronom relatif dépend de la nature de l'antécédent (personne ou chose).

→ Pronom relatif avec antécédent animé

Who s'emploie avec un antécédent animé, une personne, en position de sujet de la phrase.

The woman, **who** has just parked her car, is my neighbour. La femme, qui vient de garer sa voiture, est ma voisine.

En position de complément d'objet direct ou indirect, le pronom relatif est en général omis.

The man **Ø** she spoke to is her brother. L'homme à qui elle a parlé est son frère.

→ Pronom relatif avec antécédent inanimé

The book, **which** was on the desk yesterday, is Tom's. Le livre, qui était sur le bureau hier, est celui de Tom.

Il s'agit d'une proposition **relative appositive**, précédée d'une virgule.

→ Pronom relatif *that*

Le pronom relatif ***that*** s'emploie indifféremment avec une personne ou une chose. Il permet d'introduire une **relative déterminative**. Il n'y a pas de virgule avant le pronom relatif.

The train **that** was cancelled last Monday had a technical problem. Le train qui a été annulé lundi dernier avait un problème technique.

→ *Whose* et la possession

Whose est employé pour établir une relation de possession entre deux éléments.

The house **whose** roof is red is the mayor's. La maison dont le toit est rouge est celle du maire.

Your turn!

27 Complétez par le pronom relatif qui convient : *who, which, that, whose*.

a. The train, ... has just left the platform, is the Liverpool one.
b. Her cricket instructor, ... came from Cardiff yesterday, has already gone.
c. The suitcase ... was left unattended was finally destroyed by the customs officer.
d. The mayor ... second home was broken into reported to the police.

24. La subordonnée de but

→ Formation

La proposition de but est exprimée par l'infinitif en *to* + base verbale, ou par *in order to* ou *so as to*.

! Attention, ***for*** n'exprime pas l'idée de but en anglais et n'introduit donc pas une subordonnée de but.

→ Emploi

En cas de sujet identique, on emploie ***to / in order to*** ou ***so as to.***

I went to the station this morning to / in order to / so as to take the first train to Glasgow.

Je suis allé·e à la gare ce matin pour prendre le premier train pour Glasgow.

La proposition de but est introduite par ***so (that)*** lorsque les deux sujets sont différents (ici, ***I / you***).

I have downloaded this app so (that) you don't get lost in New York.

J'ai téléchargé cette application pour que tu ne te perdes pas à New York.

Your turn!

28 Reformulez les phrases suivantes en exprimant le but.

a. She is planning to work overtime. She wants to have more money to support her family.
b. She has bought a French dictionary for her son. She wants her son to learn French.
c. The managers have come to an agreement. They want the staff to stop striking.

25. Contraste et concession (*while, whereas, though, although*)

→ Emploi

While et ***whereas*** introduisent la notion d'opposition ou de contraste (**alors que**, **tandis que**).

David prefers the English countryside, while his wife prefers the hectic city life.

David préfère la campagne anglaise, **alors que / tandis que** sa femme préfère la vie frénétique des grandes villes.

While peut aussi vouloir dire « pendant que ».

She was cutting some slices of gammon, while her sister was preparing some jacket potatoes.

Elle coupait des tranches de jambon braisé, **pendant que** sa sœur préparait des pommes de terre en robe des champs.

Though et ***although*** sont utilisés pour formuler une subordonnée de concession et veulent dire « bien que. »

A lot of foreign students are applying for Oxbridge, though / although it is difficult to be shortlisted.

Beaucoup d'étudiant·e·s étrangers·ères envoient leur candidature aux universités d'Oxford et de Cambridge, **bien que** cela soit difficile d'être sélectionné.

Your turn!

29 Complétez par *whereas, while,* ou *although*.

a. I will accept this proposal, ... it doesn't suit me.
b. He fell off the chair, ... he was repairing the lamp.
c. ... it is too late, you can still send your application, who knows?
d. I prefer living in the countryside, ... my sister prefers cities.

26. Les verbes d'état, *like*, *think*, *imagine*, *feel*...

→ Formation

Certains verbes, appelés « **verbes d'état** », sont généralement conjugués au présent simple et s'emploient difficilement au présent en *be* + V-*ing*, notamment les verbes d'état liés à l'existence ou à l'imagination, les verbes d'opinion ou de sentiment, ainsi que les verbes faisant appel aux sens tels que l'odorat (*smell*), la vue (*see*), l'ouïe (*hear*)...

→ Emploi

Voici les verbes les plus fréquents :

Verbes d'état liés à l'existence ou à l'imagination	be (être), exist (exister), forget (oublier), imagine (imaginer), seem (sembler), look (avoir l'air), remain (rester)
Verbes d'opinion	believe (croire), think (penser), understand (comprendre), know (savoir), mean (vouloir dire), remember (se souvenir)
Verbes de sentiment	like (aimer), dislike (ne pas aimer), love (adorer), prefer (préférer), fear (craindre), hate (détester), envy (jalouser)
Verbe de perception involontaire	see (voir), hear (entendre), feel (avoir l'impression), smell (sentir), taste (goûter)

I see what you mean. Je vois ce que tu / vous veux / voulez dire.

Your turn!

30 Complétez par un verbe d'état.

a. I ... (see) you have already finished. Take a rest now!
b. I ... (understand) what you mean.
c. I can ... (hear) her playing the piano.
d. She ... (think) that it's easy to translate this text into English.

Verbes irréguliers

	Base verbale	Prétérit	Participe passé	Traduction
	Trois formes identiques			
1	bet /e/	bet /e/	bet /e/	*parier*
2	burst /ɜː/	burst /ɜː/	burst /ɜː/	*éclater*
3	cast /ɑː/	cast /ɑː/	cast /ɑː/	*jeter*
4	cost /ɒ/	cost /ɒ/	cost /ɒ/	*coûter*
5	cut /ʌ/	cut /ʌ/	cut /ʌ/	*couper*
6	hit /i/	hit /i/	hit /i/	*frapper*
7	hurt /ɜː/	hurt /ɜː/	hurt /ɜː/	*faire mal*
8	let /e/	let /e/	let /e/	*laisser, louer*
9	put /ʊ/	put /ʊ/	put /ʊ/	*mettre, poser*
10	read /iː/	read /e/	read /e/	*lire*
11	shut /ʌ/	shut /ʌ/	shut /ʌ/	*fermer*
	Prétérit et participe passé identiques			
12	bend /e/	bent /e/	bent /e/	*(se) courber*
13	bring /i/	brought /ɔː/	brought /ɔː/	*apporter*
14	build /i/	built /i/	built /i/	*construire*
15	burn /ɜː/	burnt /ɜː/	burnt /ɜː/	*brûler*
16	buy /aɪ/	bought /ɔː/	bought /ɔː/	*acheter*
17	catch /æ/	caught /ɔː/	caught /ɔː/	*attraper*
18	creep /iː/	crept /e/	crept /e/	*ramper*
19	deal /iː/	dealt /e/	dealt /e/	*distribuer*
20	dig /i/	dug /ʌ/	dug /ʌ/	*creuser*
21	dream /iː/	dreamt /e/	dreamt /e/	*rêver*
22	feed /iː/	fed /e/	fed /e/	*nourrir*
23	feel /iː/	felt /e/	felt /e/	*sentir, éprouver*
24	fight /aɪ/	fought /ɔː/	fought /ɔː/	*combattre*
25	find /aɪ/	found /aʊ/	found /aʊ/	*trouver*
26	flee /iː/	fled /e/	fled /e/	*fuir*
27	forecast /ɑː/	forecast /ɑː/	forcast /ɑː/	*pronostiquer*
28	get /e/	got /ɒ/	got /ɒ/	*obtenir*
29	have /æ/	had /æ/	had /æ/	*avoir*
30	hear /ɪə/	heard /ɜː/	heard /ɜː/	*entendre*
31	hold /əʊ/	held /e/	held /e/	*tenir*
32	keep /iː/	kept /e/	kept /e/	*garder*
33	lay /eɪ/	laid /eɪ/	laid /eɪ/	*étendre*
34	lead /iː/	led /e/	led /e/	*conduire*
35	learn /ɜː/	learnt /ɜː/	learnt /ɜː/	*apprendre*
36	leave /iː/	left /e/	left /e/	*quitter*
37	lend /e/	lent /e/	lent /e/	*prêter*
38	light /aɪ/	lit /i/	lit /i/	*allumer, éclairer*

Prétérit et participe passé identiques

39	lose /uː/	lost /ɒ/	lost /ɒ/	*perdre*
40	make /eɪ/	made /eɪ/	made /eɪ/	*faire*
41	mean /iː/	meant /e/	meant /e/	*signifier*
42	meet /iː/	met /e/	met /e/	*(se) rencontrer*
43	overhear /əʊ/ /ə/ /ɪə/	overheard /əʊ/ /ə/ /ɜː/	overheard /əʊ/ /ə/ /ɜː/	*entendre par hasard*
44	pay /eɪ/	paid /eɪ/	paid /eɪ/	*payer*
45	say /eɪ/	said /e/	said /e/	*dire*
46	sell /e/	sold /əʊ/	sold /əʊ/	*vendre*
47	send /e/	sent /e/	sent /e/	*envoyer*
48	shine /aɪ/	shone /ɒ/	shone /ɒ/	*briller*
49	shoot /uː/	shot /ɒ/	shot /ɒ/	*tirer (fusil)*
50	sit /i/	sat /æ/	sat /æ/	*être assis*
51	sleep /iː/	slept /e/	slept /e/	*dormir*
52	slide /aɪ/	slid /i/	slid /i/	*glisser*
53	smell /e/	smelt /e/	smelt /e/	*sentir (odeur)*
54	spell /e/	spelt /e/	spelt /e/	*épeler*
55	spend /e/	spent /e/	spent /e/	*dépenser*
56	spit /i/	spat /æ/	spat /æ/	*cracher*
57	stand /æ/	stood /ʊ/	stood /ʊ/	*être debout*
58	stick /i/	stuck /ʌ/	stuck /ʌ/	*coller*
59	sting /i/	stung /ʌ/	stung /ʌ/	*piquer*
60	strike /aɪ/	struck /ʌ/	struck /ʌ/	*frapper*
61	sweep /iː/	swept /e/	swept /e/	*balayer*
62	swing /i/	swung /ʌ/	swung /ʌ/	*(se) balancer*
63	teach /iː/	taught /ɔː/	taught /ɔː/	*enseigner*
64	tell /e/	told /əʊ/	told /əʊ/	*raconter*
65	think /i/	thought /ɔː/	thought /ɔː/	*penser*
66	understand /ʌ/ /ə/ /æ/	understood /ʌ/ /ə/ /ʊ/	understood /ʌ/ /ə/ /ʊ/	*comprendre*
67	weep /iː/	wept /e/	wept /e/	*pleurer*
68	win /i/	won /ʌ/	won /ʌ/	*gagner*

Deux formes identiques

69	beat /iː/	beat /iː/	beaten /iː/ /ə/	*battre*
70	become /i/ /ʌ/	became /i/ /eɪ/	become /i/ /ʌ/	*devenir*
71	come /ʌ/	came /eɪ/	come /ʌ/	*venir*
72	overcome /əʊ/ /ə/ /ʌ/	overcame /əʊ/ /ə/ /eɪ/	overcome /əʊ/ /ə/ /ʌ/	*surmonter*
73	run /ʌ/	ran /æ/	run /ʌ/	*courir*

Trois formes différentes

74	arise /ə/ /aɪ/	arose /ə/ /əʊ/	arisen /ə/ /i/ /ə/	*se lever*
75	awake /ə/ /eɪ/	awoke /ə/ /əʊ/	awoken /ə//əʊ/ /ə/	*se réveiller*
76	be /iː/	was /ɒ/-were /ɜː/	been /iː/	*être*
77	bear /eə/	bore /ɔː/	borne /ɔː/	*supporter*
78	begin /i/ /i/	began /i/ /æ/	begun /i/ /ʌ/	*commencer*
79	bite /aɪ/	bit /i/	bitten /i/	*mordre*
80	blow /əʊ/	blew /uː/	blown /əʊ/	*souffler*
81	break /eɪ/	broke /əʊ/	broken /əʊ/ /ə/	*casser*

82	choose /uː/	chose /əʊ/	chosen /əʊ/ /ə/	*choisir*
83	do /uː/	did /i/	done /ʌ/	*faire*
84	draw /ɔː/	drew /uː/	drawn /ɔː/	*dessiner*
85	drink /i/	drank /æ/	drunk /ʌ/	*boire*
86	drive /aɪ/	drove /əʊ/	driven /i/ /ə/	*conduire*
87	eat /iː/	ate /eɪ/	eaten /iː/ /ə/	*manger*
88	fall /ɔː/	fell /e/	fallen /ɔː/ /ə/	*tomber*
89	fly /aɪ/	flew /uː/	flown /əʊ/	*voler (dans les airs)*
90	forbid /ə/ /i/	forbade /ə//eɪ/	forbidden/ə/ /i/ /ə/	*interdire*
91	foresee /ɔː/ /iː/	forsaw /ɔː/ /ɔː/	foreseen /ɔː/ /iː/	*prévoir*
92	forget /ə/ /e/	forgot /ə/ /ɒ/	forgotten /ə/ /ɒ/ /ə/	*oublier*
93	forgive/ə/ /i/	forgave /ə/ /eɪ/	forgiven /ə/ /i/ /ə/	*pardonner*
94	freeze /iː/	froze /əʊ/	frozen /əʊ/ /ə/	*geler*
95	give /i/	gave /eɪ/	given /i/ /ə/	*donner*
96	go /əʊ/	went /e/	gone /ɒ/	*aller*
97	grow /əʊ/	grew /uː/	grown /əʊ/	*croître*
98	hide /aɪ/	hid /i/	hidden /i/ /ə/	*cacher*
99	know /əʊ/	knew /uː/	known /əʊ/	*connaître*
100	lie /aɪ/	lay /eɪ/	lain /eɪ/	*être allongé*
101	mistake /i/ /eɪ/	mistook /i/ /ʊ/	mistaken /i/ /eɪ/ /ə/	*se méprendre*
102	mow /əʊ/	mowed /əʊ/	mown /əʊ/	*faucher*
103	outgrow /aʊ/ /əʊ/	outgrew /aʊ/ /uː/	outgrown /aʊ/ /əʊ/	*devenir trop grand*
104	overdo /əʊ//ə//uː/	overdid /əʊ//ə//i/	overdone /əʊ//ə//ʌ/	*exagérer*
105	oversee /əʊ/ /ə/ /iː/	oversaw /əʊ/ /ə/ /ɔː/	overseen /əʊ/ /ə/ /iː/	*superviser*
106	overtake /əʊ/	overtook /əʊ/ /ɒ/	Overtaken /əʊ/	*dépasser*
107	overthrow /əʊ/ /ə/ /əʊ/	overthrew /əʊ/ /ə/	overthrown /əʊ/ /ə/ /əʊ/	*renverser*
108	ride /aɪ/	rode /əʊ/	ridden /i/ /ə/	*aller à cheval/à bicyclette*
109	ring /i/	rang /æ/	rung /ʌ/	*sonner*
110	rise /aɪ/	rose /əʊ/	risen /i/ /ə/	*se lever*
111	see /iː/	saw /ɔː/	seen /iː/	*voir*
112	shake /eɪ/	shook /ʊ/	shaken /eɪ/ /ə/	*secouer*
113	show /əʊ/	showed /əʊ/	shown /əʊ/	*montrer*
114	shrink /i/	shrank /æ/	shrunk /ʌ/	*rétrécir*
115	sing /i/	sang /æ/	sung /ʌ/	*chanter*
116	sink /i/	sank /æ/	sunk /ʌ/	*s'enfoncer, couler*
117	speak /iː/	spoke /əʊ/	spoken /əʊ/ /ə/	*parler*
118	spring /i/	sprang /æ/	sprung /ʌ/	*sauter, jaillir*
119	steal /iː/	stole /əʊ/	stolen /əʊ/ /ə/	*voler, dérober*
120	swear /eə/	swore /ɔː/	sworn /ɔː/	*jurer*
121	swim /i/	swam /æ/	swum /ʌ/	*nager*
122	take /eɪ/	took /ʊ/	taken /eɪ/ /ə/	*prendre*
123	tear /eə/	tore /ɔː/	torn /ɔː/	*déchirer*
124	thrive /aɪ/	throve /əʊ/	thrived /aɪ/	*prospérer*
125	throw /əʊ/	threw /uː/	thrown /əʊ/	*jeter*
126	undergo /ʌ//ə/ /əʊ/	underwent /ʌ//ə/ /e/	undergone /ʌ//ə/ /ɒ/	*subir*
127	undertake /ʌ//ə/ /eɪ/	undertook /ʌ//ə/ /ʊ/	undertaken /ʌ//ə/ /eɪ/ /ə/	*entreprendre*
128	wake /eɪ/	woke /əʊ/	woken /əʊ/ /ə/	*s'éveiller*
129	wear /eə/	wore /ɔː/	worn /ɔː/	*porter (vêtement)*
130	write /aɪ/	wrote /əʊ/	written /i/ /ə/	*écrire*

Précis de phonologie

Il est important de comprendre quelques notions de phonétique (sons) et de phonologie (accentuation et intonation) de l'anglais si l'on veut se faire comprendre d'un anglophone. Ce précis vous aidera à comprendre les règles générales.

I. L'alphabet phonétique international de l'anglais

Afin de savoir comment se prononce un mot en anglais, même si vous le rencontrez pour la première fois, vous pouvez vous référer à l'alphabet phonétique, dont la composition pour l'anglais est la suivante : **12** voyelles, **8** diphtongues, **5** triphtongues et **24** consonnes. Voici les transcriptions phonétiques de ces sons, accompagnés d'un mot qui intègre ce son.

Audio
CD2 piste 46
MP3 n° 134

12 voyelles

/ə/ le schwa	comm**a**	/ʌ/	b**u**tter
/ɜː/	b**ir**d	/ɑː/	l**au**ghter
/ɪ/	bisc**ui**t	/ʊ/	f**oo**t
/iː/	p**ea**	/uː/	j**ui**ce
/e/	dr**e**ss	/ɔ/	w**a**tch
/æ/	h**a**t	/ɔː/	ch**al**k

Audio
CD2 piste 47
MP3 n° 135

8 diphtongues

/əʊ/	g**oa**t	/ɔɪ/	b**oy**
/æʊ/	m**ou**th	/ɪə/	n**ear**
/eɪ/	b**ay**	/eə/	p**ear**
/aɪ/	pr**i**ce	/ʊə/	c**ure**

Audio
CD2 piste 48
MP3 n° 136

5 triphtongues

/aiə/	f**ire**	/əʊə/	gr**ower**
/ɔɪə/	empl**oyer**	/eɪə/	l**ayer**
/æʊə/	h**our**		

Audio
CD2 piste 49
MP3 n° 137

24 consonnes

/p/	**p**et	/v/	**v**et
/b/	**b**ag	/tʃ/	**ch**at
/t/	**t**ap	/dʒ/	**j**ug
/d/	**d**eck	/θ/	**th**eatre
/k/	**k**itten	/ð/	**th**is
/g/	**g**irl	/ʃ/	**sh**ell
/m/	**m**ap	/ʒ/	trea**su**re
/n/	**n**et	/l/	**l**adder
/ŋ/	park**ing**	/h/	**h**ospital
/s/	**s**uit	/j/	**u**niversity
/z/	**z**ebra	/w/	**w**ool
/f/	**f**ilm	/r/	**r**at

II. La transcription phonétique et les règles de prononciation

Lorsque vous rencontrez un mot que vous ne connaissez pas ou un nouveau mot, il est important de chercher son sens dans un dictionnaire, mais aussi sa prononciation. Un mot mal prononcé ne sera pas compris de votre interlocuteur·trice et peut donc être source de malentendu ! Il importe également de **vérifier sur quelle syllabe porte l'accent**. Par exemple, *a sheep* /ʃi:p/ (un mouton), prononcé avec un *i* long, n'est pas la même chose que *a ship* /ʃɪp/ (un navire), qui se prononce avec un *i* court.

Audio CD2 piste 50 MP3 n° 138

De même, l'anglais possède certaines **règles d'accentuation de certaines syllabes par rapport aux terminaisons** qu'il est bon de connaître (par exemple, pour les mots se terminant par *-ion*, l'accent porte sur la syllabe précédant *-ion*, comme pour *communication* /kəˌmjuː.nɪˈkeɪ.ʃən/). Bien maîtriser ces règles, c'est pouvoir anticiper sur l'accentuation d'un nouveau mot que vous rencontrez en le comparant à d'autres mots similaires.

Enfin, il convient de noter que, en phonétique et en phonologie, c'est **le son qui prime sur la graphie** : par exemple, on dira *a university* car *university* /ju:niˈvɜ˞:siti/ débute par un son consonne /j/ ; on prononcera par ailleurs *the* différemment dans *the apple* /ði/ et *the cherry* /ðə/.

Audio CD2 piste 51 MP3 n° 139

1. Les paires minimales

Qu'est-ce qu'une paire minimale ? C'est une paire de mots qui diffèrent uniquement sur **un seul son, appelé « phonème ».** Un seul phonème est différent, et pourtant la différence de sens est grande.

Audio CD2 piste 52 MP3 n° 140

Si je prononce une voyelle courte ou longue au lieu de la bonne prononciation, le sens du mot est complètement modifié.

/i:/ et /i/	leave /i:/ *quitter*	live /i/ *vivre*
/i/ et /e/	tin /i/ *boîte de conserve*	ten /e/ *dix*
/æ/ et /ʌ/	cat /æ/ *chat*	cut /ʌ/ *coupure*
/ɑ:/ et /ɔ:/	cart /ɑ:/ *charrette*	caught /ɔ:/ *attrapé·e*
h aspiré ou pas /h/	heat /h/ *chaleur*	eat /i:/ *manger*
/æ/ et /eɪ/	lack /æ/ *manque*	lake /eɪ/ *lac*
/ɪ ə/ et /e ə/	pier /ɪə/ *jetée*	pear /e ə/ *poire*
/aɪ/ et /eɪ/	pile /aɪ/ *pile*	pale /eɪ/ *pâle*

2. Les terminaisons des verbes au prétérit

Audio CD2 piste 53 MP3 n° 141

/t/	work**ed**
/id/	decid**ed**, exploit**ed**
/d/	agre**ed**, travell**ed**, plann**ed**

Après le son /k/, *-ed* se prononce /t/. Après le son /d/ et /t/, je dois prononcer /id/ et *-ed* se prononce /d/ dans les autres cas.

3. Liens entre orthographe (graphie) et prononciation (son)

La langue anglaise n'a pas de correspondance systématique entre l'orthographe d'un mot et sa prononciation. D'un côté, *horse* et *worse* ont une orthographe très proche (*-orse*) et se prononcent pourtant différemment : /hɔ:s/ et /wɜ:s/. De l'autre, *door* et *lawn* ont des voyelles bien différentes (*-oo* / *a*) et partagent pourtant le même son /ɔ:/. D'où l'importance de vérifier la prononciation d'un mot grâce à l'alphabet phonétique international, et d'apprendre la prononciation en même temps que l'orthographe et le sens du mot.

Your turn!

Recopiez le tableau, puis écoutez les mots enregistrés et classez-les selon le son entendu dans le tableau. Puis soulignez les différences d'orthographe.

E-workbook hatier-clic.fr/lmu1190

Audio CD2 piste 54 MP3 n° 142

/i/ et /iː/	leave • slip • bin • niece • heat • sea • fee • cheap • peach • hit • see • sheep • lick • leap • team • chip • wheat • wit • lead • lid	Classement /ɪ/	Classement /iː/
		Orthographe différente :	Orthographe différente :
/æ/ et /ɑː/	laugh • tap • lack • bark • heart • scar • hat • bat • dark • back • mass • mat • cat • park • ban • lap • half	Classement /æ/	Classement /ɑː/
		Orthographe différente :	Orthographe différente :
/ʊ/ et /uː/	book • youth • boot • wool • butcher • put • foot • bull • stool • stood • tuna • should • glue • juice • few • shoe	Classement /ʊ/	Classement /uː/
		Orthographe différente :	Orthographe différente :
/ɜː/ et /ɔː/	worse • horse • hawk • daughter • nurse • prawn • raw • early • learn • stir • awful • turn • work • walk • bought • bird • dawn • skirt • water • more • taught • earn • version	Classement /ɜː/	Classement /ɔː/
		Orthographe différente :	Orthographe différente :
/e/ et /ei/	beg • bet • bake • say • play • red • raid • wait • bacon • great • bell • make • mason • maid • rainy • head • leopard • many • hate • eight • faith	Classement /e/	Classement /ei/
		Orthographe différente :	Orthographe différente :
/æ/ et /ʌ/	brother • love • candle • mat • sun • son • bat • but • ugly • blood • double • magic • cat • cut	Classement /æ/	Classement /ʌ/
		Orthographe différente :	Orthographe différente :

III. L'accentuation des mots

1. Règles générales d'accentuation selon le nombre de syllabes

L'accent tonique : c'est **l'accent qui portera sur l'une des syllabes** d'un mot. Dans l'alphabet phonétique, il est graphiquement représenté par le signe ' avant la syllabe en question : par exemple, booklet **/'bʊk.lət/**, architect **/'ɑː.kɪ.tekt/**, economic **/iː.kə'nɒm.ɪk/**.

Pourquoi l'accentuation est importante en anglais : contrairement au français, les mots anglais portent **l'accent tonique**. Les noms, verbes, adjectifs et adverbes d'une syllabe portent l'accent tonique. Pour les mots de deux syllabes ou plus, seule une syllabe portera cet accent tonique. Il est difficile d'établir des règles constantes, mais en général, on retrouve les grands principes suivants :

- Les **adjectifs et les noms** de **deux** syllabes portent, en général, l'accent tonique sur la **première syllabe** : **book**let, **back**bone, **ti**cket, **bro**ther, **li**ttle, **bi**gger, **per**fect
- Les **verbes** de **deux** syllabes sont quant à eux, en général, accentués sur la dernière syllabe : for**bid**, coll**ec**t, be**gin**...

Mot d'une seule syllabe	Accent tonique si l'une des quatre catégories = noms, adjectifs, verbes, adverbes
Mot de deux syllabes	En général : noms, adjectifs = sur la première syllabe -verbes = accent tonique en général sur la deuxième syllabe
Mot de plus de trois syllabes	Une seule syllabe portera l'accent tonique et la terminaison du mot peut vous donner une indication, comme indiqué dans le tableau ci-dessous

Voici les mots qui ne sont pas accentués en général : les articles (a / **an** / the...), les prépositions (at / **in** / on / by...), les conjonctions (and / **or** / but...), l'auxiliaire *be* et *have*.

2. Règles générales de l'accentuation de mot selon la terminaison des mots

Mots se terminant par :	L'accent se porte sur :
ic : **mechanic**	La syllabe qui précède celle contenant *-ic* ***Exceptions*** : *Catholic, Arabic, arithmetic, arsenic, lunatic, heretic, politics, rhetoric*
ion : int**ention**	La syllabe placée avant le son *-ion* ***Exceptions*** : *dandelion, television*
ient : ef**ficient**	La syllabe qui précède *-ient*
ate	Verbe de deux syllabes : accent sur la deuxième syllabe : *translate* Pour les noms : accent sur la première syllabe : *the Senate* ***Exceptions*** : *debate, estate, innate* Mots de plus de deux syllabes : accent sur l'antépénultième (c'est-à-dire deux syllabes avant le son contenant *-ate*) : *accommodate*

IV. L'intonation de la phrase anglaise

En phonologie, l'intonation de la phrase est la mélodie, ou courbe mélodique, qui, selon qu'elle soit montante ou descendante, indiquera le sens voulu par le locuteur.

1. Intonation descendante : ↘

Intonation descendante pour exprimer :	
• Les phrases déclaratives	Mary is coming to the party tonight. ↘
• Les ordres à l'impératif	Sit down immediately! ↘
• Les questions en Wh-	What do you want? ↘
• Les phrases exclamatives	What a lovely day! ↘

2. Intonation montante : ↗

Intonation montante pour exprimer :	
• Les questions ouvertes en *yes* / *no*	Have you studied in England ? ↗

En plus de la phonétique, l'intonation employée sera aussi porteuse du sens de votre phrase.

V. Les variétés d'anglais dans le monde

Le **lexique** employé peut vous permettre de savoir si vous êtes en présence de l'anglais britannique ou américain.

La **phonétique** de certains mots, qui ont pourtant la même orthographe, peuvent aussi être des indicateurs du type d'anglais employé. En effet, certains mots sont prononcés différemment en anglais britannique et en anglais américain. En voici les principaux :

Anglais britannique	Anglais américain
tomato **/tə'mɑ:təʊ/**	tomato **/tə'meitəʊ/**
lieutenant **/lef'tenənt/**	lieutenant **/lu:'tenənt/**
privacy **/'privəsi/**	privacy **/'praivəsi/**
schedule **/'ʃedju:l/**	schedule **/'skedʒʊl/**
either **/'aiðə/**	either **/'i:ðə/**

VI. Des outils pour vous aider à bien prononcer

En classe :

- Le tableau d'API (Alphabet Phonétique International) anglais de votre manuel *Let's Meet Up!* que vous pouvez consulter au début du *Précis de phonologie* (p. 263).
- Les dictionnaires unilingues ou bilingues, au CDI de votre lycée par exemple.
- Votre professeur·e d'anglais.

Hors de la classe :

Sur internet, plusieurs sites peuvent vous aider à bien prononcer un mot anglais. Voici par exemple quatre sites utiles :

- https://www.youtube.com : Entrez dans *Rechercher* le mot dont vous cherchez la prononciation et *English pronunciation* ou *American pronunciation*. Vous devriez trouver une vidéo où le mot est prononcé par un·e anglophone.
- https://www.wordreference.com : Vous trouverez le dictionnaire de *Wordreference* et celui de *Collins*. Entrez le mot dans l'onglet. Vous pouvez ensuite sélectionner les accents suivants : *US / UK / UK-RP / UK-Yorkshire / Irish / Scottish / US Southern / Jamaican.*
- https://www.macmillandictionary.com : Entrez le mot dans *Search.* On vous indique si le mot est dénombrable ou indénombrable, sa prononciation, sa transcription phonétique, ainsi que le pluriel pour les dénombrables.
- https://www.linguee.fr : Entrez le mot que vous recherchez. On vous donne la traduction du mot en français. En outre, vous pouvez accéder à la prononciation britannique ou américaine, ainsi qu'à l'utilisation de ce mot en contexte dans une phrase en anglais, suivie de sa traduction.

Fiches de méthodologie

Pour mieux travailler

Pour réaliser les projets

Pour vous entraîner dans les différentes activités langagières

Fiche N° 1 Comprendre une consigne

Les consignes sont des instructions qui ont pour rôle de guider le travail sur un document oral ou écrit, pour réaliser une tâche orale ou écrite. Elles sont formulées à l'aide d'un verbe à l'impératif.

Elles progressent généralement du repérage à la réalisation d'une production orale ou écrite personnelle. Dans ce manuel, chaque document fait l'objet de 3 à 5 questions.

1 Pour commencer, vous rencontrerez des consignes de repérage ou d'identification d'éléments significatifs sur ou dans un document. Ces consignes demandent qu'un relevé soit effectué avec les verbes ci-contre, qui attirent votre attention sur des éléments précis du document.

Pick out words or expressions
Spot
Find out elements
Choose
Select
Match

2 À partir du relevé ou repérage de mot(s) ou expression(s) effectué, un travail d'analyse ou d'interprétation peut être réalisé. On vous demande de produire des énoncés complets en prenant appui sur les éléments que vous avez repérés. Ce travail est indiqué avec les verbes ci-contre.

Deduce
Explain why
Analyse
Show how
Sum up
Justify with a quote

3 À ce stade, un travail de reformulation ou de synthèse de mots ou d'expressions du document peut vous être demandé avec les verbes ci-contre.

Rephrase
Sum up / Recap

4 Ce travail d'analyse ou d'interprétation effectué, un travail de production personnel en lien avec le document étudié vous est généralement proposé. Sans le repérage, l'analyse et la reformulation, il n'aurait pas été possible. Vous le trouverez dans les consignes commençant par les verbes ci-contre.

Write
Say
Imagine
Create
Take part in

Fiche N° 2

Mémoriser

Les 3 règles d'or

- **T**riez
- **O**rganisez
- **R**eliez

La mémoire

On distingue la mémoire à court terme (savoir son cours pour l'heure qui suit, voire pour le lendemain) et la mémoire à long terme (pour la tâche finale, pour le bac, pour vos études...). Il est donc important de multiplier les exercices de mémorisation et de réviser **fréquemment**.

Pour mémoriser quelque chose, mieux vaut l'avoir compris. Donc n'hésitez pas à poser des questions à votre professeur·e et prenez des notes pour pouvoir les relire plus tard.

Entraînez-vous à l'aide des ***Memory Challenges*** proposés dans le manuel et avec les activités ludiques de la plateforme reussirenlangue.fr qui vous propose des outils de révision du lexique, de la grammaire et de la phonologie. Celle-ci vous permettra en outre de tester votre compréhension de certains documents. Utilisez les liens **Quizlet** pour mémoriser puis réviser régulièrement le vocabulaire de chaque séquence.

Pour rendre les révisions entre ami·e·s plus amusantes, vous pouvez aussi créer vos propres concours sur Kahoot.it.

Le traitement des informations

Il est toujours plus facile d'apprendre lorsque les choses sont claires. Cela commence naturellement par la **tenue de votre support** (cahier ou classeur). Plus votre **prise de notes** sera **claire** et **structurée**, et plus vous pourrez apprendre efficacement. N'hésitez pas à illustrer certains propos ou mots de vocabulaire. Respectez un code de couleurs et soyez **rigoureux·se**.

Pour mémoriser et être capable de restituer les connaissances dans plusieurs semaines, plusieurs mois ou même des années plus tard, **classez** et **reliez** les informations nouvelles à ce que vous connaissez déjà.

Appliquez la méthode **TOR** !
Trois mots-clés : **T**rier - **O**rganiser - **R**elier

Triez ce qui est utile et ce qui ne l'est pas. Inutile de retenir tout le vocabulaire d'un texte par exemple, le vocabulaire principal suffit.

Organisez les connaissances, c'est-à-dire regroupez-les par thème, par catégorie, par ressemblance, etc.

Reliez les éléments en établissant des liens logiques entre ce qui est nouveau et ce que vous connaissez déjà.

Les trois principaux modes de mémorisation

Nous apprenons tous de façon différente en faisant appel à nos sens (souvent l'ouïe et la vue mais parfois aussi par le mouvement).

Essayez tous ces moyens et voyez lequel / lesquels vous convien(nen)t le mieux. La lecture seule ne suffit pas toujours !

Mémoire visuelle ?
Lisez et écrivez, dessinez, associez des images mentales visuelles à ce que vous devez retenir (ex : mémorisez des prépositions de lieu en visualisant un lieu précis que vous aimez).

Mémoire auditive ?
Lisez à haute voix, répétez en chantant, enregistrez-vous sur votre smartphone et réécoutez dès que vous pouvez.

Mémoire kinesthésique ?
Lisez puis récitez à voix haute, en marchant, en dansant, en faisant des gestes associés (comme les acteurs qui apprennent un texte).

Ces types de mémoire sont **complémentaires** : vous devez repérer le moyen qui vous convient le mieux, mais ne devez pas négliger les autres.

Pour qu'un apprentissage soit utile, il faut bien sûr **avoir compris**, mais aussi passer par la **répétition espacée**. Comme pour les grands sportifs·ves, vous devez vous **entraîner régulièrement** pour être capable de retenir quelque chose sur le long terme.

> **Utilisez des Post-it®** pour noter les points importants et mettez-les dans des endroits où vous les verrez souvent, comme par exemple sur la porte de votre chambre !

Les outils

Les *mind maps*

Fabriquez des **aides visuelles** du type carte mentale, sur support papier ou numérique.

Classez les éléments selon leur importance **à l'aide de titres**.

Faites ressortir les éléments-clés : utilisez un code de couleurs vives, surlignez, soulignez, encadrez, entourez d'un cercle...

OUTILS NUMÉRIQUES
Xmind8
Popplet
Mindnode
Vocabulary Box pour tablettes

Placez **le thème au centre d'un cercle**. Dessinez les branches principales et indiquez les titres au bout de chaque branche. En dessous de chaque titre, listez le vocabulaire, les idées, les faits à retenir... Utilisez des couleurs pour plus d'efficacité.

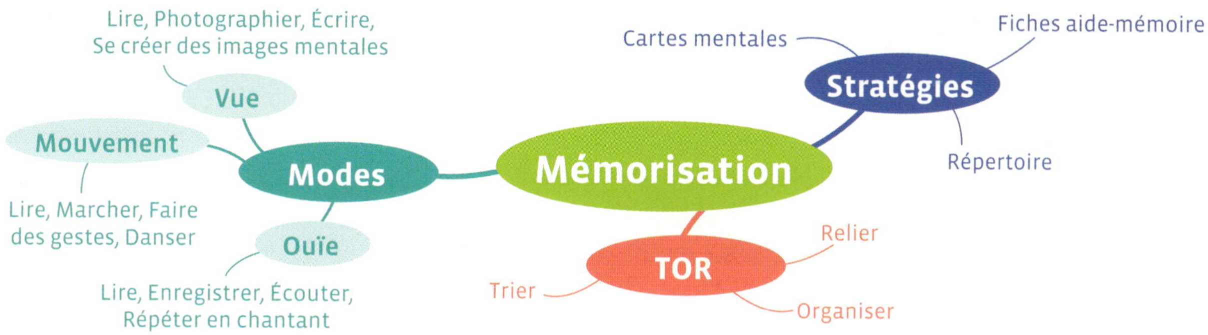

Les fiches thématiques et répertoires

Vous pouvez faire des fiches **par thème, axe ou séquence**, comprenant du lexique, des idées, des faits culturels (ou les 3) vus en classe. Ajoutez des titres, des sous-titres, des dessins... qui constitueront des repères pour la mémoire. Vous pouvez alimenter deux carnets : un en anglais, un autre en français.

Réalisez un lexique classé par ordre alphabétique.

Utilisez un carnet, une liste sur votre smartphone ou un fichier Excel par exemple.

Vous pouvez créer votre propre liste de mots avec leur traduction, leur construction, suivies d'un exemple de phrase incluant le mot. Vous pouvez ajouter la transcription phonétique si le mot pose des problèmes de prononciation.

Fiche N° 3

Relire un devoir écrit

La règle d'or

Garder le temps nécessaire pour deux relectures (minimum 5 min) !

Une relecture en 2 temps

1. Lisez une première fois pour revoir la cohérence globale et l'enchaînement des idées.

Si vous le pouvez, laissez passer quelques minutes avant la deuxième lecture pour avoir un regard neuf.

2. Faites **une deuxième lecture** en vous concentrant uniquement sur la langue (orthographe, grammaire, syntaxe), la mise en forme (alinéas, présentation propre au type de sujet : lettre, dialogue, article de journal, etc.) et la ponctuation.

Pensez à repérer tout au long de l'année les **erreurs** que vous avez tendance à faire fréquemment. Vérifiez tout particulièrement ces points dans votre **relecture**.

Les *Grammy Awards* de la grammaire !

Pour éviter les erreurs les plus courantes, voici **notre top 10 des chansons pop anglo-saxonne qui peuvent vous aider**.

Écoutez les chansons sur internet et **mémorisez les refrains** pour retenir les points de langue qu'ils illustrent.

1. **Anyone Can Play Guitar*, by Radiohead

Les auxiliaires modaux sont **toujours** suivis de la base verbale.
(auxilaires modaux : *can, could, must, may, might, shall, should, will, would*)

2. *Why Do I Feel so Sad?* by Alicia Keys

Une question se forme généralement selon le schéma suivant :
(pronom interrogatif) + auxiliaire + sujet + verbe + complément?

3. *Born To Be Wild*, by Steppenwolf

Pour exprimer le but (« pour » + verbe), on utilise *to* + base verbale.

4. *Last Christmas I gave you my heart*, by Wham

Quand vous racontez un fait passé et daté, vous utilisez le prétérit.

5. *She moves far away*, by Alle Farben

À la 3e personne du singulier du présent simple, le verbe prend un *-s*.

6. *I Don't Wanna Live Forever*, by Taylor Swift

wanna = want to (et *gonna = going to*)
« Vouloir » se dit *want* (et pas ~~*will / would*~~)

Pour dire « vouloir + verbe », on utilise *want + to +* base verbale.

7. *Single Ladies*, by Beyoncé

Les adjectifs ne prennent **jamais** de *-s* en anglais.

8. *People Are Strange*, by The Doors

Au pluriel, *person* devient *people*.
Et *people* est un nom pluriel.

9. *Give Peace a Chance*, by John Lennon

Devant un nom employé dans un sens général, on ne met pas l'article *the*.

10. *The Man Who Never*, by Maroon 5

WH☺ renvoie à une personne. *Which* renvoie à une chose ou une idée.

Ma check-list

Apprenez à créer vos propres *check-lists* le jour de l'évaluation !

Pour cela, vous devez vous concentrer sur les consignes. Vous devez en déduire des éléments spécifiques au devoir.

Observez l'exemple ci-dessous :

1 Read this extract from *Post-Mortem*, by Patricia Cornwell (1990).

2 In the style of the author, write the next chapter (30-50 lines) and include a questioning.

- Vous devrez donc **repérer** et **respecter** le schéma narratif de l'auteur·e.
- Il faudra que ce chapitre **suive** l'extrait que vous venez de lire et que l'histoire soit **cohérente**.
- Vous devrez **respecter** le nombre de lignes **minimum** (et **maximum**).
- Il vous faudra **ajouter** des dialogues (**discours direct**) et/ou du **discours rapporté** pour inclure une scène d'interrogatoire. Pour cela, vous ne devrez pas oublier de **varier** les **verbes introducteurs**.

S'il vous est demandé de « rédiger un chapitre à la manière de », vous pouvez en déduire qu'il faudra sûrement utiliser le prétérit simple et donc préciser succinctement la règle sur votre brouillon afin de procéder à la relecture une fois le devoir terminé.

De cette façon, essayez de réfléchir à **quatre ou cinq points** que vous pourrez vérifier lors de vos relectures.

Vous pouvez également vous inspirer de la check-list suivante qui vous propose des pistes sur lesquelles travailler.

Ma *check-list*

Est-ce que...

- ❑ j'ai bien traité le sujet, tout le sujet et rien que le sujet ?
- ❑ j'ai répondu aux questions posées ?
- ❑ j'ai tenu compte des consignes (type de production, nombre de mots...) ?
- ❑ j'ai fait l'effort de structurer le devoir ?
- ❑ les idées s'enchaînent-elles de façon logique avec des mots de liaison et ce que je veux dire est-il clair ?
- ❑ j'ai illustré mon travail avec des exemples concrets ?
- ❑ j'ai fait des paragraphes en allant à la ligne ?
- ❑ le contenu est intéressant (suivant le type de devoir : références culturelles, humour, originalité...) ?
- ❑ j'ai évité les répétitions d'idées ou de mots ?
- ❑ j'ai utilisé une langue riche (c'est-à-dire un vocabulaire varié, de nouvelles structures...) ?
- ❑ j'ai vérifié l'orthographe ?
- ❑ j'ai respecté la ponctuation (points, virgules...) et mis des majuscules en début de phrase et aux noms propres ?
- ❑ j'ai écrit proprement et lisiblement ?

Fiche N° 4

Utiliser un traducteur ou un dictionnaire en ligne

La règle d'or

Rechercher des mots uniquement, pas des phrases !

La rapidité d'utilisation des outils numériques facilite le travail en anglais et est une aide précieuse – à condition de savoir les utiliser.

Les sites de traduction automatique

Les sites de traduction automatique utilisent des robots qui traduisent mot à mot ou par segments de texte. Le logiciel génère une traduction en tenant compte de nombreux paramètres identifiables par les robots du site, **mais sans jamais replacer les mots et la phrase dans leur contexte**.

Vous ne pouvez donc pas vous contenter de reprendre sans aucune vérification préalable le texte obtenu avec un traducteur automatique.

Voici par exemple trois sources d'erreurs possibles avec un traducteur en ligne :

- **l'orthographe** : « amande » (le fruit) sera traduit *almond*, mais « amende » (une contravention) sera traduit *fine*.
- **les homonymes** : « avocat » pourra être traduit soit par *avocado* s'il s'agit du fruit, soit par *lawyer* s'il s'agit du métier.
- **les expressions idiomatiques** : en français, « elle a encore sauté le repas » donne *she jumped again the meal* (traduction erronée mot à mot) au lieu de *she skipped the meal.*

Ces précautions valent également lorsque vous traduisez de l'anglais vers le français : un traducteur comme ceux cités ci-après vous fournira uniquement une **idée globale, rapide et approximative** du sens d'un texte, sans pour autant le traduire correctement. Par ailleurs, ce n'est qu'en vous essayant à la traduction « manuelle » que vous pourrez améliorer votre maîtrise syntaxique, grammaticale et lexicale des deux langues française et anglaise.

Quelques traducteurs automatiques

https://www.deepl.com/fr/translator
http://www.reverso.net
https://www.linguee.fr/

Le dictionnaire en ligne bilingue

Le dictionnaire en ligne est quant à lui un incontournable du travail en et hors la classe, en avoir un dans ses favoris ou en appli téléchargée sur le smartphone est un *must*. Ils vous permettront de trouver facilement un maximum d'informations sur un mot ou expression que vous recherchez.

Par exemple, voici les informations obtenues sur un **dictionnaire bilingue** lorsque nous cherchons des informations sur le mot *desk* :

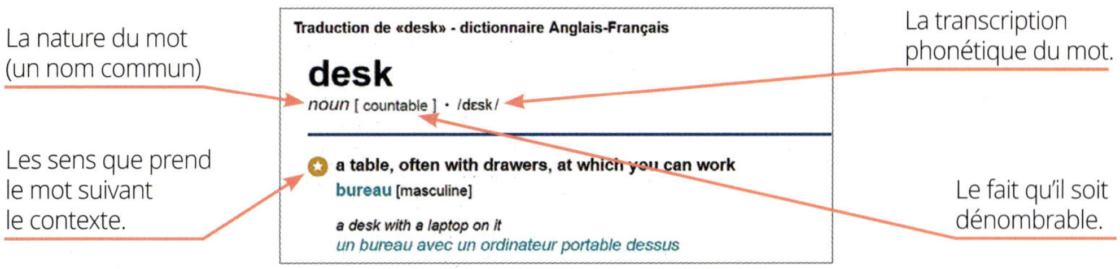

Nos recommandations de dictionnaires bilingues en ligne :

- https://context.reverso.net/traduction/anglais-francais/

Avec sa section « Contexte », ***Reverso*** vous permet, au moment où vous tapez les mots, de voir apparaître des propositions de traductions d'expressions idiomatiques.

Ex : Il pleut des cordes. → *It's raining cats and dogs.*

- https://www.linguee.fr/

Linguee vous propose des traductions dans leur contexte, vérifiées par des expert·e·s du milieu concerné (juridique, médical, etc.) – idéal pour savoir exactement quel mot utiliser en fonction de votre besoin.

- http://www.wordreference.com/enfr/

En plus d'être un dictionnaire en ligne, ***WordReference*** propose des forums pour diverses langues, où les utilisateurs·rices peuvent échanger pour mieux apprendre.

Le dictionnaire en ligne unilingue

L'utilisation **de dictionnaires unilingues** vous permettra d'accéder à des définitions **plus complètes**, en vous donnant notamment accès aux différences d'orthographe et de prononciation entre l'anglais britannique et l'anglais américain.

Dictionnaires unilingues

oxforddictionaries.com
dictionary.cambridge.org
www.merriam-webster.com

Ainsi, en cherchant *neighbour* sur le dictionnaire unilingue dictionary.cambridge.org, vous trouverez :

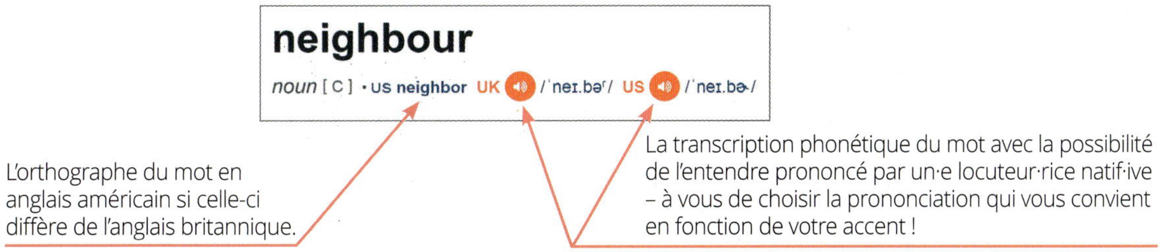

Bilingues ou unilingues, les dictionnaires en ligne sont indispensables !

> **Tip :** devenez curieux·euse des mots que vous découvrez en réalisant des **nuages de mots** avec les synonymes, antonymes ou famille de mots sur un mot recherché ou grâce aux sites gratuits suivants :
> https://nuagedemots.co/
> https://wordart.com/
> http://wordsaladapp.com/ (disponible en appli sur IOS et Android)
> https://worditout.com/word-cloud/create

Fiche N° 5

Faire une recherche internet

Les 2 règles d'or

- Repérer les *fake news*
- Se recentrer régulièrement sur le sujet

Avant de se connecter

Prévoyez un **journal de recherche**, papier ou numérique, où prendre des notes au fur et à mesure de la recherche.

Ouvrez par exemple un document Word, dans lequel vous pourrez copier-coller les informations intéressantes.

Notez le sujet de la recherche en titre. Et faites un rapide *brainstorming* autour du sujet. Les idées que vous notez sont les **mots-clés** que vous allez utiliser pour votre recherche.

Les moteurs de recherche

Commencez d'abord par une recherche large : **pas plus de trois mots**.
Ajoutez ensuite vos mots-clés pour affiner la recherche.

Vous pouvez encore orienter votre recherche grâce aux outils suivants :

Les opérateurs de recherche

- Pour chercher uniquement **sur les réseaux sociaux**, tapez **@** devant le mot recherché.
- Pour chercher un **hashtag**, tapez **#** devant le mot.
  Exemple : #hatier
- Pour **exclure un mot** de votre recherche, tapez le symbole **-** devant le mot à exclure.
  Exemple : mammifères marins -baleine
- Pour rechercher **une expression exacte**, mettez-la entre **guillemets**.
  Exemple : "the life of pi" (titre de livre ou de film)
- Pour **associer des recherches**, tapez **OR** entre chaque mot.
  Exemple : marathon OR race

Les options des moteurs de recherche

- **« Image »**
- **« Vidéo »**

} pour rechercher ce type de fichiers uniquement.

- **« Actualités / news »** pour rechercher sur les sites d'information (journaux, magazines, TV, radio...).
- **« Maps »** pour chercher un lieu, localiser.

Les principaux moteurs de recherche

www.google.fr
www.qwant.com
www.bing.com
uk.yahoo.com / us.yahoo.com

Attention, si vous êtes en France, vous avez probablement accès par défaut à la version française du moteur de recherche. Les premiers résultats sont alors en français. Mais vous pouvez modifier **la langue** pour obtenir des résultats en anglais :

- Google vous le propose sur la page d'accueil : « Google disponible en : *English* ».
- Bing vous propose dans les paramètres de limiter la recherche à une langue spécifique.

! Évitez les **traductions** automatiques proposées par les moteurs de recherche, elles sont souvent fausses ou très approximatives.

Les encyclopédies en ligne

QUELQUES ENCYCLOPÉDIES GRATUITES EN ANGLAIS

www.britannica.com
www.scholarpedia.org
www.infoplease.com
www.wikipedia.org

Vous y trouverez des informations plus structurées. Elles vous permettent d'avoir une **vision globale d'un sujet** et elles vous donnent des pistes vers des sujets voisins, ce qui vous permet d'enrichir ou corriger votre liste de mots-clés.

Wikipédia est souvent un bon point de départ. En bas d'une fiche (→ *Liens externes*), vous trouverez notamment des liens vers des sites ou des documents consacrés au sujet.

! Mais attention, Wikipédia est une encyclopédie collaborative : toutes les pages ne sont pas de qualité égale et certaines ne sont pas fiables. Il faut l'utiliser en parallèle avec d'autres sources.

Quel que soit le sujet de votre recherche, vous êtes comme un·e inspecteur·rice ou un·e journaliste d'investigation : vous menez une enquête. Si vos sources sont fiables, vous aurez des résultats solides. Sinon, vous allez suivre des fausses pistes !

Conserver les informations

À chaque fois que vous trouvez une **information intéressante**, copiez-la dans votre journal de recherche, avec quelques mots de commentaire.

Copiez toujours le lien complet vers une page qui vous intéresse.

Une page web peut vous paraître facile à retrouver quand vous êtes dessus... Mais quand vous aurez vu vingt autres pages, vous aurez oublié le chemin que vous avez parcouru !

Créez un **dossier** sur le disque dur. Vous y sauvegardez votre feuille de recherche si c'est un document Word.

Vous pouvez aussi envoyer le lien par e-mail à un·e camarade pour attirer son attention ou lui demander son opinion.

Quand vous trouvez **une image** intéressante, vous pouvez la copier-coller dans votre journal de recherche. Et vous pouvez sauvegarder les PDF, les audios ou les vidéos dans un dossier de recherche :

Clic droit
/ « Enregistrer l'image sous... »

Quand vous trouvez une information ou un document intéressant sur votre **smartphone**, gardez-en une trace. Vous pouvez par exemple vous envoyer le lien par e-mail, ou bien prendre une note écrite ou enregistrer un mémo vocal.

Fiche N° 6 Repérer une *fake news*

Les *fake news* sont de fausses informations, ou infox, qui sont propagées délibérément. On en trouve de plus en plus, et elles ne sont pas toujours faciles à identifier. Face à ce phénomène, il est important de se poser les bonnes questions pour éviter d'être piégé·e.

Les 5 règles d'or pour repérer les *fake news*

1 Vérifiez la source de l'information.

Qui a publié l'information ? Cette personne ou cette source est-elle reconnue et fiable ? S'agit-il d'un·e expert·e reconnu·e ou d'un site de référence ? Faites des recherches si vous avez un doute.

2 Lisez plus loin que les titres et méfiez-vous des images.

Certains titres ou accroches peuvent être trompeurs. On y trouve souvent des tournures de phrases ou des exagérations qui visent à attirer le ou la lecteur·rice, mais qui ne racontent qu'une interprétation de l'histoire.

Ne vous arrêtez pas à une affirmation de ce type, lisez les détails. Faites attention aux images qui accompagnent les informations et ont pour but d'influencer votre vision de l'information et peuvent vous amener sur une fausse piste.

3 Regardez la date !

Il arrive que de vieilles histoires soient republiées pour faire croire à des informations nouvelles.

4 Comparez les informations.

Si l'information vous semble trop farfelue, il peut s'agir d'une blague ou d'un canular. Faites des recherches pour comparer ou croiser les informations. Vérifiez sur les sites d'information officiels et professionnels.

5 Demandez conseil !

Si après avoir suivi ces conseils vous n'êtes toujours pas sûr·e d'une information, vous pouvez demander conseil à quelqu'un qui est en mesure de porter un jugement éclairé comme un·e professeur·e ou documentaliste. Vous pouvez aussi aller sur un site comme *CheckNews* qui vous permet de savoir si vous avez affaire à une vraie information.

Fiche N° 7 Analyser une image

La règle d'or
- Identifier
- Décrire
- Interpréter

Analyser une image, c'est la décomposer de manière à comprendre ce qu'elle représente et ce qu'elle signifie. L'objectif est de répondre à ces trois questions clés :
Que voit-on ? Quel est l'effet recherché ? Comment s'y prend l'auteur.e ?

Pour répondre à ces questions, il faut passer par trois étapes : identifier, décrire et interpréter.

1. Identifier

Repérez les informations données dans la légende.

- La nature de l'image : *a photograph, a poster, a cover, an advert, a cartoon, a drawing, a comic strip...*
- Le titre, l'auteur·e et la date s'ils sont donnés

2. Décrire

- Les lieux
- Les personnages et / ou les objets
- Les actions
- Les couleurs
- Les plans : *in the background, in the middle, in the foreground*

In the top left-hand corner — *At the top* — *In the top right-hand corner*

On the left-hand side / On the left — *On the right-hand side / On the right*

✦ *Black Panther*, dir. by Ryan Coogler, with Chadwick Boseman and Lupita Nyong'o, 2018

In the bottom left-hand corner — *At the bottom* — *In the bottom right-hand corner*

3. Interpréter

- Mes impressions personnelles : *I have the impression that...*
- La visée et l'intérêt de l'image : *This picture symbolises...*
- Le message et le point de vue de l'auteur : *The artist wants to... I think the aim is...*

Fiche N° 8

Analyser un tableau

La règle d'or

Identifier
Décrire
Interpréter

Un tableau est un type d'image, et son analyse consiste à le décomposer de manière à comprendre ce qu'il représente et ce qu'il signifie. L'objectif est de répondre à ces trois questions clés : Que voit-on ? Quel est l'effet recherché ? Comment s'y prend l'artiste ?

Pour y répondre, il faut passer par trois étapes : identifier, décrire et interpréter.

1. Identifier

Repérez les informations données dans la légende.

- Le titre, l'artiste et la date de réalisation
- Le lieu de conservation et les dimensions s'ils sont précisés
- Le contexte historique et culturel
- Le mouvement artistique : *impressionism, cubism, pop art, realism, renaissance, Dada, Art Deco, conceptual, classicism...*

2. Décrire

- Le genre : *a portrait, a landscape, a stand still, a trompe-l'oeil, a religious scene, a historical scene, a genre scene...*
- Les personnages et / ou les objets
- Les espaces et décors
- La construction du tableau et les éléments picturaux : *straight / vertical / horizontal / diagonal lines, shapes / forms...*
- Les couleurs, la lumière, l'atmosphère

✦ Charles Sheeler, *Classic Landscape*, 1931

***In the foreground**, brown and grey rail tracks draw the viewer's eye into the distance. **On the left**, we can see a white building with orange silos, and **in the top right-hand corner** there is a geometrical white building with a bright coloured smokestack. **In the background, in the middle**, there seems to be another factory in the distance.*

3. Interpréter

- Mes impressions personnelles : *It seems that... We get a feeling of...*
- La visée et l'intérêt de l'image : *The painting illustrates...*
- Le message et le point de vue de l'artiste : *The painter points out...*

Fiche N° 9 Analyser une scène de film

La règle d'or
- Identifier
- Décrire
- Interpréter

Comme pour une image fixe, analyser une image animée comme une scène de film consiste à la décomposer de manière à comprendre ce que nous montre le ou la réalisateur·rice.
L'objectif est de répondre à ces trois questions clés : Que voit-on ? Quel est l'effet recherché ? Comment s'y prend le ou la réalisateur·rice ?

Pour y répondre, il faut passer par trois étapes : identifier, décrire et interpréter.

1. Identifier

Repérez les informations données dans la légende et l'introduction de la vidéo.

- Le titre, le ou la réalisateur·rice et la date de sortie du film
- La situation du passage dans le film si elle est précisée
- Le genre de film : *a comedy, a drama, a western, a science fiction film, a historical film, an epic, a documentary...*

✦ *It's a Free World...*, dir. by Ken Loach, 2007

The scene is an extract from *It's a Free World..., a social realist drama that* ***was directed*** *by Ken Loach and released in 2007. In this scene, Angie is helping illegal immigrants by giving them passports.*

2. Décrire

- Les personnages et / ou les objets
- Les actions et événements
- Les espaces et décors
- Les plans : *a wide shot, a long shot, a medium shot, a close-up, a close shot...*
- Les mouvements de la caméra : *still frame, travelling, panoramic, zoom...*
- Les couleurs, la lumière, l'atmosphère
- La bande-son

3. Interpréter

- Mes impressions personnelles : *What strikes me most in ... is... I find the scene interesting... We get a feeling of...*
- La visée et l'intérêt de la scène de film : *The scene is about... It is a key scene...*
- Le message et le point de vue du ou de la réalisateur·rice : *The director wants to emphasise / stress the fact that...*

Fiche N° 10 Poster sur les réseaux sociaux

La règle d'or

Pensez toujours aux réactions de vos lecteurs·rices

Ce qu'on peut poster…		Quel avantage ? Quel conseil ?
sur **Twitter**	des textes limités à 280 caractères + des images et des vidéos	Réagissez en temps réel à une audience large. ! Utilisez les bons symboles : # (hashtag) pour les mots-clés et @ (arobase) pour un·e utilisateur·rice.
sur **Facebook**	tous types de documents (sauf les PDF)	Partagez en temps réel avec vos ami·e·s. ! Réglez les paramètres de confidentialité pour bien cibler vos destinataires.
sur **YouTube** et **Dailymotion**	des vidéos	Créez votre propre chaîne. ! Pourquoi ne pas créer vos propres vidéos ?
sur **Snapchat**	des photos, vidéos et messages éphémères	Personnalisez vos messages en les modifiant avec des filtres, des *smileys*, des masques… ! Réfléchissez bien avant de publier !
sur **Instagram**	des images et vidéos courtes	Partagez ce que vous voyez. ! Choisissez des mots-clés pertinents précédés de # (hashtag).

Sur toutes ces plateformes, mieux vaut **rester concis·e**. Il ne faut pas confondre un réseau social et un blog. Si vous voulez être lu·e·s par vos abonné·e·s, **évitez les textes trop longs**. Préférez également les tournures **actives** aux tournures passives, qui sont plus accrocheuses. Enfin, vous pouvez utiliser les hashtags, mais évitez de les additionner : ils servent à **catégoriser votre post**, et à indiquer à votre lecteur·rice le ou les sujet(s) principal(aux) de celui-ci.

Protéger son image et sa vie privée

Sur internet, vous laissez des traces personnelles, volontaires ou involontaires. Soyez prudent·e quand vous montrez votre vie privée, ne publiez pas toutes sortes d'images de vous. **Adoptez les bons réflexes** : utilisez un pseudo, ne révélez pas de données personnelles, vérifiez les paramètres de confidentialité de votre profil, optez le plus souvent pour le mode « privé »…

Sécurisez vos identifiants et mots de passe.
À chaque réseau, un mot de passe choisi avec soin !
Soyez aussi prudent·e avec votre smartphone, votre tablette qu'avec votre ordinateur.
N'acceptez pas des inconnu·e·s dans vos réseaux d'ami·e·s.

Avez-vous envie qu'on retrouve cette photo un peu gênante dans dix ans ? Non ? Alors **ne la publiez pas** ou bien **restreignez-en l'accès** à vos proches.

personnel·le
innovant·e
#
observateur·rice
vigilant·e
bref·ve
respectueux·euse
surprenant·e
imaginatif·ve
Soyez
@
créatif·ve
percutant·e
visuel·le
poète
bienveillant·e
vous-même
reconnaissant·e

Avoir une attitude et un langage respectueux

N'oubliez pas que vous vous adressez à un grand nombre de personnes, dont certaines ne vous connaissent pas. Demandez-vous : est-ce que je dirais telle ou telle chose et de cette manière **si j'étais face à de vraies personnes** ?
Pensez toujours aux réactions de vos lecteurs·rices. Et évitez les propos qui peuvent blesser ou les images qui peuvent choquer.
Pour indiquer le ton de votre message, il vaut parfois mieux utiliser des smileys ou des GIF animés, et ainsi éviter tout malentendu. Il ne faudrait pas que votre post soit mal pris.

> N'écrivez pas en **majuscules** : c'est comme CRIER dans les oreilles !

Ne pas propager de *fake news*

Avant toute publication, apprenez **à vérifier les sources et les contenus** afin de ne pas propager de fausses informations ou des informations erronées… Sur internet, vous trouvez des milliers d'informations, mais beaucoup sont fausses. Alors dépouillez, comparez et vérifiez l'information pour mieux publier !

Pour vérifier vos informations
factuel.afp.com
Decodex par Le Monde.fr
Checknews.fr par Liberation.fr

Rester sous la vigilance parentale

Certains réseaux sociaux demandent une **autorisation** des parents pour les mineur·e·s, il faut vous renseigner avant de vous y inscrire. Dans tous les cas, le contrôle des parents reste primordial pour utiliser les réseaux en toute sécurité, discutez-en avec eux. C'est un moyen de se protéger contre le **cyber-harcèlement**. En cas de problème, demandez de l'aide à un·e adulte.

> Pour vous renseigner sur le **cyber-harcèlement** allez sur le site officiel de la CNIL (Commission nationale de l'informatique et des libertés).

Respecter le cadre légal

Respectez le droit d'auteur et le droit à l'image. Si vous citez des extraits de texte, indiquez-en la source. Si vous voulez utiliser des documents qui ne vous appartiennent pas, assurez-vous d'en avoir le droit.
Pour cela, préférez les licences *Creative Commons* (CC) gratuites qui précisent les conditions d'utilisation.

> Si vous interviewez des personnes, demandez une **autorisation** pour diffuser leur image et leur voix.

Fiche N° 11

Réaliser une vidéo

La règle d'or

Plus le ***story-board*** est précis, plus le tournage et la vidéo seront réussis !

La préparation

Prévoyez d'abord un temps de conception pour bien définir le projet et prévoir tout ce dont vous aurez besoin.

Choisir le bon type de vidéo

Visionnez ensemble des films et des vidéos pour vous **inspirer**.

Réfléchissez ensemble à ce que sera votre film, son **objectif**, son **format**, son **genre** :

- un clip informatif ? une publicité ? un sketch ? un reportage ? un tutoriel ?
- une mini-fiction ? basée sur un scénario original ? adaptée d'un livre ?
- un documentaire ? sur un lieu, un événement, une personne ? une interview ?
- une animation ? une pixilation (image par image, comme *Wallace and Gromit*) ?

Formaliser l'idée principale de la vidéo

Rédigez un **synopsis** : une courte description de ce que sera le film (½ page).

Résumez aussi votre synopsis en une seule phrase : un ***pitch***. S'il est accrocheur, il vous aidera à présenter votre projet à tou·te·s les intervenant·e·s que vous allez solliciter !

Écrivez le scénario.

1. À partir du synopsis, découpez l'histoire en **séquences** (une séquence = 1 lieu, 1 action).
2. Écrivez pour chaque séquence les divers éléments **descriptifs** et les **dialogues**.
3. Découpez chaque séquence en différents **plans** (ou prises de vue). Décrivez-les très précisément : lieu, décor, accessoires, comédiens, répliques, cadrage, bruitages, musique…

Écrivez votre **story-board** aussi précisément que possible, plan par plan.

Plan n°	Nom du plan + description	Lieu + décor	Personnages + répliques	Costumes et accessoires
1				
2				

Vous pouvez vous répartir les séquences ou les plans pour travailler en plus petits groupes.

Logiciels d'écriture scénaristique et de story-boards

CeltX Free
StoryBoardThat
StoryBoardFountain (pour Mac)

Pour écrire et conserver les fichiers ensemble

FramaPad
Google Docs
Mega.nz

Le tournage

QUELLE CAMÉRA ?
- un caméscope
- un appareil photo hybride
- un smartphone ou une tablette

L'équipe

Pour être efficace, le mot d'ordre est « **organisation** ». Plus vous serez organisé·e·s, et plus le tournage se passera bien.

Répartissez les **rôles dans l'équipe** : acteur·rice·s, cadreur·euse, responsable des décors, des costumes, de la prise de son, etc.
Faites pour chacun une liste des tâches et du matériel dont il est responsable.

Prévoyez à l'avance **dans quel ordre vous allez filmer** les différents plans.

Soyez patient·e·s. Certains plans d'une minute demandent parfois une après-midi entière de tournage.

Vérifiez – et vérifiez **encore** – que vous n'avez oublié aucun plan. Et dans le doute, refaites-le !

N'oubliez pas de **prévenir** en amont les personnes sur le **lieu de tournage** afin d'éviter les bruits parasites ou interventions inopportunes.

Demandez conseil à votre professeur·e concernant les **autorisations** pour filmer dans un lieu public ou utiliser un extrait de film ou de musique.

Le montage

Il faut maintenant **assembler les plans** bout à bout, sans oublier la bande-son, pour former les séquences en reprenant votre story-board. Vous pouvez utiliser des **musiques** et des chansons pour accompagner vos séquences, mais assurez-vous que vous respectez les **droits d'auteur**. Vous pouvez aussi vous tourner vers des banques de musiques libres de droit comme Dig.CC Mixter ou FreeMusicArchive.

Organisez des **séances de visionnage** en commun pour prendre ensemble les décisions importantes.

Prévoyez un temps confortable pour le montage car c'est souvent à cette étape qu'on prend conscience d'oublis ou de ratés. Il faut alors parfois prévoir une nouvelle séance de tournage pour refaire certains plans ou enregistrer certains sons.

LOGICIELS DE MONTAGE
VSDC Free Video Editor
VideoPad
Movie Maker

LOGICIELS POUR FILMER SON ÉCRAN (POUR FAIRE DES TUTOS)
Apowersoft
CamStudio

POUR UNE ANIMATION EN PIXILATION
FrameByFrame
MonkeyJam

POUR NE PAS TÉLÉCHARGER DE LOGICIEL
MovieMakerOnline
FramaPad
StoryBoardThat

Quelques tips !

- Si vous devez créer une vidéo pour votre chaîne YouTube, essayez de trouver un nom pour celle-ci et une phrase accrocheuse pour commencer votre vidéo : *Hello everyone! Every day is a great day!*
- Si vous devez jouer un rôle, imaginez quels sont les sentiments et les intentions du personnage. C'est ce qu'on appelle « se détacher du texte ».
- N'oubliez pas d'articuler et de parler fort. Cela vous évitera de mauvaises surprises lors du montage.

Fiche N° 12

Les outils TICE

Utilisée à bon escient, la technologie peut vous faciliter la tâche et rendre vos productions plus ancrées dans la réalité. Vous devez toutefois choisir le bon outil et expérimenter. Vous aurez parfois besoin de créer un compte en ligne ACCOUNT NEEDED. Mais ne vous inquiétez pas, les services ci-dessous proposent une offre gratuite*. Voici quelques pistes pour vous aider à choisir !

Simulateurs de réseaux sociaux

- Instagram https://generatestatus.com/generate-fake-instagram-post/
- Snapchat https://igenerator.eu/?snapchat_image
- Facebook https://generatestatus.com/facebook-post-generator/
- Twitter https://generatestatus.com/fake-tweet-generator/
- Créateur de mèmes https://www.mememaker.net/

Simulateurs d'applications de messagerie

- Messenger https://igenerator.eu/?facebook_full_chat
- WhatsApp https://www.igenerator.eu/?whatsapp_iphone
- Messages sur téléphones Androïd https://www.igenerator.eu/?android_message
- Messages sur iPhones http://ios.foxsash.com/ ou http://ifaketextmessage.com

Éditeurs de photos en ligne

- Pixlr https://pixlr.com/editor/
- BeFunky https://www.befunky.com/create/

Éditeurs de vidéos en ligne

- MovieMakerOnline https://moviemakeronline.com/
- Adobe Spark https://spark.adobe.com/sp/ ACCOUNT NEEDED

Créer et monter sa vidéo

- Écrire son scénario https://framapad.org/fr/
- Construire son *story-board* https://www.storyboardthat.com/ ACCOUNT NEEDED
- Monter sa video https://moviemakeronline.com/
- Éditer le son (logiciel) https://audacity.fr/ ACCOUNT NEEDED

* Vérifiée en 2019

Créer un magazine
- MadMagz https://madmagz.com/fr ACCOUNT NEEDED
- Issuu https://issuu.com ACCOUNT NEEDED
- Calaméo https://fr.calameo.com/ ACCOUNT NEEDED

Posters et infographies
- Canva https://www.canva.com/ ACCOUNT NEEDED
- Genially http://genial.ly/ ACCOUNT NEEDED
- Pik To Chart http://piktochart.com/ ACCOUNT NEEDED
- Easelly https://easel.ly/ ACCOUNT NEEDED
- Glogster https://edu.glogster.com/ ACCOUNT NEEDED

Présentations vidéos
- Powtoon https://www.powtoon.com/home/ ACCOUNT NEEDED
- Biteable https://app.biteable.com/video/starters ACCOUNT NEEDED
- Adobe Spark https://spark.adobe.com/sp/ ACCOUNT NEEDED

Créer un dépliant
- Canva https://www.canva.com/ ACCOUNT NEEDED
- Desygner.com
- about.easil.com

Présentations interactives
- Prezi https://prezi.com/ ACCOUNT NEEDED
- Visme https://www.visme.co/ ACCOUNT NEEDED

Diaporamas en ligne
- Google Slides https://www.google.com/slides/about/ ACCOUNT NEEDED
- U Tell Story http://www.utellstory.com ACCOUNT NEEDED

Écrire à plusieurs de manière collaborative
- Google Documents https://www.google.com/docs/about/ ACCOUNT NEEDED
- Framapad https://framapad.org/fr/
- Padlet http://padlet.com ACCOUNT NEEDED
- Titanpad http://titanpad.com/

Organiser ses idées avec des cartes mentales
- GoConqr MindMaps http://goconqr.com ACCOUNT NEEDED
- Coggle http://coggle.it ACCOUNT NEEDED
- MindMapFree http://mindmapfree.com/
- MindMup https://www.mindmup.com/ ACCOUNT NEEDED
- Bubbl.us https://bubbl.us/0257991486588777596

Parler d'un voyage
- Tripline https://www.tripline.net/ ACCOUNT NEEDED

Réviser seul·e ou entre ami·e·s
- Quizlet https://quizlet.com/
- Kahoot http://kahoot.com ACCOUNT NEEDED
- Quizzoodle http://www.quizzoodle.com ACCOUNT NEEDED

Fiche N° 13 Travailler en groupe

GROUP WORK
PAIR WORK

Pourquoi travailler en groupe ?

- Pour **aider** ses partenaires et **être aidé·e** en retour.
- Pour élaborer **plus efficacement** des pistes de réflexion, des questions, tester vos connaissances.
- Pour **expérimenter l'anglais** d'une manière plus authentique.
- Pour construire **en commun** autour d'une tâche à mener à l'oral ou à l'écrit.

L'**esprit d'équipe** est une des composantes majeures du fonctionnement en société. Il permet de travailler en **collaboration** (travail identique sur une même tâche mis en commun) ou en **coopération** (travail différent mais complémentaire pour aboutir à une réalisation commune). Le travail en équipe vous permet de gagner en **confiance**, en **estime** de vous-même et de développer vos **compétences relationnelles** – indispensables à la réussite d'un projet scolaire, personnel et professionnel dans le futur.

Comment travailler en groupe

PAIR WORK Le **travail en binôme** vous permet d'échanger facilement sur une activité commune et de réaliser des activités d'interaction orale ou écrite en vous répartissant les rôles définis dans la consigne :

Exemple *Imagine a conversation between* ***an astronaut*** *and* ***a US president***.

Le travail effectué en amont dans l'unité vous permet de réaliser cette tâche.

GROUP WORK Le **travail en groupe** peut se faire de 3 à 6 élèves.

Pour qu'il soit efficace, vous devez respecter quelques règles :

- tous les membres doivent lire la consigne,
- tous les membres individuellement, **sans être interrompus**, expriment ce qu'ils ont compris du travail à effectuer et la manière dont il faut s'y prendre,
- chacun·e exprime son **accord ou désaccord** sur ce qui a été dit en apportant un ou des arguments pour justifier son opinion.

- Quand tout le monde est d'accord sur ce qu'il faut faire, il est temps de **se répartir les rôles**.
  - Qui effectue les recherches ?
  - Qui écrit ou rédige ?
  - Qui coordonne les tâches ?
  - Qui fera la restitution orale du travail ?
  - Qui synthétise les questions pour les poser à l'enseignant·e ?
  - Qui gère le temps et répartit la parole ?
  - Qui crée le document final (*PowerPoint*, carte mentale, affiche, article...) ?

À la fin du travail, faites votre bilan personnel sur le travail du groupe et le rôle que vous avez joué. Qu'est-ce que vous avez aimé ? Quels sont les points qui pourront être améliorés ?

! Rappelez-vous : pour améliorer votre anglais, il faut parler anglais !

Fiche N° 14 Médiation

Qu'est-ce que la médiation ?

Définition : La médiation consiste à transmettre à quelqu'un les informations contenues dans un document ou un échange écrit ou oral. Il faut avoir compris le contenu du document ou de la conversation afin de pouvoir le reformuler, en anglais ou en français. Il s'agit de jouer le **rôle d'intermédiaire**.

Les descripteurs du programme – B2

- **Transmettre une information, interpréter**
  Peut assurer une interprétation consécutive sur des sujets généraux et / ou connus, **transmettre les propos importants et les points de vue**, si l'intervenant fait de fréquentes pauses et clarifie son propos si nécessaire.
  → Écouter une conversation sur un sujet vu en cours et être capable de transmettre l'essentiel du contenu à une autre personne en anglais ou en français suivant la situation.

- **Traiter un texte ou un dossier documentaire**
  Peut (en langue Y), faire une synthèse et **rendre compte d'informations et d'arguments venant de diverses sources** orales et écrites (en langue X). Peut **comparer, opposer et synthétiser** (en langue Y), des informations et points de vue différents (en langue X).
  → Expliciter un fait culturel (Thanksgiving par exemple) à une personne qui ne connaît pas ce fait, en anglais ou en français suivant la situation.

- **Faciliter la coopération**
  Peut mettre en évidence le problème principal à résoudre dans une tâche complexe. Peut **agir comme rapporteur·euse du groupe**, noter les idées et les décisions, les discuter avec le groupe et faire ensuite en plénière un résumé des points de vue exprimés.
  → Participer à un travail de groupe et guider ses camarades à travers des reformulations, des commentaires afin d'accomplir la tâche demandée.

- **Mener un travail collectif**
  Peut **organiser et gérer un travail collectif de façon efficace**, inciter les membres d'un groupe à décrire et développer leurs idées et recentrer habilement l'attention des participants en sollicitant des propositions.
  → Expliquer à un camarade une consigne dans ses propres mots en anglais ou en français.

- **Faciliter la communication**
  Peut aider les parties en désaccord à mieux se comprendre et à obtenir un consensus en reformulant leurs positions, en présentant les principaux points de désaccord, en repérant les terrains d'entente, en établissant des priorités de besoins et d'objectifs.
  → Animer un débat et faciliter les échanges en clarifiant les malentendus et en faisant émerger les différents points de vue.

- **Établir un espace pluriculturel**
  Peut, **à l'occasion de rencontres interculturelles**, reconnaître des points de vue différents de sa propre vision du monde et en tenir compte, **clarifier les malentendus** et discuter des ressemblances et des différences de points de vue et d'approches **afin de détendre l'atmosphère** et de permettre à la discussion d'avancer.
  → Rencontrer des personnes de cultures et de langues différentes (en voyage scolaire, en vacances) et être capable de tenir compte de leurs différences, savoir comparer sa culture à celle des autres et lever les ambiguïtés afin de favoriser les échanges.

⚠ La médiation n'est pas de la traduction, le passage par la traduction est une stratégie parmi d'autres.

Stratégies

> **Faire des repérages** pour bien comprendre le contenu des documents ou de la conversation (lexique, dimension culturelle…).

> **Synthétiser et identifier** ce que l'on veut communiquer.

> **Écouter activement** pour vérifier que son interlocuteur·rice comprend ce que l'on dit et reformuler si besoin.

> **Se mettre à la place de l'autre** pour anticiper ses problèmes et trouver des solutions.

> **Être capable de trouver les mots dans une autre langue** que celle des documents ou de la conversation (de l'anglais vers le français par exemple).

Fiche N° **15**
Compréhension orale

Les descripteurs du programme – B2

- Peut **suivre l'essentiel** d'une conférence, d'un discours, d'un compte rendu et d'autres formes d'exposés complexes du point de vue du fond et de la forme.
- Peut comprendre des annonces et des messages sur des **sujets concrets et abstraits**, s'ils sont en langue standard et émis à un débit normal.
- Peut comprendre la plupart des reportages et des autres enregistrements ou émissions radiodiffusées en langue standard et peut **identifier correctement l'humeur, le ton, etc., du ou de la locuteur·rice.**
- Peut **comprendre la plupart des films, des journaux et des magazines télévisés** en langue standard.

Faites une expérience

1. **Prenez** le document F page 51 : *Rom-coms for everyone.*
2. **Anticipez** à partir du titre : quel sera le sujet ? Connaissez-vous tous les mots du titre ?
3. **Écoutez et notez** les mots que vous connaissez, les mots-clés, les mots accentués, tous les éléments qui vous semblent importants.
4. S'il y a des blancs ou des éléments manquants : **imaginez ce qui manque** et ce que vous allez devoir écouter.
5. **Réécoutez et vérifiez** vos hypothèses.
6. **Récapitulez** tout ce que vous avez compris.

Que vous apprend cette expérience ?

Comprendre un document audio ne veut pas dire en faire la traduction intégrale, l'important est de comprendre l'essentiel et s'il vous manque des éléments ce n'est pas le plus grave. Avec de l'entraînement et en étant actif·ve en classe, vous pouvez vous améliorer.

Ce qui est important est de noter les mots-clés, les noms propres etc. pour comprendre l'essentiel du message.

Avant l'écoute

À partir des éléments accompagnant le document audio (titre, introduction ou chapô, légende), vérifiez les termes que vous comprenez. Vous pouvez faire une petite **liste de mots en rapport** qui pourront vous aider, vous pouvez émettre des **hypothèses** et préparer votre brouillon.

Voici des idées de brouillon : dessiner des colonnes qui correspondent au nombre d'écoutes, utiliser une couleur différente correspondant à chaque écoute pour les notes.

Voici les informations que nous avons pour le document p. 51 :

1 ***PAIR WORK*** Listen to Greg Berlanti, the director of *Love, Simon*, interviewed on NPR (National Public Radio).

On en déduit :

- qu'il s'agit d'un support authentique, puisqu'il s'agit d'une interview radio.
- le réalisateur va sûrement parler de son film. Il y a sûrement deux locuteurs puisqu'il s'agit d'une interview.
- que le film s'adresse à un public adolescent et qu'il parle d'amour (pour tout le monde).

La première écoute

Les questions à se poser

Ces questions sont à écrire **en amont** et vont vous aider à écrire votre **brouillon.**

- Quelle est la **nature du document** ? (Un discours, une bande annonce, une interview, un extrait de journal télévisé, une émission de TV ou de radio…)
- **Qui** parle ? (Identité, sexe, nombre de voix, leur métier / occupation, les liens entre les personnes, personnes présentes ou seulement mentionnées, attitude…)
- Est-ce qu'il y a des **données chiffrées** ? (Âge, somme, pourcentage, date…)
- Quel est **le sujet principal** ? (Les éléments accompagnant le document ont-ils déjà donné une piste ?)
- Y a-t-il des **indices sonores** ? (Musique, bruits de fond, quelque chose ou quelqu'un.)
- Est-ce qu'il y a des **aides visuelles** ? (S'il s'agit d'une vidéo, vous pouvez voir apparaître des noms, des mots etc. Ces éléments peuvent vous aider et vous pouvez faire le lien avec ce que vous entendez.)

Qu'avez-vous noté ?

typical teenage Greg Berlanti directed
big reveal
major studio Simon is gay romantic comedy
changing the gender myself
power of representation
evocative coming of age

Il faut noter tout ce que pouvez le long du document : ce que vous entendez ou ce que vous voyez. S'il reste des blancs, vous pourrez les compléter pendant les pauses ou lors des écoutes suivantes. Ne notez pas des phrases entières, utilisez des abréviations ou seulement des mots-clés, des initiales etc.

Les écoutes suivantes

Réécouter le document plusieurs fois

Qu'allez-vous devoir écouter ensuite afin de compléter vos notes ?

- **À qui** s'adresse le document ?
- Quel est **le ton** des personnes qui parlent ? neutre ? en colère ? passionné ? triste ? Cela va vous aider à comprendre l'implicite du document (ce qui n'est pas dit).
- Quels sont les **sujets** ? Quel est le **but** en l'abordant ? Quels sont les **enjeux** ?

Love Simon is your typical teenage romantic comedy.
big reveal is revealed right away Simon is gay

Why want to set this story up to look like a typical teenage romantic comedy?
changing the gender of the romantic interest
having a gay protagonist at the center of it
had been a closeted teen myself just realized just
the power of representation evocative for him
great coming of age movie, not see himself or his storyline

Après les écoutes

Relisez vos notes et rédigez-les en étant synthétique mais en ayant tous les éléments repérés.

Après ces écoutes, vous êtes capable de prendre la parole et dire ce que vous avez compris du document à l'écrit ou à l'oral.

Fiche N° 16 Compréhension écrite

Les descripteurs du programme – B2

- Peut comprendre **tout type de courriel ou publication** sur les réseaux sociaux même s'ils sont rédigés en langage familier.
- Peut parcourir rapidement plusieurs textes en parallèle (articles, rapports, sites internet, ouvrages, etc.) et en **relever les points pertinents**.
- Peut reconnaître si un texte donne de l'information factuelle ou bien s'il cherche à convaincre les lecteurs·rices. Peut reconnaître la **structuration d'un texte**.
- Peut **lire pour son plaisir de façon très autonome**, en adaptant le mode et la rapidité de lecture à différents textes (magazines, romans assez simples, livres d'histoire, biographies, carnets de voyage, guides, passages de chansons, poèmes), en utilisant les références adéquates.

Faites une expérience.

1. Prenez le texte p. 97 : *This Is What Social Media Had to Say About the March for Our Lives.*
2. Barrez tous les mots inconnus et surlignez tous les mots connus.
3. Essayez de résumer le texte à partir des éléments non barrés.
4. Lisez maintenant le texte en entier. Cherchez les mots inconnus dans un dictionnaire.
5. Comparez ce que vous avez compris avec le résumé à l'étape 3.

Que vous apprend cette expérience ?

Avez-vous besoin de chercher tous les mots dans un dictionnaire pour pouvoir comprendre un texte ? Ne pouvez-vous pas vous appuyer sur les éléments connus ? Comprendre un texte ne signifie pas le traduire dans son intégralité. Comprendre en détail peut traduire une compréhension **fine** mais saisir le sens **global** peut certaines fois suffire.

Avant la lecture

Anticiper à partir du paratexte

Lisez le **paratexte** et les éléments accompagnants le texte (chapô, image, légende) et posez-vous les questions suivantes :

- Quelle est la **nature** du document ? (Article de journal, extrait de roman, poème, etc.)
- Quelle **date** ? (Date d'écriture et / ou de parution) Quel **contexte** historique ? (Si cela vous semble pertinent.)
- Quel est le **titre** ? (Possibilité d'émettre des hypothèses à vérifier au moment de la lecture. Vous pouvez le connaître ou il peut vous évoquer des choses : nom propre, date, etc.)

Paratexte : informations autour du texte, souvent situées en bas de page.

- **Qui** a écrit le texte ? (Vous pouvez connaître d'autres œuvres de l'auteur·e ou il·elle peut vous évoquer des choses comme le contexte historique, le courant artistique, etc.)

S'il s'agit d'un **texte littéraire** on parlera **d'auteur·e** (*writer*) qui peut se décliner par type de texte : un·e dramaturge (*playwright*), un·e romancier·ère (*novelist*) etc. On parlera de **journaliste** pour **un article de presse**.

Y a -t-il un chapô ? (Qu'apprenez-vous des personnages, de l'intrigue ? Possibilité d'émettre des hypothèses à vérifier au moment de la lecture.)

Lecture du texte

Il est essentiel de faire plusieurs lectures du texte.

Lisez les questions **en amont** pour savoir ce que vous allez devoir **repérer**. Choisissez la méthode qui vous convient : différents surligneurs, tableau à remplir, etc.

Lecture 1

Elle correspond à la compréhension globale et permet de répondre aux hypothèses émises avant la lecture.

Lectures suivantes

Elles correspondent à la compréhension détaillée du texte.

Dans un extrait littéraire

Les personnages	Le nombre de personnages, les relations entre eux·elles. Interviennent-ils ou elles dans le texte ou sont-ils ou elles seulement mentionné·e·s ? Faites un travail de repérage des pronoms personnels.
Les lieux	Ville, pays, lieu public, lieu privé, etc.
Une date	Date précise, époque, période, etc.
La narration	Externe, interne ou omnisciente.

Attention à ne pas confondre l'auteur·e : celui ou celle qui écrit et le ou la narrateur·trice : celui ou celle qui s'exprime dans un texte. Ils ou elles peuvent être différent·e·s.

Dans un article de presse

Les personnes	Le nombre, leur fonction, les paroles prononcées ou rapportées ?
Les nombres	À quoi correspondent-ils (année, pourcentage...) ?
Les objectifs principaux	Dénoncer, annoncer, montrer, etc.

Stratégies pour comprendre

Il s'agit de comprendre la **structure interne** du texte. Voici ce qu'il faut repérer : les mots de liaison, les différents paragraphes ou les retours à la ligne également quand il s'agit d'un texte littéraire.

Les **mots de liaison** ainsi que les **paragraphes** sont aussi à repérer dans les articles de presse. Souvent une idée ou un argument correspond à un paragraphe.

Vous pouvez donner un **titre** à chaque paragraphe ou bien donner la liste des **thèmes principaux**.

Vous tombez sur des mots inconnus ? Regardez si vous avez une aide lexicale, si vous connaissez un mot de la même famille ou bien si vous pouvez en déduire le sens avec le contexte. On appelle cela **l'inférence.**

+ Trouver le mot **racine** : il faut enlever le préfixe et / ou le suffixe pour comprendre comment le mot est formé.

+ S'aider du **contexte** pour comprendre le sens du mot.

+ Comprendre le **rôle** du mot dans la phrase.

Fiche N° 17

Expression orale en interaction

Les descripteurs du programme – B2

- Peut exposer ses idées et ses opinions et **argumenter** sur des **sujets complexes familiers**, identifier avec précision les arguments d'autrui et y réagir de façon convaincante en langue standard.
- Peut **échanger ou négocier pour trouver une solution,** présenter ses conditions et poser des questions détaillées sur des **sujets complexes.**
- Peut conduire **un entretien ou une conversation téléphonique avec efficacité et aisance**, en s'écartant spontanément des questions préparées et en exploitant et relançant les réponses intéressantes.

Il y a deux types d'interaction : à deux et à plusieurs.

expliquer
raconter
questionner
négocier
exprimer un point de vue
Dialoguer
formuler une opinion
réagir et rebondir
argumenter
relancer
exprimer des émotions

L'interaction préparée

Dans le cas d'une interaction préparée (jeu de rôle, saynète), prenez en note quelques mots-clés qui vous serviront de base lors de l'interaction. À cela, ajoutez quelques informations qui vous paraissent utiles. Par exemple :

- Vérifiez la prononciation et l'accentuation des mots dont vous n'êtes pas sûr·e avec un dictionnaire en ligne (*WordReference*, *Cambridge*...)
- Préparez quelques phrases idiomatiques et des *gap fillers*.

Adaptez votre **niveau de langue** à la situation (plus ou moins familier). Évitez par exemple de mettre des *like* ou *I'm gonna* si vous faites un jeu de rôle avec une situation formelle comme un entretien d'embauche.

Par ailleurs, essayez d'anticiper les arguments de l'autre. Dialoguez avec votre partenaire à partir des mots-clés et entraînez-vous à refaire le dialogue même si certaines formulations changent.

L'interaction spontanée

Dans le cas d'une interaction **spontanée** (comme dans la vraie vie), ce qui compte c'est **d'oser** se lancer directement en anglais sans écrire ! Vous pouvez prendre une minute pour réfléchir chacun·e dans votre tête, puis lancez-vous !

- Mettez le **ton** si vous jouez un rôle et dans tous les cas, soyez impliqué·e.
- Si vous ne comprenez pas ce que dit votre interlocuteur·rice, n'hésitez pas à le·la faire répéter : *Sorry?* (intonation montante), *I beg your pardon? Could you say that again? What do you mean?*
- Pensez aux réponses courtes du type : *Yes, I do. No, I can't.* Mais développez dès que vous le pouvez !

> Si vous ne trouvez pas un mot ou une formulation, pensez à **paraphraser**, **simplifier** ou **illustrer** ! Vous ne connaissez pas *cover letter*, vous pouvez dire *a letter for a job*. Vous ne connaissez pas le métier de *advertiser*, vous pouvez illustrer par *the person who promotes products on TV*.

- Relancez votre partenaire en lui posant des questions, en lui demandant son avis, etc.
- Regardez votre interlocuteur·rice.
- Surtout, laissez-le ou laissez-la prendre part à la conversation !

Le débat

Avant le débat

- Choisissez votre position suivant le point de vue à défendre.
- Prenez des notes (pas de phrases complètes) qui résument vos arguments.
- Faites une liste de mots de liaison que vous devrez utiliser.

Pendant le débat

- Utilisez un niveau de langue assez soutenu.
- Pratiquez l'écoute active : soyez attentif·ve à ce que disent les autres pour pouvoir rebondir sur leurs arguments, placez vos idées au bon moment.
- Demandez la parole et respectez la parole des autres.

> **Après le débat**, revenez sur les mots qui vous ont manqué et apprenez-les !

Voici **des expressions et des phrases** que vous pourriez utiliser lors de vos prochains dialogues, débats, entretiens… *Help yourself!*

Gap fillers

Well,…
So… Er…
You know/see,…
You know what I mean,…
What I'm trying to say is…
How can I say this,…
Let's see,…
Anyway, the point is…

Disagreement

I don't agree with you…
I'm not sure about that…
I agree up to a point, but…
We don't seem to agree here…
That's not always true…

Expressing opinions

I believe…I feel…
It seems to me that…
From my point of view…
As far as I'm concerned…
Personally, I think…
I'd like to point out that…

Agreement

I agree with you…
Definitely…
I see your point…
I think so too…
That's a good point…
Actually, I think you're right…
That's true…

Phone conversations

Hello, this is Mary. May I speak with John?
Brian speaking.
Could you slow down a little?
Sorry, I didn't quite catch that. Could you repeat it, please?
Can I leave a message?

Fiche N° 18 Expression orale en continu

La règle d'or

Connaissances
Méthode
Entraînement

Les descripteurs du programme – B2

- Peut faire une **description claire et détaillée** d'une gamme étendue de sujets en relation avec son domaine d'intérêt.
- Peut dire de façon détaillée en quoi des événements et des expériences le / la touchent personnellement.
- Peut **développer méthodiquement une argumentation** en mettant en évidence les points significatifs et les éléments pertinents.
- Peut **développer un exposé de manière claire et méthodique** en soulignant les points significatifs et les éléments pertinents.
- Peut **s'écarter spontanément d'un texte préparé** pour suivre les points intéressants soulevés par des auditeurs·rices.

La préparation des notes

Étape 1 : Mobilisez vos idées et vos connaissances.

- **Culturelles** : en fonction du sujet.
- **Lexicales** : un vocabulaire riche et précis lié à la présentation.
- **Grammaticales** : les structures vues en classe.

Étape 2 : Commencez à préparer vos notes.

Vous pouvez créer une **carte mentale** avec les mots-clés qui se lisent dans le sens des aiguilles d'une montre ou bien faire une **liste** avec :

- des abréviations : ex ; i.e.
- des signes (⚠).
- des couleurs différentes pour les titres de parties et sous-parties.
- des espaces entre chaque partie et des alinéas pour les sous-parties.
- des flèches pour indiquer les exemples ou les conséquences.

Étape 3 : Préparez le passage à l'oral.

- Mettez dans la marge les connecteurs logiques et *gap fillers*.
- Surlignez les points importants.

L'entraînement

Entraînez-vous avec un dictionnaire en ligne pour bien prononcer les mots-clés.

Puis, faites la présentation orale :

- à voix haute (de préférence),
- devant le miroir ou mieux, devant un·e camarade ou un membre de votre famille,
- dans le temps imparti,
- plusieurs fois pour ajuster.

Filmez-vous puis regardez votre prestation pour trouver des points à améliorer.

> Pour un **entraînement régulier**, vous pouvez regarder des tutos sur la prise de parole en continu, vous entraîner à prendre la parole sur toutes sortes de sujets ou encore vous parler à voix haute à la maison dès que vous le pouvez.

La présentation en classe

- Contournez les difficultés d'expression.
  - Dites la même chose en faisant une phrase (*I'm thirsty.* → *I want to drink.*).
  - Utilisez un équivalent approximatif (*a vet* → *a doctor for animals*).
  - Simplifiez votre formulation (*I feel like sleeping.* → *I want to sleep.*).
- Parlez suffisamment **fort et distinctement** pour être compris·e.
- L'erreur est humaine ! Inutile de vous focaliser sur les erreurs.
- Essayez de prononcer les phrases correctement en pensant à la musique de la langue anglaise.

Pendant la présentation :

- Gardez les pieds bien ancrés au sol.
- Utilisez la gestuelle.
- Parlez avec conviction et enthousiasme.
- Laissez un petit temps de silence avant de commencer.
- Faites des pauses pendant votre présentation.
- Essayez de regarder tou·te·s vos interlocuteurs·rices.
- Faites attention à votre posture.

Fiche N° 19 Expression écrite en interaction

Qu'est-ce que l'expression écrite en interaction ?

Définition : Il s'agit d'**échanges généralement courts** entre interlocuteurs·rices **à l'écrit**.
Ex : échanges personnels (lettre, messagerie instantanée, messages téléphoniques, ...) ou impersonnels (formulaires, ...).
Forme : Le langage est souvent **informel**, il peut être emprunté au langage oral. Structurer le texte n'est pas la priorité. Il est même possible de demander de clarifier un propos.

Les descripteurs du programme – B2

- Peut maintenir une relation à travers une correspondance personnelle dans une **langue fluide et efficace**.
- Peut **se procurer par lettre ou par courriel les informations** dont il·elle a besoin. Peut **prendre des messages** personnels et professionnels **complexes** et en laisser, à condition de pouvoir demander des compléments d'information.
- Peut intervenir en ligne pour relier ses contributions à d'autres déjà publiées, saisir les implications culturelles et réagir de façon adéquate.
- Peut **s'engager dans des échanges en ligne entre plusieurs participants**, relier efficacement ses contributions à d'autres déjà publiées, à condition qu'un·e modérateur·rice aide à gérer la discussion.

Faites une expérience.

1. **Réfléchissez à votre support** : est-ce un texto ? un e-mail ? plusieurs messages sur un forum de discussion ?
2. **Qui écrit ?** Allez-vous utiliser votre **nom** et **prénom** ou bien un **pseudonyme ?**
3. **Prise de notes** : quelle longueur ? quel registre de langue ? quel sujet ? à qui cela s'adresse-t-il ?
4. **Utilisez un dictionnaire** (papier ou en ligne) pour traduire des mots mais surtout pas des phrases entières.
5. **Entraînez-vous** d'abord sur un brouillon en utilisant des **couleurs différentes** pour chaque participant·e.

Que vous apprend cette expérience ?

Il ne s'agit pas seulement de rédiger mais de réagir à l'écrit à ce que votre interlocuteur·trice vous a écrit ou bien à ce que vous lui avez écrit.

N'oubliez pas que vous pouvez demander des précisions à votre interlocuteur·rice si vous n'avez pas compris ses propos.

Essayez d'adopter un langage correct, mais ne vous concentrez pas trop sur la forme. Vous pouvez vous corriger en temps réel, comme à l'oral.

Communiquer efficacement

Assurez-vous toujours de :

- vous faire bien comprendre en reformulant au besoin (*What I meant is..., I'm sorry, I didn't mean...*).
- prendre en compte la ou les réponses précédentes et les réactions de votre ou vos interlocuteurs·rices.
- mettre en place des stratégies pour communiquer : la coopération, l'illustration, la négociation, etc.

Organiser sa prise de parole à l'écrit

1. **Bien définir le contexte de cette interaction à l'écrit :** pourquoi écrivez-vous ? À qui ? Quelles questions vous posez-vous ? Sur quel support (en ligne, par voie postale, par courrier électronique ...) ? Répondez-vous à quelqu'un, ou bien êtes-vous à l'origine de ce questionnement ?

2. **Préparer son sujet :** prenez des notes et rassemblez les outils dont vous avez besoin. N'écrivez pas de phrases complètes mais réfléchissez au lexique dont vous aurez besoin.

3. **Répéter ses interventions :** imaginez les questions ou les réponses que vous pourriez formuler. Quels éléments pouvez-vous apporter à cette conversation ?

4. **Anticiper une clarification :** rassemblez les outils et expressions que vous pourrez utiliser pour reprendre et clarifier un propos si celui-ci n'a pas été compris par votre interlocuteur·rice.

5. **Mettre le ton :** réfléchissez aux moyens de mettre le ton dans vos écrits (ponctuation, mais aussi symboles, GIFs, images et smileys s'il s'agit d'une conversation personnelle). ☺

Entraînez-vous à plusieurs !
Vous venez de devenir ami·e sur Instagram avec une célébrité que vous adorez. Imaginez la conversation privée que vous pourriez avoir elle. Présentez-vous, expliquez pourquoi vous l'aimez, la suivez sur les réseaux sociaux, etc.

Veillez à adopter le bon **registre de langue** et à adapter votre **ton**.

SIMULATEURS D'APPLICATIONS DE MESSAGERIE EN LIGNE
igenerator.eu
ifaketextmessage.com

Fiche N° 20 Expression écrite

Les descripteurs du programme – B2

- Peut écrire des **descriptions claires et détaillées** sur une variété de sujets en rapport avec son domaine d'intérêt.
- Peut écrire une **critique** de film, de livre ou de pièce de théâtre.
- Peut écrire **un essai ou un rapport qui développe une argumentation** de façon méthodique en soulignant de manière appropriée les points importants et les détails pertinents qui viennent l'appuyer.

Faites une expérience.

1. D'instinct, comment traduiriez-vous en anglais les deux expressions suivantes ?
   - Il me fait chanter.
   - Il me fait marcher.

   Des énoncés de type **He makes me sing* ou **He makes me walk* ne sont pas recevables dans ce contexte.
2. Cherchez maintenant ces expressions dans le dictionnaire.
3. Que remarquez-vous sur la démarche même d'écriture ? Pouvez-vous toujours traduire mot à mot ?

Que vous apprend cette expérience ?

Afin d'éviter les confusions, il faut garder en tête qu'écrire ce n'est pas traduire. En effet, penser comme cela évite de passer par le mot à mot et permet d'utiliser une langue de plus en plus authentique. Il convient donc de **penser directement en anglais** et d'acquérir une logique de la langue, en participant activement en classe par exemple, pour se faire corriger.

L'anglais est très global alors que le français est très spécifique. C'est pourquoi le même terme en anglais peut traduire plusieurs idées. Pour chaque mot appris, essayer de retenir trois sens différents est très utile.

Le fond et la forme

Réussir une expression écrite, c'est assurer un équilibre entre **le fond** (les idées) et **la forme** (la façon de les articuler), le tout en répondant à un sujet donné.

Pour cela, appliquez la méthode **COOL** :

C	pour **comprendre** : bien comprendre le sujet est essentiel (→ Fiche N° 18 Compréhension écrite p. 276).
O	pour **obéir** : il faut suivre la direction donnée par les mots-clés du sujet.
O	pour **organiser** : plus vos idées seront organisées, plus votre devoir sera clair.
L	pour **lire** : lire et relire sa production en entier à la fin sont des étapes capitales.

Écrire un e-mail ou une lettre

Dans ce type d'échanges écrits, tout dépend du **destinataire**. En effet, une lettre à quelqu'un de sa famille sera à distinguer d'une correspondance avec une institution ou encore à un potentiel employeur.

Attention, le langage SMS ne sera pas recevable dans ce type d'écrit.

Présenter un courrier formel

Nom et adresse
de l'expéditeur·rice

Date

Nom et adresse
du·de la destinataire

Dear Madam, Sir

Lettre
...
...

Formule de politesse

Signature

	Un email	Une lettre
Fond	**Pour amener l'objet du courriel** • *I'm writing to you today...* • *The reason why I'm writing is...* • *I really wanted to tell you about...* • *The purpose of my email is to know...* • *I'm writing to find out if...*	**Pour amener l'objet du courrier** • *If I may, I would like to + V* • *I am writing to inform you about...* • *The subject of my letter is...* • *With all due respect, I would like to inform you that...* • *I wanted to tell you how I was doing.*
Forme	**En ouverture :** • *Dear X* • *Dear Mr / Mrs X* • *Hi (to a friend)* **Pour conclure :** • *Yours sincerely* • *Regards (to someone you esteem)* • *See you soon (to a friend)* • *Xo Xo (to a very good friend)* **Pour parler d'une pièce jointe :** • *You will find the document attached* • *As promised please find the document attached*	**En ouverture :** • *Dear Madam, Sir* • *To whom it may concern* **Pour conclure :** • *Yours faithfully* • *Kind regards* • *Love from LA* **Point de vigilance :** • Aérer son courrier au maximum. • Changer de ligne ou de paragraphe chaque fois que vous apportez un élément nouveau (dans une lettre formelle). • Utiliser les mots de liaison. • Pas de présentation particulière pour une lettre à un·e proche.

Écrire un dialogue

Attention, un dialogue n'est pas un script. Il ne suffit donc pas d'écrire des répliques échangées entre deux personnages (comme au cinéma ou au théâtre). Il est important de **contextualiser**.

Commencez par **une courte phrase d'introduction** puis donnez des précisions sur **les expressions faciales ou l'atmosphère**, cela permet de rendre le dialogue visuel pour le ou la lecteur·rice et donc authentique.

Dans le fond comme dans la forme, un dialogue en anglais s'avère assez différent d'un dialogue en français. Dans le premier cas, le dialogue s'imbrique davantage dans le récit et n'est visible que grâce aux guillemets.

Présentation d'un dialogue	
en français	**en anglais**
« – Un jour je partirai et tu ne me reverras plus jamais ! cria-t-il. – Calme toi d'abord, » répondit-elle choquée.	"Someday, I'll run away, and you will never see me again!" he shouted. "First, calm down," she answered, shocked.
• Les guillemets sont ouverts au début du dialogue et ne sont fermés qu'après la dernière réponse. • Des tirets sont utilisés à chaque ligne pour marquer le changement de personnage.	• Les guillemets sont utilisés au début et à la fin de chaque intervention. • Pas d'inversion sujet/verbe pour les introducteurs de paroles. • Pas de tirets.

Said is dead!
Évitez la répétition du verbe *said* à chaque ligne, remplacez-le par un autre verbe.
Parler : *tell, say, ask, answer, reply, explain, admit, deny…*
Crier : *scream, shout…*
À voix basse : *mumble, whisper…*
Avec émotion : *cry, laugh, argue…*

Écrire un article

Attention, il faut distinguer l'article du paragraphe argumentatif. Le premier se base sur des faits et non sur l'opinion. Même si un article est rarement objectif, l'opinion n'est pas donnée directement : l'enjeu est de faire comprendre ce que l'on pense dans la manière et pas dans les mots.

À partir du **thème** qui vous est donné, vous devez trouver **un sujet** (un aspect caractéristique ou problématique du thème) autour duquel votre article sera construit.

Le paragraphe introductif doit permettre aux lecteurs·rices de répondre aux questions en *Wh-* (*Who? What? Where? When?*…) et d'imaginer clairement la situation que vous allez développer dans la suite.

Vous devez maîtriser **les mots de liaison**, rechercher le **vocabulaire spécifique** au sujet que vous traitez, et **répartir vos idées** tout au long de l'article.

Chaque nouveau paragraphe doit apporter des éléments supplémentaires.

N'hésitez pas à utiliser des **citations** de gens connus ou qui interviennent dans les faits relatés.

Pour plus de cohérence et d'inspiration donnez **un titre** à votre article après l'avoir écrit.

Utilisez des formules passives (équivalent du pronom neutre « on ») pour donner à votre article un ton plus objectif.

Écrire un paragraphe argumentatif

Le paragraphe argumentatif n'est pas un plaidoyer. Vous ne devez pas présenter une seule et unique vision de problèmes amenés par le sujet. Il s'agit de **peser le pour et le contre**.

Construisez votre texte en suivant le **principe de l'entonnoir** : de l'argument le plus évident à l'argument le plus réfléchi.

Tout l'enjeu de l'exercice est d'**argumenter**, **relativiser**, **réfuter**, **critiquer**…

Pour cela vous devez maîtriser **les mots de liaison** afin que votre développement soit structuré et suivi de bout en bout par votre lecteur·rice, sans aucune gêne.

Faites bien attention à **trouver les mots justes** pour vous exprimer de façon claire et concise.

Ne confondez pas vos arguments (les idées qui répondent au problème posé en introduction) **et les exemples** (qui rendent les arguments plus concrets en les illustrant).

Vos phrases introductive et conclusive ne doivent pas excéder une à deux lignes.

Notez les guillemets différents :
« … » : guillemets français,
"…" : guillemets anglais

CREDITS TEXTES

p. 16 *Tea Tuesdays: How Tea + Sugar Reshaped The British Empire*, by Maria Godoy, April 7, 2015 © NPR. D.R ; **p. 18** *The great tea robbery: how the British stole China's secrets and seeds – and broke its monopoly on the brew*, by STUART HEAVER, 27 MAY 2017 © Stuart Heaver ; **p. 19** *Why do the British love the taste of tea so much?*, by Veronique Greenwood, 3 June 2016 © BBC ; **p. 24** *Congo Square*, Prime Media & The Ponderosa Stomp Foundation © A Closer Walk, D.R. ; **p. 26** *South London Memories – Jazz singer Adelaide Hall sang as bombs fell*, 3rd July 2018, ©londonnewsonline.co.uk, D.R. ; **p. 27** *'Tremé Was Empty': How Musicians Are Helping New Orleans Heal From Katrina*, by CARIMAH TOWNES, AUG 26, 2015, © 2019 ThinkProgress, D.R. ; **p. 35** *Pot luck: tea researchers find Britain's oldest cuppa*, Maev Kennedy, Tuesday 26 May 2015 © 2018 Guardian News and Media Limited. All rights reserved. ; **p. 37** *The British jazz explosion: meet the musicians rewriting the rulebook*, by Kate Hutchinson, 8 April 2018, © Guardian News & Media ; **p. 42** *Depraved Heart*, 2015 Reprinted by permission of HarperCollins Publishers Ltd © 2019 Patricia Cornwell ; **p. 43** *Why do we enjoy reading about female detectives?*, by Alexander McCall Smith, 7/11/2012 © The Independent ; **p. 49** Excerpts from news report titled *"Remembering Hollywood's Hays Code, 40 Years On"* by Bob Mondello were originally published on npr.org on August 8, 2008, and is used with the permission of NPR. Any unauthorized duplication is strictly prohibited. © National Public Radio, Inc. ; **p. 51** *LGBTQ representation in Hollywood is still 'bleak,' GLAAD report finds*, DEVAN COGGAN, May 22, 2018 © Meredith, D.R. ; **p. 59** *The Fall: The Most Feminist Show on Television* by Amy Sullivan, The Atlantic, Jan 23, 2015 ; **p. 61** *Isn't It Romantic?' is only pretending to be a different kind of rom-com*, by ANGIE HAN, FEB 12, 2019 © MASHABLE.COM, D.R. ; **p. 65** *Street art: Crime, grime or sublime?*, by Bethan Bell, 16/12/2016 © BBC News ; **p. 67** *dRMM's Hastings Pier Wins 2017 RIBA Stirling Prize*, by Patrick Lynch, 31 October, 2017 © ArchDaily, D.R. ; **p. 73** *THE GRAPES OF WRATH: 75TH ANNIVERSARY EDITION* by John Steinbeck, copyright © 1939, renewed © 1967 by John Steinbeck. Used by permission of Viking Books, an imprint of Penguin Publishing Group, a division of Penguin Random House LLC. All rights reserved. ; **p. 83** *Can we trust the government to judge what's beautiful?*, Oliver Wainwright, 15/01/2019 © Guardian News & Media ; **p. 85** Christopher Paul Curtis, *Bud, not Buddy*, (1999) © Penguin Random House ; **p. 90** *Trump Has Changed How Teens View the News*, by Taylor Lorenz, 29/08/2018 © 2018 The Atlantic Media Co., as first published in TheAtlantic.Com. All rights reserved. Distributed by Tribune Content Agency ; **p. 97** *This Is What Social Media Had to Say About the March for Our Lives*, by CHRISTIAN ALLAIRE, MARCH 24, 2018 © Vogue, D.R. ; **p. 99** *Philanthropy That Comes From a Click*, by Clyde Haberman, Nov. 13, 2016 © The New York Times ; **p. 107** *How Social Media Has Changed How We Consume News*, Nicole Martin, Nov 30, 2018 © Forbes ; **p. 109** *Youth Activism and the #NeverAgain Movement*, by Carolyn Davis, Feb 21, 2018, PRRI © medium.com, D.R. ; **p. 113** *1984*, Georges Orwell © Random House UK ; **p. 114** *The Handmaid's Tale*, Margaret Atwood © Houghton Mifflin Harcourt ; **p. 121** *PIRACY*, © National Museum of the Royal Navy 2018 ; **p. 121** *Pirates in the Age of Sail*, by Robert J. Antony. © 2007 Used by permission of W.W. Norton & Company, Inc. ; **p. 122** *The Timeless Allure Of Pirates*, by Roger Luckhurst, 21 June 2017 © BBC ; **p. 131** *Twentieth Century Dystopian Fiction*, ANTHONY BURGESS © 2019 International Anthony Burgess Foundation, D.R. ; **p. 133** *More Than a Pirate, a Rebel With a Democratic Spirit*, by Colin Woodard, 22/11/2018 © The New York Times ; **p. 137** *Elon Musk: regulate AI to combat 'existential threat' before it's too late*, Samuel Gibbs, 17/07/2017 © Guardian News & Media ; **p. 139** *Facial recognition software can spot liars and could help bust airport terrorists*, by Joseph Archer, 24 May 2018 © Telegraph Media Group Limited 2018 ; **p. 145** *Apollo 11: First Men on the Moon*, by Nola Taylor Redd, December 19, 2017 © Space.com / PURCH ; **p. 147** *"Mars City: Human missions to space colony will start in 2024, Elon Musk says*, by James Titcomb 29 September 2017 © Telegraph Madia Group Limited 2017" ; **p. 155** Isaac Asimov, *Robbie* (1940), D.R. ; **p. 157** *Mars, Our First Outpost on the Final Frontier*, James Fallows, APRIL 2013 © 2018 The Atlantic Media Co., as first published in TheAtlantic. Com. All rights reserved. Distributed by Tribune Content Agency ; **p. 161** *Black Americans mostly left behind by progress since Dr. King's death*, by Sharon Austin, 7 février 2018, © The Conversation France, Creative Commons ; **p. 163** *A Place to Come Together on Matters That Divide Us*, SUSAN GOLDBERG © National Geographic ; **p. 168** Neil Mitchell, *Where to begin with kitchen sink drama*, August 4, 2016,©2019 British Film Institute. D.R. ; **p. 169** *This is England, British Working Class on Film, Working Class Heroes: British Working Class on Film* © www.watershed.co.uk, D.R. ; **p. 170** *Film-maker Amma Asante on race, Brexit and meeting Prince*, by Emma Jacobs, NOVEMBER 10, 2016 © Financial Times, D.R. ; **p. 179** *The #BlackLivesMatter Movement: Marches And Tweets For Healing*, June 9, 2015 © National Public Radio, Inc. ; **p. 181** *An Introduction To British Social Realist Directors*, 8 JANUARY 2017 © 2019 The Culture Trip, D.R. ; **p. 184** *Map: The rise and fall of the British Empire*, by Adam Taylor, September 8, 2015 © Washington Post ; **p. 187** *Irma: Caribbean overseas territories condemn UK Government's 'disgraceful' lack of help as Hurricane wreaks devastation*, by Samuel Osborne, 7/09/2017 © The Independent ; **p. 192** *Why celebrating Juneteenth is more important now than ever. It's time for America to truly grapple with its legacy of slavery.* By P.R. Lockhart © Vox Media ; **p. 194** Bob Marley, *Redemption Song*, 1980 © Blue Mountain Music ; **p. 203** *Ahoy there! Mutiny island grabs tourist bounty lifeline*, Anthony Browne, 25/03/2001 © Guardian News & Media ; **p. 203** *Mutiny on the Bounty: The true story of Captain Bligh's mutineers*, by Caroline Alexander, 12/03/2017 © Telegraph Media Group Limited 2018 ; **p. 205** *United Nations unveils slavery memorial*, By Jacqueline Charles, March 25, 2015 © Miami Herald, D.R.

TABLE DES ILLUSTRATIONS

p. 6 -h ph © Vadim Georgiev / Shutterstock ; **p. 6** -mh ph © Josh Brasted / WireImage / Getty Images ; **p. 6** -mb ph © SunsetBox / AllPix / Aurimages ; **p. 6** -b Coll. Christophel © MGM ; **p. 8** -h ph © Charles Bowman / Robertharding / Alamy Stock Photo ; **p. 8** -mh ph © Everett Collection / Aurimages ; **p. 8** -mb ph © Mira / Alamy Stock Photo ; **p. 8** -b ph © Bill Clark / CQ Roll Call / Getty-Images ; **p. 10** -h Coll. Christophel © Holiday Film Productions Ltd ; **p. 10** -mh ph © SuperStock / Leemage ; **p. 10** -mb ph © Universal Pictures / SunsetBox / AllPix / Aurimages ; **p. 10** -b Coll. Christophel © Twentieth century fox film corporation ; **p. 12** -h ph © Volkan Furuncu / Anadolu Agency / AFP Photo ; **p. 12** -mh Coll. Christophel © Warp Films / Big Arty Productions ; **p. 12** -mb ph © Daisy Gilardini / Science Faction / Getty-Images ; **p. 12** -b ph © Michelle Gilders / Alamy Stock Photo / © Josh Sarantitis and Eric Okdeh ; **p. 15** -h ph © Vadim Georgiev / Shutterstock ; **p. 15** -b ph © Josh Brasted / WireImage / Getty Images ; **p. 16** © Pirates of the Caribbean at world›s end, Gore Verbinski, 2007. Coll. Christophel ; **p. 17** -h ph © Akg-Images / Pictures From History ; **p. 17** -b © « Les aventures de Robert Fortune ou comment le thé fut volé aux chinois » Un film de Charles-Antoine de Rouvre & Jérôme Scemla © ARTE France - La Compagnie des Taxi-Brousse – 2016 ; **p. 18** -g ph © Fancy Photo / Getty-Images ; **p. 18** -d ph © Humphrey Spender / Picture Post / Getty-Images ; **p. 19** -g ph © Popperfoto / Getty-Images ; **p. 19** -d ph © Eric McNatt / FoodPix / Getty-Images ; **p. 23** -h ph © Greg Balfour Evans / Alamy Stock Photo ; **p. 23** -b ph © Maximilian Stock Ltd / Photononstop ; **p. 24** ph © Ilpo Musto / Alamy Stock Photo ; **p. 25** -h ph © The Art Institute of Chicago, IL, USA / Restricted gift of Mr. and Mrs. Marshall Field, Jack and Sandra Guthman, Ben W. Heineman, Ruth Horwich, Lewis and Susan Manilow, Beatrice C. Mayer, Charles A. Meyer, John D. Nichols, and Mr. and Mrs. E.B. Smith, Jr.; James W. Alsdorf / Bridgeman Images ; **p. 25** -b ph © Harry Warnecke / NY Daily News Archive via Getty-Images ; **p. 27** ph © Mario Tama / Getty-Images / AFP Photo ; **p. 31** -h ph © David Gahr / Getty-Images ; **p. 31** -b ph © Historic Faubourg Treme Association ; **p. 33** -hg © Princeton University Press© Walt Disney ; **p. 33** -hd ph © Robert Fortune, The Tea Thief, Diane Perelsztejn, 2001 © Les Films de la Memoire / BBQ_DFY / Aurimages ; **p. 33** -mg © Anchor Publishers, 2016 ; **p. 33** -bd1 ph © New York, New York, Martin Scorsese, 1977. Prod DB © United Artists / Allpix / Aurimages ; **p. 33** -bd2 © Whiplash, Damien Chazelle, 2014. Coll. Christophel © Bold Films / Blumhouse Productions / Right of Way Films ; **p. 33** -bd3 ph © Bird, Clint Eastwood, 1988. © Warner Bros / The Kobal Collection / Aurimages ; **p. 33** -bd4 © Treme, 2012. Coll. Christophel © Paul Schiraldi / HBO ; **p. 33** -bd5 ph © The Halcyon, created by Charlotte Jones, 2017. ph © ITV - Left Bank Pictures / Prod DB / Allpix / Aurimages ; **p. 33** -bd6 ph © Dancing on the Edge, TV série, Stephen Poliakoff, 2013. © Endgame Entertainment / Playground Entertainment / BBC Worldwide / BBQ_DFY / Aurimages ; **p. 34** -h ph © Pictures from History / Woodbury & Page / Bridgeman Images ; **p. 34** -b ph © Bob Whitaker / Getty-Images ; **p. 35** ph © Print Collector / Getty-Images ; **p. 36** -h ph © Pantheon (Knopf Doubleday Publishing Group), 2018 ; **p. 36** -b ph © Naum Chayer / Alamy Stock Photo ; **p. 37** ph © Craig Lovell / Eagle Visions Photography / Alamy Stock Photo ; **p. 39** -h ph © SunsetBox / AllPix / Aurimages ; **p. 39** -b Coll. Christophel © MGM ; **p. 40** -g © Elementary, TV serie, Robert Doherty, 2012. Ph © CBS / BBQ_DFY / Aurimages ; **p. 40** -mg © Harpercollins Publishers, 1997 ; **p. 40** -md Doc. Archives Hatier ; **p. 40** -d ph © Blue Steel, Kathryn Bigelow, 1990. Prod DB © Lighting Pictures / Aurimages ; **p. 41** © Ill. Hannah Firmin. Publisher, Abacus, 2005 ; **p. 42** -h © HarperCollins, 2016 ; **p. 42** -b © Trailer FBI © CBS 2018 ; **p. 43** ph © British Library Board. All Rights Reserved / Bridgeman Images ; **p. 47** -h ph © vadimguzhva / Getty-Images ; **p. 47** -b © "Creatures of the Night" CSI: NY, TV Serie. ph © Ron Jaffe/ CBS Licensed by Channel 5 Broadcasting / Mary Evans / Aurimages ; **p. 48** -hg ph © Prod DB © Selznick International Pictures / AllPix / Aurimages ; **p. 48** -hm ph © Tri-Star / The Kobal Collection / Aurimages ; **p. 48** -hd Coll. Christophel © Twentieth Century Fox / Paramount Pictures / Lightstorm Entertainment ; **p. 48** -bg ph © Focus Features / The Kobal Collection / Aurimages ; **p. 48** -bm Coll. Christophel © Universal ; **p. 48** -bd Coll. Christophel © Black Label Media / Gilbert films / Impostor Pictures / Marc Platt Productions / Summit Entertainment ; **p. 49** ph © 20th Century-Fox / Getty-Images ; **p. 50** -h ph © 20th Century Fox / Prod DB / AllPix / Aurimages ; **p. 50** -b Coll. Christophel © CBS Films / Escape Artists ; **p. 51** © Love Simon, Greg Berlanti, 2018. Coll. Christophel © Fox 2000 pictures / New leaf literary and media ; **p. 55** -h ph © Daniel Ernst - stock.adobe.com ; **p. 55** -b ph © fabioderby - stock.adobe.com ; **p. 57** -hg1 ph © Paperjacks, 1988 ; **p. 57** -hg2 ph © Vintage Crime / Black Lizard, 2018 ; **p. 57** -hd1 ph © Nancy Drew, Andrew Fleming, 2007. © Jerry Weintraub Productions / Warner Bros. / The Kobal Collection / Aurimages ; **p. 57** -hd2 ph © Fargo, Joel Coen, 1996. ph © Working Title / Polygram / The Kobal Collection / Aurimages ; **p. 57** -hd3 © The Silence of the lambs, Jonathan Demme, 1991. Coll. Christophel © Strong Heart / Demme Production ; **p. 57** -hd4 © Prime Suspect, Serie TV, 2011. Coll. Christophel © NBC / Universal ; **p. 57** -hd5 © The Bletchley Circle: Season 1, directed by Andy DeEmmony. DVD's cover © PBS ; **p. 57** -hd6 © The Fall, Serie TV, 2013. Coll. Christophel © Artists Studio / BBC Northern Ireland ; **p. 57** -bg1 © Cover designed by Francis Cugat © Charles Scribner's Sons, 1925 ; **p. 57** -bg2 ph © Pamela Dorman Books / Viking, 2012 ; **p. 57** -bd1 ph © The Notebook, Nick Cassavetes, 2004. ph © New Line / The Kobal Collection / Aurimages ; **p. 57** -bd2 ph © Moonlight, Barry Jenkins, 2016. © A24 / Plan B Entertainment / BBQ_DFY / Aurimages ; **p. 57** -bd3 © Romeo and Juliet, Baz Luhrmann, 1996. Coll. Christophel © Bazmark Films / Twentieth Century Fox ; **p. 57** -bd4 ph © The Perfect Holiday, Nancy Meyers, 2006. © Sony Pictures / The Kobal Collection / Aurimages ; **p. 57** -bd5 © Isn't It Romantic, Todd Strauss-Schulson, 2019. Coll. Christophel © Bron Studios / Netflix / Warner ; **p. 57** -bd6 © Brokeback Mountain, Ang Lee, 2005. Coll. Christophel © Focus Features / River Road Entertainment ; **p. 58** -h © Berkley Publishers, 2011 ; **p. 58** -b ph © SunsetBox / AllPix / Aurimages ; **p. 60** -h ph © Netflix / Kobal / REX / Shutterstock / Aurimages ; **p. 60** -b ph © New Line Cinema / Netflix / BBQ_DFY / Aurimages ; **p. 63** -h ph © Charles Bowman / Robertharding / Alamy Stock Photo ; **p. 63** -b ph © Everett Collection / Aurimages ; **p. 64** © Cover Artwork Credit: PichiAvo / Cover Photo Credit: Nick Clague ; **p. 65** © Stik in Shoreditch: the artist's hidden tribute to a sold-off London - video, Guardian News & Media. ; **p. 66** ph © London Legacy Development Corporation ; **p. 67** -g ph © Laurie Noble / Dorling Kindersley / Getty-Images ; **p. 67** -d ph © Paul Lawrenson (Sussex) / Alamy Stock Photo ; **p. 71** -h ph © Rawpixel Ltd / Alamy Stock Photo ; **p. 71** -b ph © Jon Arnold Images / hemis.fr ; **p. 72** -h ph © Courtesy of the Cedar Rapids Museum of Art ; **p. 72** -b ph © Lange, Dorothea / Private Collection / Bridgeman Images ; **p. 73** ph © Elmer Hader / Christie's Images / Bridgeman Images ; **p. 74** -h ph © Granger / Bridgeman Images ; **p. 74** -b ph © Collection of Barney A. Ebsworth / National Gallery of Art ; **p. 75** -h ph © Sheldon Memorial Art Gallery and Sculpture Garden, Univ. of Nebraska-Lincoln Nebraska Art Association Collection ; **p. 75** -b ph © The Museum of Modern Art, New York / Scala, Florence / Adagp, Paris, 2019 ; **p. 79** -h ph © Scott Olson / Getty-Images / AFP Photo ; **p. 79** -b ph © Ridofranz / Getty-Images ; **p. 81** -hg1 ph © Publisher Cornerstone – Century , 2006 ; **p. 81** -hg2 ph © Publisher Dokument Press, 2013 ; **p. 81** -hg3 ph © Prestel Publishing, 2017 ; **p. 81** -hd ph © Exit Through The Gift Shop, Banksy, 2010. © Paranoid Pictures / BBQ_DFY / Aurimages ; **p. 81** -bg1 ph © Penguin Books Ltd, 2019 ; **p. 81** -bg2 ph © Candlewick press, 2011 ; **p. 81** -bd1 © Modern Times, Charlie Chaplin, 1936. © United Artists ; **p. 81** -bd2 © The grapes of Wrath, John Ford, 1940. © The Advertising Archive / Aurimages ; **p. 81** -bd3 ph © Bonnie and Clyde, Arthur Penn, 1967. Prod DB © Tatira-Hiller / AllPix / Aurimages ; **p. 81** -bd4 ph © Seabiscuit, Gary Ross, 2003. © Universal - Dreamworks / Prod DB / AllPix / Aurimages ; **p. 82** -h © The Hull Beermat Photography Festival © BBC Look North ; **p. 82** -b ph © Anh Nguyen / Moment / Getty-Images ; **p. 83** ph © mpworks / Alamy Stock Photo / © John Bancroft (architect), 1967-70 ; **p. 84** -h ph © New York, Whitney Museum of American Art. Gift of Dr. Hartley Neel / © Estate of Alice Neel © 2019. Digital image Whitney Museum of American Art / Licensed by Scala ; **p. 84** -b ph © Peter Newark American Pictures / Bridgeman Images ;

p. 87 -h ph © Mira / Alamy Stock Photo ; **p. 87** -b ph © Bill Clark / CQ Roll Call / Getty-Images ; **p. 88** ph © Tim UR - stock.adobe. com ; **p. 89** ph © IFLA (The International Federation of Library Associations and Institutions ; **p. 90** ph © Frédéric Cirou / Altopress / AFP Photo ; **p. 91** -h ph © From American Government, Power and purpose, Brief 14E by Stephen Ansolabehere, Benjamin Ginsburg, Theodore J. Lowi & Kenneth A. Shepsle. Copyright © 2017, 2015, 2014, 2013, 2012, 2011, 2010, 2009, 2008, 2006, 2005, 2004, 2002, 2000, 1998, 1997, 1996, 1995, 1994, 1993, 1992,1990 by W. W. Norton & Company, Inc. Used by permission of W. W. Norton & Company, Inc ; **p. 91** -b ph © Wikileaks ; **p. 95** -h ph © monkeybusinessimages / istock / Getty-Images ; **p. 95** -b ph © Lazyllama / Alamy Stock Photo ; **p. 96** ph © Change.org: Starbucks, we know you can make a #BetterCup ; **p. 97** ph © Nicholas Kamm / AFP Photo ; **p. 98** -h © How online social movements translate to offline results, PBS NewsHour Weekend, #699 Twitter and Tear Gas, 10 june 2017 © WNET ; **p. 98** -b ph © Patrick LaMontagne ; **p. 103** -h ph © kate_sept2004 / E+ / Getty-Images ; **p. 103** -b ph © Linda Davidson / The Washington Post via Getty-Images ; **p. 105** -mg ph © Ten Speed Press, 2017 ; **p. 105** -hd1 ph © All the President's Men, Alan J. Pakula, 1976. © Warner Bros / Prod DB/ AllPix / Aurimages ; **p. 105** -hd2 © The Insider, Michael Mann, 1999. Coll. Christophel © Blue Lion Entertainment / Touchstone Pictures ; **p. 105** -hd3 ph © The Newsroom Serie TV 2012 - 2014, Aaron Sorkin. © HBO / BBQ_DFY / Aurimages ; **p. 105** -hd4 ph © The Post, Steven Spielberg, 2017. © Amblin Entertainment - DreamWorks - Pascal Pictures - Star Thrower Entertainment / Prod DB / AllPix / Aurimages ; **p. 105** -hd5 ph © Snowden, Oliver Stone, 2016. © Endgame Ent, Vendian Ent, KrautPack Ent / BBQ_DFY / Aurimages ; **p. 105** -hd6 ph © House Of Cards, 2013. © Media Rights Capital / The Kobal Collection/ Aurimages ; **p. 105** -b1 ph © Tundra Books, 2010 ; **p. 105** -b2 ph © Bloomsbury YA publishers, 2019 ; **p. 105** -b3 ph © The Internet's Own Boy: The Story of Aaron Swartz, Brian Knappenberger, 2014. © FilmBuff / Participant Media / BBQ_DFY / Aurimages ; **p. 106** -h © How media literacy can help students discern fake news, Jun 6, 2017, PBS NewsHour © Editorial Projects in Education ; **p. 106** -b ph © Vincentho / Dreamstime.com ; **p. 107** ph © Jean Glueck / F1online / Getty-Images ; **p. 108** ph © Allison Joyce / Getty-Images / AFP Photo ; **p. 109** ph © Steve Schapiro / Corbis via Getty-Images ; **p. 111** -h Coll. Christophel © Holiday Film Productions Ltd ; **p. 111** -b ph © SuperStock / Leemage ; **p. 112** -hg © Harpercollins Publishers, 2017 ; **p. 112** -hd ph © Grafton, 1976 (illustration : Steve Crisp) ; **p. 112** -bg ph © Penguin Classics, 2017 ; **p. 112** -bd ph © Penguin UK, 2008 (design: Separd Fairey) ; **p. 114** ph © Hulu / BBQ_DFY / Aurimages ; **p. 115** -h ph © David Dettmann / Zeppotron / Channel 4 / BBQ_DFY / Aurimages ; **p. 115** -b Coll. Christophel © Imagenation Abu Dhabi FZ / Likely story / Playtone ; **p. 118** Coll. Christophel © Blue Tulip ; **p. 119** -h ph © Sean Prior / Alamy Stock Photo ; **p. 119** -b ph © Tomorrowland, Brad Bird, 2015. © Walt Disney Pictures/ The Kobal Collection / Aurimages ; **p. 120** -h ph © James Brey / iStock Getty-Images ; **p. 120** -b ph © National Geographic Creative ; **p. 121** -1 Coll. Christophel © Dangerous Films / BBC ; **p. 121** -2 ph © Heritage Images / Leemage ; **p. 121** -3 ph © Private Collection / Peter Newark Historical Pictures / Bridgeman Images ; **p. 121** -4 ph © Black Sails (T.V. 2017-Season 4). Pers: Clara Paget / © Film Afrika Worldwide / Platinum Dunes / Quaker Moving Pictures / © David Bloomer / 2017 Starz Entertainment, LLC ; **p. 122** ph © Private Collection / Peter Newark Historical Pictures / Bridgeman Images ; **p. 123** -h ph © Pictorial Press Ltd / Alamy Stock Photo ; **p. 123** -b Coll. Christophel © Film Afrika Worldwide / Platinum Dunes / Quaker moving Pictures ; **p. 127** -h ph © Richard Ellis - www.agefotostock.com ; **p. 127** -b © Taneos Ramsay / Courtesy of the Pirates Week Festival Office ; **p. 129** -hg ph © Greg Rucka / © Image Comics, 2013 ; **p. 129** -hd1 ph © Logan's run, Michael Anderson, 1976. © M.G.M / PictureLux / The Hollywood Archive / Alamy Stock Photo ; **p. 129** -hd2 ph © Brazil, Terry Gilliam, 1985. © Universal / Embassy / The Kobal Collection / Aurimages ; **p. 129** -hd3 ph © Gattaca, Andrew Niccol, 1997. © Columbia / Prod DB / Allix / Aurimages ; **p. 129** -hd4 ph © Minority Report, Steven Spielberg, 2002. © Mary Evans / Aurimages ; **p. 129** -hd5 © The Children Of Men, Alfonso Cuaron, 2006. Coll. Christophel © Universal ; **p. 129** -hd6 ph © Idiocracy, Mike Judge, 2007. © 20th Century Fox / The Kobal Collection / Aurimages ; **p. 129** -b 1 © Treasure Island, ill. Louis Rhead and Frank E. Schoonover. Published by Evertype. First edition, 2010 ; **p. 129** -b 2 © Illustrations by Minalima. © 2015 Minalima Ltd. Reprinted by permission of Harpercollins Publishers ; **p. 129** -b 3 ph © Anne of the Indies, Jacques Tourneur, 1951 © 20th Century Fox / The Kobal Collection / Aurimages ; **p. 129** -b 4 © Blackbeard, terror at sea (Dir: Richard Dale, Tilman Remme. Pers: James Purefoy), TV 2006. Coll. Christophel © Dangerous Films / BBC ; **p. 130** -h ph © Aaron Davidson / WireImage / Getty-Images ; **p. 130** -b Coll. Christophel © Color Force / Lionsgate ; **p. 132** -h ph © Ill. by Howard Pyle, 1900. Private Collection / Costa / Bridgeman Images ; **p. 132** -b ph © The Advertising Archives / Bridgeman Images ; **p. 133** ph © Pan Macmillan, 2014 ; **p. 135** -h ph © Universal Pictures / SunsetBox / AllPix / Aurimages ; **p. 135** -b Coll. Christophel © Twentieth century fox film corporation ; **p. 136** Coll. Christophel © Bad robot / Jerry Weintraub productions / Kilter films ; **p. 138** -h © Jon Carter / Kd-nuggets ; **p. 138** -b © ELLIQ - The active aging companion © Intuition Robotics ; **p. 139** ph © gece33 / iStock / Getty-Images ; **p. 143** -h ph © 1000 Words / Shutterstock ; **p. 143** -b ph © SeventyFour / iStock / Getty-Images ; **p. 144** -h ph © Collier's Magazine Cover - October 18, 1952 ; **p. 144** -b ph © Collier's Magazine Cover – June 27, 1953 ; **p. 146** -h ph © Paul Fearn / Alamy Stock Photo ; **p. 146** -b ph © Nasa ; **p. 147** ph © Patrick T. Fallon / Bloomberg Finance LP via Getty-Images ; **p. 151** -h ph © Nasa / S.Dupuis / Alamy Stock Photo ; **p. 151** -b ph © Cultura Creative (RF) / Alamy Stock Photo via hemis.fr ; **p. 153** -h1 ph © Blade Runner, Ridley Scott, 1982. © Ladd Company/Warner Bros / The Kobal Collection / Aurimages ; **p. 153** -h2 ph © I, Robot, Alex Proyas, 2004. © 20th Century Fox / The Kobal Collection / Aurimages ; **p. 153** -h3 ph © Ex Machina, Alex Garland, 2015. © Dna Films / Film4 / The Kobal Collection ; **p. 153** -h4 © A.I. Artificial intelligence, Steven Spielberg, 2001. Coll. Christophel © Amblin / Dreamworks / WB ; **p. 153** -h5 © Ghost in the shell, Rupert Sanders, 2017. Coll. Christophel © Arad Productions / DreamWorks / Paramount pictures ; **p. 153** -h6 ph © Battlestar Galactica, Michael Rymer, 2003 (US TV Series), DVD's cover © Universal Pictures Home Entertainment ; **p. 153** -h7 © Humans (TV Series), Jonathan Brackley and Sam Vincent, 2015. Coll. Christophel © AMC ; **p. 153** -b1 ph © A Space Odyssey, Stanley Kubrick, 1968 © MGM / The Kobal Collection / Aurimages ; **p. 153** -b2 ph © Gravity, Alfonso Cuaron, 2013 © Warner Bros / The Kobal Collection / Aurimages ; **p. 153** -b3 ph © Interstellar, Christopher Nolan, 2014 © Paramount / Warner Brothers / The Kobal Collection / Aurimages ; **p. 153** -b4 ph © Mars Attack, Tim Burton, 1996. © Warner Bros / The Advertising Archive / Aurimages ; **p. 153** -b5 ph © The War of the Worlds, adaptaded by Mary Ann Evans (Publisher: A Stepping Stone Book(TM)), 1991 / Random Penguin House ; **p. 154** -h ph © Faculty of Engineering at UNSW (The University of New South Wales), Sydney, Australia ; **p. 154** -b ph © Reuters / Francois Lenoir ; **p. 155** ph © Allan Tannenbaum / Getty-Images ; **p. 156** -h ph © Images Etc Ltd / Getty-Images ; **p. 156** -b ph © e71lena / iStock / Getty-Images ; **p. 157** ph © Ramin Talaie / Corbis / Getty-Images ; **p. 159** -h ph © Volkan Furuncu / Anadolu Agency / AFP Photo ; **p. 159** -b Coll. Christophel © Warp Films / Big Arty Productions ; **p. 160** -h ph © Underwood Archives / Getty-Images ; **p. 160** -b ph © Michael Zagaris / San Francisco 49ers / Getty-Images / AFP Photo ; **p. 162** -h ph © Black Lives Matter / D.R. ; **p. 162** -b Coll. Christophel © Marvel Studios / Walt Disney Pictures ; **p. 163** ph © Pamela Au / Alamy Stock Photo ; **p. 167** -h ph © Associated Press / via Sipa Press ; **p. 167** -b ph © Max Herman ; **p. 169** -h © This Is England Trailer, © Ad Vitam ; **p. 169** -b Coll. Christophel © Warp Films / Big Arty Productions ; **p. 170** Coll. Christophel © Awol Films Ltd / Tantrum Films Ltd ; **p. 171** -hg © "I, Daniel Blake" is very real, 9/01/2017© The Economist / Wild Bunch ; **p. 171** -hd ph © Les Films du Fleuve / Sixteen Films / Aurimages ; **p. 171** -b © Free World, Ken Loach, 2007 © Orange ; **p. 175** -h ph © John Phillips / Getty-Images / AFP Photo ; **p. 175** -b Coll. Christophel © BBC Films / UK Film Council / Limelight Communication ; **p. 177** -hg ph © Top Shelf Productions, 2013 ; **p. 177** -hd1 © Malcolm X, Spike Lee, 1992. Coll. Christophel © 40 Acres & a Mule Filmworks ; **p. 177** -hd2 ph © If Beale Street Could Talk, Barry Jenkins, 2018. © Annapurna Pictures / BBQ_DFY / Aurimages ; **p. 177** -hd3 ph © Green Book, Peter Farrelly, 2018. © Universal Pictures / BBQ_DFY / Aurimages ; **p. 177** -hd4 ph © Inside Look: The People v. O.J. Simpson - American Crime Story, Serie TV, Joel Knoernschild and Cuba Gooding Jr., 2016. © FX Network / BBQ_DFY / Aurimages ; **p. 177** -hd5 ph © Seven Seconds (Mini-serie TV), Veena Sud, 2018. © Netflix / BBQ_DFY / Aurimages ; **p. 177** -hd6 ph © Dear White People, Serie TV, Saison 2, 2018. © Netflix / BBQ_DFY / Aurimages ; **p. 177** -bg ph © Faber & Faber, 2009 ; **p. 177** -bd1 ph © Fish Tank, Andrea Arnold, 2009. © BBC Films / The Kobal Collection / Aurimages Fish Tank ; **p. 177** -bd2 ph © A kind of loving, Stan Barstow (TV Serie 1982) DVD's cover, 2009. © Network / Granada Television ; **p. 177** -bd3 © Angel's share, Ken Loach, 2012. Coll. Christophel © Entertainment One / © Sixteen Films ; **p. 177** -bd4 © This is England ' 86, Shane Meadows, 2007. Coll. Christophel © Warp Films ; **p. 178** -h © Reniqua Allen on the Struggles of Young Black Americans, 01/21/2019 © CNN ; **p. 178** -b ph © Bettmann / Getty-Images ; **p. 180** -h Coll. Christophel © Film Four International / Rosen ; **p. 180** -b ph © Mary Evans / StudioCanal Films LTD / Alamy Stock Photo ; **p. 181** ph © Mary Evans / Aurimages ; **p. 183** -h ph © Daisy Gilardini / Science Faction / Getty-Images ; **p. 183** -b ph © Michelle Gilders / Alamy Stock Photo / © Josh Sarantitis and Eric Okdeh ; **p. 184** ph © Chris Radburn / PA Archive / PA Images ; **p. 185** © Overview of Britain's Treasure Islands TV documentary series, Stewart Mcpherson, 12 April 2016, © Warehouse Productions 51, D.R ; **p. 186** -h ph © Conor King Devitt ; **p. 186** -b © La Dame de Fer © Pathe UK ; **p. 189** -h, b ph © yuoak / DigitalVision Vectors / Getty-Images ; **p. 189** -m ph © Arizzonadesign / Adobe.stock ; **p. 191** -h ph © B.A.E. Inc. / Alamy Stock Photo ; **p. 191** -b ph © Matt Cardy / Getty-Images / AFP Photo ; **p. 193** -h ph © Richard Levine / Alamy Stock Photo ; **p. 193** -b ph © JoeFoxBerlin / Radharc Images / Alamy Stock Photo / © Rodney Leon (Architect) ; **p. 194** ph © Hulton Archive / Getty-Images ; **p. 195** -h ph © Martin Moxter / Zoonar GmbH / Alamy Stock Photo / © Clara Sornas (sculptor) ; **p. 195** -b © Amazing Grace © Momentum Pictures ; **p. 199** -h ph © Sandy Carson / Zuma Press, Inc. / Alamy Stock Photo ; **p. 199** -b ph © Eugenio Marongiu - adobe stock ; **p. 201** -hg1 ph © Three Rivers Press, 2001 ; **p. 201** -hg2 ph © Redfern Natural History, 2016 ; **p. 201** -hd1 ph © Gibraltar: My Rock, Ana Garcia, 2013. © Under The Milky Way / D.R. ; **p. 201** -hd2 ph © Britain's Distant Lands, the UK Overseas Territories by Stewart McPherson. DVD's cover. © Redfern Natural History, 2019 ; **p. 201** -bg1 © Amistad - HarperCollins Publishers, 2003 ; **p. 201** -bg2 ph © John Jennings (illustration) / © Abrams ComicArts, 2017 ; **p. 201** -bd1 ph © Glory, Edward Zwick, 1989. ph © Tri Star / The Kobal Collection / Aurimages ; **p. 201** -bd2 © Belle, Amma Asante, 2013. Coll. Christophel © DJ Films ; **p. 201** -bd3 ph © Twelve Years A Slave, Steve McQueen, 2013. © Regency Enterprises / The Kobal Collection / Aurimages ; **p. 201** -bd4 ph © Roots, TV Serie, Mario Van Peebles, 2016. © History (A&E Television Networks) / D.R. ; **p. 202** -h ph © St.Helena, a remote island in the Atlantic. © SWR ; **p. 202** -b ph © Michael Dunning / Getty-Images ; **p. 204** ph © Muratani / iStock / Getty-Images ; **p. 205** ph © BJ Warnick / Newscom / Alamy Stock Photo ; **p. 207** ph © vukrytas / Adobe Stock ; **p. 208** © This Map Shows Where American Accents Come From, Science Insider, 10/06/2018© 2019 Insider ; **p. 209** -h ph © Alastair Grant - WPA Pool / Getty-Images / AFP Photo ; **p. 209** -mg ph © Nuwan / Moment / Getty-Images ; **p. 209** -md ph © oversnap / iStock / Getty-Images ; **p. 209** -bg ph © SKLA / E+ / Getty-images ; **p. 209** -bd ph © Prasit photo / Moment / Getty-Images ; **p. 210** -1 ph © Look and Learn / Bridgeman Images ; **p. 210** -2 ph © Poster by Hilda Dallas, 1909, Museum of London. © Heritage Images / Getty-Images ; **p. 210** -3 ph © William Vandivert / The Life Picture Collection / Getty-Images ; **p. 210** -4 © Harpercollins Publishers, 1997 ; **p. 210** -5 ph © Penguin UK, 1954 / The Advertising Archives / Alamy Stock Photo ; **p. 210** -6 ph © Granger Historical Picture Archive / Alamy Stock Photo ; **p. 210** -7 ph © Private Collection / Prismatic Pictures / Bridgeman Images ; **p. 211** -1 ph © Tim Graham / Getty-Images ; **p. 211** -2 ph © Patrick Kovarik / AFP Photo ; **p. 211** -3 ph © Woodfall / Kestrel / The Kobal Collection / Aurimages ; **p. 211** -4 ph © Daniel Tomlinson / iStock / Getty-Images © Foster & Partners (architects), 2003. ; **p. 211** -5 ph © Denis Charlet / AFP Photo ; **p. 211** -6 ph © Colin McPherson / Corbis via Getty-Images ; **p. 211** -7 ph © incamerastock / Alamy Stock Photo ; **p. 212** -1 ph © Manifest Destiny, by John Gast, 1872 / © Universal History Archive / UIG / Bridgeman Images ; **p. 212** -2 ph © Tim Page / Corbis / Getty-Images ; **p. 212** -3 ph © Bettmann / Getty-Images ; **p. 212** -4 ph © George Rinhart / Corbis via Getty-Images ; **p. 212** -5 ph © Bettmann / Getty-Images ; **p. 212** -6 ph © © The Art Institute of Chicago, IL, USA / Friends of American Art Collection / Bridgeman Images / © Adagp, Paris, 2019 ; **p. 213** -1 ph © MEPL / Bridgeman Images ; **p. 213** -2 ph © Everett Collection / Aurimages ; **p. 213** -3 ph © Reuters / Sean Adair ; **p. 213** -4 ph © Julie Dermansky / Corbis via Getty-Images ; **p. 213** -5 ph © Akg-Images / © The Andy Warhol Foundation for the Visual Arts, Inc. / Licensed by / © Adagp, Paris 2019 ; **p. 213** -6 © Nasa ; **p. 213** -7 ph © Vincent Fournier / Gamma-Rapho via Getty-Images ; **p. 213** -8 © Apple Inc. ; **p. 214** -h1 ph © Icon / Ladd Co / Paramount / The Kobal Collection / Aurimages ; **p. 214** -h2 ph © R.P. Productions - Runteam Ltd./ Prod DB / AllPix / Aurimages ; **p. 214** -h3 Coll. Christophel © BBC Films / Cross street films ; **p. 214** -b1 ph © New Line Cinema / BBQ_DFY / Aurimages ; **p. 214** -b2 Coll. Christophel © Morgan Creek Productions ; **p. 214** -b3 Coll. Christophel © Twentieth Century Fox ; **p. 214** -b4 ph © Mary Evans / Aurimages ; **p. 215** -h1 ph © Warner Bros / Ratpac-Dune Entertainment / BBQ_DFY / Aurimages ; **p. 215** -h2 Coll. Christophel © Pathé ; **p. 215** -h3 Coll. Christophel © Baffin Media / Channel 4 ; **p. 215** -b1 Coll. Christophel © Twentieth Century Fox Film Corporation ; **p. 215** -b2 ph © Mary Evans / Aurimages ; **p. 215** -b3 ph © Orion / The Kobal Collection / Aurimages ; **p. 232** -g ph © Joana Kruse / Alamy Stock Photo ; **p. 232** -m ph © S. Greg Panosian / compassandcamera / Getty-Images ; **p. 232** -d ph © Sergey Borisov / Alamy Stock Photo ; **p. 279** Coll. Christophel © Marvel Studios / Walt Disney Pictures ; **p. 280** ph © Collection of Barney A. Ebsworth / National Gallery of Art ; **p. 281** © Free World, Ken Loach, 2007 © Orange ; **p. 290** Coll. Christophel © Fox 2000 pictures / New leaf literary and media

Achevé d'imprimer en Italie par L.E.G.O. S.p.A. Lavis (TN) - Dépôt légal : 05298 - 7/01 - Avril 2019